I0458236

Unforgettable Years

Mingqing Wu

Canada International Press

Title: Unforgettable Years
Author: Mingqing Wu
Copyright © 2025 by Mingqing Wu
Cover Design by: Mingqing Wu
Text Design by Mingqing Wu
Publisher: Canada International Press
www.intlpressca.com
Email: service@intelpressca.com
ISBN: 978-1-998479-27-6
E-book ISBN: 978-1-998479-28-3
First Edition in Canada, Feb.2025
First Printing, Feb. 2025
Unauthorized reproduction prohibited.

 All rights reserved.

No part of this publication may be reproduced, stored in a retrieval system, of transmitted in any form or by any means--- electronic, mechanical, photocopying, recording, or otherwise without prior written permission from the copyright owner, except for brief quotations used in a review or critical analysis.

Summary

This memoir by Mingqing Wu, a former researcher at the Institute of Geochemistry, Chinese Academy of Sciences, chronicles his extraordinary life journey. Born in a remote village in Guizhou, China. The author experienced significant historical events such as the Anti-Rightist Movement, the Great Leap Forward, the Three Years of Economic Hardship, and the Cultural Revolution. During this turbulent period, he worked as an educated youth in the countryside and later attended Guizhou University as a worker-peasant-soldier university student. After the fall of the "Gang of Four," the author became the first graduate student at the University of the Chinese Academy of Sciences in 1978, studying rare earth element geochemistry under the guidance of Professor Chengji Guo, a renowned mineralogist and geologist specializing in Rare and Rare Earth Elements and an Academician of the Chinese Academy of Sciences. He achieved remarkable success, earning national recognition as a leading expert and receiving special government allowances of the State Council. His career included a fruitful international collaboration at the Geological Survey of Canada, where his research was highly praised. Despite his achievements, author faced political suppression, which ultimately led him to settle in Canada. His memoir vividly portrays his resilience, dedication, and optimism while offering insights into rural Chinese life, fieldwork in Xinjiang, and scientific expeditions in the Okinawa Trough. Blending personal narrative with popular science, the book provides an engaging and thoughtprovoking account of a life shaped by history and driven by passion for learning.

Prologue

More than seventy years of life are like a fleeting moment. Now life is like golden autumn. After experiencing the vicissitudes of life, I have tasted the warmth and coldness of the world and seen the good and evil of human nature. Therefore, I have already washed away the lead and dust, and my heart is as pure as a steel knife, and I am free and easy. It is also like a steel knife that has been quenched by fire. If you want to change yourself, you can only sharpen yourself to the utmost. Although you don't want to become a Longquan sword, you want to have no regrets in this life. In life, I only wish that poetry and wine will set off the years and cook out the four seasons like spring; cherish what you once had and endure the eternity; talk about the years, drink with time, look at the three thousand vanities lightly, and enjoy the passing years quietly.

For the rest of your life, cut a period of leisure time, slow down your hurried pace in time, look at the scenery along the way, and listen to the voice from the depths of your heart. Read the books you like, do the things you like, go where you want to go, love the people you like, make friends you like, and turn every moment of your time into a shallow love or deep love in your eyes.

Preface

— —Reading Notes on *Unforgettable Years*

Du Du

Unforgettable Years is a book I came across unexpectedly. After a Chinese language activity, Mr. Xiang Wang stuffed it into my hands, like an inevitable homework falling from the sky, "Take a look, it's worth reading!" In Ottawa, a smaller city that local Chinese self-deprecatingly call Ottawa Village, there are many Chinese technology talents, and any new book published in the native language of Chinese cannot be ignored. Weighing its heavy weight, I wondered: What kind of life is wrapped in this thick spine? I wanted to flip through it casually, but after turning a few pages, I couldn't put it down, as if I had been injected with anesthetics. I flipped through the pages from beginning to end for two nights, my eyes followed my heart, and I was immersed in Mr. Mingqing Wu's rich and varied life journey, like riding a roller coaster, with ups and downs in my mood.

In a macro sense, this book is Mr. Wu's personal biography, and the process of reading is just like walking into the author's personal life journey. This book spans more than 70 years of the author's life, and the whole book focuses on these 70 years, taking readers into the history of China's modern social development over the past 70 years. The social evolution and changes experienced by the author, including the Great Leap Forward, the Three Years of Hardship, the Cultural Revolution, the geological surveys in Xinjiang and the Loess Plateau, marine scientific research in the East China Sea, visits abroad for academic exchanges, etc., are vividly depicted on paper. If you are a person who is not very familiar with China's modern history over the past 70 years, by reading this book, I believe you can have a general impression and understanding of this series of social changes and the evolution of the times in China from the level of the common people.

On a micro level, the author reflects his personal life journey on the big screen of the development of the times through his own memories, and then slowly unfolds them one by one. The work covers the author's experiences and feelings in various stages of life, from childhood, adolescence, youth, middle age to old age, in chronological order. It successfully portrays the growth process of a farm child who came out of a mountain village in a remote mountainous area of Guizhou, how he grew up step by step through his own hard work to become an outstanding scientist with both perseverance, courage, real talent and outstanding achievements. At the same time, the natural geographical environment of his hometown in Guizhou, Shanmu (i.e., Firwood) Village, the small mountain village, the detailed conditions of his original family, the living conditions of the people in the mountainous areas of Guizhou at that time, and the many folk customs and customs of the local people are all described in detail. By reading this book, I believe that anyone who has never set foot in the mountainous areas of Guizhou will have a clear understanding of the humanistic, social and geographical conditions of Guizhou.

The main thread of this book is based on the author's cultural and knowledge growth. The author's education and the practical process brought by education are a solid main thread. It regards the important events in the author's life as precious pearls one after another. This educational main thread slowly and steadily connects these pearls one by one through text narration, and finally forms a complete and vivid chain of life. This vivid chain of life connects the author's various learning stages of elementary school, middle school, university and graduate school, and also connects his rich and diverse scientific research and party and mass management work in the Institute of Geochemistry of the Chinese Academy of Sciences, as well as his life trajectory of being treated unfairly and suppressed after he went abroad as a visiting scholar and finally got an international cooperation project across borders and returned to China.

The personal character of being active, diligent, hardworking, and optimistic is appropriately reflected in this very dedicated scientist, without exaggeration or modesty. The book has neither gorgeous words nor delicate and artificial plots, but presents the author's life experience perfectly in the most authentic way. However, it is regrettable that when the author reached the middle of his life, an outstanding scientist who returned to China with an international cooperation project from abroad was outrageously suppressed by some leaders in the institute, so the author was forced to leave his country. However, fate played a trick on him. After returning to Canada, the author suddenly encountered the blow of the death of the boss of the international cooperation project. Faced with a major setback in life, the author gave up his scientific skills with great courage and chose to start a new business and do general work. Whenever reading this chapter, readers see this shining pearl in the author's life course, as if it had unfortunately fallen into the mud. At this time, readers all sighed and sighed. Fortunately, the author, who has an optimistic and open-minded character, finally ushered in a peaceful, warm, happy and healthy old age through his own hard work in this difficult transformation process.

From the family level, in addition to talking about his ancestors and his father, the author also briefly talked about his own small family, as well as the growth of his daughter after he settled in Canada in middle age. Therefore, this memoir spans four generations of life, from his parents, he and his wife, his daughter and his grandchildren. Of course, the focus of the biography is to record the fate of the generation of his peers in the Republic that he represents. However, even so, whether it is a reader older than the author or a middle-aged person who is more than 20 years younger than the author, they will find fragments of the times in this memoir that overlap with their own experiences. Therefore, many contents in the book are very intimate and touching to read, and many of the backgrounds of the times are completely familiar to people of our age group born in the 1960s.

From the perspective of writing techniques, this book adopts a purely documentary style. The narration of the article is completely based on objective facts, and the narration of historical events is also very accurate and detailed. From the author's memoirs, the accuracy of each era and each event is amazing to read. It is not difficult to see that the author's careful thinking and accurate writing must have been done before writing a lot of data collection and sorting work, or the author has a long-term diary habit, otherwise it is difficult to accurately cover the decades of historical events covered in the book. From this level, it is not difficult to see that a scientist who has been professionally influenced and strictly trained for a long time has such a serious and meticulous attitude towards writing. Therefore, this autobiographical memoir, which is as rigorous and true as a scientific paper, has won the favour of readers as soon as it came out. In addition, there are a large number of photos inserted in the book, which are precious image records of the author's life from childhood to old age. These photos can not only leave readers with a more intuitive visual experience, but also make the book less boring to read. Readers can look at the inserted photos while reading, which not only increases the readers' intuitive impression of the author's life course, but also releases the mental pressure brought to readers by reading dense text.

One of the main features of this book is that it unfolds slowly in chronological order. When readers read this book along the main line of time, it seems as if they are constantly walking along a long river that flows from the author's childhood to old age. This river is not only a long river that flows from the mountains to the outside of the mountains, from the countryside to the city, but also a long river that flows from China to the world. At the same time, it is also a long river that flows from the author's ignorance to his erudition. This long river has been flowing forward persistently and steadily since its origin. Due to the high degree of integration between time and the plot, when reading this book, readers seem to be riding on a large ship built by the author and going downstream. Along the way, they can enjoy the gorgeous scenery, and at the same time, the readers and the author have a spiritual resonance, which makes people feel very intimate and natural to read. In addition, there are several mysterious descriptions of the author's personal experience in this memoir, which are very interesting to read. For example, the author's near-death physical examination during the life-saving process due to a gallbladder surgery error, as well as the telepathy experienced by the author and his family during his mother's critical illness and death, and other strange phenomena are all described in detail in the book. These stories seem absurd, but they are actually full of philosophy and humanistic atmosphere. Moreover, these mysterious experiences flowed from the pen of a senior natural scientist, which suddenly reminded me of the mysterious scientific problem of quantum entanglement that has been popular in recent years, that is, between two particles or quanta that are not controlled by time and space distance, when one changes state, no matter how far apart they are, the other almost changes state at the same time, and this is not a coincidence, but a scientific phenomenon that has been verified by scientific experiments in the scientific community. Therefore, the near-death experience experienced by the author and the strange phenomena such as telepathy between him and his mother can be roughly regarded as the specific manifestation of quantum entanglement in daily life. Obviously, the reason why the author recorded all the mysterious experiences he experienced truthfully is that he is also very awed by the mysterious world, which makes me feel very cordial, because I am also a person who is very awed by gods. It can be said that the author's unique and precious unexpected mysterious experiences not only cast an unusual halo on his life experience, but also greatly changed his outlook on life and values, and also greatly enhanced the interest and readability of this memoir.

The last point worth pointing out is that when readers read about the author's experience of being suppressed by some leaders in the institute for no reason in the process of reading this book, they are all indignant and sighing, and even speechless and choking with a long sigh! However, the author's experience should not be an isolated case in China. It can be said that he is just one of some scientists who have suffered injustice in China and were forced to go abroad in recent years. Imagine that in our motherland, if every scientist can get due respect and treatment, and all scientists' intelligence and wisdom can be fully utilized, then scientists can devote themselves to scientific research without distraction, and make greater contributions to the motherland. If that were the case, there would not be so many top scientific talents in our motherland drifting abroad.

Reading this book is an experience that makes people unable to stop. Mr. Wu's life experience is a small person who sees the great era, and a person's fate reflects the trend of the group. It reflects a period of history full of changes, China's social changes and the survival trend of senior intellectuals. His overseas life after migration in the second half of his life is also very typical, and it condenses the common characteristics of a large number of overseas Chinese who are tenacious and flexible in seeking survival overseas. In front of the strong, there is no word "failure" in life. Mr. Wu is such a strong man. With his unique and rich life, he depicts the vivid appearance that a tenacious life can have. Although the author has experienced many setbacks and blows in his decades of life, the vicissitudes of time do not seem to leave too many traces on his face. So when I had the honour to meet Mr. Wu later, I was surprised by his very young frozen face, which looked at least 10 to 20 years younger than his actual age. At that time, his bright smile was radiant, just like the smile in the photo in his book, sincere and contagious. Obviously, it is the positive emotions that cannot be concealed by the optimistic attitude emanating from his heart, as well as the happiness brought by the real satisfaction of life. A person is like his book. It is this positive and optimistic attitude towards life that has made his remarkable life journey. However, although I have written three or four thousand words here, after all, words are weak. Readers can still experience the many charms of his extraordinary life by reading Mr. Wu's book in person!

Du Du
May 20, 2023
Ottawa, Ontario, Canada

[Note]: Dudu, a Chinese female writer living in Ottawa, Canada, has published more than 10 Chinese literary works with more than 3 million words over the years. Her novels, poems, and essays have won the Chinese Literature Awards in the United States, China, and Canada. Among them, the novel "China Lake" won the 2021 Overseas Chinese Writings Award Novel Gold Award. She is currently a member of the Canadian Chinese Writers Association, the North American Chinese Writers Association, and the Canada-China PEN Club.

CONTENTS

Introduction

I am a very ordinary person. Although I've received a good education in my life, worked at a professional research institute for almost thirty years, and later chose to settle abroad, I have not made any significant achievements or contributions. I never thought of writing a memoir. However, truth be told, compared to my peers, my life experience has been rather rich and full of twists and turns. Over the years, as time passed, I accumulated many memories based on my life experiences. While these memories don't encompass all my life events, they do record my life's journey, interpret the changes of the times, and reflect the characteristics and imprints of the era. Recording these memories would undoubtedly offer some reflection and inspiration for both the present and future generations. Thus, the idea of writing a memoir occasionally crossed my mind. But I always believed that writing memoirs or autobiographies was the privilege of famous or great people, and it had little to do with someone as ordinary as me. So, the idea of writing a memoir was only a fleeting thought, never turning into action. After retiring in 2016, during occasional gatherings with friends, classmates, or family when I visited China, my past experiences, being somewhat representative in my hometown, often sparked their interest. Some stories or experiences even became frequent topics of discussion. As a result, many people urged me should record these memories in writing. This would not only leave behind a precious written record for my family and future generations, but also serve as a comprehensive reflection and summary of my life. Thus, after the Lunar New Year in 2021, I finally picked up my pen and began to document my memories of the past. This is the origin of this memoir book.

I was born in a small, remote, and impoverished mountain village in Guizhou. As common people say, I was just an ordinary farm kid, without any family background, and who lost his father in childhood. However, as I progressed, not only did I attend middle school and university, but I also went to graduate school, eventually being assigned to work at a national research institute and later going abroad. To my fellow villagers, I undoubtedly became a successful figure, and over the years, they often used me as an example to educate their children. On the other hand, many of my fellow villagers didn't fully understand my journey and wondered how I managed to leave the mountains. In this book, I will tell them that my success was not because I possess any extraordinary talents, nor because I had grand ambitions or lofty aspirations from my young age. Rather, at each stage of my education, I was naturally inspired by certain circumstances, leading to a simple desire to learn. In modern terms, one could say I always had a "dream" or "pursuit" in my heart. Once a person has dream and pursuit, his learning or life would have a goal, and their action will have motivation. It was precisely this dream and pursuit that drove me to steadily climb upward in my academic journey, one step at a time.

I remember clearly when I was in the second or third grade of elementary school, every time we received new textbooks at the start of the new term, I noticed that the covers of the higher-grade students' textbooks had "Advanced Elementary Textbooks," while my textbooks were labeled "Primary Elementary Textbooks." I thought to myself, once I finish primary school, I want to go to advanced elementary school too. In the fifth grade, our arithmetic teacher, Mr. Yunpu Cai was explaining a problem when a classmate curiously asked, "Mr. Cai, what will we learn in math in middle school?" He replied:
"In middle school, arithmetic will be called mathematics." He then wrote some equations like $X+Y=Z$ and $a + b + c = d$ on the blackboard. While we students were puzzled, he explained:
"This is algebra, which you'll study in middle school." I found it fascinating and mysterious, and I made a firm decision in my heart that after finishing elementary school, I would definitely go to middle school.

When I attended the Second Middle School of Puding County, people in my village mentioned the Yang brothers from Dixi village (the elder brother was probably named Dengguo Yang and the younger brother was Dengju Yang), both worked in the provincial government in Guiyang. I was curious and wondered how they managed to work in the city. Later, I learned that the Yang family were wealthy landowners, and both brothers had studied hard before the libration, eventually attending university in Guiyang. After graduation, they were assigned jobs in the city. That's when I realized that for people from the mountains like us, the only path out was through education. If we studied well and attended university, we had a chance to work in the city. So, when I graduated from middle school, I was determined to go to high school and then university. After graduating from university, I seized the opportunity to pursue graduate studies, driven by a constant pursuit of dreams.

Of course, having dreams or pursuits is one thing, but having the opportunity to achieve them is another. Opportunities are crucial in realizing one's dreams, and the ability to seize them is essential. In my life, three opportunities were particularly important, and I seized them all. The first was in 1960, when I was in the fifth grade. Due to my excellent performance, I had the chance to take the middle school entrance exam a year early. If I had graduated in 1961, I would have missed the opportunity to attend middle school, as admissions were reduced or stopped, and I would have had to return home to farm. The second opportunity came in 1972 when Guizhou began admitting worker-peasant-soldier students to university. I was working at the commune office and had performed quite well in the eyes of my superiors, so I was recommended to attend Guizhou University. If I had not worked at the commune office back then, but instead had been assigned to rural areas to do farm work or had taught in an elementary school, I would have missed this opportunity to attend university, and like many of my peers, I would have had no chance to accept a higher education. The third opportunity came after I graduated from university. In 1978, when graduate admissions resumed nationwide, I boldly applied and was accepted, marking another leap in my life. Of course, objectively speaking, there were not the only three opportunities in my life, but compared to others, these three had the greatest impact and were the most crucial. I can say that with each opportunity I seized, my life was elevated to a new level.

In recent years, whenever I return to China, some old classmates and friends often ask me: "why did you choose to settle abroad before, and now that our country has developed, why have't you come back". Mentioning settling abroad, it's a long story. When I first went to Canada as a visiting scientist in June 1995, it was through a Chinese Academy of Sciences (CAS) scholarship for a six-month research project with the Geological Survey of Canada, later extended to a year. The so-called collaborative research involved bringing my own project and geological samples, and using the advanced equipments and conditions at the Geological Survey of Canada to analyze and test my samples. At the time whether success of the collaboration research depended entirely on my own capabilities and academic level. In other words, working at an internationally advanced research institution with leading experts from abroad was the true test of my scientific ability and academic knowledge. To be honest, when I first arrived in the Geological Survey of Canada, I felt a great deal of mental pressure and faced significant challenges in my work. I was unsure whether I could complete the research project successfully. However, retreat was not an option. I think that "Once you draw the bow, there was no chance to turn back. Whether it's a mule or a horse, now is the time to take it out for a walk." Right now it was time to see if I was up to the task. It turned out that by the end of my year at the Geological Survey of Canada, relying on the analytical chemistry skills and academic research experience I had honed at the Institute of Geochemistry of the Chinese Academy of Sciences, I worked tirelessly and successfully completed several complex Laboratory tasks agreed upon with my collaborative professors. Despite the challenges, I finished analyzing over 200 geological samples and obtained lots of valuable data, including isotopic and trace element analysis, which would have taken two to three years to complete in China. Although I only had time to submit one paper, the work was highly praised by my Canadian counterparts.

When I returned to China on schedule after the visit, I brought back an international collaborative project authorized by the International Union of Geological Sciences' Commission on Stratigraphy, and I also was appointed as the head of the Chinese working group for this project. However, after successfully completing my project and returning to China, I was unexpectedly and repeatedly suppressed by certain individuals in power at our institute. Faced with this situation, I had no choice but to leave again and return to Canada. To be fair, as a peer of the new China, I had received free education from primary school through middle school, university, and graduate school. We should be grateful to and serve our country in return. Actually, after completing my education, I had always planned to stay in China and to serve our country. When I first went to abroad as a visiting scientist in 1995, although I witnessed the stark contrast in material living conditions between China and abroad, I had no intention of staying abroad. At the end of my visit, I returned to China on schedule and even brought back an international collaborative project, with the hope of setting down and focusing on my academic research in China. However, the bad circumstances upon my return led me to reconsider my options. Thus, my second move to Canada and eventual decision to settle there was not by choice but by necessity. Although I faced the loss of my project leader after returning to Canada, I decided to stay and seek a better life for my children, as I did not want them to endure the struggles I faced.

Looking back, as a peer of the People's Republic of China, I witnessed and experienced nearly every major political movement since the mid-20th century. I endured a bitter childhood, a challenging adolescence, worked as a sent-down countryside youth, and became a worker-peasant-soldier student of university. I had worked on the Gobi desert wilderness of Xinjiang and faced the turbulent waves of the East China Sea. I served as a dedicated party official and a competent scientific researcher. I studied diligently in China's ivory towers and later gained international experience. I also survived a near-death experience due to a botched surgery. Nearing fifty, I chose to emigrate and live an ordinary life abroad. My life journey has been filled with ups and downs, with unforgettable struggles and moments of triumph. There have been both high points and low valleys, hardships, and unexpected opportunities. Yet, despite all the twists and turns, everything I've experienced is the result of choices and fate. Although in the eyes of my fellow villagers, I may appear to be a "successful person," but I am well aware that success is just a perception. True success, in my view, does not comes from others' recognition or evaluation but rather from a sense of inner peace, calm, and happiness that comes from personal contentment. Therefore, it's unnecessary to dwell on whether one has achieved success by external standards. As long as you have strived and worked hard, that is enough.

Truth and accuracy are the soul and lifeblood of written records, especially memoir and they are the source of their value. Without truth, any memoir is worthless. Thus, faithfully and authentically recounting past events without embellishment has been my guiding principle in writing *Unforgettable Years*.

However, due to the erosion of time has inevitably blurred some memories, and there may be discrepancies in the description of certain details of events. Therefore, I sincerely ask for the understanding of those who may know the real facts.

During the writing process, I received encouragement and support from many old classmates and friends. Special thanks go to my dear friends Kaiyuan Li and Xiang Wang, who provided numerous valuable suggestions and advice during the drafting process. At the same time, I would like to extend my special thanks to Ms. Dudu for taking the time out of her busy schedule to write a very touching preface for this book.

Chapter 1   A Bitter Childhood

（Ⅰ）

On the night of the third day of the first lunar month of the Year of the Rat (1948 AD), I was born in a small, remote village called Shanmu (i.e., Firwood) Village (杉木寨), located on the southwestern edge of Puding County, Guizhou Province, near the border of Langdai County (now part of the Liuzhi Special District). At that time, our village had only about 20 to 30 households. Apart from a few families who had moved in from elsewhere to stay with relatives, most of the villagers shared the surname Wu and belonged to the same extended family. When I was a child, my parents told me that the ancestors of the Wu family in our Shanmu Village had migrated from Bijie in Guizhou Province. According to the genealogy of the Wu  family in Bijie, the founding ancestor of the Wu clan in Guizhou was Liangbi Wu (吴良弼), the 90th generation descendant of Taibo Wu (吴泰伯), the progenitor of the Wu surname. Liangbi Wu was born in 1348 (AD) in Macheng County, Huguang (present-day Macheng City, Hubei Province). He was a military officer who followed General Youde Fu (傅友德), appointed by Yuanzhang Zhu (朱元璋), the first emperor of the Ming Dynasty, to lead a military expedition to Yunnan and Guizhou in 1381 (AD). Due to his military accomplishments Liangbi Wu (吴良弼) was awarded the title of Marquis of Bijie and was stationed in Guizhou, where his descendants settled and thrived in the border region of Guizhou, Yunnan, and Sichuan three provinces. Over the past 600 years, the Wu family has expanded into more than 20 generations, with a population of over 200,000, making it the largest Wu family in southwestern China. Liangbi Wu (吴

良弼) had three sons: Gonghua Wu (吴公华), Gongpu Wu (吴公普), and Gongrong Wu (吴公荣). Our branch of the Wu family in Puding descends from Gonghua Wu (吴公华), the eldest son. Our founding ancestor, Guosi Wu (吴国思), was the 7th generation descendant of Liangbi Wu (吴良弼), and I am the 10th generation descendant of Guosi Wu (吴国思) and the 17th generation descendant of Liangbi Wu (吴良弼). Based on these calculations, I am the 106th generation descendant of Taibo Wu (吴泰伯), the progenitor of the Wu surname. The Wu family of Shanmu Village has been settled here for at least 300 to 400 years, though there are no written records to confirm the exact time of migration.

Shanmu Village overlooking

Shanmu Village, though remote, is considered a scenic and favourable place compared to other villages in the surrounding area. The village is nestled in a basin formed by a "厂"-shaped ridge, which serves as the natural border betweenPuding Countyand Liuzhi Special District. The village itself is situated on a flat terrace in the centre of the basin, with rice paddies extending for several kilometres on either side. Unlike much of the rugged, steep terrain common to the Wumeng Mountains of the Yunnan-Guizhou Plateau, our Shanmu Village benefits from an abundance of trees, coal deposits, and water sources, making it a highly favourable place to live. The region's acidic soil and humid climate are ideal for the growth of large trees, particularly Chinese fir, which is both fast- growing and the most commonly used timber for building houses. It was this abundant resource of

Chinese fir that gave the village its name, Shanmu (meaning "Chinese fir wood"). In the early 1950s, Shanmu Village was still a primitive, underdeveloped place, surrounded by dense forests and streams flowing year round through the lowlands. Thanks to its unique natural conditions, Shanmu Village was a place that never suffered from drought or floods, making it an ideal environment for the families who lived there.

Aerial view of Shanmu Village

Our Wu family in Shanmu village has been making a living by farming for generations. When it came to my father's generation, there were four brothers in his generation, and my father was the third oldest. My father was born in the eleventh year of the reign of Emperor Guangxu of the Qing Dynasty (1885 AD), and his zodiac sign was Rooster. Since he was young, my father has married three wives, including my mother. My father had five children with his first two wives, but they all died of illness in childhood. After the first two wives died, around 1938, my father married my mother again. My mother's surname is Tan and her name is Fengying. She was born in the year of the Xinhai Revolution (1911 AD), and her zodiac sign was Pig. My mother brought my sister (my sister was about two years old at the time, her zodiac sign was Rat, and she was 12 years older than me) to marry my father because my mother's exhusband (my sister's father) died of illness. After my mother married my father, in previous years she also had three children, but they all died. When I was born, my father was already in his early sixties. Because I was born in my father's old age, my parents were very happy. They see me as the apple of their eye since I was a boy. When it's hot they worry I might be overheat, and when it's cold, they fear I might get too cold. According to our local customs, if a couple's children always die before they grow up, in order to make the newborn child grow up healthily and safely, the child cannot call his father "Daddy" or "Dad", but "Uncle" (the villagers believe that after changing the father's appellation, the disease devil will think that the child is not born by the "hard-luck" father, and will let the child grow up safely). Therefore, I have called my father "Uncle" since I was a child, and of course, my mother's appellation has not changed. My father's name is Huagao Wu (吴华高), my eldest uncle is Huaqing Wu (吴华清), my second uncle is Huayi Wu (吴华益) and, my fourth uncle is Huaxing Wu (吴华兴). When I was born, all my uncles were dead. Among my father's brothers, my father is considered to be an educated person, because I heard that my three uncles are not well educated, they are all farmers who can only farm. My father not only had education and farming skills, but also knew a lot about Chinese herbal medicine (when I was a child, he often took me to the mountains to dig herbs, and taught me what was a lotus, a wormwood, a plantain, etc.), and he also himself studied Yin and Yang to be a geomancer. Every now and then, fellow villagers from all over our countryside would come to our house to invite my dad to treat illnesses or look after graves, bury the dead, etc. For this reason, my father earned the title "Mr. Wu" and became quite well-known in our local area. Every time he went to other places for ten days or half a month to treat people or perform a Taoist ritual, he would always bring back a few liters of rice and a few dried chickens and ducks (chickens and ducks that were slaughtered and half-dried by the victim's family to offer sacrifices to the gods), or one or two lamb legs (according to the local customs of my hometown, when my father buried the dead for the deceased, the victim's family had to kill chickens and sheep to offer sacrifices to the gods, and give my father a liter of rice and a chicken or a duck, or a lamb leg as a reward). Therefore, our family's life in the local area was quite comfortable at that time.

When I was born, there were five people in our family. In addition to my parents and me, there was an older brother and an older sister. My older brother was adopted by my father from outside. His family name is Hu, and he is my aunt's nephew. There are five brothers in his family, and my brother is the second oldest. His father farms when he is busy, and takes several sons to sell clay pots in the village market to make some money supporting their household expenses when he is free. Because there are many children in the family and few fields, their family lives in poverty. My sister and I have the same mother but different fathers. I heard from my mother that my sister was only about one year old when her father died of a sudden illness. After that, my mother took my sister to remarry and live with my father. Because my father and his previous two wives had four or five children who did not survive, and later the three children born to my father and mother after they got married also died one after another, so my parents were particularly sad and distressed. You know that in the old rural areas, if there was no boy in the family, it was much despised. The so-called "there are three unfilially acts, and the greatest one is to have no descendants" is deeply rooted in people's ideas. Seeing that he was already in his early sixties, my father discussed with my mother and planned to adopt a boy from outside to inherit the family business. In addition, there is a custom in our local area that when a couple has been married for many years and the child born is not easy to survive, they need to adopt a boy from outside to come to the family to act as a "Ya Zhang (押掌)" (meaning to suppress or drive the disease devil away in the family), so that the children born in the future will be easier to survive and grow up. It was with this idea that my parents decided to adopt a boy from outside to come to our family, firstly to act as a Ya Zhang, and secondly, in case there is no boy, the stepson can take care of them in the future and inherit the family business. Later, with the promotion of my aunt, around 1946, my fourth aunt's eldest brother's second son named Changyuan was adopted into our family. My brother was born in 1931, with the zodiac sign of the sheep. He was 15 years old when he came to our family, but my parents treated him as their own son. In the beginning, my father sent my brother to study in the village private school and gave him a literary name:

"Chaogang Hu (胡朝纲)". My brother went to a private school for one or two months, but because he was already fifteen or sixteen years old, he had been used to farm work since he was a child, and missed the best age for studying. He was not interested in studying at all, and he had a headache when he picked up books. In addition, my father was over sixty years old, and the family was in urgent need of male labor, eventually my brother quit school to help my father on the farm. Later, more than a year later, my parents thought that since my brother was an adopted son to carry on the family line, it would be better for him to change his surname to my father's. So they obtained the consent of my brother and his parents, and specially asked a master to choose an auspicious day. With the participation and witness of some respected elders in our Wu's family and relatives and friends in the village, a grand ceremony for changing my brother's surname was held publicly. An important part of the surname change ceremony was that when my brother knelt in front of the altar (Bodhisattva) in the centre of our main hall and accepted the congratulations of relatives and friends, he solemnly swore to the Bodhisattva: he would never regret changing his surname and would be loyal to the Wu family for the rest of his life. Even if the third generation are return to his original surname in the future (according to our local custom, the adopted stepson can restore the original family name when it is passed to the third generation, so it is called "three generations return to the clan"), but if possible, he would still keep a male with surname Wu. After the surname change ceremony ended that day, my father officially named my old brother "Mingfa Wu (吴明发)" according to our Wu family's character generation.

In the early days of liberation, my brother was in his early twenties and reached the age of marriage, but he failed to get married after being introduced to several girls by matchmakers. My sister was also sixteen or seventeen years old at the time and had grown into a graceful young lady. So people in our Wu's family and many relatives came to my parents to give them advice. They all said: "Your eldest son was adopted from outside, and your daughter was also brought from outside. There is no blood relationship between them. Why not let this young couples get married?" My parents thought: That's right! If the young boy and the young girl agree, wouldn't it be a happy marriage?

Originally, my brother and sister were very close. After my parents and relatives urged them to get together, they were naturally very happy. So around 1952, my brother and sister got married. This was also a good story in our remote mountain village at that time.

(II)

I was born less than two years after my brother came to our family. Because my father had a son in his old age, I was regarded as a treasure in the eyes of my parents. It's not too much to say that "Holding it in the palm is afraid of falling, holding it the mouth is afraid of melting." The whole family revolved around me, and gave me the best food and clothes first. In addition to my mother taking care of me, my sister took care of me the most. When I just learned to walk, my sister held my hand and followed me closely, fearing that I would fall or get hurt. My mother told me that when I was about eight or nine months old, one morning in the twelfth month of winter, my mother was cooking at home. She had just used a fire tong to burn a piece of bacon pig skin (a necessary step to remove the residual hair on the pig skin before cleaning the bacon), and the fire tongs were placed on the stove. After a while, my sister brought me home from outside and casually held me and sat me on the stove with the fire tongs. Because infants and young children in the old days all wore open-crotch pants with their buttocks exposed, as soon as I was put down, I was immediately burned by the fire tongs and cried heartbreakingly. Seeing this, my mother thought: This precious boy is clearly the apple of his father's eye. What if something goes wrong?! So my mom immediately picked me up and started to curse my sister: "You damn girl! You burned your youngest brother already. If your father was at home, he would beat you half to death!" My sister was also frightened and burst into tears. Fortunately, my father was taken away to do a ritual l for others in other places during those days, otherwise if he was at home, he might really beat my sister severely. After three or four months of treatment, the burn on my right thigh root was healed, but a four to five-inch long scar was left. After this incident, my sister took extra care to take care of me. Originally, this was an accident that happened when I was an infant, and I had no memory of it at all. After I went to middle school, when I was swimming in the river once, a classmate saw from behind that I had a four to five-inch long scar on my right thigh root, so he asked me what happened. I felt puzzled at the time, and asked my mother after returning home. My mother then told me the ins and outs of the scar. Since I was

A Guizhou farm-woman is grinding with a millstone.

the youngest and most favored boy in the family, my mother weaned me very late. I was still breastfeeding when I was about three or four years old. I remember one time when my mother was grinding corn grits with a mill, and I pestered her for breastfeeding. My mother was too busy grinding the mill to stop working, so I kept crawling into her clothes and sucking her nipple. In order to save me, my mother had to stop working and let me suck for more than ten times. One afternoon in a summer, my childhood playmate Xiaobao Yuan (a distant relative and nephew, one year older than me) came to my house with a sickle in his hand and asked me to go outside with him to cut grass and play. I said: "Wait a minute, let me have some milk before we go!" So I ran to my mother's arms and started to breastfeed again. When I grew up, my physique seemed to be better than other children of the same age, and I rarely got sick. Many people said that it might have something to do with the fact that I drank a lot of breast milk when I was a child.

This is a stone mortar for bulling rice

When my father was alive, our family had five or six acres of paddy fields and three or four acres of dry land. During the land reform at the beginning of liberation, our family was classified as middle peasants. Because there were not many people in the family, and my father often went out to treat people or bury the dead, he would bring some rice and chickens and ducks back home every month. In addition, our family would kill at least one pig weighing about two hundred kilograms every winter, and smoke the pork into bacon to eat all year round. Therefore, our family's life was quite good in the local area when I was a child. I remember that every time my family stewed chicken soup, my parents would always leave the chicken liver and chicken legs for me. When I ate chicken legs, I would always peel off the chicken skin for my mother first, and then eat the chicken meat myself, but my mother never complained. Even if my parents got a piece of candy or fruit or something delicious when they went out, they would always be reluctant to eat it and bring it home to me no matter how far it was. Although my parents loved me, they did not over-pamper me. When I was very young, my parents asked me to learn how to dress and button my clothes (my clothes were handmade by my mom, and the buttons were Chinese-style buttons made of cloth strips. Especially the buttons of new clothes were usually very tight, which was very difficult for children to button). When I was a little older, my parents taught me to sweep the floor and the yard. In the past, there was no electricity in the countryside, nor rice machine or flour-machine. The rice and flour that farmers ate were respectively husked with stone mortar and ground with stone mills. Therefore, whenever the adults husked rice and ground flour, my parents would ask me to help step the stone mortar, or help push the stone mill. In addition, my parents also asked me to go up the mountain with my child-friends in the village to herd cattle, cut grass or chop firewood, which was also what I often did in my childhood. When my parents taught me to work, they often told me: "We are farmers. Farmers must learn any kind of work from a young age. No matter what kind of work or what kind of things we do, we must do it seriously and never perfunctorily." So I remembered my parents' teachings from a young age. Not only did I develop a habit of loving labor from a young age, but I also took it seriously no matter what I did.

The reason why I say my father is a well-educated person is that when I was a child, I saw a large wooden box in the attic of our house, which was two or three feet square and finely crafted. It was filled with various books, some of which were handwritten books that my father bought white cotton paper and made it himself. The small regular script written by my father with a brush in the book was very neat and beautiful. There was a handwritten book that my father might have made for my brother to write. There were three words "Chaogang Hu" on the cover, but there was no any word written in the book. In addition, most of the books were thread-bound books printed by woodblock printing, and some were so-called foreign books printed and published by modern printing factories. Among them, there is a modern printing book with yellowed paper, which looks particularly old, and the pages are broken and the cover is missing. There are all kinds of ghost pictures in the inner pages of this book, such as the ghost of impermanence with a long and big tongue, and the ghost of impermanence is divided into white impermanence and black impermanence. There are also horrible pictures such as the ox-headed and horse-faced ghost, the ten kings of the Yan Palace, the little ghost in the oil pot, the little ghost sawing people's heads, and people crossing the Naihe Bridge after death. When I saw these pictures, I felt creepy all over my body, my heart was pounding, and I was very scared; but soon after, I wanted to look at it again, so every two or three days, as long as my father was not at home, I would sneak upstairs to open the box and peek at this ghost book. I think this is probably why this book rotted so quickly. Unfortunately, these books and wooden boxes were taken away by someone when no one was at home during the Great Leap Forward in 1958.

My father started my enlightenment education at my early age. When I was about two or three years old, he began to teach me to read children's enlightenment books such as *Hundred Family Names*(《百家姓》) and *Three Character Classic* (《三字经》). In addition to these two children's books, my father also taught me to recite: "*Shang Daren, Confucius, Hua Sanqian, Qishier*" ("上大人，孔夫子，化三千，七十二。"). I don't know whether it was compiled by himself or some formal reading material, anyway, these sentences are still firmly in my mind. I remember that my father not only taught me to read, but also wrote the characters on the wall of the house with chalk to teach me to recognize them, and sometimes explained them to me. But a two or three-year-old child has no ability to understand, so I can only follow him and parrot. Once my father asked me to recite the *Hundred Family Names* (《百家姓》). When I recited "*Zhao Qian Sun Li* (赵钱孙李), *Zhou Wu Zheng Wang* (周吴郑王), *Feng Chen Zhu Wei* (冯陈褚卫), *Jiang Shen Han Yang* (蒋沈韩杨)", I suddenly jumped to "*Xi Fan Peng Lang* (奚范彭郎)". My father laughed and said: "My little youngest, are you hungry and want to eat porridge? Why did you jump to the 'porridge basin wolf' all of a sudden?" My father usually collected waste paper with words on it or discarded manuscripts very well. He never threw waste paper with words on the ground. Occasionally, when he saw a little bit of waste paper on the ground, he would immediately pick it up and put it in the trash can, and then burn it. He often said to me: "Those waste papers with words on them must not be thrown on the ground for people to step on, otherwise it would be a waste of saints!" He even scared me, saying: "If you step on the paper with words on it, you will go blind in the future! So don't throw the paper with words on it on the ground and step on it." In fact, I know my father's good intentions, which is to teach me to respect knowledge and culture since I was a child. My father said this and did this. Through words and deeds, he instilled some correct concepts of respecting knowledge in my young mind.

Because I was influenced by my father since I was a child, by the time I was four or five years old, I had basically memorized the children's books such as *Three Character Classic* (《三字经》) and *Hundred Family Names* (《百家姓》) taught by my father. Although I didn't know many words and didn't understand what he was saying, as long as my father asked me to recite *Three Character Classic* (《三字经》) or *Hundred Family Names* (《百家姓》), I could recite thirty or forty sentences in one breath without stopping until my father asked me to stop. For this reason, my father often boasted to me in front of others: "My youngest son has a good memory and will definitely be a good student in the future!" When my father was alive, some cousins or nephews in our Wu's family often liked to come to our house in the evening to chat with my father during the slack season. Among them, I have a cousin who is not yet out of the fifth mourning period and is relatively close to our family. His name is Mingliang Wu (吴明亮). He had received a lot of education before, had seen the world, and was very good at making up stories. Whenever there was a wedding or funeral in the village, he would always come to the scene to tell the villagers stories about *Romance of the Three Kingdoms* (《三国演义》) or *Water Margin* (《水浒传》). He was recognized by the whole village as the most educated and eloquent young people. When I was four or five years old, one night, he came to my house as usual to chat with my father. Besides my father, there were also my brother and two or three cousins next door. A total of six or seven people sat together to warm themselves by the fire. At the beginning, my father asked me to recite the "Three Character Classic" for everyone. After I recited the "Three Character Classic", my father asked me to recite a few *Tang poems*(唐诗) he had just taught me, such as Bai Li's (李

白) "*Quiet Night Thoughts*" (静夜思) and Zhihuan Wang's (王之涣) "*Climbing the Stork Tower*" (登鹳雀楼). I memorized them all by heart. After I finished reciting them, everyone clapped and praised to me, saying :   "little brother, your memory is very good. You will definitely be very good at studying in the future!" At this time, Mingliang Wu (吴明亮), my cousin brother, pulled me to his chest, let me sit on his knees, and then said to me: "Little brother, come here and let me touch your head!" Then he used his big hands to touch my forehead to the top of my head, and then from the top of my head to the back of my head, and then his two hands touched from both temples to the back of my ears and ended. After touching my head, Mingliang cousin smiled and said to everyone: "Ouch! This little brother has an incredible brain! He is very smart and will be very good at studying in the future!" Everyone burst into laughter, and I embarrassedly broke away in the laughter.

Although I liked to recite *Three Character Classic* (《三字经》) and *Hundred Family Names* (《百家姓》) with my father since I was a child, there was one thing that made me feel resistant to going to school. When I was about four years old, there was a private school in the main hall of my eldest uncle's house next door. There were 10 to 20 elementary school students in the classroom. The teacher was my cousin's husband named Mingru Ye (叶明儒). One morning, when I was playing in the yard in front of my uncle's house, I suddenly heard the sound of reading in the main hall of my uncle's house, so out of curiosity I lay down through the crack of the door and looked into the classroom. At that time, the teacher was teaching students to recognize Chinese characters. One of the students was called to read a new character. Since he didn't know the character, he couldn't read it. So the teacher called the student to stand in front of the blackboard, and then used a stick made of palm strips to severely whip the student's palm. The number of whips depended on the number of strokes in the character. The more strokes, the more whips. At that time, I saw that the student whose palm was hit looked very painful. Every time the palm was whipped, student's hand would immediately retract to his chest. But the teacher said that it was not enough and it had to be beaten again. So the student reluctantly stretched out his palm and let the teacher continue to beat until the number of strokes was counted. In the end, the student's palm was beaten red and swollen. After the beating, the student's face became red and swollen, and tears welled up in his eyes and he almost cried out. Seeing such a scene, I was very scared at that time. Because my father saw that I was young, he mainly taught me to read and recite, and rarely taught me to recognize words. Even if he taught me to recognize words, I couldn't remember them. I thought that if I went to school and couldn't recognize the new words taught by the teacher, I would definitely be beaten. The palm stick hurt a lot when it hit people, and I couldn't bear it. The next spring, when I was about five years old, one morning, my father wanted to send me to my cousin's husband's private school to start learning, but I was afraid of being beaten and refused to go. As a result, my father was so angry that he picked up a small bamboo stick and chased me around to beat me. While chasing me, he kept cursing: "Damn it, since you don't want to go to school, then you can just carry a hoe and follow me to the mountains to open up wasteland!" Although I was young at that time, I was as light as a swallow and ran very fast. My father, who was nearly 70 years old, how could he catch up with me?! I remember that it was late spring, and the wheat seedlings had already grown taller than me. After my father chased me out of the house, I went straight to the wheat field outside the village. At this time, my father could not see where I was hiding, and there was no way to catch me. Seeing this, the neighbors persuaded my father: "Grandpa, forget it! The child is only five years old and does not understand. If he does not want to go to school, let him be. Wait for one or two years until he is older. You chase him like this, if he runs away, won't you be even sadder?" My mother also persuaded my father anxiously, asking him not to force me anymore. After hearing someone's persuasion my father gave up. But I thought that my father might not have completely given up the idea of letting me go to school and I wanted to make him more anxious, so I hid in the wheat field until lunch that day. I was hungry, so I sat in the wheat field and picked the peas to eat. My parents looked for me everywhere in the morning and couldn't find me. They seemed very anxious. Finally, my brother found me in the middle of the wheat field

and carried me back home. From then on, my father never dared to force me to go to school again. In this way, I played at home for another one or two years. By the autumn of 1955, I was more than seven years old. One night, Mingliang Wu (吴明亮) cousin brother came to my house to chat. He told my father: "Grandpa, I'm going to Mirun village to teach in September. The township has set up a primary school in Mirun village, and they invited me to be a teacher. You can let the youngest brother go to Mirun Primary School with me! What do you think?" My father said:
"That's very good! Your youngest brother is now more than seven years old, and it's time for him to go to school. Since you are teaching there, he can go with you!" When my father asked me if I was going to school, I thought that my cousin Mingliang Wu (吴明亮) liked me so much, and when he taught me to recognize words, if I couldn't recognize them, he would probably not beat me, so I agreed very readily. But I didn't know that the new-style schools run by the government did not allow beatings. Therefore, in early September of that year, I went to Mirun Primary School happily with a dozen of child friends in the village.

My childhood times before I went to primary school was relatively happy, because at that time, farming was still done by each household, and the rural people lived a simple and natural with quiet and peaceful life. In addition, my father was still alive at that time, and the family life was relatively comfortable, and it can be said that we had no worries about food and clothing. In addition, during my childhood, I often went up the mountain with my child friends to herd cattle, cut grass, chop firewood and play, which was very interesting. Although it has been more than 60 years, I often have good memories in my mind. In the early 1950s, the mountains near our hometown were full of primitive forests. In the forest, not only wild boars, hedgehogs, pangolins, weasels or yellow muntjacs and other wild animals could be seen everywhere, but also golden pheasants flying in the forest with beautiful long tails, as well as magpies, cuckoos, thrushes, yellow warblers, turtledoves and other various tits, and there were beautiful scenery all year round. Due to the good vegetation, the sweet and clear mountain spring water is continuous all year round. In summer, when the villagers came back from the Township market in Liuzhi Xiayingpan, they often sat in groups at the mouth of the Liangshuijing on the ridge of Laohei Mountain to rest. At this time, people would pick a large, thick fresh leaf from the bushes on the roadside, fold it into a funnel-shaped gourd, and then scoop a few gourds of cool and sweet mountain spring water to enjoy it slowly. The taste seemed to be more delicious than the popular cola now. In spring, not only are there fiery red azaleas blooming on the edge of the field and on the roadside, but also azaleas and wild flowers of various colors are blooming all over the mountains. The whole mountain village is like a beautiful landscape painting. In summer, when various wild fruits such as bayberry, peach, and plum are ripe, friends will invite each other to go up the mountain to pick bayberry or peach and other wild fruits. Among them, the big and purple-red charcoal bayberry in the small well is the most popular. The scenery in autumn is even more beautiful. At this time, not only are the maple leaves all over the mountains red like fire, but also wild fruits such as chestnuts, persimmons and kiwis can be seen everywhere on the mountain. At that time, there were fruit trees such as persimmons, walnuts and chestnuts in the corners of the fields near the Guojia Village and Shadijiao near the village. In the autumn, a few of us would often run to the foot of a chestnut tree on a mountain at dawn on a rainy morning to pick the largest and sweetest chestnuts. Sometimes we would take baskets up the mountain to pick kiwis or persimmons, and put them in the attic at home, and then we could eat them for ten days, a half month or even more than a month. The winter at that time was particularly cold. When we went out, we could often see the snow on the ridge of Laohei Mountain(老黑山), and the eaves of every house were covered with one or two feet long icicles. The paddy fields next to the village were covered with a thick layer of ice, so the child friends would use the small stools of home as ice sleds. They would turn the small stools upside down and lay them flat on the ice, and then sit in the middle of the belly of the stools to paddle and play. During the Spring Festival, we children not only eat all kinds of baba or snacks, but also wear new clothes. In addition, there are several high swings in the village for adults and children to play. Sometimes, my child friends will make a swing similar to the Korean swings to play with, that is, a one or two-meter-high pillar is erected on the flat ground, a rotating beam is placed on the top of the pillar, and then a small swing is hung on each end of the beam. Two children sit on each end, and when the side people help them turning, the adults and children are so happy that they clap their hands and cheer. In autumn or winter, when my friends and I go to the mountains to herd cattle, we always play the game of "hitting chicken sticks" on the flat ground (chicken sticks are two wooden sticks, one long and one short, one thick and one thin. Then we use one hand hold the big stick to hit the small stick, and the distance the big stick hits the small stick to determine the winner. This game

has strong skills and entertainment). This game is both safe and enjoyable. There are running and jumping, which not only exercises the brain, but also exercises the coordination of the body. My child friends like it very much. In different seasons of each year, various wild mushrooms will grow on the mountains in our hometown. For example, in early winter or early spring, large white winter mushrooms will grow on the dead tree stumps on the mountain. In summer, the thatched ground on the mountain will grow delicious collybia albuminosa. In the bushes, you can also pick morels, boletus, yellow silk mushrooms, etc. In autumn, there are fragrant mushrooms on the dead trees. In short, you can pick all kinds of mushrooms almost all year round. In winter, almost every family in our village would kill a pig for the New Year. When the pig was killed and smoked for bacons, when our family sat by the fire, my parents would always cut a large piece of lean meat from the pig leg that had not yet been smoked, and then put it on a bamboo stick and roast it for me to eat. The fresh and fragrant taste of the roasted meat was so delicious indescribable. I still drool when I think about it. In short, my hometown in my childhood is a place that I will always be haunted by, and there are many beautiful memories of my childhood.

(III)

Besides the beautiful natural scenery of my hometown at my childhood times, there were many local rural customs and habits, which also left me an indelible impression. With the changes of the times and the advancement of technology, many of these customs and habits have changed a lot, and some have completely disappeared already. Now even in the local rural areas, they may no longer be seen. Here I will briefly record a few so that our next generation can understand the original customs and habits of our hometown.

In the past, our local villagers used wood to build houses, because there was nothing else in our mountains except forests, and there was high-quality wood for building houses---fir wood all over the mountains. When people in the mountains build new houses, they usually decide how big the house should be based on the family's wealth, and the size of the house is judged by the "number of heads". The so-called number of heads refers to the number of columns in a row of fans composed of columns. The smallest house generally has 7 heads (that is, the highest column in the middle is used as the central column of the roof, and there are 3 columns on each side arranged symmetrically), and the largest house has 13 or 15 heads. The average small family builds a house with 7 heads, and there are also houses with 9 or 11 heads. Ordinary houses are generally three rooms long and two floors, that is, in addition to the middle room used as the main room, each side has a room as a bedroom or kitchen, and the upstairs is used as a warehouse for storing grain or for other purposes. A wealthy family usually builds a two-story house with 13 heads or more and five rooms. The middle room is used as the main room, and the four rooms on both sides are used as kitchens or bedrooms too. The main room is usually used to worship gods. In other words, each household will set up a shrine in the main room, on which there are tablets of *"Heaven, Earth, King, Parents, and Teachers* (天地君亲师)", which are commonly known as of ferings to Bodhisattvas. At the same time, the main room is also the place where important family affairs are handled. Therefore, the main room is a sacred place for a family. In addition, people often build wing rooms on the side of the main room to use as cattle (or horse) stable for raising livestock and to store firewood, plows, farm tools and other sundries.

For farmers, building houses is one of the major affairs of the family besides weddings and funerals. Therefore, farmers in the old days attached great importance to this. From choosing the foundation to when to build a house, they would ask Feng Shui masters to consider and choose a good day. On the day of building a house, the host usually had to organize a banquet to entertain relatives and friends. When people build a house, they usually hire two or three carpenters to supervise the construction, and no any nails can be used during the entire process. When building a new house, after the foundation is levelled, the carpenter will first use the firwood that has been cut and stored for a period of time to make a wooden bracket with 7, 9, or even more heads according to the owner's requirements. After the wooden bracket is finished, the carpenter (commonly known as the master builder) will offer sacrifice to **Master *Ban Lu* (鲁班)**[1] on an auspicious day and time (usually at about 5 a.m. on an auspicious day when it is just getting light). At this time, the master builder will come to the wooden bracket with a rooster in his left hand and a hatchet in his right hand, and gently knock the different pillars of the wooden bracket lying on the ground one by one with the back of the hatchet, while chanting loudly: *"The purple clouds in the sky have opened, and Ban Lu has come down to earth. Ban Lu came here when it was time to fell wood. One felling lasts forever, twice felling also last forever, three times of felling are the triple first-class honours, and four times of felling are constant prosperity and auspiciousness*! (天上紫云开，鲁班下凡来；鲁班来到此，正是伐木时。一伐天长地久，二伐地久天长；三伐三元及第，四伐常发吉祥！)" After the master

---

[1] *Ban Lu (**鲁班**) was a famous skilled craftsman and a great inventor in ancient China. Throughout his life, he invented many woodworking tools and constructed various architectural structures. His contributions had a profound impact on China's civil engineering and architecture, and he is revered by later generations as the "Patron of Carpentry and Architecture." Honouring Lu Ban before beginning work has become a unique cultural tradition in China. Carpenters offer rituals to Lu Ban in hopes of receiving his protection, ensuring safety and smooth progress during construction.*

builder offered sacrifice to Ban Lu, people immediately set off firecrackers, and then set up the wood frames of the house. At this time, young and mid-aged men in the whole village will come to the scene uninvited to help, so the scene is very spectacular. After the wooden brackets are erected, the carpenters immediately use some mortises and tenon structural parts of the wood to connect and fix several brackets together, so that the roof frame of the new house is established. After lunch, the wooden crossbeam is put up at the chosen auspicious time (usually around 1 pm on the day of the house building). The so-called beam-putting is to erect a specially selected large and thick beam on the two central pillars of the main hall in the centre of the new house. This wooden beam is carefully selected and presented by the wife's brother of the host's family. The wife's brother's family usually asks four young men to carry the beam covered with red or colourful decorations in the evening before the house building, and a group of drummers blow the Shona horn and beat the gongs and drums along the way to deliver it to the host's family. When they arrive at the village entrance of the host's family, they will also set off fireworks and firecrackers. The ceremony is quite grand.

贵州山民立新房上梁

Before the beam-putting at noon, the master builder first draws the **Bagua Tai Chi Diagram** (太极八卦图) in the middle of the beam sent by the wife's brother's family, and wraps several copper coins (or silver dollar coins) with red cloth and fixes them on the beam. At the same time, one or several red cloths about ten feet long and two or three feet wide, symbolizing auspiciousness and festivity, are folded in half and hung in the centre of the beam. Before the auspicious time to put up the beam, the master builder must first kill a rooster to offer sacrifice to the beam. At this time, the master builder first holds the wings of the rooster with his left hand, then uses his right fingernail to pinch the comb and squeeze out the chicken blood, and then smears the comb blood on the two ends and the middle of the beam, while smearing the chicken blood and chanting the sacrificial text loudly: *"My boss gave me a good rooster, and now I have it in my hand. One sacrifice to the east, house owner's sons and grandchildren will be in the imperial court; two sacrifices to the west, house owner's sons and grandchildren will wear imperial court clothes; Sacrifice the head of the beam, house owner's sons and grandchildren will be regional rulers; sacrifice the waist of the beam, house owner's sons and grandchildren will wear dragon robes; sacrifice the tail of the beam, house owner's sons and grandchildren will pass the imperial examinations!* (东家给我一只大雄鸡，而今拿在我手里。一祭东，儿子儿孙坐朝中；二祭西，儿子儿孙穿朝衣；祭梁头，儿子儿孙做诸侯；祭梁腰，儿子儿孙穿龙袍；祭梁尾，儿子儿孙高中举。）"

After the sacrifice to the beam, everyone tied the beam with a rope and lifted it up, and then placed it horizontally on the two central pillars in the middle of the hall. At this time, a group of drummers immediately played cheerful music, and people set off firecrackers on the wooden frame of the new house. The owner also sent people to throw some Liangba (a kind of sticky-rice cakes) and a small amount of clean water from the top of the frame to the crowd on the ground, indicating that the owner's house will be prosperous and auspicious after it is built. The people on the ground scrambled to grab the Liangba thrown from the top of the frame and the firecrackers that had not yet exploded, and the whole new house was full of joy. After the frame was erected, the interior and exterior house decoration, including the floor and walls, were all completed with wooden boards made from firwood. (Before bricks and tiles were fired in our area, our villagers just lived in the thatched wooden houses. In the late 1960s, our local area began to invite Sichuan brick-makers to guide the firing of bricks and tiles, and then people all lived in tile houses.) After such a wooden house was built, it was warm in winter and cool in summer, and it felt very comfortable to live in it. However, after entering the new century, although our area is still rich in timber, due to the closing hillsides to facilitate afforestation and the high price of timber, people no longer use timber to build houses. Instead, they have built sturdy and durable two or three or four-story reinforced concrete buildings. Every household lives a happy life with televisions and telephones upstairs and downstairs.

Secondly, there was a custom of "crying at the wedding ceremony" in our hometown. In the old days, when young men and young women reached the age of thirteen or fourteen, their parents would start to look for a partner in marriage for them. After finding a partner, the both families would *"Exchange the Eight Characters"* of man and woman.

【 *"Exchanging the Eight Characters" is a traditional Chinese marriage custom, mainly aimed at predicting whether a marriage will be harmonious by exchanging both parties' birth dates and times. This ritual typically takes place after the initial discussion of marriage between the two families, where the matchmaker exchanges the birth details (year, month, day, and time) of the couple to perform a compatibility assessment.*

A. *Specific Process and Purpose of Exchanging Eight Characters:*

(1). Exchanging Birth Details: Both parties exchange birth information through the matchmaker. The girl's birth details are written on red paper and given to the boy's family, while the boy's birth details are provided to the girl's family.

(2). Compatibility Assessment: Once the boy's family receives the girl's birth details, they will consult a fortune teller or a knowledgeable person to calculate whether the couple's Eight Characters are compatible, which helps determine whether the marriage is suitable.

(3). Choosing an Auspicious Date: The date for the exchange of eight characters is usually selected as a lucky day to ensure a smooth marriage.

B. Regional Differences in Exchanging Eight Characters: The customs related to exchanging Eight Characters may vary in different regions. For instance, in some places, this practice not only involves exchanging birth details but also includes engagement and the giving of betrothal gifts.】

After the fortune teller's calculations, if the boy's and the girl's Eight Characters are compatible, the boy's family will choose an auspicious day and send the matchmaker to the girl's family to deliver the compatibility of the Eight Characters of two parties, along with a betrothal gift. If the girl's family accepts the betrothal gift, the marriage is considered officially confirmed. One or two years after the girl's family accepted betrothal gift sent by boy's family, when both men and women were eighteen or nineteen years old, the both families would start to arrange their wedding ceremony again. As for the festive day for the wedding, it was generally chosen by the man's family and a fortune teller. When the man and woman got married, both families would organize a banquet to entertain their own guests, and the close relatives would generally give big gifts to the family holding the wedding. The first day of the marriage is the day when the bride's family prepares a banquet to entertain her relatives and friends. On this day, the bride's family would cook hundreds of eggs, dye the eggshells with rouge red, and then distribute these red eggs to the children of the neighbours to eat, which means joy and auspiciousness. The second day, the day of the marriage, is the day of the groom's family's celebration. On this day, the groom's family usually holds a grand banquet to entertain guests from all directions. The groom's family usually arrives at the bride's house in the evening of the first day when the bride's family holds a banquet. In addition to the groom, there are also a group of young people who deliver gifts to pick up the bride. The more particular the family is, the more it hires a sedan chair for the bride to ride. On the first day of a girl's wedding, she usually has to dress up carefully at home. The bride's sisterin-law or good girl-friend will use a red silk thread to help the bride remove the thick and conspicuous sweat hair on her lips (this is the so-called "twisting face" before the bride gets married), and also help her make her eyebrows into beautiful willow-shaped eyebrows. The hair should also be carefully combed, so that the bride looks more delicate and beautiful. At that time, there were no various cosmetics on the market. In families that were more particular, brides or girls often used rouge powder or vanishing cream. On the morning of the wedding day, whether it was the people from the bride's family or the people from the groom's family who came to pick up the bride, they got up very early before dawn. Before the sedan chair was lifted, the bride had already cried quietly in the boudoir, and when the sedan chair was lifted and left her parents' home, the bride cried even more sadly. Her original intention was that she felt that her parents had raised her for so many years, and now she was leaving her parents to start her new life, and she felt very reluctant in her heart. Therefore, the bride's crying before leaving home was very normal in the eyes of ordinary people, and no one would interfere or dissuade her. When the bride leaves her parents' home, in addition to setting off fireworks, the bride's family will usually invite a group of people (including two children as escort boys) to deliver the dowry sent by her parents' family to the groom's

A wedding team in the mountainous areas of Guizhou.

home along with the bride. The dowry sent by her parents' family usually includes: a bed, a wardrobe, a suitcase, several sets of brand new bed sheets and quilts, as well as the bride's clothes, etc. At the same time, in the wardrobe used as dowry, the bride's family often puts some nuts such as peanuts, walnuts and sunflower seeds, as well as some candies which symbolizes many children and good fortune, and secondly, after the bride is brought to her husband's home, when the young people make trouble in the bridal chamber on the wedding night, the bride will take them out as a reward to the young people to eat, so as to ease the embarrassment encountered during the wedding. After the bride's escort arrives at the groom's house, the bride's escort returns to her parents' home after the wedding banquet. The bride's escort boys and two or three direct relatives will stay at the groom's house for two days, and then return to her parents' home together on the third day when the bride and groom return to the bride's home. When I was four or five years old, I was a bride's escort boy because a niece got married. The scene at that time is still vivid in my mind.

In addition, in the old days, there was a bad custom of Shaman's dancing to cure diseases in our local rural areas and a funeral custom of "scattering joss-paper for the road" when burying the dead. In the old days, there were neither hospitals nor doctors in our hometown area. When people were sick, if they caught a cold, they would usually make a large bowl of hot chilli water or ginger soup and drink it while it was hot, then cover themselves with a quilt and sleep to sweat, and they might get better soon. If a headache or fever does not go away after a long time, or if there are some unidentified illnesses, people think that the patients might bump into a ghost, so they often invite a Taoist priest or a shaman to perform a shaman dance, and then take some Chinese herbal medicines to boil water to drink. After a week or so, the disease may be cured. People call this method of treatment "the two solutions of gods and medicine". In other words, just performing a shaman dance may not be effective, and some Chinese herbal medicines should be taken at the same time. People believe that shaman dance can cure diseases. In today's view, it actually plays a role of a mental placebo, because the patient may not have a serious illness. Even if there is no shaman dance, the disease may be cured after a period of time (of course, it may be relatively slow to heal). But after the shaman dance, the patient will naturally have the wish of "my disease will be cured soon after the shaman dance", and then the patient's immunity way be enhanced, so the disease could be cured faster. Therefore, in the old days, the villagers were very superstitious about the effect of shaman dance to cure diseases, and asking shamans to perform shaman dance to cure diseases was quite popular in rural areas at that time.

In my infancy time, I witnessed the shaman performing the shaman dance in my hometown many times. The scene of the shaman performing the shaman-dance is still vivid in my mind. Generally speaking, the shaman-dancing was holding in the evening, and it was divided into three steps, namely, inviting the gods, gods perform, and sending the gods away. When the shaman performed the god dances, people from the village would come to watch. When the shaman sat on the bench in the middle of the main hall of the host's house and chanted to invite the gods, the main hall of the host's house was often crowded with people. Some middle-aged men around the shaman would also chant along with the shaman to help invite the gods. After about ten minutes of chanting, the shaman's whole body began to tremble, and his emotions immediately became excited. At this time, the shaman said that he was "possessed" by a certain god, and then he danced in the middle of the main hall. At this time, the spirit possessed by the god can often do somethings incredible, such as reaching into the fire pit to get fire, stepping on the redhot fire tongs with bare feet without being burned, or eating burning paper balls soaked in vegetable oil, etc. At this time, the spirit possessed shaman will ask the host if he needs help from the god. The host will answer that someone in his family has been possessed by evil spirits and is sick, and hopes that the god can help the host to exorcise the evil spirits and cure the disease, etc. After the host helps the sick person to sit in the middle of the main hall, the shaman will ask the host to take a basin and put it on the ground in front of the patient, and pour some mild Baijiu (a kind of bulk alcohol) into the basin. The shaman then uses some joss-paper (ghost money) to light the Baijiu in the basin, and then repeatedly picks up the burning Baijiu in the basin with both hands and smears it back and forth on the patient's face. People call this operation of the gods washing the patient's "oil fire (油火) (actually washing the "wine fire" (酒火)). Since the alcohol content of bulk alcohol in rural areas is generally not high, the flame will go out immediately when the shaman applies liquor on the patient's face. The patient only feels a heat on his face, so it generally does not cause burns. After the shaman washes the "oil fire" for the patient, the patient goes back to the bedroom to rest. Next, the shaman will tell the fortune or predict the good and bad luck of the host family. At this time, the shaman will generally say that there are some problems in the host family that need to be rectified, such as the grave of the host's ancestor needs to be relocated and buried or a sheep needs to be killed for sacrifice, or there is a tree at the front door of the host's house that blocks the fortune and needs to be cut down, etc. After the shaman finishes dancing, the last step is to send god back. When sending back start, the sending words must be recited. After the shaman and the crowd recite the sending words for three to five minutes, two or three big barbarians will help the shaman stand upside down and climb up the closed door of the host's main hall with his feet. The shaman seems to stretch on the top, and after coming down, the spirit completely retreats, and the shaman returns to being an ordinary person. My third uncle(i.e, my mother's third sister's husband) from Zhangjiaping Village, Liuzhi, was an honest farmer who could not read or write, but he could actually perform the shaman dance and tell fortunes with ventriloquism (commonly called as "Lingge"(灵哥)), which was said to be very effective. Therefore, he was very popular in Liuzhi and Xiayunpan area. He was often invited by one family after another, and sometimes he was even too busy to handle it. When I was very young, someone in my family was sick and invited him to perform the shaman dance. I witnessed him performing the shaman dance with my own eyes. In front of everyone, he not only ate a lot of burning paper balls soaked in vegetable oil, but also bent the red-hot fire tongs that had just been taken out of the stove with his bare feet. The squeaking sound of the red fire tongs when they burned his bare feet and the smelly green smoke that came out are still vivid in my mind. Obviously, this is my third uncle's unique performance that makes people believe that he is possessed by a real god. But what I still find difficult to understand is how his feet could withstand such high temperatures of more than 600 or 700 degrees Celsius without getting burned. It is not difficult to see that the practice of healing illness by shaman-dancing was obviously the result of the poverty and backwardness of the rural areas in the old days, as well as the lack of medical care and medicine, and the ignorance of the people. In the 1950s, shaman-dancing to cure illness was quite popular in rural areas, but in the 1960s, with the government's education on "breaking superstition" in rural areas and the crackdown on superstitious activities during the Cultural Revolution, by the 1970s, the bad custom of shaman-dancing to cure diseases had basically disappeared in rural areas of Guizhou Province.

In the old days, when rural people got sick, there were no doctors to hire, and the people were poor and backward and had no money to treat them. Therefore, in addition to hiring a shaman to dance with gods, most people would persist or endure themselves after getting sick to see if he (she) would get better. Villagers believed that the death of an old person due to illness was inevitable in life, especially when the elderly over 60 or 70 years old person fell ill. Most families would not rush to treat them, but would be busy preparing for their funeral, such as preparing coffins, looking for a fortune teller to look at the land for the grave, preparing funeral items, etc. After a person dies,

The traditional burial customs for deceased individuals in rural areas of Guizhou Province.

they are usually buried in a coffin. For ordinary people, this is one of the major affairs of life, such as "marriage and funeral", so the common people have always attached great importance to it. When looking for a cemetery and choosing a burial date for the deceased, a geomancer should also be invited to repeatedly consider and determine the date of birth of the deceased. At the same time, when burying the deceased, the host family will also invite a Taoist priest to perform a Taoist ceremony, that is, invite the Taoist priest to chant Buddhist scriptures to help the deceased's soul transcend. We call this chanting ceremony "accompanying the spirit" (伴灵) in our local area. When the Taoist priest performs a ceremony to accompany the spirit, it is usually held in the main hall of the host's house. If the main hall of the host's house is too small or there are too many guests, a temporary mourning hall will be built outdoors to accompany the spirit. Most people only chant Buddhist scriptures for the deceased just for one night, while more sophisticated wealthy families may hold a ceremony for three days and three nights, but this is extremely rare. When the Taoist priest chants Buddhist scriptures and performs a ceremony, the filial sons and grandsons of the host's family must wear mourning clothes and kowtow around the coffin of the deceased on a regular basis under the guidance of the Taoist priest. When the Taoist priest performs a ceremony to accompany the spirit that night, most men in the village will come to support the ceremony. When the coffin is carried up the mountain early the next morning before dawn (on an auspicious day and time), there will be crowds of people along the way, and young and middle-aged men from the whole village will come forward to help. This is the second important moment when people come uninvited after repairing and building a house. At this time, under the arrangement of the Taoist priest, the host family will scatter a large amount of joss-paper (ghost money) along the road as tolls. After the coffin is put into the tomb, the Taoist priest will kill a sheep to sacrifice to the gods and scatter some joss-paper money to "buy land" (i.e. to buy a cemetery for the deceased). At this time, one person will walk in front of the tomb on behalf of the land owner, and will continue to shout loudly while walking: "Selling the land! Selling the land!" Another person will lead the sheep and follow closely behind, scattering joss-paper money while walking and constantly answering on behalf of the host family: "Buying the land! Buying the land!" Such funeral customs are only for us Han people in Guizhou. The local Yi, Miao or Gelao and other indigenous peoples do not need to scatter joss-paper money to buy land and to buy roads when burying their deceased. It is said that this custom originated from when our Han ancestors first came to Guizhou hundreds of years ago. Guizhou was not only a wild land, but also ruled by chieftains of the Yi (彝族), Miao (苗族) or Gelao (仡佬族) ethnic groups. At that time, they were the majority of the aboriginal people, and we, the Han (汉族) people who came from outside, were the minority, so the Han people had to accept their rule. Since the local land and mountains belonged to the aboriginals, when a Han person died and the family of deceased wanted to carry the coffin of the deceased to the mountain for burial, they had to first use silver to buy a cemetery from the chieftains, and when carrying the coffin up the mountain, they had to pay a toll to the chieftains too, otherwise the chieftains would not allow Han people to bury the dead. Later, as the number of Han people migrating from other provinces gradually increased, the power of the Han people also grew. The Tusi (i.e, chieftain) felt that it was inappropriate to collect money from the Han people to bury the dead, so the Han leaders reached a new agreement with the Tusi leaders, that is, before the Han people buried the dead, they no longer had to pay money or other physical presents, but only had to symbolically throw some joss-paper (ghost money) to the deceased ancestors of the chieftains as money to buy cemeteries and pass through, so both sides were happy. From then on, the custom of Han people in Guizhou throwing josspaper (ghost money) along the way as tolls and cemetery purchases when burying the dead became a custom passed down from generation to generation, and this custom has never changed until today.

(IV)

In the past, there was no formal primary school in the villages near our hometown. It was not until 1955 that the township opened a public primary school in Mirun Village, adjacent to our Shanmu village. In early September of that year,

I went to school happily with the colourful rattan schoolbag my brother bought for me. Mirun Primary School is about one and half kilometres away from our village, and it takes about 15 minutes to walk there. At that time, this primary school was newly opened, and there was no readymade school building, nor any tables, chairs and benches for formal teaching. Except for a public house built by the township at the beginning of liberation, the rest of the classrooms were temporarily borrowed from the main hall of the villagers' homes, and the tables, chairs and benches were also brought by the students themselves. Not only was there a shortage of classrooms, but there were also not enough teachers, so the first and second grades shared a classroom and a teacher. When the teacher taught, he taught the first grade first, and then the second grade, and each grade had half a class. Our first and second grade Chinese teacher happened to be my cousin Mingliang Wu (吴明亮), and it was he who gave me my full name "Mingqing Wu" (吴明清). On the first day of school, he gave names to the students in our class who didn't have a name. When it was my turn to be named, he said, "Since you are from the Ming generation, I'll give you the name Mingqing Wu (吴明清)! Mingqing means to be a clear person and do things clearly. Do you understand?" From then on, I had the name "Mingqing Wu (吴明清)", and it has been used to this day.

There were about 30 students of grade one and two in our classroom. Our classroom was a public house built by the township government in Mirun Village in the early days of liberation. There were no formal chairs and benches in the classroom. The so-called desks were just a few thick wooden boards of 40 to 50 cm wide and two meters long placed on square stools or stones. As for the chairs, they were small benches brought by the students from home. The school conditions were extremely simple. In addition, the classroom was ventilated on all sides, the windows were empty, not to mention glass, there was no paper to paste the windows, and there was no celling in the room. At first glance, it was just beams and tiles. In spring, summer and autumn, it was not a big problem for students to sit in class, but in winter, the classroom was very cold. In order to solve the problem of students keeping warm during winter classes, the school initially required students to bring their own fire baskets (a bamboo basket with a small charcoal brazier inside) to school for heating. However, only a few students had fire baskets, and most students did not have them at home, so

A group photo with my nephews, nieces and great-nephew in Puding, Guizhou in May, 2000. (The author is the middle person).

many students used old pottery jars or old casseroles to bring charcoal fire to school for heating. During class, some students often made fires, which made the whole classroom smoky and full of students' coughs. The teachers had to wait until the students were quiet before they could start the class. Not long after, the school paid for coal, so they burned several large fires around the classroom, which made the classroom much warmer, and students no longer had to bring their own fire baskets or braziers.

Our first and second grade combined class mainly had Chinese, arithmetic, physical education, writing big characters (brush calligraphy) and music courses at that time. Among them, Chinese and writing classes were taught by Teacher Mingliang Wu (my cousin). Teacher Wu had a very loud voice during class and very strict classroom discipline. He first wrote the new words for the new lesson on the blackboard, then taught the students to recognize and read them word by word, and finally taught us to read the lesson. After teaching the new lesson once or twice, he asked the students to read it aloud by themselves. After reading the lesson aloud, he asked students to stand up and read the new words. Although corporal punishment was not allowed in new-style schools, students who could not recognize the new words would often be called up to stand or severely criticized. I remember that when we are in Chinese class, I not only recognized all the new words that the teacher taught in our first-grade Chinese class, but also all the new words that the teacher taught in the second-grade Chinese class. So whenever there were individual students in the second grade who could not recognize the new words, Teacher Wu would always call me up to read them to the whole classroom. Whenever I finished reading new words fluently, Teacher Wu would always say to the second-grade students who stood up and could not read new words: "I think you are really a fool! Look at Mingqing Wu, who is so young and has just started school, and can recognize them. Why can't you recognize them? Is your head full of tofu dregs? Tell me, is it true?!" I knew that Teacher Wu was criticizing the student who could not recognize new words, but in fact he was also praising me, so I felt shy and happy at the time, and my interest in learning became stronger.

Author was in Kunming, Yunnan, China with great-great-nephew Shilong Wu ((right) in April, 2019.

We had just finished one semester in the first grade of elementary school, and it was the beginning of 1956 in a blink of an eye. The Spring Festival would come soon after the winter vacation in mid-January. I remember that my father had many rules for celebrating the Chinese New Year. First of all, the Kitchen God (灶神) should be worshipped on the 23rd day of the twelfth lunar month, and the worship of the Kitchen God was mostly done at night. Around 11 or 12 o'clock at night (most of us kids were asleep), my parents would put a bowl of knife meat (a three-inch square piece of fresh pork belly or bacon with skin and fat that had been cooked) on the stove, pour a small cup of liquor, and then light three incense sticks and stick them on the stove. My father would first kowtow three times on the floor in front of the stove, then bow twice after getting up, and then chant: "Bodhisattva (菩萨)! When you go to heaven to report to the Jade Emperor, please say speak well of our family and bless our whole family to be safe and sound, and have good weather and good harvests in the coming year." The 24th day of the twelfth lunar month is the day for general cleaning. On this day, not only the clothes and quilt covers of the whole family, including tables, chairs, benches, etc., must be taken out and cleaned, but also the inside and outside of the house must be cleaned, especially the dust and spider webs on the roof, etc., all of which must be cleaned. After cleaning, the next few days are spent preparing for the New Year. For example, the men are busy slaughtering the New Year pig, and the women are busy making tofu, pounding sticky rice powder, and making various grain cakes or pure sticky rice cakes, etc., all the way until New Year's Eve. On the morning of New Year's Eve, the women are busy steaming sticky rice early in the morning, and then the men beat the steamed sticky rice into glutinous rice cakes. At noon, the whole family eats glutinous rice cakes. When eating glutinous rice cakes, the whole family sits around the eight-immortal table, each holding a ball of hot glutinous rice cake that has just been kneaded into a ball in both hands, and then pinching the glutinous rice cake into small pieces, and then dip them in brown sugar water or honey, and wrap them in roasted and ground sesame powder or roasted soybean flour, and finally put the glutinous rice cake into the mouth. Such hot glutinous rice cakes taste unique and are especially filling. In the evening, there was a big table of chicken, duck, fish and meat, and more than 20 dishes for the sumptuous New Year's Eve dinner. When my father was alive, there was a small land temple below our village. Before eating the New Year's Eve dinner, each household would carry a knife head meat to the land temple to offer to the land bodhisattva, and this task mostly fell on us children. Since the time to offer to the land bodhisattva was mostly during dinner time, there were many families going there at the same time, so when we arrived, we often had to wait in line and then offer in order. When offering to the land bodhisattva, we first put the knife head meat on the offering board of the land temple, inserted three lit incense sticks, and then burned a few pages of joss-paper, then made two bows, then knelt down and kowtowed three times, and then stood up and made two more bows, and the ceremony of offering to the land bodhisattva was over. After offering to the land bodhisattva, we hurried home with our own knife head meat, eager to get home early to eat delicious food. In those days, offerings to the Earth Bodhisattva usually started on New Year's Eve and continued until the Lantern Festival on the 15th day of the first lunar month. Offerings were made twice a day, at lunch and dinner. After offerings to the Earth Bodhisattva before the New Year's Eve dinner, the family had to offer sacrifices to the Bodhisattva and the ancestors in the family before eating. In those days, every household in our rural area had an altar of *"**Heaven, Earth, King, Parents, and Teachers** (天、地、君、亲、师)"* in the main hall, and they would offer sacrifices to this Bodhisattva before eating during every festival (at that time, when people talked about *"Bodhisattva"* (菩萨), they believed that Bodhisattva was omnipotent, and that Bodhisattva knew everything people did, and they were also blessed by Bodhisattva. Therefore, no matter adults or children, everyone was very awed by Bodhisattva). After offering to the Bodhisattva on New Year's Eve, the next step is to offer to the ancestors of the family. At this time, the bowls on the table should still be filled with rice, chopsticks and stools should be placed, and the wine glasses should be filled with wine. Then the male host of the family stands at the front of the square table and recites the names and titles of the ancestors in the family one by one. This means that all the ancestors in the family are invited to come and have the New Year's Eve dinner. We hope that the ancestors will eat and drink well and bless the men, women, old and young in our family to be safe and healthy. After reciting, about 5 minutes later (meaning that the ancestors have finished their New Year's Eve dinner already), some joss-paper (hell money) will be burned for the ancestors. At this time, the male host will also call all the children in the family to kowtow to the ancestors together, so we will first do two bows under the square table, then kneel down and kowtow three times, and then stand up and do two bows. The ceremony of offering meal is completely over, and the New Year's Eve dinner officially began.

After eating the New Year's Eve dinner on the 30th of the 12th lunar month, every household will stay up all night as usual. There is a local saying during the New Year that goes "*Fire on the 30th night, lights on the 15th* (三十夜的火, 十五的灯)." The so-called fire on the 30th night means that every year on the night of the 30th of the twelfth lunar month, every household will burn a basket of coal or firewood that is bigger and more prosperous than usual, and then the whole family will sit around the fire hall, eating all kinds of snacks or melon seeds, peanuts, etc., while chatting and laughing. And "lights on the 15th" means that on the 15th day of the first lunar month, the Lantern Festival, every household will hang lanterns or light lights indoors and outdoors, making the house brightly lit and festive. In addition, after eating the New Year's Eve dinner on the night of the 30th of the twelfth lunar month, every household will boil hot water to wash their feet as usual. When it was our turn to wash our feet, the parents would always say to us: "Be careful when you wash your feet tonight! You must wash your feet to the knees, so that when you visit other people's homes in the future, you will happen to see them eating, and you will have food to eat. If you don't wash your feet to the knees, then you may go to other people's homes too early and it's not time to eat; if you wash your feet above the knees, then you may go to other people's homes too late, and they have finished their meal, and then you will not have a chance to eat!" At that time, we children always half believed and half doubted, always thinking that the parents were joking, and the purpose was to coax us to wash our feet more cleanly. However, most of us still did what the parents said. Every night on New Year's Eve, we would wash our feet more seriously and carefully than usual, and we would definitely wash our feet to the knees. It is not difficult to see from this custom that, first, it shows that the issue of eating has always been the most concerned issue for the people; second, it shows that the folk customs in the past were still relatively simple and honest. In those days, whenever you went to a house, if you saw someone eating, the host would definitely treat you. If you refused, the host would always say, "Why are you being polite? It's just an extra pair of chopsticks and an extra bowl." Whenever such a situation occurred, the host had already scooped up all the rice and put it on the table, and the guests often couldn't refuse. Even if they had just finished their meal, they would pick up the bowl and eat a bowl or half a bowl. I witnessed such scenes many times in our home when I was a child. If the guest insisted on not eating, he would be considered ungrateful, or that he thought the host's food was not good enough, etc. If it got out, such a person would be looked down upon. In addition, when staying up at night on the 30th night, the adults often asked us children not to sleep or doze off, and to stay with the adults by the fire. But how could we children stand it? We often fell asleep by the fire before midnight, so our parents had to carry us to bed. In addition, every year on the night of New Year's Eve, my father had another must-do job, which was to fetch "silver water" from the well. Usually on the night of New Year's Eve, around 2 or 3 o'clock in the middle night before daybreak, he would carry two small-mouthed ceramic jars with corks (usually wine jugs) to the well near the village to fetch two pots of spring water, and then bring them home and hang them in the attic of our house. My father called these two pots of spring water "silver water", which indicated and prayed that our family would have more money in the coming year. After bringing these two pots of "silver water" home and hanging them up, no one knew how long they would be kept or what to do with them, because no one had ever touched them while they were hanging there (because my father had told the family that no one was allowed to touch the "silver water" he brought back, and what my father said was often like an imperial decree in our family, and the family members never dared to disobey). As far as I can remember, my father would go to the well to fetch "silver water" in the middle of the night on New Year's Eve every year. Even though our family didn't make much money every year, but he still enjoyed doing it.

Just after the Spring Festival in 1956, my father fell ill on the seventh day of the first lunar month. At first, I heard that he had caught a cold and had a fever, and he coughed in the middle of the night. At that time, there was no hospital or doctor in our hometown. We just found some herbs to boil water for him to drink, but his condition not only did not improve, but worsened day by day. After the tenth day of the first lunar month, not only did he have a high fever, but he also had diarrhea. He even had diarrhea after eating anything. Vomiting and diarrhea made him thinner day by day. At that time, the countryside had already become a primary cooperative of agricultural cooperation. Shortly after the New Year, the members were busy accumulating fertilizer and preparing for farming. Even the children participated in collecting fertilizer. Most people carried a dustpan or a basket and went all over the mountains and fields to pick up cow dung and horse dung, and then handed them over to the production team. I remember that the fifteenth day of the first lunar month, the Lantern Festival, was a sunny day. The weather was particularly good. Not only was the sun shining brightly, but it was also very warm. That afternoon, I was picking up cow dung in the rotten fields above the village with a few child-friends. At this time, someone came to the wild to find me. When he saw me, he said to me: "Little youngest, go home quickly! Your mother asked me to come and find you and she said that your father is dying. You should go home quickly!" After hearing the news, I ran all the way back home. It was about five or six o'clock in the afternoon. I saw my mother, sister, second aunt, fourth aunt and other women, wiping tears in front of my father's bed. When my mother saw me coming back, she quickly pulled me to my father's bed. At this time, my father could hardly speak, but when he saw me, he held on. My mother and I quickly bent down and threw ourselves on the bed to support his shoulders. My father held my hand and said hoarsely: "My little youngest boy, I am afraid that I will die. You must study hard!" Then he could no longer speak, and soon my father died. At this time, my mother, sister, second aunt and other women began to cry loudly. I heard the crying and felt sad and scared, tears kept falling. I knew my father had died. He was 71 that year, and I was just 8 years old.

(V)

After we finished the first grade of Mirun Primary School, the township government decided to abolish Mirun Primary School when the new school year started in September, 1956, because Mirun Primary School did not have the good conditions to run a school. All the students were merged into Laliu Primary School, which was located in the Laliu Township Government. After merging with Laliu Primary School, there was only one complete primary school in the entire Laliu Township. At that time, there were two classes in each grade from the first to the third grade of Laliu Primary School, and one class in each grade from the fourth to the sixth grade. There were 30 to 40 students in each class, so there were about 350 students in the whole school. After transferring to Laliu Primary School, students were commuters at the beginning, that is, all students, no matter how far away from the school, walked to school in the morning and walked back home after class in the afternoon. Our village was about four km away from the school, and it took about 45 minutes to walk to school. Of course, our village is not the farthest from the school. The farthest students, such as Shabao and Taojialanba villages, live more than 15 km away from the school, and the roads are all mountainous. The school starts at about 8:30 a.m. in the morning. Those students who live far from the school have to get up before dawn to travel. The school ends at about 4:30 p.m. in the afternoon. If it is winter, when those students who live far away get home from school in the afternoon, it is already completely dark. Therefore, it is more difficult for them to go to school. It is dark both at the beginning and the end. In comparison, the students in our village are obviously much luckier.

When I was in the second grade of elementary school, the teacher who taught us Chinese and music was a tall, beautiful, and very fashionable young female teacher. Her name was Guolan Chen (陈国兰). She lived in Dabatou Village. I heard that she came from Guiyang and was the daughter-in-law of a wealthy family in Dabatou Village. Teacher Chen is not only beautiful, but also a good teacher. She speaks softly in class and never loses her temper. Therefore, the students like her very much. We had a music class every week, and she also taught us. She sang very well and taught us many songs, including

"Kangding Love Song" (《康定情歌》), *"Blue Sky White Clouds Floating"* (《蓝蓝的天上白云飞》, *"Kajusha"* (《喀秋莎》) and other songs that she taught us to sing. Teacher Chen taught us for one semester, and she stopped teaching in the second semester of the second grade. I didn't see her in the school. Later, I heard that she went back to Guiyang. After my cousin Mingliang Wu (吴明亮) transferred to Laliu Primary School, he still taught the first grade of primary school, but after one semester, I also didn't see him again. Later, I heard that the school cleaned up and reorganized the teaching staff. Some people said that Teacher Guolan Chen (陈国兰) was the child of a landlord, and my cousin Mingliang Wu (吴明亮) was a landlord member, so the school didn't let them teach. For this reason, I still felt a little disappointed, because Teacher Wu was my cousin after all, and he had a very good relationship with my family. Later, although Mingliang Wu (吴明亮) stopped teaching, he never stopped concerning about my study in the school. Until I was in junior and senior high school, he often come to my house during the vacations to see my academic transcripts and understand my learning situations at school.

I had been a study committee member in my class since the third grade of primary school, because my Chinese and arithmetic grades were always among the best in the class, and the monitor was Minghua Hu (胡明华) from Dabatou village. Minghua Hu (胡明华) has an older brother named Mingde Hu (胡明德), who also studied in Laliu Primary School and was the monitor of the fifth grade. Minghua Hu (胡明华) was four or five years older than me. He was tall in the class and had good academic performance, always ranking in the top one or two. Although I had good academic performance, I was young and short, and I didn't like to talk, and I blushed when I talked, so the head teacher said to me: Mingqing Wu, you should be a study committee member. In fact, the duty of the study committee member is to help the teacher collect and distribute homework books in the class, and there is nothing else to do.

The first political movement I have experienced and still remember in my mind should be the "Anti-Rightist (反右派)" in

1957. I remember it was around June to July of 1957. At that time, the countryside was in the advanced stage of agricultural collectivization. Our Shanmu Village, including Indigo Mountain, Qingjiao and Tanziyao villages, was a production brigade. At that time, the township sent cadres to each production brigade to organize and mobilize members to hold meetings to launch *"**the Great Debate Movement**"* (大鸣大放运动) and *"let people speak freely and openly"*, to give opinions to the leaders and to write big-character posters. At that time, behind our house was Denggao Yang's house. Denggao Yang (杨登高), who was born in a poor and lowermiddle peasant family (Yang was my cousin's husband), was a brigade cadre of our Shanmu Brigade. The brigade office seemed to be set up in his house. At that time, Denggao Yang was very enthusiastic about his work. When the brigade held meetings, he was often the host of the meeting, and his voice was very loud when he spoke to people. Most of the cadres who came from the township stayed in his house, and the brigade meetings were held in his house too. When the brigade organized members to hold meetings to "let people speak freely and openly" to the leaders, most of them were held at night, and the venue was behind our house. Out of curiosity, we children would sometimes go to join in the fun. One night, after I entered the main hall of my cousin's husband Denggao Yang's house, I saw that not only were the walls covered with big-character posters, but there were also several rows of big-character posters hung horizontally in the middle of the hall with ropes. The brigade member representatives sat on the benches, and everyone gave their opinions to the brigade cadres, the head of the cooperative team, or the various policies of the party. When the brigade members gave their opinions, they often expressed them in the form of rhymes. Although it has been more than 60 years already, I still remember one or two of them. At that time, the rural advanced agricultural cooperatives had already implemented a rationing system of grains for the members. In the meantime, cooperative production team required members to go to work and leave work together. Thus, people think that individuals have no freedom. I remembered that at that time, regardless of adults or children, each person was allocated 430 Jin(215 kg) of raw grain (whether rice or corn) per year. This amount should be enough for some families with many children, but for most families with a large population and few children, this amount was obviously insufficient. Therefore, in response to this grain rationing policy, the farmers composed a few rhymes to express their opinions at the *"Great Debate"* meeting:

"人人定量四百三，吃了不够望拿来添；
若是吃完不得添，群众将饿得打偏偏！"

"Everyone's ration is 430 Jin (215 kg), but it's not enough, and we hope for more; If we finish and get no more, people will starve and fall."

Another rhyme criticized the lack of freedom under collectivization:

"合作化来好是好，可是社员不能到处跑；
若是领导找不见，抓回来就脱不了爪爪！"

"Collectivization is fine, but you can't go anywhere; If the leader can't find you, you will be dragged back in trouble!"

At the "Great Debate" meeting, the brigade or team cadres who were exposed by the members of the production team with corruption problems would sometimes be caught by the people attending the meeting, tied up and criticized, and such criticism meetings were often held at night. When we children saw such scenes at that time, we felt very scared. We thought how could those critics be so cruel and do such things? The adult world is really cruel. The arms of the person being criticized were tied tightly with brown ropes by two or three men. Soon, the palms and fingers of the person being tied turned black, and his face showed a painful expression. During the criticism, whenever the person being criticized did not admit the accusation, the critics would take out two twothree-foot-long wooden sticks, pry them on the left and right arms of the person being criticized, and press them down hard to make the brown ropes tighter. At this time, the person being criticized would scream "Ouch! Ouch!" in pain. When we saw such a scene, we would be so scared that we dared not even look at it and quickly ran back home. After returning home, because the criticism meeting was right behind our house and it was particularly quiet at night, when I woke up in the middle night, I would often hear the painful screams of the person being criticized when he was beaten for not admitting the accusation, so I would quickly cover my ears with a quilt.

However, although the "Anti-Rightist" movement of that year also affected the countryside, the superiors may think that the farmers only have little culture, and even if they put forward some radical opinions or posted some "unreliable" big-character posters, it would not have much impact in the countryside. Therefore, no one in our village was labeled a rightist. However, our Laliu Primary School was not so lucky. There was a Chinese teacher in our school named Xinghe Long (龙 兴 和). His hometown was Yanjiao Town, Langdai County. He went to Guizhou University before liberation. He was a well-mannered and slow-talking intellectual. I don't know what opinions he gave to the school leaders at that time or the various policies of the Communist Party during the Anti-Rightist Movement in 1957. As a result, he was labeled the only rightist in Laliu Primary School that year. At the same time, he was also the only primary school teacher with a university degree in Laliu Primary School. Not long after being labeled a rightist, Teacher Xinghe Long (龙 兴和) was "cleared" from the teaching team and was not allowed to teach in Laliu Primary School. For this reason, many parents of students in our school felt deeply sorry for the loss of such a knowledgeable teacher in Laliu Primary School.

In the second half of 1957, when I was in the first semester of the third grade of primary school, there was a wave of major water conservancy project repairs in rural areas. Two or three reservoirs were planned to be built near our hometown in Tanziyao and Dadichong, and the township government organized the labor of each production team to concentrate on the repair regardless of gender, age or status. At that time, it was already the advanced stage of agricultural cooperation, and collective canteens were set up in various places according to production teams. Since the rural labor force was drawn to build water conservancy projects, there was no one to take care of the children at home, so nurseries and kindergartens were also popular in rural areas at that time, and some old and weak women were drawn to serve as aunts. The two children of my brother and sister also were sent to kindergartens at that time, so my mother also worked as an aunt in the nursery for a period of time. Since collective canteens had been opened in various places, we elementary school students had no place to eat when we went home from day school, so the school decided to let all day students change to live in school and eat in the collective canteen set up on school campus.

Speaking of opening collective canteens in rural areas, the enthusiasm of farmers was very high at the beginning. Because they heard that they could eat delicious food every day in the collective canteen without paying, so as soon as the propaganda was made, every household handed in all the delicious food at home, such as bacon, sausage, lard, vermicelli, tofu, as well as all the rice and flour, to the collective canteen. The canteen of our production team was set up in the home of my cousin Minggang Wu (吴明刚), and the meat, grain, rice and other foods handed in by all the members of the production team were stored upstairs and downstairs in his house. The canteen also selected the two brothers Shaowu Li (李少伍) and Chongru Li (李崇儒), who were recognized as good cooks in the production team, as chefs, and my old brother was the cashier. When the canteen was first opened, meals were served like a banquet held by farmers. More than 10 large square tables were lined up in the courtyard in front of the kitchen. Nearly a hundred members of the production team, including adults and children, sat at each table with eight people. There were about twenty dishes on each table, such as sausages, bacon, chicken, duck, fish, meat, etc. Adults and children laughed and talked while eating. The scene was very lively, and the dishes were different every two or three days. However, after all, the material reserves and economic conditions of rural families were limited, and the production capacity of rural areas was very low. The days of feasting and drinking in the collective canteen did not last long. The chickens, ducks, fish, meat, bacon, sausages, etc., handed in by each household were basically eaten up, so the food in the collective canteen gradually became worse day by day. Later, as the food supply became increasingly tight, the collective canteen also gradually transitioned from eating and drinking with an open belly to weighing the food according to the number of people. At this time, the attitude of farmers towards the collective canteen also dropped to the lowest point.

As for the elementary school students living in the school dormitory, none of the rural children had any decent luggage. The whole belongings were an old quilt, a straw mat, a cloth bag filled with two litres of rice husk as a pillow, and a small wooden basin, which was used as a wash basin for washing faces and sometimes as a foot basin for washing feet. As for the enamel wash basin, it was a luxury product at that time. At that time, I only saw the cadres of the township government using it. Enamel wash basins were not only expensive, but also unavailable, not to mention that the rural people could not afford them. When sleeping, a bundle of straw was laid under the straw mat, which felt soft and warm. Twenty or thirty boys in our class slept on the wooden floor. At that time, no one in our rural Guizhou had a mosquito net on the bed. Before going to bed in the summer night, every household would light some firewood that could produce smoke in the house and open all the doors and windows. At this time, the mosquitoes in the house could not stand the smoke and flew out of the house. After about ten minutes of fumigation, almost all the mosquitoes in the room flew away, so all the doors and windows were closed, and then people went to bed. So the villagers called this magical operation before going to bed as "repelling mosquitoes". However, we couldn't repel mosquitoes when we slept in school, because we lived in a wooden house, the bed was on the wooden floor, and it was straw under the bed. If we burned some grass to repel mosquitoes, it might cause a fire disaster, so repelling mosquitoes was absolutely not allowed in school. Fortunately, around 20 or 30 of us students slept in a large room, and since we were just kids who slept deeply, even if there were mosquito bites, each of us would only get a few bites on average. Often, we would sleep soundly until dawn, so no one really cared whether there were mosquito bites. But it was very cold to sleep in winter, because the dormitory was ventilated on all sides, and the straw mat was very thin and cold. However, when it was cold, we also had a way to deal with it. At this time, we would squeeze two, three or even three or four students to sleep together, and then press several quilts together, which felt much warmer.

After living on campus, students eat in the school-run canteen. At that time, we don't have to pay for meals, which means our meals were completely free. But we can only eat two meals a day, lunch at around 12:00 o'clock noon and dinner at 5 to 6 p.m. When it's time to eat, the chefs in the canteen carry the big steamer for steaming rice to the courtyard outside the canteen and put it there. After the lid is opened, a few wooden ladles are placed in each rice steamer for scooping rice. You can scoop as much or as little as you want. At the beginning, we only ate rice, and we could also eat meat in the dishes. Later, coarse grains were gradually added to the rice, such as cornmeal or corn grits mixed with rice. Later on, vegetables were added to the rice, and the food gradually became insufficient. The dishes that the students ate were cooked vegetables in enamel basins and placed on the ground in the courtyard. Seven or eight students shared a basin, and everyone squatted on the ground to eat. After the basin of vegetables was finished, no more was added. At the beginning, there was meat in the dishes, but gradually there was no meat, and the cooking oil became less and less. Most of the time, we ate eggplant, old pumpkin or Swiss chard. Due to the lack of cooking oil, these vegetables were hard to eat, but we had to eat them because we were hungry. Since children in their teens were growing and developing, they were not only active but also consumed a lot of food. However, due to the lack of oil and meat, they ate more rice. Therefore, when it was time for dinner, the students ate like hungry wolves, and everyone was scrambling for food. We kids not only ate quickly, but we also invented a "little trick" in the process of scooping rice. In the beginning we eat at the canteen, the quality of the food was good, so we could eat full whether we use a big bowl or a small bowl. But later, as the quality of the food became worse and worse, the food was cooked less than before. Many people had just eaten half full and there was no rice in the rice cooker when they scooped rice. To deal with this, most students later bought large enamel mugs to use as rice bowls. When eating, they would first scoop half or three-quarters of a mug of rice first to eat. After finishing that, they would scoop a second full mug of rice. Sometimes they would even use a rice ladle to pack the rice down tightly before filling the mug to the brim. In this way, even if people who eat with large mugs eat slowly, as long as there are some rice in the rice cooker when they scoop the second time, they will definitely be full. Until today, I still eat quickly and in large quantities, a bad habit I developed in elementary school when I was in third or fourth grade, competing for food at school. Although I am already over seventies years old, I still haven't been able to change this bad habit.

(VI)

During the *Great Leap Forward (大跃进)* in 1958, almost all people were under quasi-military management, and rural labor was uniformly deployed. Today, commune members might be sent to this commune to build a reservoir or a road, and tomorrow they might be sent to another commune to make steel. In the alleys and lanes of rural villages, there were large slogans written with white lime everywhere, such as *"Work hard, strive for the best, build socialism quickly, efficiently and economically! "* *(鼓足干劲，力争上游，多快好省地建设社会主义)*, *"Long live the three red flags of the general line, the Great Leap Forward and the people's commune! "* *(总路线、大跃进、人民公社三面红旗万岁!)*, *"Take grain as the key link, take steel as the key link!"* *(以粮为纲，以钢为纲)*, *"Surpass UK and catch up with the USA in 15 years! "* *(十五年超英赶美!)*, etc. At that time, in addition to the construction of water conservancy projects, there was a wave of steel production all over the country, and earthen blast furnaces were built everywhere; secondly, rural areas in various places were *"launching satellites "*(放卫星) to create *"ten thousand catties of grain per mu "*(亩产万斤粮), *"the bolder the people, the more productive the land "*(人有多大胆，地有多大产), and newspapers often reported that the per mu yield of wheat in some places reached several thousand catties, and the per mu yield of rice in some places reached tens of thousands of catties. The exaggerated style of fraud was prevalent everywhere. At that time, there were two things in our local rural production team that left the deepest impression on me, one was deep plowing, and another was burning soil fertilizer. The so-called deep plowing means that some cadres assigned by superiors were sent down to guide agricultural production, requiring farmers to dig 3 to 4 feet deep into the cultivated soil when plowing the land, until the old soil under the cultivated soil was turned to the surface. Those cadres told the farmers that deep plowing would allow the roots of crops to grow deeper, so that the seedlings would grow stronger and the crops would have a good harvest. In the first year, some production teams took a small part of the cultivated land and did so. The result was not only timeconsuming and labor-intensive, but also the crops did not grow well and the yield was reduced (because the old soil below had no fertility after being turned up, so how could the crops grow well), so no production team did deep plowing the next year. Speaking of burning soil fertilizer, in winter and spring, the above cadres required the farmers to go up the mountain to cut some firewood and grass and put it in the dry fields, and then burn the firewood into piles of bonfires, and then let the farmers press the soil around the bonfires and roast them. After the bonfires burn out, the bonfireroasted soil will be scattered in the fields on the second or third day. The rice seedlings in the fire pits that had been burned to fertilize the soil did grow very lush in the summer of the second year. However, the problem was that burning a few firewoods could not solve the problem of poor soil. If a large area of firewood was to be burned, where would there be so much firewood on the mountain? It was also timeconsuming and laborious, and the labor paid was far from proportional to the harvest. Therefore, after a small amount of experiments for one year, no production team was willing to do it again after the second year. These are two typical examples of blind command in agricultural production that we saw when we were very young.

Another most impressive memory is the *Great Steel Making Campaign* (大炼钢铁运动). The slogan advocated during the Great Leap Forward in 1958 was "*Taking grain as the key link and Taking steel as the key link* " (以粮为纲，以钢为纲), and in terms of industry, China was required to "*Surpass UK and catch up with the USA within 15 years*" (十五年超英赶美). In other words, at that time, the whole country first focused on grain production and, secondly, focused on steel production. Therefore, when the Great Leap Forward was launched in 1958, the craze for the steel production campaign was everywhere in the country. In the early 1950s, the mountains around our village were full of virgin forests. Liquidambar trees, birch trees, and oak trees that could be surrounded by several people could be seen everywhere. Every autumn, the mountains and fields were covered with red leaves and wild fruits. In the year of the Great Leap Forward, a large number of migrant workers were transferred from somewhere. Some of them went up the mountain to cut trees. For those large trees that could be surrounded by several people, they cut the trees into three or four-meter-long tubes after cutting them down, and then hollowed out the inside of the trunks to make bellows, which were used to blow the charcoal fire in the earthen blast furnace to smelt iron. Smaller trees were cut down, split, burned into charcoal, and transported to the place where the earthen blast furnace was built for iron smelting. Others built six or seven earthen blast furnaces in the flat area called Dapingzi below our village. People built many temporary sheds with trees and thatch grass cut from the mountains, and the migrant workers transferred from other places lived in these sheds. After the earthen blast furnace was built, the commune mobilized the masses to smash all the iron farm tools and cooking utensils, such as iron pots, iron shovels, and old plowshares, and send them to Dapingzi for iron smelting in the earthen blast furnace. At the same time, the commune also mobilized production members to pick up iron ore all over the mountains and fields. We primary school students also joined the ranks of going up the mountain to find iron ore during holidays. After the earthen blast furnace in Dapingzi was successfully ignited and tested, the person in charge of the construction site also organized the migrant workers to beat gongs and drums to report the good news to the commune, so the craze for steel production was in full swing, and the scene was thriving. However, since there were no iron mines in our area, only a small amount of pyrite was occasionally seen in some coal mining areas, and soon these scattered pyrites were quickly dug up. At the same time, there was no iron ore to be found in the mountains, so the earthen blast furnaces in Dapingzi soon became a waste of resources. Less than half a year after the start of construction, these earthen blast furnaces were declared shut down. However, the bad consequence is that the original forests on the mountains around our village have been basically cut down completely during the Great Steel Production Campaign.

In addition to participating in the Great Steel Production Campaign, we primary school students also have one or two busy farming leaves every year during the summer and autumn harvest seasons. The school organizes students to go to various parts of the commune to help production teams harvest crops. Each busy farming leave lasts for about two or three weeks to a month, and the teacher leads students to the relevant production team. There are 20 to 30 students in our class. Every two students (boys and boys, girls and girls) bring a quilt, a straw mat, and each person brings a bowl and a pair of chopsticks. The teacher takes us to this village to break off corn today, and to another village to cut rice tomorrow; we work wherever we go, and we eat and live there too. After finishing the work in this village today, we will move to another village tomorrow; we will go wherever the production teams need help to work, until the commune agency believes that the harvest season has ended and no longer needs students to help, and then the teacher will take us students back to school.

In 1959, when I was in the fourth grade of elementary school, it was said that the school canteen was out of food supply and later the canteen was closed. So the school decided not to let students live on campus and resume day schooling, and our students had to eat in the collective canteen of the production team in our hometown. At this time, the food in the collective canteen of the production team was no longer good. Not only was there a lack of cooking oil, but also the food supply was insufficient. The rice cooked in the canteen not only had a lot of coarse grains, but also mixed with a lot of vegetables, and the rice was cooked very soft. At this time, the canteen of the production team was no longer like before, where everyone ate together in a big pot. Instead, it was changed to a family unit, and the rice was weighed according to the amount of adults and children, and each family ate at home after taking the food home. I remember that the adult's meal was 1.7 Jin (0.85 kg) per person, and the children's meal was weighed according to their age. I was 11 years old at the time, and the meal was one Jin (500g). Because the rice was mixed with planting vegetables or wild vegetables, the rice seemed very watery and soft, and the dishes from the canteen lacked oil. The adults also had to work, and the 1.7 Jin (0.85kg) per meal was not enough. For us children, one Jin (500g) of rice was only two small bowls. Although we didn't have to work, children were very active, so one Jin (500g) of rice was not enough for each meal too. For this reason, after we got the rice from the collective canteen, our family would mix some wild vegetables or planting vegetables into the rice again to fill our stomachs. In addition, the collective canteen of the production team also stipulated that when primary school students returned home from school in the afternoon, they had to collect 2 to 3 Jin (about 1.5kg) of wild vegetables on the way home and hand them in to the collective canteen every day. Only then would they be eligible to get rice after school. Students who did not hand in or handed in less wild vegetables would not be given weighed rice or would have less rice weighed. Once, because I didn't hand in enough wild vegetables, the canteen manager Guoyou Deng wanted to deduct my food. For this, I had a big quarrel with him and called him Mazi Deng (because his face is pockmarked). Since it was the first time that I handed in less wild vegetables, my mother came to be careful with him, and later weighed out one Jin (500g) meal for me. From then on, I would never dare to deliver less wild vegetables to the canteen, otherwise I would go hungry. This kind of life was basically like this from 1959 to 1960, before I went to middle school.

Although life was very difficult, study conditions were very tough, and classes were not normal, my academic performance was basically not affected much, and I was always among the best in the class. In April or May of 1960, when I was in the second semester of the fifth grade of elementary school, the school received a notice from the Bureau of Culture and Education of the Puding County, saying that students with excellent academic performance in the fifth grade of elementary school could graduate one year in advance and apply for middle school together with the current sixth grade school graduates. So, there were three students in our fifth grade, including me, who were qualified to graduate early and apply for middle school. As a result of the exam, the three of us who applied for middle school in advance were all admitted to middle school. Among them, our class monitor Minghua Hu and another classmate, Yongxiang Wang, were admitted to Huachu

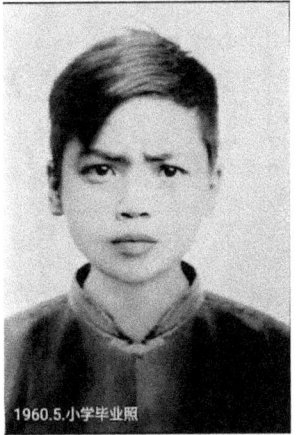

1960.5.小学毕业照

Agricultural Middle School, and I was admitted to Puding No. 2 Middle School. As a result, in September 1960, I graduated from elementary school one year in advance and entered the gate of middle school. That year I was exactly 12 years old.

My childhood should have been relatively happy before I went to elementary school. At that time, my father was still alive. Not only was our material life relatively superior, but my spiritual life was also rich and colourful because my father had enlightened me very early. Therefore, my childhood can be said to be carefree and happy. However, since I went to primary school, I happened to catch up with the national agricultural cooperative movement. I started living in the school and eating in the collective canteen from the third grade of primary school. Then I experienced the Great Leap Forward and the People's Commune, and we primary school students were also involved. At that time, we not only went up the mountain to pick iron ore, but also during the two busy farming leaves a year, we, the primary school students in our teens, were like adults. We always were sent to this village today and to that village tomorrow. We worked wherever we went. Sometimes, in order to earn work points, we had to participate in the work of the production team even during winter and summer vacations. The most puzzling thing is that after eating in the collective canteen from the third grade of primary school, not only did I lack nutrition, but I also often didn't have enough food. Such a childhood life is indeed very bitter. However, it was precisely the hardship experienced in childhood that strengthened my willpower and unleashed my potential. Going through tough times as a child made me more grateful and taught me to cherish what I have. Therefore, it is no exaggeration to say that the hardships I endured in my childhood have been invaluable assets in my life, benefiting me for a lifetime.

Chapter 2   Hardship in Youth

（ I ）

Around July 1960, when Xingzhi Wu, my distant nephew, and I received our admission letters from Puding No. 2 Middle School by mail, the notice instructed us to report to the Baifen Branch of Puding No. 2 Middle School. At the time Xingzhi Wu and I felt quite puzzled. Since we had been admitted to Puding No. 2 Middle School, why were we asked to report to the Baifen Branch instead of the main campus in the county town? What was the origin of the Baifen Branch School, and where was it located? At the time, we were just 12 or 13 years old kids and naturally had no knowledge of the Baifen Branch School's background. It was only later, through what we learned, that we fully understood its origins. It turned out that during the Great Leap Forward of 1958-1959, while the country was fervently engaged in mass steel production, every sector of society, including education, was also swept up in the movement. Across the nation, new primary and secondary schools were being built, and student enrolment was expanded. Puding No. 2 Middle School was established under this broad national initiative, growing out of what was originally the Puding County Agricultural Middle School, which had been founded during the Great Leap Forward in 1958. At the time, the agricultural school consisted of just one old brick-and-wood teaching building, covering only a few dozen square meters. In 1958, it had admitted a single class of about 30 to 40 students, and by 1959, another class had been enrolled, bringing the total student population to around 70 to 80 by the beginning of 1960. When the county decided to upgrade the agricultural school into Puding No. 2 Middle School, they also planned to construct a new, larger teaching building. Since the new campus construction would take quite some time, the county authority decided to temporarily convert the abandoned factory and office buildings left over from the Baifen Ironworks into the Baifen Branch of Puding No. 2 Middle School. These facilities were available after the Baifen Ironworks had been shut down following the failure of its short-lived steel production efforts during the Great Leap Forward. The abandoned buildings provided a ready-made solution, and the county issued the necessary documents to authorize the school's temporary use of the facilities. Thus, when Puding No. 2 Middle School admitted about 400 new first-year students in 1960, all of us received admission notices directing us to report to the Baifen Branch, and I was one of these around 400 new students.

The Baifen Branch was located in the Baifen Brigade of Boren Commune, near the seat of the Huachu District government, about 5 kilometers from the district offices and around 20 kilometers from my hometown. The name "Baifen" came from a large, stately white tomb in the area. In 1958, during the height of the nationwide steel production craze, the county had built over a dozen small blast furnaces at the foot of Longzi Mountain near Baifen. At its peak, the Baifen Ironworks employed three to four hundred workers, who worked in three shifts around the clock. Many of the workers in the nearby mountains, including those near my hometown, spent their time chopping trees to produce charcoal, which was used to fuel the blast furnaces at Baifen. The large wooden bellows used in the furnaces were reportedly made from large trees cut down from the mountains near our village. However, like many other hastily conceived projects during the Great Leap Forward, the Baifen Ironworks had not undergone a proper feasibility study. There was no iron ore in the area, nor was there an adequate water supply. As a result, the ironworks struggled to operate and shut down within less than a year, leaving behind the abandoned office buildings and factories that would later serve as the temporary campus for the Baifen Branch of Puding No. 2 Middle School. Because state assets were centrally managed at that time, there was no need for the school to pay for the use of the abandoned facilities---the county simply issued an order. As a result, preparations for the Baifen Branch were completed quickly, and by early September 1960, we, the newly admitted students, reported to the Baifen Branch as instructed.

At that time, the Baifen Branch had 13 classes of first-year students, totalling around 400 students. I was assigned to Class 3 of the first year. Among my classmates were Xingzhi Wu (吴兴志), who was a distant nephew of mine and four years older than me, and Yuchang Tao (陶玉昌) from Laliu Village. The three of us had all come from Laliu Elementary School. The person in charge of Baifen Branch was the deputy principal of

Puding No. 2 Middle School, Yucai Lou (娄育才), a middle-aged man of medium build and robust physique who often wore a faded yellow military uniform. It was said that he was a retired military officer. My homeroom teacher, Xianzhong Huang (黄显忠), was a recent graduate from the Chinese Department at Guiyang Normal Institute and had just been assigned to Puding No. 2 Middle School. He taught us Chinese and also served as our class advisor.

In early September 1960, when the school year began, the school cafeteria had not yet been built, so a temporary kitchen was set up besides the office building, with a simple earthen stove made from bricks and a large iron pot to cook food for the students. At that time, middle school students were allotted 23 Jin (11.5 kg) of grain and 3 Liang (150 grams) of cooking oil per month. Our monthly meal fee was ¥3.60 yuan, which meant that each day we received less than 8 Liang (400 grams) of grain. Breakfast consisted of just over 1 Liang (50 g) of food, while lunch and dinner provided 3 Liang (150 g) each. The daily meal cost was a mere 12 cents. When the students lined up for meals, Principal Lou personally served us each a large ladle of rice and a ladle of vegetables. The vegetables mainly consisted of old pumpkin, eggplant, and cowpea leaves, with cowpea leaves being the most common. Due to the lack of cooking oil and the small amount of grain, coupled with the fact that we were teenagers in our growth years, we were often hungry after meals. After school, during the autumn harvest season, we would go to the nearby cornfields and tobacco fields to scavenge for leftover or dropped corn and beans, which we would then bring back to school and cook to eat. Sometimes, we would cut fresh corn stalks and chew them like sugarcane to stave off hunger. We also foraged for tobacco seeds in the harvested tobacco fields, and some students even picked wild cotton, mixing it with rice to make rice cakes, which they then roasted to eat. In short, we tried to find and eat anything we could from the wild to fill our stomachs. By October, the school cafeteria was completed, and starting in November, the meal fee increased to ¥4.80 yuan per month. The cafeteria switched to serving students steamed "pot meals." Each student was given a small earthenware pot with their name painted on it. The pots were filled with rice and water, then steamed in a large steam cooker. When it was time to eat, the cafeteria staff would pull the pots out of the steam cooker, call out the names, and students would collect their pots and go get their vegetables. Initially, we were served plain rice, but as grain supplies dwindled, coarse grains like cornmeal and beans were mixed into the rice, making the food even more difficult to eat. Students who lived nearby could often go home to bring back some vegetables or carrots to supplement their meals, but for those of us who lived farther away, it was only every three or four weeks that we could return home. Each time I went home, I brought back some potatoes, vegetables, or chilli peppers to help fill the gaps in my diet.

When the school year ended, and it was time to go home for winter break, my brother and I went to the district's grain station in Huachu to purchase our allotted grain and oil for the winter vacation. I remember that for the one-and-a-halfmonth winter break, I was able to buy over 30 Jin (15 kg) of grain, which included about 10 Jin (5 kg) of rice and 5 Jin(2.5 kg) of glutinous rice (since there was a special supply of glutinous rice for the Chinese Spring Festival). The rice cost 8 cents per Jin, and the glutinous rice was 12 cents per Jin. I was also allocated 5 Jin of beans and 5 Jin of corn as part of the coarse grain ration. Additionally, I bought 4 Liang (200 g) of cooking oil, which I stored in a small glass bottle. We ended up needing several small bags to carry all the food home. When I brought the grain home, my family was quiet envious, as my mother, brother, and sister, who were farmers, only received a monthly ration of 17 Jin (8.5 kg) per person, far less than what I, a student, was allotted. For the farmers who couldn't get enough to eat, their only solution was to forage for wild plants in the mountains to supplement their food. Families would send their strongest members to the mountains throughout the winter to dig up fern roots, which they mixed with cornmeal to make the food last longer. Fortunately, in our area there was abundant with ferns, which provided some relief during the harsh winters. Since our area was in a mountainous region known as coal-bearing stratum, the mountains were covered with bracken ferns. In the spring, tender fern shoots could be collected and eaten as vegetables, and in the winter, people could dig up the roots of the ferns to stave off hunger. As a result, during those years, every winter the mountains were full of people digging up fern roots. Once dug up, the roots had to be taken to the small streams near the village and washed repeatedly to clean off the dirt. After being washed, the roots were dried by the fire and then chopped into small pieces. These pieces were then ground into powder using a stone mortar. The powdered fern roots were sifted and mixed with cornmeal in a certain ratio, then moistened with water to form a dough, which was shaped into cakes and either steamed in large rice steamers or cooked in pans. The resulting fern root cakes were dark in colour, hard in texture, and slightly bitter. They were somewhat tolerable when eaten warm but became extremely hard and nearly inedible when cold. However, when hunger set in, there was little choice, if you didn't to eat, you would starve.

Not only did we eat fern root cakes, but we also ate loquat bark cakes, made from loquat tree bark mixed with cornmeal. The process for preparing the loquat bark was similar to that of the fern roots---it had to be dried and ground into powder first. However, fern root cakes were somewhat easier to digest compared to loquat bark cakes. After eating the latter, digestion became difficult. Since the loquat bark was astringent, had few long fibers, and wasn't mixed with much cornmeal, it often resulted in constipation, sometimes lasting for days. Eventually, people stopped eating loquat bark altogether. In addition to ferns, the mountains, wastelands, and fallow fields in our area were home to many types of wild vegetables. These included houttuynia, bracken ferns, toon leaves, wild celery, shepherd's purse, qingming herb (also known as "hairy coriander"), and lamb's quarters. Throughout the year, villagers would frequently go up the mountains to gather wild vegetables to mix into their meals. On the other hand, because our area was remote, perhaps the higher authorities couldn't keep a close watch or chose to turn a blind eye. After the collective canteens were disbanded in the first half of 1961, the villagers secretly opened up land in the remote mountains and forests to grow potatoes or early-maturing crops like buckwheat, helping them get through the food shortages. As a result, during the "Three Years of Economic Hardship," not many people in our area starved to death. However, other parts of the country were not as fortunate. Those regions may not have had as much mountainous land or as many wild vegetables, and combined with the extreme leftist policies being enforced, it's said that many people in other areas died of hunger during the food shortages.

The so-called "Three Years of Economic Hardship" from 1959 to 1961 left a lasting impression on me. In our region, there was no significant natural disaster during that period. In other words, there were neither major droughts nor floods. In fact, the older generations would often say that 1958-1959 had been bumper harvest years for agriculture. So why did the people go hungry? In addition to the government's explanation that the country was repaying debts to the Soviet Union, one contributing factor, in my opinion, was the government's policy of unified grain purchase and distribution. Starting around 1957, all the grain harvested by rural production teams had to be transported to state granaries, leaving no grain in the hands of the production teams or individual farmers. The grain stored in these state granaries was often shipped to other provinces, and due to poor storage management, much of it was wasted due to rodents, insects, or mold. Consequently, grain had to be rationed for the entire population. Although farmers grew the grain, they couldn't store it. The grain they consumed had to be purchased from the state granaries. Moreover, under the extreme leftist policies of collectivization, the small amount of private land that farmers had under the earlier cooperative system was confiscated and absorbed into the collective during the formation of communes. Aside from the rationed grain, there was no surplus, and the ration allocations for farmers were generally low. In our area, for example, each farmer was allotted only 17 Jin (8.5 kg) of grain and 3 Liang (150 grams) of cooking oil per month, leading to widespread hunger. I remember around 1961, several young, able-bodied men in our village died due to prolonged malnutrition and weakness. Three men, in particular, Liangqing Xiao (肖亮清), Qisheng Guo (国启盛), and Deguang Hu (胡德光), all passed away from hunger in 1961. Under such difficult living conditions, some of the older students at school couldn't bear the hardship and never returned after going home. School life meant constant hunger, whereas at home, in addition to the rationed grain, one could dig up wild vegetables from the fields or mountains to supplement meals. Many students who stayed in school were distracted by the difficulties of daily life. Some frequently took days off or simply didn't come back to school after leaving, and it was common for students to skip classes or not complete assignments. As for me, after experiencing constant hunger from the time I started eating in the collective canteen during elementary school, my physical development was stunted, leaving me short and small in stature. When I took the middle school entrance exam early in fifth grade, I was only 1.33 meters tall and weighed just 32 kilograms. Farming was clearly beyond my physical capabilities, so my only goal since childhood was to study hard in hopes of one day escaping rural life and securing an urban residency, where I could eat government-supplied grain. That way, I wouldn't have to toil in the fields year after year like a farmer. Being a farmer was simply too exhausting and difficult. As a result, once I started middle school, I rarely went home. Even on weekends, if I went home and I would return to school promptly on Sunday afternoons. I never skipped classes without reason, and I always completed my homework diligently. My academic performance remained among the top in my class, leaving a favourable impression on my homeroom teacher.

(Ⅱ)

In March 1961, after the second semester of my first year of middle school began, everything in terms of academic life continued as usual. However, around April, some students began hearing rumours that the main campus of Puding No. 2 Middle School had completed construction and was now fully capable of accommodating all the students from our branch campus. But the school leadership had decided to wait until the new school year starts on September 1st in the second half of the year to move the students off the Baifen branch to the main campus. Since the school conditions at Baifen Branch were too poor. First, the school grounds were too small and the terrain was uneven. The school lacked places for physical exercise. Second, the students' living conditions were very difficult. Not only was there no running water supply in the student living area, but even the student cafeteria had to rely on horse-drawn carriages to fetch water for cooking from several kilometers away. Moreover, Baifen was located in a remote rural area, far from any towns, making it extremely difficult for both students and staff to purchase daily necessities. As a result, both the students and staff wanted to leave and return to the main campus as soon as possible. However, in those days, nothing could be done without the approval of the school leadership. To express their demand, groups of students during the day would gather to the branch office to petition for the school to move back to the main campus in Puding county town. In the night, after the lights-out whistle blew at ten o'clock, the students would lie in bed and shout: "We want to move back to the main campus!", "We want to move back to the main campus!" These chants would echo throughout the dormitories, which were made of wooden planks, and the students slept in large communal rooms with dozens of others. As soon as one dorm finished shouting, another would immediately respond. This nightly chorus of "We want to move back to the main campus!" would continue for half an hour to an hour, until the students eventually fell asleep.

The students' demands to return to the main campus were much stronger than the branch campus leadership had anticipated. To calm the situation, the branch campus leaders reported the matter to the main campus administration, requesting an expedited move back to avoid further disruption to the school's order. The main campus leadership sent a senior official to Baifen to assess the situation. When the leader from main campus arrived, he saw that the students' emotions had become uncontrollable. Fearing that something serious might happen if branch students didn't relocate, the main campus administration held a meeting and decided to immediately close the Baifen Branch and transfer all students and staff to the main campus in the county town. Thus, in April 1961, we were finally moved from the Baifen Branch back to the main campus of Puding No. 2 Middle School in Puding County Town.

When I first started attending Baifen Branch School, the school was about 40 li (20 km) away from my hometown. Except when my old brother carried my luggage to school at the beginning of the semester, I would go home occasionally on weekends, and I would walk back with my classmate and nephew Xingzhi Wu. 40 li (20 kilometers) of mountain roads was no big deal for us 12- or 13-year-old kids who grew up in the countryside because we were used to farm work and walking in the mountains from a young age. However, after the school moved to the county town, it was now 60-70 li (around 30-35 kilometers) away from home, and that distance made it much harder for a young child like me to walk to school. Fortunately, I had my older brother to help me; otherwise, getting to school in Puding County would have been even more difficult. I remember before we moved from the branch school to the county town main campus, Xingzhi Wu and I took our bedding back home and informed our families that the school had moved to the county town already. On the day we headed to the main campus, Xingzhi Wu and I went together. My older brother and Xingzhi Wu's father carried our luggage, while we walked behind them, empty-handed. Early in the morning, after having breakfast, the four of us set off from home. After walking 40 or 50 li (around 20-25 kilometers) to the **Fifteen-li Dry Flat** (十五里干坝) area of Puding's **Houzhai Village** (后寨), my feet were aching terribly. However, I had to endure the pain and push through to finish the remaining 20-30 li (10-15 kilometers). Seeing that I was struggling, my brother and Xingzhi Wu's father slowed their pace. By the time we arrived at the school, it was probably around 4 or 5 p.m. This was my first time traveling far from home and the longest I had ever walked. After finding our homeroom teacher and getting settled in, my feet hurt so much I could barely stand. Fortunately, the school had hot water available. After dinner, my old brother fetched a basin of hot water for me, and I soaked my feet. That night, I had a good sleep, and the next morning, I was able to walk again, although still with some pain.

Speaking of beddings we rural students brought to middle school, it wasn't much different from what we had taken to elementary school for boarding. The main items were still a quilt, a pillow stuffed with grain husks, and a straw curtain. The only difference was that my family had spent ¥4 or ¥5 yuan to buy me an enamel basin. In elementary school, we slept on a bundle of straw, but in middle school, the straw was replaced by a straw curtain made by my old brother. It was about five feet long, three feet wide, and about ten centimetres thick, and it could be rolled up for easy transport. To make the bed, I would unroll the straw curtain and lay it on the bamboo bed frame, spread the straw mat over it, and then put the quilt and pillow on top, Ok, my bed was made. Of course, after starting middle school, we began to use toothpaste and a toothbrush like the students from the towns. As for mosquito nets, they were a luxury for us rural students. Throughout my entire time in middle school, and even during my time as a "sent-down youth," spanning seven or eight years, I never used a mosquito net, nor did I see any of my classmates using one. At that time, everything was rationed by coupons, and mosquito nets were made from gauze, which required fabric coupons to buy. Even though mosquito nets weren't expensive, we didn't have extra fabric coupons. Not only were we short on money, but my brother and sister kept having five or six children in a row. With so many mouths to clothe, the fabric coupons were never enough, let alone having extras for a mosquito net. Our family never had mosquito nets, so I never even thought about needing one for sleeping at school. As for shoes, during elementary school, I wore cloth shoes made by my mother and sister. But in middle school, since I had to walk more, cloth shoes wore out too quickly. So, my brother and sister bought me a pair of "liberation shoes" (shoes with yellow canvas uppers and rubber soles, priced at ¥3-5 yuan per pair). When it came to clothes, after I started middle school, my mother and sister felt it was time for an upgrade which means that I couldn't keep wearing their handmade coarse fabric clothes to school. They saved up some money and fabric coupons and bought blue khaki cloth, which they took to the tailor in our village to make me a set of Zhongshan suits using a sewing machine. One of my older cousins, Mingquan Wu, worked for the township government after the liberation and later became a secretary at the commune, working there for several decades until his retirement. He was the only official in our village. His wife, my cousin-in-law Fuzhen Zhou, was a skilled seamstress, and their family had owned a sewing machine since the late 1950s. My cousin-inlaw would sew clothes for the nearby villagers, charging ¥2-3 yuan for a full set of clothes (jacket and pants). However, whenever we brought fabric to her to make clothes for me, she never charged us for her sewing. Every time I went, she would say: "Little brother, it's not easy for you to go to middle school. I don't have much to offer, but I'll make your clothes for free--- consider it my way of helping you. I just hope you study hard!" Her words were deeply moving and have stuck with me to this day. It's something I'll never forget. Unfortunately, I never had the chance to repay her kindness, which I deeply regret. Over the years of middle school, I had several more sets of Zhongshan suits made by my cousin-in-law, and she never charged us a single cent for the sewing.

(Ⅲ)

A little over a month after we moved from the Baifen branch to the main campus in Puding County Town, sometime in May 1961, a major event happened at the school. The county received a notification from higher authorities regarding adjustments to schools across the country, which required reducing or merging various types of schools at all levels. It also mandated the return of many students with rural household registrations back to their homes to participate in agricultural production, leaving only a small number of students in school. As a result, the county decided to abolish Puding No. 2 Middle School. The small number of remaining students were to be merged with Puding No. 1 Middle School, and Puding No. 1 would be renamed Puding Middle School. Even before this announcement, life at school had been very difficult. When the new semester started in March, some of the older students had already voluntarily given up their studies to return home and farm, while many of the students who remained were often unable to focus on their studies due to hunger. Therefore, when the school announced the government's decision to shut down Puding No. 2 Middle School and send students back home to farm, most students welcomed the news and enthusiastically volunteered to be sent home. By that point, classes had already been suspended entirely. As for deciding which students would stay, aside from those who volunteered to leave, the final decision rested with the homeroom teachers and the school administration. Personally, I felt torn at the time. On the one hand, life at school was incredibly tough, and the biggest problem was that we were always hungry. On the other hand, the school was far from home, and walking back was difficult for me. However, given my small size and young age, it was obvious that working on a farm back home would be just as challenging for me. I really wanted to stay and continue studying. So, while other students were rushing to volunteer to be sent home, I didn't go to talk to my homeroom teacher. I wasn't sure if I would be allowed to stay, and I felt anxious and uneasy. In the midst of my anxiety, my homeroom teacher Xianzhong Huang came to talk to me. When we met, he said: "Mingqing Wu, I want to talk to you. Although your family is from the countryside, you're young and small in stature. If you go home to farm, I think it will be really hard for you. So, I think it's best for you to stay and continue your studies. What do you think?" Hearing that my teacher wanted me to stay, I was overjoyed. I immediately replied: "Teacher Huang, that sounds great! I'd like to stay. Thank you!" Teacher Huang smiled and said: "Alright then. Since you've agreed, I'll put your name on the list of students staying behind." After saying that, he left. A little while later, my classmate and nephew Xingzhi Wu came to ask if Teacher Huang had spoken to me. I told him that Teacher Huang had talked to me and asked me to stay, and I had agreed. Xingzhi Wu then said that Teacher Huang had also asked him to go home, and he had agreed. He added: "Well, going home isn't so bad, at least we won't be hungry all the time like we are here." Shortly after that, another classmate from our class, Yuchang Tao, who lived in Laliu Village, told me that Teacher Huang had also told him he would be staying. By late May, of the 13 classes and about 400 students who had moved from the Baifen branch to the main campus, only about 30 students, most of whom were younger and had good grades and behaviour, were allowed to stay. More than 90% of the students were sent home. The remaining 30 or so students from our school were grouped into one class, which was then merged into Puding No. 1 Middle School. After Puding No. 2 Middle School was abolished, Puding No. 1 Middle School reverted to being called Puding Middle School. When my mother learned that my nephew Xingzhi Wu, who lived in the same village, had been sent back home, while I stayed at school to continue my studies, she said to me with great affection: "My little youngest, why don't you come back home too? It's so far to go to school, and you're not even getting enough food there." I replied: "Mom, while I'm at school, I get 23 Jin (11.5kg) of rationed grain per month, but you in the countryside only get 17 Jin (8.5kg) each. I get several Jin more than you do!" My mother knew how much I loved studying, and no matter what she said, she couldn't persuade me. So, she eventually stopped insisting.

Puding Middle School was located on top of a hill behind Puding County Town. It was funded and built during the

Republic of China period by a well-known wealthy gentleman, Mr. Xiaogao Wu. The entire campus had white walls and black tiles, and its prominent buildings could be seen clearly from 10 km away from the county town. Puding Middle School was famous even before the libration, and children from wealthy families in the surrounding counties came to study there. In 1960, when Puding No. 2 Middle School was established, Puding Middle School was renamed Puding No. 1 Middle School. However, in less than a year, Puding No. 2 Middle School was abolished, and Puding No. 1 Middle School was reverted back to Puding Middle School. Before the student reduction and relocation, Puding No. 1 Middle School had established a branch at Wangjiawan in the county town, with more than 1,000 students across the entire school. Each grade had several classes, with the most first-year students in junior high school. After the student relocation, our first-year class from No. 2 Middle School remained as one class, while No. 1 Middle School retained two classes of first-year students. When we merged into No. 1 Middle School, our class was still designated as Class 3, Grade 1. My classmates in Class 3 included Yuchang Tao from the same commune, as well as Mingjun He from Shuimu Commune and Guiquan Yan and Fuhao Yan from Boyu Commune. Although Yuchang Tao and I had both been admitted to middle school from the same elementary school, we weren't from the same village, and he was several years older than me. As a result, we rarely hung out together, and I often felt quite lonely and homesick after class.

I remember that year's Dragon Boat Festival was on a Saturday in early June. Since I was feeling particularly homesick, and it was also the time for eating zongzi (rice dumplings), I decided to walk home by myself to see if there might be something delicious at home. Early on Saturday morning, just as the sky was beginning to lighten, around 6 a.m., I set off from school alone. The Dragon Boat Festival season coincided with the rice transplanting season in our area, and it was the rainy season, so it had been raining almost every day leading up to cause floods. However, that Saturday turned out to be a sunny day. By around 9 a.m., I had walked near the Moxiang River in the vicinity of Old Shuimu. As I was about to cross a stone arch bridge, I found that the river had risen due to the recent heavy rains, and the floodwaters had completely submerged the bridge, making it impossible to cross. At that point, I had already walked about one-third of the way home and didn't want to turn back to school halfway. So, I decided to follow the river upstream in search of another crossing bridge. After walking 1 or 2 km along the riverbank, I still hadn't found a bridge, and I was getting quite anxious. Just as I was hesitating, I spotted a wooden aqueduct spanning a narrow part of the river, only about 10 meters wide. I knew this type of aqueduct was used by rural production teams for irrigation, and there was one near my home as well. The aqueduct looked quite old, but since it was currently dry (because the rice seedlings had just been transplanted and didn't need water yet), I figured I could use it to cross the river. The aqueduct was covered in moss, so to avoid slipping and falling into the river, I cautiously bent down, gripping the sides of the aqueduct with both hands, and slowly made my way across. Once I had safely crossed, my heart, which had been in my throat, finally settled down. I could feel my heart still pounding, but I was incredibly relieved. Having crossed the river, I knew there were no more major rivers along the way, so I quickened my pace, even running at times. When I finally arrived home, my mother was shocked to see me. She exclaimed joyfully, "My little youngest, I just dreamt about you last night, and now here you are today!" I replied: "Mom, I haven't been home in so long, and I've been missing you all so much at school!" My mother responded: "I've missed you even more! Weren't you scared coming back alone?" I told her: "It was daylight, so I wasn't scared, but the water had risen." At that moment, my mother and my sister had just finished lunch, and it was probably not even noon yet. The coal stove on the kitchen hearth had just been sealed up, so my mother quickly opened it to prepare some food for me.That evening, as we sat together chatting, I recounted the thrilling experience of crossing the river to my mother and sister. My mother exclaimed: "Oh my goodness that was so dangerous! The river flooded and submerged the bridge, you should have just turned back to school! Why did you cross on the aqueduct? What if it had broken halfway? You would have fallen into the river!" She was so worried that tears nearly came to her eyes, and she kept saying: "My little youngest, next time if you encounter something like that, don't take any risks!" Looking back, I realized how dangerous that river crossing had been. Although the river was narrow where the aqueduct was, the water was deeper and faster, and if the aqueduct hadn't been sturdy enough and had collapsed, I could have been swept away. What made it even more dangerous was that I didn't know how to swim. In the end, I was able to cross safely because the aqueduct was still solid, I was small and lightweight at the time, and I lowered my centre of gravity by crouching down while crossing. I also walked very slowly, which likely prevented the aqueduct from vibrating too much. If a larger person had tried to cross, or if the aqueduct had been filled with water, it might have collapsed. If that had happened, whoever fell into the river would have almost certainly lost their life. After my mother's repeated warnings, I no longer dared to travel home alone. From then on, whenever I wanted to go home, I would arrange to go with my classmate, Yuchang Tao, from Laliu Village. After all, the journey home was 60 or 70 li (about 35 km) of mountain roads, requiring us to cross mountains and rivers and pass through many forests. At the time, wild animals often appeared along the narrow mountain paths, and the journey was full of dangers. My mother's concerns were certainly justified.

Not long after that incident, when my mother went to the town market at Xiayingpan in Liuzhi, she also visited my eldest aunt's home in Ganhe village. When my eldest uncle and aunt asked about my studies in Puding Town, my mother recounted in detail the dangerous situation I encountered during the Dragon Boat Festival when I returned home alone. She worriedly said: "Our youngest insists on studying, but he's so young, and Puding County Town is so far from home. What are we going to do?" My eldest uncle replied: "It would be great if your Mingqing Wu could study here in Xiayingpan! It's only about ten li (5 km) from your home, and his cousins Yingwen Tan and Zhongbin Yu (my two cousins) are both studying at Liuzhi Middle School here. It would be lively if they could study together." My mother said: "But we're from different counties. How could my youngest study here? If he could study here, it would be wonderful!" At this point, my eldest cousin (my eldest uncle's eldest son), Zhongmei Yu, chimed in: "Second Aunt, there's someone in our village named Zhongxue Guo, and he is the teaching director at Yingpan Primary School. I'll look for a chance to ask him if he knows anyone in charge at Liuzhi Middle School. If he does, maybe he can help transfer your youngest cousin to study at Liuzhi Middle School." My mother responded: "That would be fantastic if it could happen!" At that time, my eldest cousin, Zhongmei Yu, was the accountant for their village's production brigade, and he was well-known in the nearby villages. He also had a good relationship with Zhongxue Guo, who was from the same village. So later, I heard that when my eldest cousin approached Zhongxue Guo and explained my situation, Zhongxue Guo said that he frequently represented Yunpan Primary School at middle and primary school directors' meetings at the Liuzhi County Education Bureau. He was quite familiar with the teaching director at Liuzhi Middle School and promised to help. During the summer vacation in July-August of 1961, when Zhongxue Guo attended one of the education meetings, he approached the teaching director of Liuzhi Middle School and explained my wish to transfer. The teaching director readily agreed and promised to arrange everything by the start of the new school year in early September. When the new term of the second year of junior high school began in early September, I had just attended two weeks of classes at Puding Middle School when the transfer approval from Liuzhi Middle School came through. Around September 20, my older brother came to Puding Middle School with the transfer approval document from Liuzhi Middle School. It took us a day or two to complete the transfer procedures. On September 23, my brother and I returned home, and on the 25th, I officially reported to Liuzhi Middle School, thus becoming a student at Liuzhi Middle School. After I transferred, the only remaining student from our entire Laliu Commune studying at Puding Middle School was Yuchang Tao. Later, whether because he had no companions or because he was always hungry while at school, Yuchang Tao dropped out after completing the first semester of the second year and returned home to farm. For the next three to four years before the Cultural Revolution, no other students from our commune were admitted to middle school.

(IV)

Liuzhi originally belonged to Langdai County in Guizhou Province and was a district within Langdai County. There were no middle schools in the Liuzhi area at that time. In the late 1950s, the National Geological Survey discovered rich deposits of high-quality coal in the Liuzhi, Shuicheng, and Panxian areas of Guizhou (what is now known as the Liupanshui region). As the *"Third Front Construction"* (三 线 建 设) industrial development strategy advanced, the government planned to develop the Liupanshui region into a major energy production base for southwestern China. To support this construction, in 1960, Guizhou Province decided to relocate the Langdai County government from Langdai Town to Xiayingpan in Liuzhi and renamed Langdai County to Liuzhi County (although it was later briefly renamed Liuzhi City before reverting to Langdai County again). Consequently, Langdai Middle School also moved to Xiayingpan Town in Liuzhi and was renamed Liuzhi Middle School. When I transferred to Liuzhi Middle School, it was a full middle school, but each grade in the high school division had only one class, while the junior high division had two classes per grade. After I enrolled, I was placed in Class 1 of the second year of junior high, with more than 30 students in total. My younger cousin Zhongbin Yu, who was the youngest son of my eldest aunt, was also studying at Liuzhi Middle School, but he was in the third year of junior high, so he was one year ahead of me. My aunt and uncle's home was about four li (2 km) from the school, so Zhongbin Yu lived at home and commuted to school daily. When I transferred to Liuzhi Middle School, my aunt and uncle suggested that I also live with them and commute to school with my younger cousin. Thus, beginning in the first semester of my second year of junior high, I moved into my aunt and uncle's home and became a day student, commuting to school with my younger cousin.

My mother's family was from Naqi Village in Dianzi Township, Liuzhi, and she had three sisters, with my mother being the second eldest. My eldest aunt lived in Ganhe village near Xiayingpan town, and she had always have a very close relationship with my mother, so our two families were in frequent contact. By the first half of 1961, after the public canteens were dissolved, farmers had been given back small plots of private land, and life in the countryside had started to improve. Since all the government offices of Langdai County had relocated to Xiayingpan town, my aunt and uncle's entire commune had been turned into a vegetable production base to supply the county town. As a result, my aunt and uncle's household conditions were relatively better than ours. I lived with my aunt and uncle for almost a year, and they never charged me any board or lodging fees. Sometimes, my aunt would even secretly slip me a few yuan for pocket money. I felt they treated me incredibly well, so during school vacations, I would help out with housework and farm work, such as collecting coal for cooking in the spring or cutting grass to feed the cows and pigs in the summer. During school days, my younger cousin and I walked to and from school together. This daily commuting routine continued throughout the second year of junior high. In September 1962, after my younger cousin, Zhongbing Yu, graduated from junior high without passing the high school entrance exam, he stopped his studies and returned home to farm. When I entered the third year of junior high, I began boarding at the school.

When I started my third year of junior high in September 1962, the school canteen's meal fee was ¥4.8 yuan per month, and junior high students were allotted 27 Jin (13.5 kg) of grain per month, while high school students were allotted 33 Jin (16.5 kg). The quality of the food at the school had improved somewhat. However, since my family had no steady income, even the monthly meal fee of ¥4.8 yuan was a considerable burden for me. To help cover my school meal fees and provide me with a bit of pocket money, my mother and sister would gather wild vegetables (such as houttuynia, wild celery, bracken fern, and bamboo shoots) from the mountains during their spare time. On town market days at the weekend, they would carry these vegetables in bamboo baskets to sell at the market in Xiayingpan town (which was located on Yunpan Old Street, near Liuzhi Middle School). Every weekend, before the market closed around 4 or 5 p.m., I would meet them at the market. My mother and sister would give me all the small change they had earned from selling the wild vegetables (mostly coins worth two or five cents or a dime, twenty cents, or fifty cents), which I would use for my meal fees and pocket money. Despite only earning around two or three yuan each week, my mother and sister tirelessly supported me in my studies. They also brought homemade bracken root cakes from home for me to eat at school. My mother and sister endured years of hardship to support my education, and they continued to do so until I graduated from high school. In my heart, I was determined to study hard and not disappoint them. I vowed to repay their kindness and love in the future, and I knew that their sacrifices would stay with me for the rest of my life.

It was under such harsh living conditions that I was able to attend middle school, and I knew how hard it was. Therefore, I made a firm resolution to study diligently, as I didn't want to let my mother and sister down. Through hard work, my academic performance gradually improved from the second year of junior high onward. In a class of over thirty students, by the first semester of the third year, my grades had steadily climbed from around 20th place in the second year to the top 10. By the time I graduated from junior high, I had risen to the top five in the class. Before graduating from junior high, many of my classmates from rural areas, due to financial difficulties, opted to apply for technical secondary schools, where tuition and meal fees were covered. Several close friends, such as Guowei Song, Lianghui Song, Zhonghao Yu, and Tingbi Tao, planned to apply for technical schools. Among them, Zhonghao Yu (a cousin of my cousin Zhongbin Yu) was my closest friend. He intended to apply for the Xingyi Teacher's Secondary School and invited me to apply with him, but I refused. I told him: "Zhonghao, I don't want to apply for a technical school. I want to go to high school." After hearing that, he left somewhat disappointed. In the end, he was successfully admitted to Xingyi Teacher's Secondary School and became a middle school teacher after graduation, while I also achieved my goal of getting into Liuzhi High School.

(V)

Since Liuzhi Middle School had only been established in 1959, the school's early years were marked by weak infrastructure, limited teaching staff, and a relatively inexperienced leadership team. As a result, the quality of education in those initial years was quite poor. In the senior high school graduating class of 1962, the first graduating class since the establishment of Liuzhi Middle School, only one student who was admitted to university at that year. By 1963, the second graduating class of more than 20 students had only four students

1963.5. 初中毕业时留影(前排左为作者)

admitted to university. These results placed Liuzhi Middle School among the lower-performing schools within the Anshun region's education system at the time. In response to this, the Anshun Region Education Bureau began making changes in the second half of 1963 to improve the school's teaching standards. They made adjustments to the leadership, bringing in Guanghui Zhou, an experienced administrator from the provincial education department, to serve as the school's principal and Party secretary, and Hong'en Qin, from the Anshun Region Education Bureau, as the vice principal. At the same time, the school sought to strengthen its teaching staff by recruiting outstanding young teachers from across the country and transferring experienced teachers from other regions. Among the new teachers were Shide Zhang, a graduate of the Southwest Normal University with a master's degree in history, and Yuji Zhuang, a history graduate from Eastern China Normal University. Other teachers included and Jingkang Wu, Xianfu Deng, Shifu Li, Wanyi Peng, Wanying Ren, and Jichu Huang, all graduates of Guiyang Normal University. Additionally, some seasoned educators like Shaoyong Li and Zongma Zhou were transferred in, bringing their wealth of teaching experience. Under the leadership of Principal Guanghui Zhou, the school implemented a series of regulations, including mandatory morning exercise, collective morning reading, and evening self-study sessions. Classroom discipline was enforced rigorously, and a strict attendance system was introduced. These measures led to noticeable improvements in both the school's teaching management and the students' learning atmosphere.

When I started high school in September 1963, I found myself in the midst of these efforts to raise academic standards. Our first-year high school class had 48 students (there was only one class per grade in the high school division). Each day began at 6:30 a.m. with a 15-20 minute collective run for morning exercise, followed by washing up and breakfast. We then gathered in the classroom for collective morning reading of Chinese or foreign languages at 7:30 a.m. Formal classes started at 8:00 a.m., with 45 minute sessions in the morning and three in the afternoon. In the evening, from 7:30 p.m., we had self-study sessions where we completed homework assignments or previewed new lessons. Our daily schedule was packed. At the same time, the school promoted the concept of striving to become well-rounded students who were both "red" (politically aware) and "expert" (academically strong). The call to be exemplary in academics, character, and physical education was constantly emphasized, and students were urged not only to excel in their studies but also to maintain "red" political beliefs. By then, the extreme leftist "class background theory" was already being widely promoted in schools, with students from "good" family backgrounds being prioritized for Party and Youth League development. The student leaders and cadres of the Youth League mostly came from these "good" families. Since my family was classified as "middle peasant," I naturally wasn't among the students that the class Youth League branch focused on for development. Additionally, I was introverted and shy by nature, often blushing when speaking in public. I didn't speak much at class meetings or in the classroom, and although my academic performance was decent, I didn't attract much attention. However, I paid close attention during lessons, took thorough notes, and completed all homework assignments on time. Beyond that, I made sure to review my lessons and prepare for upcoming classes. For subjects requiring memorization, like Chinese, political science, history, and foreign languages, I adopted a method of intensive reading and recitation. Sometimes I would study alone or with two or three classmates, heading to the hills near the school to loudly read and memorize long passages until I had committed them to memory. This method proved effective, and my academic performance improved significantly. By the end of the first semester of my first year in high school, I scored over 80 points in five of the six main subjects, i.e., Chinese, physics, chemistry, Russian, and political science, with the exception of mathematics. At the end of the first year, my grades in all six main subjects surpassed 80 points, with physics exceeding 90 points, and my overall ranking in the class climbed into the top five. This finally drew the attention of both my classmates and teachers. However, at the end of the school year, 15 of my classmates failed to pass the final exams and had to repeat their school year again. The fact that one-third of our class was held back reflected the school's strict academic standards and the intense competition among students.

After hard work in the first year of high school, I had made significant academic progress. However, due to my introverted personality, I rarely interacted with my classmates, spoke little at class meetings, and focused primarily on academics rather than politics. At the end of the first year, when I received my transcript report, my homeroom teacher commented: "Diligent and hardworking, with excellent academic performance, but lacking in openness and insufficient attention to current political events. I hope you can strive for political progress while continuing your academic efforts." When I returned home for the summer vacation, my cousin Mingliang Wu, as usual, came over to chat and inquire about my studies. One evening, he asked to see my transcript report, which I handed to him. After reviewing it, he said seriously: "Youngest brother, your academic performance is outstanding! You scored over 80 points in all six main subjects. However, there's something you need to pay attention to. The teacher mentioned that you're not very outgoing and don't pay enough attention to politics. You need to work on this! Your class has a Youth League branch, right? Besides excelling in your studies, you should also build good relationships with the class leaders and Youth League members. Strive to join the League, it will greatly benefit your future!" Initially, when I received my transcript report and saw my high scores, I was quite pleased. I knew my personality wasn't very open and that I wasn't also paying enough attention to politics, but I thought those issues could be addressed slowly. I believed that as long as I continued to focus on my studies, everything would be fine. However, after my cousin's advice, I realized the importance of these areas and knew what I needed to work on in the coming school year. After that when I started my second year of high school, I made a conscious effort to build better relationships with class leaders and Youth League members. I also submitted my application to join the Youth League and began participating more actively in class discussions and collective activities. After nearly a year of effort, I made significant progress in overcoming my shyness and began speaking more confidently in public. I also received recognition from my teachers and classmates for my increased engagement in collective activities and political affairs. By the end of the second year, my overall academic performance had risen to the top three in the class. In November 1965, after being recommended by Chaoming Wang, a classmate and Youth League group leader, I was finally accepted into the Communist Youth League and officially became a member.

During the early 1960s, the Chinese central government, recognizing the abundant high-quality coal reserves in the Liupanshui (六盘水) region, decided to develop this area into a key energy base in Southwest China as part of the *Third Front contraction* (三线建设) efforts. Liupanshui was selected for this strategic focus not only because of its coal resources but also because of its proximity to Panzhihua (攀枝花) in Sichuan, where large deposits of vanadium-titanium magnetite were discovered. These metals, vanadium and titanium, had significant applications in the aerospace industry and were considered "strategic metals." The synergy between the coal resources in Liupanshui and the iron ore in Panzhihua was crucial: coal was essential for steel production, and steel was needed to manufacture weapons like planes and cannons. As the country was preparing for potential conflicts, the Liupanshui and Panzhihua regions naturally became the focal points of the Third Front construction in the southwest. After the establishment of the Liupanshui region, it was administratively part of Guizhou Province but operated under the direct supervision of the Central Ministry of Coal of China. Due to its critical role in the Third Front construction, the area was highly secretive. For instance, Liupanshui was not referred to by its name; instead, it was publicly called the "**Dahua Farm**" (大华农场), and the three districts within it, Liuzhi, Panxian, and Shuicheng, were referred to as "farms" as well. Liuzhi, for example, was known as the "**Motianling Farm**" (摩天岭农场). Even the Guiyang Mining School was renamed "**Dahua Agricultural School**" (大华农校) for confidentiality. The administrative ranks of officials in Liupanshui and its districts were unusually high, reflecting the central government's emphasis on the region. In 1965, the *Southwest Coal Construction Command* (西南煤炭建设指挥部) was established in the area, with Ziyun Zhong (钟子云), the thenvice minister of coal, serving as the party secretary, and Dan Ding (丁丹), the party secretary of Liupanshui region, acting as commander. Dan Ding held an administrative rank equivalent to that of a deputy provincial governor. Similarly, Wanshan Shen (沈万山), the party secretary of Liuzhi District, held a rank equivalent to a prefecture committee secretary.

After 1963, with the creation of various districts within Liupanshui region and the launch of construction projects, the entire country provided extensive support for the region's development. Large numbers of coal miners and mining machinery were relocated from the northeast and north China (e.g., from Fushun and Fuxin in Liaoning Province, Pingdingshan and Jiaozhuo in Henan Province, and Kailuan in Hebei Province) to Liuzhi District. In the narrow valley stretching about 10 kilometers from Liuzhi to Xiayingpan, a new mining city gradually rose. Although Liuzhi District was relatively small, covering parts of the former Langdai County and some coal-rich areas transferred from Puding County, it rapidly expanded during the early 1960s. Key infrastructure, including coal machinery factories, construction companies, power plants, hospitals, and water supply facilities, were quickly established. During this period, cultural and entertainment activities also flourished, with art troupes such as the Central Coal Workers' Art Troupe regularly visiting the region for performances, and classic films being shown in open-air theatres. As students, we had many opportunities to watch many of these performances and films. Liuzhi Middle School, though not initially under the jurisdiction of the Liuzhi District (it fell under

Langdai County in the Anshun region), served as the school for children of workers in the district's various state-owned enterprises. This meant that the school enjoyed special privileges from both the district and the county. It wasn't until the eve of the Cultural Revolution in 1966 that Liuzhi Middle School was officially placed under the administration of Liuzhi District and renamed "Liuzhi District First Middle School."

While we were studying at Liuzhi Middle School, Xiaoping Deng's (邓小平) third brother, Xuchu Deng (邓徐初), was serving as the deputy county magistrate of Liuzhi County. Xuchu Deng, whose original name was Suchu Deng, was Xiaoping Deng's half-brother. Xiaoping Deng had another brother named Ken Deng (邓垦), with Xuchu Deng being the youngest. After Xiaoping Deng left for France at the age of 16 to study and join the revolution, Xuchu Deng remained at home to help manage the family's assets. Following the liberation of Sichuan by the Liu-Deng army (刘邓大军) in early 1950, Xuchu Deng entered the Southwest Military and Political University (西南军政大学) in Chongqing in May 1950. After graduating, he was assigned to work in Guizhou Province, where he adopted the name Xuchu. He held several positions, including town mayor of Qingshan in Pu'an County, fiscal officer of Anshun County, and finally, deputy magistrate of Liuzhi County in 1960. In November 1965, Xiaoping Deng(邓小平), accompanied by senior leaders such as Fuchun Li(李富春), Yibo Bo(薄一波), and Mu Gu(谷牧), visited Liuzhi District as part of an inspection tour of the Liupanshui region. During this visit, Xiaoping Deng met with the region's leaders, including his brother Xuchu Deng and Liupanshui's party secretary Dan Ding. That December, our school invited Deputy Magistrate Xuchu to give a lecture on revolutionary traditions. I recall that Xuchu Deng bore a striking resemblance to his brother Xiaoping Deng, especially in terms of his voice, though he was slightly taller, standing around 1.65 meters. In his lecture, Xuchu Deng shared stories about Xiaoping Deng's youth, emphasizing his love for reading, his courage, and his strong sense of justice and responsibility. He mentioned how Xiaoping Deng had learned to swim as a child and how, at the age of 16, he had left home for Europe, where he met Enlai Zhou (周恩来) and joined the revolution. After that, Xiaoping Deng never returned to his hometown. When the Cultural Revolution broke out in 1966, Xuchu Deng faced severe persecution, particularly after his brother, Xiaoping Deng (邓小平), and Shaoqi Liu (刘少奇) were denounced as the country's top capitalist-roaders. Accusations surfaced claiming that Xuchu Deng had been an "escaped landlord bully" back in Sichuan, with threats to drag him back for public struggle sessions. As a result, he became a frequent target for public humiliation and was forced to wear a placard as he was paraded through the streets. In March 1967, overwhelmed by the physical and emotional abuse, Xuchu Deng tragically took his own life by drowning in a spring well near the Langdai County Party Committee guesthouse. Thankfully, his case was posthumously cleared in 1978.

As mentioned earlier, Liuzhi Middle School was established during the Great Leap Forward, and its early years were marked by limited resources and low academic quality. However, through the tireless efforts of the school's staff and students, the school's academic performance improved steadily over the years. In 1962, only one student from the first graduating class was admitted to university. By 1963, four students from the second graduating class were admitted, and by 1964, the number had increased to nine. In 1965, 16 students from the fourth graduating class were admitted to university. Our class, the fifth graduating class in 1966, was under pressure to meet the school leadership's goal of producing 25 university admissions. The school leadership required that the number of students in the graduating class each year who are admitted to universities increase by the square of a natural number, reflecting the progress of Liuzhi Middle School. At the same time, following higher-level directives and drawing on experience from other areas, the school planned to recommend a few outstanding students with good family backgrounds for admission to key national universities. Starting from the first semester of our senior year in the winter of 1965, the school secretly began investigating the family and social backgrounds of a select few candidates. This task was assigned to two party members, Bao Wang and Qiwu Wang, who were responsible for conducting political background checks. I was unaware of this at the time because the investigation was confidential and not publicly discussed. Additionally, the school didn't inform the students involved. Given that my family's social network was relatively extensive (my father had four brothers, two aunts, and my mother had four sisters and two brothers), the investigation was complex and spanned several regions. The two teachers spent two to three weeks conducting background checks in both Liuzhi and Puding counties to thoroughly understand my family's history. During the winter break, when I went back home already, the Party Secretary of our village production brigade, Yusheng Tao (陶玉盛), visited my home and mentioned to me: "Mingqing Wu, let me tell you something. In November, two teachers from your school, one of them an older man wearing glasses named Bao Wang, came to our Party branch with an introduction letter from your school. They asked me about your family's background and social relations. I gave them a detailed explanation, emphasizing that your family has always been honest farmers, with a clean history and no political issues. The two teachers were very satisfied with the information." I was surprised and asked: "Why did those two teachers come to investigate my family?" Tao replied: "I asked them, and they said that your academic performance at school is excellent, and the school is considering recommending you for admission to a key national university next year. So, they came to conduct a political review." After hearing this, I finally realized that the school had a recommendation plan in place and that I was one of the candidates. However, despite learning about the possibility of being recommended for a top university, I didn't get carried away and didn't share this information with anyone. I believed it was better to focus on studying hard to ensure I could pass the entrance exam for an university on my own merit. Finally, after all my hard work, when the senior high school graduation exams came in late April and early May of that year, I scored around 90 points in five out of the six main subjects. I specifically remember scoring 96 in Russian and 93 in Physics, though my Chinese score was only in the 80s because my essay didn't turn out as well as I'd hoped. Although I didn't find my exam results particularly outstanding, my classmates and subject teachers all congratulated me warmly. In fact, many of my teachers encouraged me to apply to the universities in their respective fields. My Chinese teacher, Mingyang Yuan (袁名扬), even told me: "Mingqing Wu, no matter which major you choose, once your university admission letter arrives during the summer break, I'll personally bring it to your home the next day!" (As Teacher Yuan was from Machang Town in Puding County, he often passed by our village on his way home, which is why he offered to deliver my admission letter himself.) Despite their affection and support, my aspiration at the time was to apply for a physics major.

However, just as the 1966 graduating class was fully focused

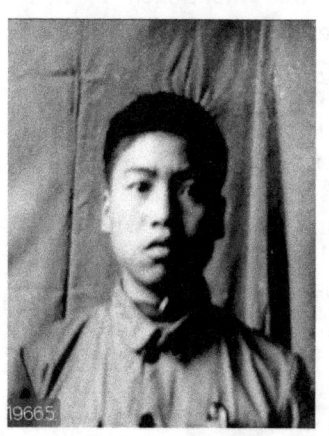

on preparing for the national university entrance exams in June, on May 16, 1966, the Central Committee of the Communist Party issued the "May 16 Notice," marking the official beginning of the Cultural Revolution across the nation. Shortly after, newspapers and radio stations announced that the national exams would be postponed for six months. The school immediately suspended classes, and all students and faculty were organized to study central government documents. Our school, like others, was swept into the fervour of the Cultural Revolution. Little did we know that the unprecedented force of this movement, its lengthy duration, and its far-reaching impacts would not only shatter our dreams of attending university but also irrevocably alter the course of our generation's lives. Moreover, it would bring significant disaster to the entire country.

Middle school is the golden phase of life for learning and knowledge acquisition. It marks the transition from childhood to youth and plays a key role in shaping one's character and knowledge base. While family and parents may have a significant influence on a child during their early years, during adolescence, the school environment becomes the most crucial factor in a young person's development. Whether one attends a good middle school and receives a solid education can have a profound impact on one's future.

Fortunately, despite the hardships I faced during my middle school years, the overall learning environment and social atmosphere at the time were still conducive to the healthy development of young people, allowing us to complete our six years of middle school in a relatively stable manner and laying a strong foundation for our future studies and careers. However, personal goals and career plans, while theoretically achievable through individual effort, are often deeply intertwined with the political and social climate of the country. In other words, personal ambitions and career plans can only be realized if the nation is in a state of political and social stability. Otherwise, in a politically turbulent environment, personal goals and aspirations may become irrelevant. Just as in May 1966, when our graduating class was preparing for the national university entrance exams, the sudden onset of the Cultural Revolution not only destroyed our dreams of attending university but also radically changed the trajectory of our lives. It is no exaggeration to say that, in the vast current of history, an individual is merely a small ripple, with little room to resist the larger forces at play.

Chapter 3   Lost and Confused Days

(I)

On May 16, 1966, the Central Committee of the Chinese Communist Party issued a notice (referred to as the *"May 16th Notification"* (五·一六通知), calling for a nationwide Cultural Revolution. It urged a fierce attack on *"bourgeois representatives"* (资产阶级代表人物) in the Party, government, military, and cultural sectors. Shortly after, on June 1st, the People's Daily published an editorial titled *"Sweep Away All Monsters and Demons"*(横扫一切牛鬼蛇神), which officially launched a **nationwide** *Cultural Revolution movement* (文化大革命运动).

At the beginning of the Cultural Revolution, the focus was on the movement to *"Break the Four Olds"* (破四旧): old ideas, old culture, old customs, and old habits. Anything connected to traditional culture or foreign influences was targeted for elimination. For example, all old books, calligraphy, paintings, antiques, and jewelry found in teachers' homes were confiscated and destroyed. Temples, Buddha statues, and elaborately designed tombstones were smashed. In a particularly absurd case, during street demonstrations, students would force people to remove their plastic sandals for inspection. If the soles had a pattern resembling the character "共" (similar to the character for "Communism"), the students would make them destroy the shoes on the spot, reasoning that "Communism" should not be trampled underfoot. Following this, teachers and students were encouraged to write big-character posters to expose and denounce others, and the "monsters and demons" among the teachers were targeted. The hallways and walls of the school were soon covered with big-character posters. Many diligent and strict teachers were severely impacted. Teachers with unfavourable family backgrounds were labeled as "monsters and demons," and students shaved their heads into a halfbald, half-haired style to represent their label, forcing them to stand in the sun to publicly "show their shame." Teachers with strong professional skills were branded as "reactionary academic authorities" and subjected to insults and humiliation. Some older teachers were accused of being historical counter-revolutionaries or unrepentant rightists, forced to wear tall hats while paraded through the streets, bound, and even beaten during public criticism sessions. Around late July 1966, a group of Red Guards from Beijing's Sixth Middle School visited our Liuzhi Middle School to stir up trouble. The leader was a girl named Lu Lu. In August 1966, Chairman Mao published his famous bigcharacter poster *"**Bombard the Headquarter---My Big Character Poster** "*(炮打司令部---我的一张大字报), marking the beginning of a direct attack on Shaoqi Liu (刘少奇) and Xiaoping Deng (邓小平) by Qing Jiang(江青) and the **Central Cultural Revolution Group** (中央文革小组). They claimed that there was a bourgeois headquarters within the Party Center, and soon Liu and Deng were accused of being the top two capitalist roaders in the country. As a result, across the nation, government agencies, enterprises, and schools began to expose and attack capitalist roaders. At our school, Liuzhi Middle School, the rebels followed the call from the Central Cultural Revolution Group and launched a campaign against the school leadership, identifying the principal and Party Secretary, Guanghui Zhou, and Vice Principal, Hong'en Qin, as capitalist roaders. The rebels then subjected these officials, as well as some "historical counterrevolutionaries" and "rightists" in the school, to endless criticism and struggle sessions. In mid-August, the school formed a **Red Guard** (红卫兵) organization and a Cultural Revolution leadership group. Zhengyou Wang, a classmate from our senior class, was appointed as the head of the school's Cultural Revolution Committee due to his family background as poor peasants, which was considered ideologically pure. He was now in charge of leading the school's Cultural Revolution activities. In August and September 1966, the *"Red Guard Great Link-Up"* (红卫兵大串联) movement spread nationwide. Red Guard reception stations were established across the country to accommodate Red Guards traveling to other regions for revolutionary exchanges. In early September, as Chairman Mao repeatedly greeted Red Guards from all over the country at Tiananmen Square, our school also organized Red Guards from poor peasant, revolutionary carders, and working-class families to take a train to Beijing to be reviewed by Mao. Although I was a Red Guard at the school, my family background as middle peasants disqualified me from being selected to go to Beijing to see the great leader. Around late September or early October 1966, I, along with my classmate Minfu Yu and others, took a train to Guiyang for our first revolutionary exchange. We stayed at the Liuguanmen Sports Stadium, where the Red Guard reception station provided food and lodging. As it was our first time traveling far from home and our first time in a big city like Guiyang, everything seemed particularly novel to us. During the day, we roamed the streets to read big-character posters and collect flyers. We also took buses to visit scenic spots like Qianlingshan Park and Huaxi Park. After dinner at the reception station, we would walk to bustling areas like the Grand Cross and Fountain Plaza to read posters and watch the excitement. At that time, the most fashionable attire for young people was a set of (or at least a top half) yellow military uniforms, a yellow military cap, and a military belt. Girls all had their hair cut shorter to the ears. However, not all Red Guards could afford such outfits---those who wore military uniforms were mostly from military families. Yellow military caps could occasionally be found for sale, and I managed to buy one for two or three yuan somewhere in Guiyang. I felt immensely proud wearing it. However, one night while Minfu Yu and I were at the Grand Cross looking at big-character posters and grabbing flyers, my yellow military cap was snatched by someone in the crowd due to my short height. I was frustrated for a long time over that loss. After returning from Guiyang to Liuzhi, Minfu Yu and I went to Kunming for another revolutionary exchange. For us young students, these so-called revolutionary exchanges were little more than an excuse to join the fun and travel for free. Red Guard reception stations were set up nationwide, and we could travel by train or bus and stay at these stations for free, as long as we had a letter of introduction from our school's Cultural Revolution committee. We could go anywhere we wanted, without having to pay for food or lodging. Some Red Guards, after traveling north and finding their clothing inadequate for the cold weather, even borrowed leather or military coats from the reception stations. Some even borrowed cash and national food coupons. It was said that most of these borrowed items were never returned.

After the revolutionary exchange in Kunming, when my classmates and I returned to Liuzhi, it was already early November 1966. Yet, many of us still felt unsatisfied. So, in mid-November, I, along with my classmates Zhihong Li, Jingwei Chen, and others, took the train to Guiyang again. After spending a few days in Guiyang, we were planning to take the train to Beijing for another revolutionary exchange. However, we suddenly heard a nationwide broadcast on Central People's Radio, relaying a notice from the Central Cultural Revolution Group that ordered an immediate halt to nationwide Red Guard travel by train. The document called for students to stop traveling across the country and instead focus on local walking exchanges. With that, we had no choice but to return to school by train. After we returned to Liuzhi Middle School, some of my classmates in our senior class thought: "Since we can't travel by train, why not organize a walking exchange instead?" After discussing the idea with a few teachers, we decided to form a walking exchange group and continue the revolutionary activities on foot. With approval from the school's Cultural Revolution committee, we, mostly from the senior class, formed a team of 15 students and teachers to walk to Beijing. Our team leader was Teacher Tingkuan Li, and the members included my classmates Jiuyun Wu, Caifeng Dai, Xuhe Dong, Minfu Yu, Weiyou Sun, Qingsu Li, and myself, as well as several students from junior high and first-year high school. To ensure we would be able to present something to Chairman Mao when we arrived in Beijing, our walking group made a special trip to the Lizhi Mining Bureau's Dizong Coal Mine. We selected a shiny piece of coal weighing four to five kilograms. We wrapped it in layers of cotton and white gauze, then covered it tightly with a piece of bright red silk, placing it in a special backpack. The plan was to walk all the way to Beijing and present this as a precious gift to the great leader, representing the people of the Liupanshui region of Guizhou. In early December of that year, the school held a send-off ceremony for our walking exchange team. Our group of 15 people set out from Liuzhi, carrying backpacks and wearing leg wraps, marching with our red flags held high. People often say: "Idealism is full, but reality is bony," and this is indeed true for us. On the first day, we walked about 25 kilometers to reach Luobie town, where we stayed overnight. The next day, we walked to Dingqi, then to Yaopu on the third day, and finally arrived in Anshun city on the fourth day, covering about 75 kilometers in total. Within just a few days, everyone's feet were covered in blisters, and our pace slowed more and more each day. The first ten days or so of the walk were the hardest, as not only did our feet blister, but the physical exhaustion also took a mental toll, leaving us feeling extremely fatigued. However, since we were all in our teens and twenties, we were full of youthful "revolutionary enthusiasm," eager to endure hardship for the cause. After two or three weeks, we gradually adjusted, and walking became easier. As for the five-kilogram coal block we were carrying, although no one was officially assigned to carry it, everyone wanted a chance to bear it, knowing it was a "precious gift" for Chairman Mao. This shows just how pure and idealistic we young people were at the time. It was this sense of youthful revolutionary spirit that carried us from Liuzhi, walking through Anshun, Pingba, Guiyang, and then from Guiyang through Xifeng to Zunyi, over the Loushan Pass, through Tongzi, Qijiang, and finally to Chongqing. From Chongqing, we followed the Yangtze River upstream, passing Jiangjin and Hejiang, crossing the Yangtze River to Neijiang, and finally reaching Chengdu, covering close to 2,000 kilometers in total. In every city or historical site with revolutionary significance, we stopped to visit and learn. For example, in Anshun, we visited the former residence of Ruofei Wang (王若飞); in Xiuwen, we visited the place where General Xueliang Zhang (张学良) was imprisoned--Yangming Cave. When we reached Zunyi (遵义), we stayed for two days, visiting the Zunyi Conference Site and the Red Army Cemetery. In Chongqing (重庆), we visited the Zhazidong (渣滓洞) and Baigongguan (白公馆) prisons on Gele Mountain. In Hejiang, Sichuan, we not only learned about the heroic drilling team "32111" but also stayed with local farmers, participating in agricultural work with the local production teams and experiencing the daily life of the local people.

Although walking every day was exhausting and difficult, our team remained united, and not a single member dropped out or quit. Sometimes, cars would stop and offer us rides, but despite our fatigue, we always politely declined, maintaining our enthusiasm for walking. I still remember the final day of our walk. Chengdu (成都) was already in sight, and to reach our destination as quickly as possible, we set out early from Jianyang County Town and walked all the way to Chengdu, covering over 140 li (approximately 70 kilometers) in one day, the longest distance we had walked in a single day. By the time we arrived in Chengdu, it was late January 1967. We planned to rest for a few days, visit the city's historical sites, and then continue north. However, just a day or two after we reached Chengdu, the Central Cultural Revolution Group issued another notice ordering the cessation of all forms of revolutionary exchanges, including walking tour exchanges. With that, our walking journey came to an abrupt end in Chengdu. Before heading home, we visited Liu Wencai's Manor in the outskirts of Chengdu, in Dayi County, and then went to Dujiangyan (都江堰) to see the ancient waterworks built by Li Bing and his son during the Qin Dynasty. Back in Chengdu, we toured famous sites such as Du Fu's Thatched Cottage (杜甫草堂) and the Wuhou Shrine (武侯祠). After spending about a week in Chengdu, we all took the train back to Liuzhi, arriving in early February 1967, just in time for the Spring Festival.

Looking back on this walking journey with today's perspective, it might seem laughable that we were so naive-- choosing to walk hundreds of kilometers instead of riding in a car, enduring hardships that seemed disproportionate to the rewards. But in retrospect, the hardships we endured actually helped to strengthen our will and enrich our life experiences. From this perspective, the lessons learned from the walk-journey were valuable. Still, it is clear that much of the thinking and behaviour of us youth during the Cultural Revolution, in hindsight, was indeed absurd and laughable.

During the time we were away participating in the *Great Link-Up* (大串联) around November 1966, several classmates in our grade, including Peiding Feng, Quanli Zheng, Weifu Wang, and Xiangui Zhou, formed a rebel organization at school called the "Zunyi Combat Team" (later renamed to the "Zunyi Combat Regiment"). They also began publishing a weekly mimeographed newspaper titled "***Drive Out the Tigers and***

Leopards" (《驱虎豹》), which was distributed both inside and outside the school. The content of this small fourpage newspaper mainly consisted of critical articles, as well as essays and satirical pieces written by students to critique social issues. These were not aimed specifically at any school leaders or teachers; the newspaper was more a way to satisfy the artistic and literary interests of some of the students in our class. Peiding Feng, who had a talent for art and calligraphy from a young age, had his artwork published in the nationally distributed *Middle School Student* (《中学生》) magazine during his high school years. He also enjoyed writing poetry and short satirical pieces, and his calligraphy was well-known throughout the school. He was widely regarded as a multi-talented literary figure, not just in our class but across the entire school. Naturally, Feng took on the roles of planner and chief editor for the newspaper. He also contributed illustrations and was primarily responsible for engraving the mimeograph stencils. After our walking tour exchange ended in early February 1967, when we returned to school, my classmate Minfu Yu and I joined the editorial team of "Drive out the Tigers and Leopards", contributing several critical articles and essays. Sometimes, I also helped with the stencil engraving and mimeograph printing.

From January 1967 onward, the Cultural Revolution had reached the stage where rebels nationwide began seizing power from those identified as capitalist roaders. It began with the Red Guards and worker rebels in Shanghai, who took control of the Shanghai Municipal Party Committee, sparking a movement known as the "*January Storm*" *(一月风暴)*. Soon after, rebels in Heilongjiang Province seized control of the provincial government and established the Heilongjiang Revolutionary Committee. The rebel movement in Guizhou quickly followed suit, and Guizhou's rebels took control of the provincial government, forming the Guizhou Revolutionary Committee and taking over full authority. The People's Daily published a special editorial congratulating Guizhou's rebels, likening their actions to a "*Spring Thunder in the Southwest*" *(西南的春雷)*. After this, rebel groups across provinces and cities nationwide successively seized power, and by March or April 1967, the phrase"*The Whole Country is Red*" (全国山河一片红) was used to describe the situation, as every province, city, and autonomous region had been taken over by the rebels. As for our school's leadership, they had already been overthrown in July or August 1966, replaced by the school's Cultural Revolution Committee and the entire campus had become a sea of red. Slogans such as *"Long live the Great Proletarian Cultural Revolution!"* and *"Long live Mao Zedong Thought!"* were painted everywhere on the exterior walls of school buildings, especially the *"Four Greats"* (四个伟大)(Great Teacher, Great Leader, Great Commander, Great Helmsman). Songs like *"The East is Red"* (《东方红》) and *"Sailing the Seas Depends on the Helmsman* (《大海航行靠舵手》)" could be heard everywhere. Everyone carried a pocket-sized red book of Chairman Mao's quotations, referred to as the *"Little Red Book"*(小红书), and we were required to conduct daily rituals, such as *"Morning Greetings"* (早请示) *and "Evening Reports"* (晚汇报) to Chairman Mao. In addition to studying central directives, students participated in class discussion meetings focused on Mao's quotations, where we *"struggled against selfishness and criticized revisionism"* (要斗私批修), fiercely combating any trace of selfish thoughts. During class breaks, students would gather to perform the *"Loyalty Dance"* (忠字舞), expressing their devotion to Chairman Mao. These actions, which seem absurd today, were widespread revolutionary practices at the time. No one dared to question or disobey the fervour of the Cultural Revolution, for fear of being labeled a "counterrevolutionary" and persecuted.

By April and May of 1967, the nationwide Red Guard movement had begun to wane, and various rebel organizations began to emerge in its place. Workers and government employees became the main force in the Cultural Revolution, and different rebel factions often splintered due to differences in opinion or strategy, leading to conflicts between opposing groups. These conflicts, which began as verbal disputes, gradually escalated into violent clashes. A notable example of this was the armed conflict in Wuhan between two major rebel factions, *"Workers' Headquarters"*(工人总部) and *"Million Heroes"*(百万雄师), which started in February 1967 and became a classic case of rebel factions across the country escalating from verbal battles to physical violence. In response to this growing violence, many factories, government agencies, and schools were placed under military control, with **military propaganda teams** (军宣队) **or** **worker propaganda teams** (工宣队) stationed to maintain order. At our school, the higher authorities sent in a military representative, and workers from the Dizong Mine of the Liuzhi Mining Bureau formed a propaganda team to assist the school's Cultural Revolution committee in organizing students for the continued study of central directives and large-scale criticism sessions.

(Ⅱ)

Objectively speaking, during the Cultural Revolution---a movement that seemed intense on the surface but was in fact an internal chaos---I wasn't a particularly active participant, nor was I a passive bystander. Instead, I was more of a "**gowith-the-flow**" (随大流) kind of person. In the early stages of the movement, I didn't participate in ransacking homes, nor did I write big-character posters targeting teachers or school leaders. I neither insulted nor physically attacked any teachers, and I never spoke at the criticism sessions where teachers and school leaders were publicly denounced. My involvement was mainly limited to editing the school newspaper, writing big-character posters, and penning critical articles, none of which specifically targeted any individual teacher or leader. In other words, I never did anything that would later trouble my conscience. The reason I was a follower rather than a prominent figure in the movement was primarily due to my family background. During the ultra-leftist period of the Cultural Revolution, the extreme "**theory of bloodline**" (血统论) dominated, with sayings like, "**Dragons give birth to dragons, phoenixes give birth to phoenixes, and rats give birth to children who can dig holes**" (龙生龙，凤生凤，老鼠生儿会打洞). This meant that only the children of the "**Red Five Categories**" (红五类) -- revolutionary soldiers, revolutionary cadres, poor peasants, lower-middle peasants (or tenant farmers and hired labourers), and workers---were considered to have an inherent revolutionary superiority and were the main force relied upon in the movement. On the other hand, the children of the ***"Black Five Categories"*** (黑五类) --- landlords, rich peasants, counter-revolutionaries, bad elements, and rightists---were all marginalized. Students like me, from families of middle peasants, small urban craftsmen, employees, freelancers, or urban poor, did not belong to either group and were disparagingly referred to as the *"Grey Five Categories"* (麻五类). We were in an awkward position during the Cultural Revolution, considered only "united" but not trusted. Secondly, I had a particularly introverted personality back then. I would often blush just trying to speak in public, so making a public appearance was not in my nature. It is precisely these subjective and objective factors that determined I could never become a prominent figure of that time, but only a follower who goes with the flow. Upon reflection, I realize I wasn't the only one swept along---most of the students at the time were young and inexperienced, and when faced with the unprecedented and overwhelming force of the Cultural Revolution, we couldn't grasp its full scope, much less question or resist it. We were simply caught up in the immense historical tide, carried forward helplessly like debris in the current. In truth, only a very small number of students were truly active and charged ahead in the movement.

By the time the Cultural Revolution had progressed to 1967-1968, students in schools were growing increasingly bored with it. Apart from studying central documents, attending criticism meetings, and occasionally participating in street protests, there was little to do. As a result, we grew tired of the movement. Intellectuals had been labeled as the *"stinking old ninth class"* (臭老九), and the idea that *"studying is useless"* (读书无用论) became widespread in society. Left with nothing to do, many of us students began playing cards or secretly playing mahjong (麻将). Playing cards, in particular, became the main way we passed time. Regardless of whether it was day or night, if you walked into any student dormitory, you would find students playing cards. Some played "100 points," others played "Find the Friend," but the most popular game was "**Pushing the Pig**" (拱猪), which became one of the students' favourite pastimes. Those who lost at "Pushing the Pig" were not only drawn with moustaches as punishment but also had to crawl under tables or beds. For more than two years, we students wasted our time like this, with our precious youth slipping away.

In the confused and aimless atmosphere of the Cultural Revolution, as a high school graduate, I often felt anxious and uncertain about the future. I had no idea when the movement would end, and I wondered what would become of us if this went on indefinitely. By the end of 1967, as the Vietnam War intensified and China was called upon to support Vietnam in its fight against American aggression, a nationwide conscription campaign began. Our school actively promoted enlistment. At the time, I thought, since the university entrance exams had been canceled, there was no hope of going to university, and no end to the Cultural Revolution was in sight, why not join the military? As a young man in my twenties, serving in the army for a few years might lead to unexpected opportunities. So, I decisively signed up for the military at the school's recruitment office. After passing the physical examination and political review, I received notice that I was about to enlist. I was ecstatic! Along with me, several classmates from different grades, Zerong Li, Weiyou Sun, Rongpeng Xie from the second-year class, and Yongguang Yuan from the first-year class, were also selected to join the military. When I went home on the weekend, I shared the "good news" with my mother, brother, and sister, expecting them to be happy about my decision. To my surprise, my mother was vehemently opposed to the idea. She said: "You're the only boy in our family. How can you go into the army? Haven't you heard people say, 'Good iron isn't made into nails, and good men don't become soldiers'? Why would you want to become a soldier? I'm going to talk to your teachers at school about this tomorrow!" I had never seen my mother so angry with me, and I thought she was just having a fit and would get over it in a few days. But to my surprise again, she really did go to the school the next day. She found my former homeroom teacher, Zongma Zhou, who was also the head of the school's Cultural Revolution committee, and explained our family situation in detail: that my brother was adopted, my sister was from a different father, and so on. In short, she made it clear that "Mingqing Wu is the only son in our family, and I don't agree with him joining the army!" Upon hearing this, Teacher Zhou immediately responded:

"Madam, you make a good point! Don't worry, I've now understood your family's situation, and since Mingqing Wu is your only son, we won't allow him to enlist." After listening to what Teacher Zhou said, my mom returned home with peace of mind. Next day when I returned to school, Teacher Zhou called me to his office and explained that my mother had spoken to him about our family circumstances. Since I was the only son and my mother didn't agree, the school had decided to cancel my enlistment. Hearing this, I was extremely disappointed. It felt like I had missed a great opportunity to realize my ambitions. I even harboured some resentment toward my mother for this. As I watched my classmates happily preparing to enlist, I couldn't help but feel frustrated and regretful. In January 1968, the selected students from our school cheerfully went off to join the military, while I remained at school, feeling dejected. I continued with the monotonous daily routine of studying documents and participating in criticism sessions. In the evenings and on weekends, I passed the time playing cards and mahjong with my classmates, leading a dull and aimless life that felt increasingly pointless.

Starting from June 1966 until the end of 1968, like middle school students all over the country, we spent two to three years idling around in school. During that time, schools of all level---elementary, middle, and university---had been completely shut down for two or three years. Factories had ceased hiring workers, and many government institutions and factories had suspended their operations. The national economy experienced a severe decline. Originally, after the hardships of the "Three Years of Difficulties," the economy had undergone significant improvement due to the three years of adjustment from 1962 to 1964. By 1965, the economic situation across the country had greatly transformed, with abundant supplies, stable prices, and a notable increase in the living standards of the people. However, after two to three years of chaos brought by the Cultural Revolution from 1966 to 1968, the country once again faced a situation of material shortages and skyrocketing prices. Amidst this situation, the government probably realized that it was impossible to reasonably manage the tens of millions of middle school students gathered in the schools. The only feasible solution was to send them to the countryside to settle and participate in agricultural production. Thus, at the end of 1968, the People's Daily published Chairman Mao's directive: "It is necessary for educated youth to go to the countryside to receive re-education from the poor and lowermiddle peasants." Immediately afterward, a vigorous movement was launched across the country to send educated youth to rural areas. In response to this directive, our school quickly began promoting the campaign for students to go to the countryside. At that time, the approach was that graduates from three consecutive classes, both junior and senior high school, who held urban household registrations were organized by the government to be collectively sent down to production brigades in designated areas to settle. As for students who lived in rural areas and held rural household registrations, they were instructed to return to where they originally came from, with each returning to their hometown's production brigade to participate in agricultural work. My family was in a rural area, and my household registration was also rural, so naturally, in late January 1969, I returned to the production brigade in my hometown. After painstakingly studying for more than ten years and finally making it to high school graduation, I had hoped that by getting into university, I could escape the life of a farmer. But who would have thought that the tumultuous Cultural Revolution not only shattered my dream of attending university but also sent me back to the countryside, to the very place where I was born and raised? The sense of loss I felt at that time is hard to describe with a single, precise word. It was truly like "after years of hardship and struggle, just in one night, I was back to square one!"

(III)

At the end of January 1969, I returned home in a deeply dejected state. Although I was returning to the place where I was born and raised, surrounded by my closest family and familiar neighbours, I had become accustomed to the collective life of school, so back home I felt incredibly lonely and isolated. My mind was blank, filled with thoughts like, "My future is completely ruined. What will I do now?" Since it was winter and there wasn't much agricultural work for the production team, I spent most of my time at home reading novels. I don't remember exactly where I got the books, but I had a few, including ***Dream of the Red Chamber*** (《红楼梦》), ***A History of the Qing Dynasty*** (《清史稿》), and ***Romance of the Sui and Tang Dynasties*** (《隋唐演义》). I would sit by the stove all day reading, not wanting to go out or interact with anyone. Because I was feeling so down, I hardly spoke to my mother or my siblings. My mother and siblings were initially happy to see me return home after finishing school. My mother, especially, was overjoyed to have her precious son home to stay. She smiled all day long, clearly delighted. However, when they saw that I was in a gloomy mood and spent all my time reading with little to say, they became puzzled. One day, my mother asked me about the situation at school and how my classmates were doing. Feeling downcast, I told her: "All the students have gone to the countryside now. There are no more students at the school. It might even be closed by now. I don't know what I'm going to do now that I'm back home." My mother replied: "Well, now that you're back home, you should just do farm work!" I immediately responded: "Mom, you worked so hard to support me through more than ten years of schooling, and in the end, I still have to come back to do farm work. Doesn't that mean all my schooling was for nothing? Wasn't all your hard work wasted too?" She said: "It doesn't matter to us. But right now, the state's policy is for you to go to the countryside and participate in agricultural production. There's no other option at the moment. Just settle down in the countryside for a few years and see what happens. Maybe in a few years, the policy will change again." After hearing my mother's words, I had nothing more to say. The reality was that there was no other path available. Since I had already returned home after being sent to the countryside, I had no choice but to stay and work with the production team.

When I returned home, my biggest concern was figuring out how to earn pocket money. Back when I was at school, whether I was studying or "making revolution," I could still ask my mother or my sister for money for food and small expenses. But now that I was home, I had no reason to keep asking them for money. Besides, it wouldn't make sense for a man in his twenties to keep asking his mother for money. But I couldn't think of any way to earn money on my own. Just when I was feeling frustrated and at a loss, my former classmate from the White Grave Branch School in junior high, who was also my distant nephew, Xingzhi Wu, came to visit me. He said: "Youngest uncle, I heard you're back home. I've teamed up with Shengfu Li from our village to buy a popcorn machine. We want to invite you to join us in going around the nearby villages to make popcorn for people and earn some extra money. What do you think?" At first, I hesitated. I felt that as a high school graduate, it was a bit embarrassing to take on such a job. But then I thought: "There's no other way to earn money right now, so why not give it a try?" So, I agreed to join them. The next day, the three of us took turns carrying the popcorn machine to nearby villages, making popcorn for the local farmers. We charged 20 cents per batch of popcorn, and we could make around 30 or 40 batches per day. Each of us earned about two or three yuan a day. For the next three to four weeks, we worked from dawn to dusk, making popcorn for the farmers in the surrounding villages. By the end of it, each of us had earned ¥40 or ¥50 yuan. But by the time April came around, the production team's farm work started to pick up, and we had to stop the popcorn business.

When it came to farm work, despite having spent most of my time away studying, I had grown up in the countryside and often helped out on our family's private plot during school breaks. Occasionally, I even joined the production team for some of their work. As a result, I was capable of handling most general farm tasks, such as planting crops, transplanting rice seedlings, and carrying or lifting things. However, the truly challenging farm tasks traditionally done by men---like plowing fields with oxen---were things I hadn't done before. Particularly when plowing flooded rice fields, the soil beneath the water is hard to see, and without experience, it's easy to miss areas. If parts of the field aren't plowed properly, the soil compacts, preventing rice seedlings from taking root, and the crops won't grow well. So, I had to learn plowing from scratch. The production team leader was kind enough to select an old, docile ox for me to work with and personally taught me how to plow. He showed me how to command the ox, what to shout to make it turn left or right, and how to handle the plow when encountering rocks, like quickly lifting the plow to avoid breaking the blade. He also taught me how to manage the plow at the edges of the field to ensure that all the soil was turned over. After about a week of practice, I finally learned how to plow, and before long, I mastered the task of plowing flooded fields with oxen.

The busiest times on the farm were during the summer and autumn harvest and planting seasons, especially when it came time to transplant rice seedlings, which happened around the Dragon Boat Festival. During this period, the women were mainly responsible for harvesting wheat and rapeseed, while the men took care of plowing and transplanting rice. The production team had many highland fields, which lacked irrigation and relied entirely on rainfall. The period around the Dragon Boat Festival coincided with the heavy rains of the flood season, making it the best time for the men to work from dawn to dusk, rushing to plow and transplant rice before the rains stopped. If they missed this window, the highland fields would have to be planted with dry-land crops instead. This kind of work lasted for three to four weeks, and once the rice was transplanted, the men's workload lightened considerably. During this busy season, I worked hard and proved myself. The skin on my back and neck peeled from the sun, and I kept pace with the production team members without issue. The team leader and the other members would often say: "Mingqing, you look like this 'intellectual' hasn't forgotten your roots! You work just as well as the rest of us old farmers." Hearing this made me happy, though I remained modest, saying: "Oh no, I'm still far from being as good as you!" Fortunately, I was young and full of energy, barely 20 years old, so I had both the strength and endurance. After a day of hard work, all it took was a good night's sleep, and I'd wake up feeling refreshed and ready to go again.

Before I knew it, more than half a year had passed, and I had become accustomed to the farm work. My feelings of isolation gradually faded. Then, in August 1969, the leaders of the two production teams in our village had a discussion and thought: "We have a high school graduate here. Isn't it a waste to have him just doing farm work? Why don't we start a village school and have Mingqing Wu teach the children instead?" So, the two team leaders came to my house and explained their idea of starting a village school, asking if I was willing to teach. As for compensation, they said that aside from receiving the same grain rations as a strong labourer, each student would pay ten yuan per semester in tuition. At the time, I thought, "Sure, I can handle farm work, but it's exhausting. If the two production teams want to open a school and have me teach, why not?" So, I agreed to their proposal. The school was set up in the main hall of my old brother's new house, which was behind our family's old home. The tables and chairs were makeshift, with students bringing their own tables and benches from home. A large blackboard was purchased and hung on the wall, and we even found a half-pipe to use as a bell, tying it with wire to the outside pillar of the house to signal the start and end of classes. After two weeks of preparation, the school officially opened on September 1st, 1969. Once the school was up and running, it attracted not only children from the two production teams in our village but also children from nearby teams, like Qingjiao and Tanziyao villages. In total, the school had more than 30 students, divided into three grades. Most were first-year students, including Shunyi Wu, Xingrong Wu, Dongsheng Wu, Zhengxiang Ye, Zhengding Ye, and others from our village, along with Xinglin Wu and Shunlin Wu from Dianshan. Second and third-grade students included Taihe Deng, Manrong Guo, Manhua Guo, and Manfu Guo from Tanziyao village. Since there were about 15 first-grade students, the remaining second and third-grade students, around five to eight in each grade, were all taught together in a multi-grade classroom. I taught the first grade first, followed by the second and third grades, with each lesson lasting 45 minutes. Classes started at 8:30 in the morning, with a 15-minute break between periods. After three periods, we had lunch at noon, followed by a two-hour break, and then resumed with three more periods in the afternoon, ending the day at 5:00 p.m. The core subjects, Chinese and arithmetic, were taught separately by grade, while music and physical education were combined for all three grades. Since I was teaching first through third grade, I didn't have to use much of the knowledge I had learned myself, but most of my energy was spent managing classroom discipline. Most of the students were from the Wu family clan in our village, and since I was considered an elder within the family, the children had a certain level of respect for me at first, and the classroom discipline was quite good. However, as they became more familiar with me over time, they grew less restrained, and some began to lose focus during lessons. As a result, I had to spend more time and energy maintaining order in the classroom. After teaching five or six periods each day, I often felt mentally exhausted and would fall asleep as soon as I lay down.

By November of 1969, the Amy recruitment drive for the spring 1970 enlistment began again. I thought to myself: "This is a great opportunity! I need to find a way to enlist this time. I can't just keep staying at home doing nothing." Back in the spring of 1968, I had passed the physical examination and political review, but just before I was set to leave, my mother had opposed my enlistment, and I missed out. I had complained to her about this many times. After I returned from being sent to the countryside, my mother knew I still held a grudge over the matter and was often in a bad mood, so she tried to appease me in many ways. However, I wasn't sure if she would agree to let me enlist again this time. To ensure I could convince my mother, I thought of my cousin Mingliang Wu, knowing that he would be the one person who could persuade her. So, one evening, I invited him to our house, where my mother, brother, and sister were all present. Once Mingliang Wu sat down, I got straight to the point and said to my mother: "Mom, the Amy recruitment drive has started again this year, and I'm preparing to enlist. I hope you won't stop me this time." My mother responded: "I don't want you to join the army because I'm afraid something will happen to you. You're only son in our family, and you haven't even gotten married yet. What if something goes wrong in the military?" My sister chimed in, agreeing with my mother: "Youngest brother, why do you need to join the army? You're teaching at home now, isn't that good enough? What's the point of being a soldier?" At this point, Mingliang Wu spoke to my mother. He said: "Aunt, since Mingqing brother wants to enlist, I think you should let him go. We're living in peaceful times now, so there's no need to worry. Mingqing has studied so much, if he joins the military, he might be given a position as a clerk or a cultural officer, and it's unlikely he'll be sent to the front lines. Besides, it's always been said that loyalty and filial piety can't both be achieved. In the new society, young people are encouraged to pursue their ambitions. Mingqing wants to go out and serve the country, and if he does well, it will bring honour to our Wu family. So, I suggest you let him go, rather than keep him at home where he's unhappy. You've seen how he's been, and it's not good for anyone." My brother also spoke up: "Mom, If my brother doesn't want to stay at home, just let him join the army. We'll take care of you, Mom." Seeing that everyone was in agreement, my mother finally relented. She said: "Alright, if you really want to join the army, then go. But make sure you stay safe, and after two or three years in the military, come back and start a family." Overjoyed, I replied: "Okay! I'll serve for two or three years and then come back." But in my heart, I thought, "Once I'm out there, I'll stay as long as I can. I don't necessarily have to come back." Two days later, I happily went to the commune and signed up for the military. People often say: "The skies are unpredictable, and misfortune can strike unexpectedly." In early December, the commune notified those who had signed up to enlist to go to the Huachu District Hospital for medical examinations. About a week later, I received a notice from the commune's revolutionary committee asking me to come in. I thought my medical checkup and political review must have passed, and I would soon be enlisting in the army. However, when I arrived at the commune, the leader in charge of recruitment told me that during the medical exam, the doctor found that I had an anal fistula, which made me ineligible for military service. Hearing this felt like being struck on the head with a heavy blow, I could hardly stand on my legs. I thought to myself: Why has my fate been so full of misfortune? Two years ago, my mother opposed it; now, I was disqualified due to a medical issue. Why is fate playing such cruel tricks on me? I had always been physically strong and healthy, but a couple of months after returning home from the school in 1969, I began experiencing itching and pain around my anus, sometimes with foul-smelling yellow liquid oozing from the side of my anus. The pain worsened when walking. Being young and careless, I didn't pay much attention, thinking it would heal over time, so I never sought medical help. But this seemingly small issue cost me a major opportunity during the military medical exam. Still unwilling to give up, I decided to go to Huachu District and talk to the Instructor Zhang, the officer in charge of recruitment, to see if there was any chance of leniency. To show my determination to enlist, I bit my right index finger the night before, and with the blood from the wound, I wrote a brief letter of appeal on a piece of white paper, insisting on my desire to serve in the military army. When I met Instructor Zhang the next day, I handed him the blood letter, expressing my earnest wish to enlist. Zhang called me into his office and kindly said: "Xiao Wu, your determination to serve in the military is admirable. With your education, you're exactly the kind of talent we need in the army. However, your medical exam didn't pass, and the standards for enlistment cannot be changed. Don't be discouraged, once you've had this issue treated, you can still try again next time if the opportunity arises." Despite my repeated requests, Zhang remained firm, and I had no choice but to return home dejected and continue teaching at the village school. By the time the summer of 1970 arrived, my mother found a private doctor in Zhangjiapingzai village, Liuzhi, who specialized in treating hemorrhoids. We spent ¥20 to ¥30 yuan, and finally, my issue was completely cured.

(IV)

Mr. Zongma Zhou was my homeroom teacher during my second and third years of high school, and we had always shared a close teacher-student bond. Even after I was sent to the countryside, I would occasionally visit him on weekends when I went to the town market in Xiayingpan Town. Around March or April of 1970, Mr. Zhou had been promoted to the Director of Cultural Revolution Committee of the Liuzhi Special District Education Bureau, where he oversaw educational and cultural work throughout the district. One weekend, when I went to visit him, Mr. Zhou heard that I had been teaching elementary school in our village. He asked me: "Mingqing, would you be interested in coming to our Liuzhi Special District to teach? A new school called Kangda Middle School has been established behind Dazhai village in Xiayingpan, and they urgently need teachers. If you're willing, I can arrange a teaching position for you." Hearing the opportunity to teach at a middle school, I was overjoyed and agreed immediately. Mr. Zhou continued: "Since you're now considered a 'zhiqing' (educated youth) under the jurisdiction of Puding County and not part of Liuzhi, I'll write a letter of inquiry from the Liuzhi Special District Education Bureau to Puding County, asking for permission. You'll need to take this letter to your production brigade, the commune, and finally the county personnel bureau for approval. If they agree to release you, bring the reply back to me, and I'll arrange for your teaching job in Liuzhi." I said happily: "Great! Thank you Teacher Zhou." Mr. Zhou quickly wrote the letter of inquiry from the Liuzhi Special District Education Bureau to the Puding County Personnel Bureau and handed it to me. He urged me to complete the process quickly and bring the reply back to him. I started by presenting the letter to our production brigade, who had no objections. However, when I reached the commune, the head of the revolutionary committee was not around, and I could only find the deputy director. After reading the letter, the deputy said: "You're one of our Educated Youth why should Liuzhi be the one arranging your job? Plus, our leader isn't here, and I don't know when he'll be back. You'll have to wait until he returns." Sensing his attitude, I figured I wouldn't get through this level easily. If I waited for the main Revolution committee leader to return and he wrote "Not Approved" on the letter, the whole process would be blocked. Thus, I decided to try the county level first, hoping to get support there. The next day, I walked to the county seat and sought out a distant relative from my mother's side, Wenming Zhang, who worked as the head of the trial court at the Puding County Court. I had met him before when I studied in Puding County in 1961. When I found Mr. Zhang, I showed him the inquiry letter from the Liuzhi Special District Education Bureau and asked if he could help me at the county personnel bureau. He agreed to give it a try the next morning. That evening, I stayed at his home, and the next morning, Mr. Zhang took me to the county personnel bureau. In the personnel director's office, I handed over the inquiry letter and requested approval to transfer to Liuzhi. And Zhang also explained my situation to the director: how I had studied in Liuzhi before and returned to the countryside for re-education, and asked the director to approve the transfer. After reading the letter, the personnel director paused for a moment and said: "This is going to be difficult. Your production brigade agreed, but the commune hasn't signed off. You need their approval first. Once the commune revolutionary committee signs off, then we can consider it at the county level. Without the commune's approval, how can we proceed? Besides, you're already one of our educated youth. We have our own plans for our educated youth, so why would we let Liuzhi arrange your job?" With that, Mr. Zhang and I had nothing more to say. Seeing that there was no way to resolve the issue, Mr. Zhang had no choice but to take me back home. A few days later, I returned to the Liuzhi Special District Education Bureau to meet with Mr. Zhou and explained the situation to him. After hearing my story, he sighed and said regretfully: "Since the county won't release you, there's nothing more I can do. It looks like you'll have to figure things out on your end." I knew Mr. Zhou had done everything he could to help me, so I thanked him for his efforts and once again returned home with a heavy heart, continuing my career as a village teacher.

In no time, a full academic year had passed teaching elementary school in my hometown, and it was already mid-August 1970. With the new school term approaching on September 1st, one afternoon, our production brigade party secretary passed along a verbal notice from the commune's revolutionary committee, informing me that the director wanted to have a word with me. The brigade party secretary didn't specify the reason for the meeting, which left me feeling somewhat uneasy. The next morning, I walked to the commune office in Bogai Village, as instructed. By then, our Laliu Commune had merged with the neighboring Duobei Commune in the mid-1960s, and the newly combined entity was known as Duobei Commune. The office was about seven or eight kilometers from our village. The director of the commune revolutionary committee was Delong Ma, a man in his fifties from Dayong Town in Liuzhi Special District. There were two deputy directors: Yuhuai Li, also from Dayong Town, and Shunyi Li, a local from Tianba Brigade. Shunyi Li came from a poor peasant family and was an old land reform cadre who could barely read but had a phenomenal memory. I had met him on my last visit to the commune office. Another official, who wasn't formally a deputy director, was Chaohuan Wang from the Shuimu Town. When I met Director Ma, he invited me into his office. After I sat down, he said: "Xiao Wu, I heard you came to see me last time, but I wasn't available. We didn't know you well before, but now we've realized that you're the only high school graduate in our commune! Since you've returned to your hometown after being sent to the countryside, I don't think you need to continue teaching elementary school. The commune revolutionary committee has decided to transfer you to the commune office for some administrative work. What do you think?" Initially, I had some lingering resentment from my last visit when my application for the teaching position in Liuzhi was rejected. I thought this meeting would be about that. But hearing Director Ma's proposal took me by surprise. I thought to myself: "If I refuse this transfer, what if future opportunities arise and the commune refuses to release me? That would be even worse." So, I decided to accept the offer and try to build good relationships with the commune leadership, hoping that things would work out better in the future. After considering it for a moment, I agreed. Director Ma, pleased with my response, said: "You'll be treated as a part-time cadre here at the commune office. Your household registration will remain in your original production team, and you'll still receive your grain distribution from them. The commune will pay you a monthly living stipend of ¥25 yuan. When you get back, let your production team and brigade know about the commune decision. After you've wrapped up your responsibilities at the elementary school, report to the commune office with your belongings in early September." I agreed and, upon returning to the production team, informed them of the commune's decision. I also arranged for all the elementary school students to transfer to Yunheng Yuan's school in Duimen Village. After settling everything, I packed my belongings and reported to the commune office.

At the time, besides Director Ma and the two deputy directors, my cousin Mingquan Wu also worked at the commune office. He was the secretary responsible for the office seal and phone communications. The entire country was in the midst of the "*One Strike, Three Antis*" (一打三反) Campaign, a political movement aimed at cracking down on counter-revolutionary sabotage while fighting corruption, theft, speculative trading, and wastefulness. In the countryside, corruption and theft were rampant, particularly in the form of illegal logging, cattle theft, and the sale of collective farming equipment. Certain areas experienced severe illegal logging. Several cases had already been opened across the commune, with a few major criminal cases transferred to the county public security bureau for investigation. The smaller cases were handled by the commune's revolutionary committee. Because there were many cases to investigate, and the commune had limited staff, even with my addition, the manpower still felt insufficient. As a result, the commune pulled another person from Tianba Brigade to assist with the investigations and report writing. This individual, named Daihe Zheng, was about 30 years old and had graduated from Puding Middle School in 1960. He was admitted to Beijing Petroleum Institute but had to drop out after a year due to illness in 1961. He never returned to his studies and ended up farming in his hometown. Later Daihe Zheng came, the commune split the two of us into separate teams. Each team consisted of a cadre from the production brigade and one of the commune's deputy director, forming two three-person groups. We were assigned to different production brigades with unresolved cases, where we investigated incidents of corruption and theft. Our work involved collecting witness statements and physical evidence and conducting interrogations of those involved. After completing the investigations, we returned to the commune office to write detailed reports, analyze the severity of each case, and propose initial recommendations for handling them. These reports were then discussed and finalized by the commune's revolutionary committee, stamped for approval, and submitted to the Puding County Revolutionary Committee for review and archiving. My reports, which were clear, wellevidenced, and thoroughly analyzed, received high praise from both the commune and county revolutionary committee leadership. Over the course of the year-long "One Strike, Three Antis" campaign, I was involved in investigating and drafting reports on about 20 cases. Some of the more serious cases, involving theft and sexual assault, were forwarded to the Puding county public security bureau, where they drew the attention of law enforcement. After further investigation and supplementary evidence collection, the suspects in these cases were eventually brought to justice.

In September 1971, following the *Biao Lin "9.13" incident* (林 彪 "9.13"), the Chinese Central Communist Party Committee's documents on the matter were distributed to the commune level in October. As a result, the commune formed a propaganda team to deliver and explain the documents to the masses in various production brigades. I was assigned to this team as one of the key speakers and participated in the month-long campaign to spread the documents across the commune. During this period, I, alongside Deputy Director Yuhuai Li, hosted more than twenty mass meetings across more than a dozen production brigades, where I explained the Central Committee's documents to the villagers. After dozens of these meetings, I gained valuable experience in public speaking, which helped me build the confidence to address large crowds without fear---an experience that laid the foundation for my later involvement in university and social work. After working alongside the commune revolutionary committee leadership for over a year, several commune leaders expressed their appreciation for my work ethic and capabilities. They commended me for my sincerity, straightforward character, and optimism, and they recognized my strong writing skills. During my time at the commune, Director Ma also encouraged me to apply to join the Communist Party, pushing me to actively align myself with the Party. In addition to guiding me toward Party membership, Director Ma was deeply invested in my future. At one point, he tried to have me promoted to a full-time government cadre, hoping I could work permanently at the commune office. However, due to a lack of hiring quotas, his plans could not materialize. Despite this, Director Ma kept a close eye on any opportunities for secondary and higher education admissions.

Around June or July 1971, a teaching secondary school in Anshun started recruiting students from among the sentdown youth. Our commune was allocated one spot. Upon hearing this, Director Ma immediately approached me, he said: "Xiao Wu, I know you're a capable young man, and we at the commune really like you very much. We'd love to keep you working with us, but it seems we won't be able to hold on to you. We can't stand in the way of your future. Right now the Anshun Teacher's Secondary School is recruiting, and I wonder if you're interested?" While I was keen on furthering my education, when I heard it was a secondary technical school, I told Director Ma: "I've already graduated from high school, and my level should be on par with a technical secondary school graduate. I don't think it's necessary for me to attend a technical school. I'd rather wait for a university opportunity." Director Ma agreed, saying: "That's fine. If any university opportunities come up, I'll be sure to let you know as soon as possible." Then, in March or April of 1972, Director Ma returned from a county meeting one afternoon, excitedly telling me: "Xiao Wu, I have great news for you! University admissions have opened! Our commune has been allotted one spot, and the program is for the Department of the Physical Education at Guiyang Normal University. Would you be interested? If you are, we'll recommend you." I was overjoyed to hear this news, as going to university had been my lifelong dream. I didn't care what major it was, so even though it was a physical education program, I immediately agreed. "I'm fine with it," I said, "I'd be happy to study physical education." Director Ma said: "Great! We'll submit your name to the county right away." By mid-May, the county education bureau notified each commune to send their recommended candidates for interviews and medical examinations. When I arrived for my interview at the county, the interviewer was a professor from the Physics Department at Guizhou University, Professor Yang. He first inquired about my educational background and then gave me a few middle and high school math problems to solve, which I completed without difficulty. After the interview, Professor Yang said: "Xiao Wu, just wait for your acceptance letter." At the time, I found it a bit odd that a physical education program would test my math skills, but I didn't dwell on it. The medical examination also went smoothly, as my previous health issues had been completely resolved after surgery in the summer of 1970. After the interview and physical exam, I returned to the commune to resume my work. Two or three weeks later, around early June, I received an acceptance letter from Guizhou University, informing me that I had been admitted to the Chemistry Department of Guizhou University and should report to campus in mid-July. I was completely surprised. However, upon reflection, I realized that Professor Yang must have seen that I wasn't suited for physical education due to my stature and had recognized my solid academic foundation as a high school graduate. He must have decided to transfer me from the Physical Education program at Guiyang Normal University to the Chemistry Department at Guizhou University.

When the commune leaders learned that I had received an acceptance letter from Guizhou University and would be leaving for school in mid-July, they were overjoyed and decided to help expedite my application to join the Communist Party before I left for university. The commune's Party committee immediately instructed the Party secretary of my production brigade, Yusheng Tao, to quickly convene a meeting to formalize my Party membership. Following the Commune Party Committee's directive, the brigade Party branch held a meeting to discuss my application, and the decision to admit me to the Party was unanimously approved. My Party sponsors were Yusheng Tao and committee member Youheng Wang. After the brigade's decision was reported to the commune Party committee, a formal review was held on the evening of June 12, 1972, where the commune Party committee unanimously approved my membership and held a formal induction ceremony. Given that during the Cultural Revolution, new Party members no longer had a probationary period, once the Party committee approved membership and the oath was taken, I became a full-fledged member of the Chinese Communist Party. To be honest, after receiving the university admission letter, I was so overwhelmed with joy that I didn't think much about joining the Party. My mind was preoccupied with my upcoming university life, a long-cherished dream finally coming true after years of struggling to find my path, especially after the challenges of being sent to the countryside. Still, since the commune leaders cared so much, I thought, "Why not?" When I returned home with the admission letter, I shared the news with my mother, brother, and sister. They were all overjoyed. As I reflected on the six years since my high school graduation, especially the trials of more than three years in the countryside, I realized that I had finally achieved my dream of going to university. The emotions were overwhelming, and I wept tears of joy, crying freely at home for the first time in a long time.

People often say: "Fate separates us into different tiers, but at times, it is also fair." When one door closes, another opens. If I hadn't returned to my hometown in January 1969 as part of the re-education campaign, instead had joined my classmates in settling elsewhere, I might have ended up as a coal miner in the Liupanshui region when recruitment took place in 1970. Similarly, if the Puding County Personnel Bureau had approved my transfer to work at the Liuzhi Special District Education Bureau, I might have spent my life as a middle school teacher and missed out on the chance to attend Guizhou University in 1972. My life would have taken a completely different path.

Chapter 4   Striving in Golden Years

(I)

After the release of the "**May 16 Notice**" in May 1966, the Cultural Revolution immediately led to the cancellation of national university entrance exams. After four to five years of disruption, by 1970, despite constant calls from leadership to *"Grasping revolution to promote production"* (抓革命促生产), the national economy had severely declined, and living standards were falling year by year. With universities having ceased admissions for several years and no new graduates entering the workforce, various sectors were suffering from a severe shortage of knowledge and specialized talent. Faced with this critical shortage, the central leadership gradually realized that keeping universities closed indefinitely was not a viable option. However, simply reverting to the old system was not acceptable; educational reform was needed. In 1970, Chairman Mao summarized the experience of the Shanghai Machine Tool Plant's training of technical workers, stating that *"Universities must still be run, but the academic duration should be shortened, and education must be revolutionized. Workers and peasants with practical experience should be selected to study for a few years in school and then return to production practice."* This became Mao's famous *"July 21 Directive"* (七.二一指示). Based on this directive, in 1970 and 1971, universities such as Peking University and Tsinghua University began admitting small numbers of students with a three-year academic program. Starting in 1972, admissions expanded across all universities in the country, marking the arrival of the "worker-peasant-soldier students" era. Statistics show that from 1970 to 1976, a total of over 920,000 worker-peasant-soldier students were admitted to institutions of higher education across China, and I was one of them.

 In mid-July of 1972, I arrived at the Chemistry Department of Guizhou University with great joy and excitement. Had the Cultural Revolution not interrupted university admissions, I should have already graduated from university and been working for two years already by this point. In reality, our generation was delayed for six years by the Cultural Revolution, wasting precious yearsof youth. Nevertheless, we finally entered university, which at least made us fortunate compared to many of our peers. For this reason, I felt incredibly happy and also developed a strong desire and sense of urgency to pursue knowledge. I secretly resolved to make the most of my time at university and learn as much as I could.

A group photo of some students from our class (The 1st person from the right in 2nd row is the author) in Aug., 1972.

Our class was the first cohort of worker-peasant-soldier students admitted by Guizhou University's Chemistry Department after a six-year hiatus due to the Cultural Revolution, with a focus on analytical chemistry. At the time, Guizhou University had seven departments: Chinese, Mathematics, Physics, Chemistry, History, Philosophy, and Foreign Languages, with each department admitting one class. In total, the university admitted about 300 students that year. Our chemistry class had 41 students, with 23 male students and 18 female students. The students not only varied significantly in age but also in educational background. The class included students who had completed as little as one year of junior high school to those who had completed three years of high school. Around 60%

of the students had only a junior high school education, while about 40% were high school education, with only two or three of them having fully completed their studies in the 1966 cohort and I am one of them. Most students were recommended by their rural communes as sent-down youth, while a few were workers recommended by factories or mines. At the time, workerpeasant-soldier students attending university were exempt from tuition and fees, and the government provided a monthly stipend of CNY ¥19.5 per student. Of this, ¥13.5 was issued as meal tickets for the school cafeteria, and the remaining ¥6 was given as pocket money. Students who had previously been employed and had five or more years of work experience could also study with full pay. As our Chemistry Department was part of the sciences, there were no soldier students in our class. In contrast, departments such as Chinese, History, and Philosophy admitted a few soldier students, who were usually officers with the rank of platoon leader or higher. These military students enjoyed the same benefits as officers of their rank in the army, making their treatment among the best of the students.

Due to the significant disparity in educational levels among the students in our class, with most students having only completed junior high school and lacking a solid academic foundation, the department decided to spend the first three months providing supplementary lessons to cover basic middle school-level knowledge. This meant that the subjects taught in the first three months, such as mathematics, physics, and chemistry, all focused on middle school-level content, while English started from the most basic level, including the alphabet and phonetics. Since I was one of the few students who had graduated in high school in 1966, with a relatively strong foundation in middle school subjects, the teachers often asked me to help my classmates with questions after they had completed their lessons. Sometimes, I even stood at the front of the class to explain concepts, almost serving as a teaching assistant for math, physics, and chemistry. After about three months of remedial classes, our studies transitioned to regular university-level courses. However, some students have to struggle to keep up due to their weak academic backgrounds, and a few of them had no choice but to transfer from our science department to the humanities.

Given the radical leftist influence during the Cultural Revolution and the fact that worker-peasant-soldier students were being admitted to universities, there was a prevailing belief that these students should not only attend university but also "manage and reform" universities. In this environment, the expectations for students were markedly different from those before the Cultural Revolution. Teachers typically assigned very little homework, and regular tests or quizzes were rare. There were only mid-term and final exams, and even then, the questions were relatively easy, allowing nearly all students to pass. As a result, the overall academic pressure on students was not particularly high.

Our class was focused on analytical chemistry, a practical and highly applicable field that plays a critical role in industries such as cement, mining, metallurgy, environmental protection, food, medicine, geological exploration, and even criminal investigations. Given the halt in university admissions during the Cultural Revolution, there was a dire need for talent in this area. Consequently, when universities reopened, many chemistry departments chose to offer this major. During my time at university, despite the relatively low academic expectations from the school and teachers, I remained committed to my studies. As one of the four Communist Party members in our class and one of the few high school graduates, I was appointed as the Party Branch Secretary for our class by the Party Committee of the department. Another Party member, Wanzhi Li, was appointed class monitor. As Party Branch Secretary, in addition to managing my own studies, I had to assist our class instructor (who was referred to as the "guide") in overseeing various class activities, including student ideological education, academic progress, Communist Youth League activities, and the recruitment of new Party members. These responsibilities required a significant amount of my time outside of class, so I had to focus on making the most of my in-class learning to maximize efficiency. Although I was often busy, I found the experience fulfilling, and my academic performance did not suffer. I understood that the department's decision to appoint me as Party Branch Secretary reflected their trust and high expectations of me. Additionally, since my classmates knew I had graduated from high school in 1966 and had an academic advantage, I felt a responsibility to set a good example in both conduct and academics. I continued to apply the study methods I had used in high school: I paid close attention to key points during lectures and took detailed notes, completed assignments promptly, and reviewed the material afterward. For new lessons, I tried to preview the content at least once or twice in advance to familiarize myself with it. For English, I dedicated extra time in the mornings or during my free time to practice reading and speaking. Thanks to my solid middle school foundation and effective study methods, I consistently ranked at the top of my class throughout my three years at university. My strong academic performance and quick problem-solving skills earned me the playful nickname "**The Great Prodigy**" (大神童) from my classmates, while another younger classmate, Weiming Chen, who had a weaker academic background but also achieved excellent results, was affectionately called "**The Little Prodigy**" (小神童). However, in reality, there were no "prodigies"---it was simply a matter of putting in more time and effort behind the scenes.

Since it was a newly emerging things for workers, peasants and soldiers to go to university introduced after the abolition of the university entrance exam during the Cultural Revolution, praised as a great initiative in educational reform at the time. It emphasized integrating education with the three revolutionary movements, encouraging students not only to attend university but also to manage and reform it. Students were expected to engage in both agricultural and military training, in addition to their academic studies. To meet the agricultural trainingrequirement, our class was assigned a plot of land, about four or five acres in size, near Leizhuang Airport of Guiyang, located several miles from the university. We planted vegetables like potatoes, peppers, and eggplants, and our class regularly walked to the farm with tools to participate in agricultural labor. In the fall, during the harvest season, we would deliver the vegetables we harvested to the school cafeteria to improve the meals for both students and staff. To better organize the agricultural work, our class elected a Labor Committee member from the rural students, and that person was Zhihai Pan. Although Zhihai Pan wasn't very old, he was tall, strong, and sincere, so everyone called him "Old Pan." He was a Miao from Majiang County in Guizhou Province and was an expert in farming, not only physically capable but also knowledgeable about agricultural practices. He was a highly competent Labor Committee member, well-respected and trusted by both students and teachers.

A group photo of some classmates in Huaxi Park, Guiyang, Guizhou in July, 1973 (The 4th person from the left is the author).

The second aspect of the *"open-door schooling"* (开门办学) initiative was the practical activity of learning through work. Since our major was analytical chemistry, in the first year of this program, the department specifically arranged for our class to visit chemical laboratories in chemical and metallurgical industries. This allowed us to experience firsthand the practical applications and importance of analytical chemistry, thereby enhancing our professional studies. During the summer vacation of 1973, our class, led by our professors, visited the analytical chemistry laboratories at the Zunyi Alkali Plant and Zunyi Ferroalloy Plant for a two-week observational learning experience. To further improve our practical skills in analytical chemistry, in August 1974, the university organized a one-and-a-half-month internship for our entire class at the analytical chemistry laboratory of the Zhuzhou Smelter in Hunan Province. In mid-August, under the leadership of our department's professors, we traveled by train through Liuzhou and Guilin in

Guangxi to reach Zhuzhou, Hunan Province (as the Xiang-Gui Railway connecting Guiyang to northern China was not yet open at that time, we had to detour through Guangxi). During the journey, we stopped in Guilin, where we took the opportunity to explore the scenic beauty of the city. Zhuzhou Smelter was a large lead-zinc mining and smelting plant with thousands of workers. In addition to producing lead, zinc, and other non-ferrous metals, the plant also recovered and produced rare metals such as germanium, gallium, indium, and thallium. The laboratory at the smelter was vast, with both chemical and instrumental analysis laboratories. The chemical analysis lab was further divided into groups for gravimetric analysis, volumetric analysis, and atomic absorption spectroscopy. Our class rotated between different groups, applying our theoretical knowledge to practical industrial work. During the internship, we had the opportunity to apprentice under the lab technicians at the smelter, learning from these experienced professionals and

strengthening our bond with them. This experience effectively achieved the goals of "learning through work" and "opendoor schooling." When we conducted our internship in Zhuzhou, it was during the peak of summer in August and September, with daily temperatures exceeding 35-36°C, a level of heat we had never experienced in Guizhou. It was only after arriving in Zhuzhou that we, having grown up in the highlands of Yunnan and Guizhou, truly experienced the humid and hot climate of the central-southern region of China.

In the mid-1970s, during the downturn in the economy that had followed the Cultural Revolution, rationing of grains, oil, and other foodstuffs was implemented across the country. However, as Hunan was an agriculturally prosperous region with abundant lakes, rivers, and fertileland, the supply of pork was far more plentiful than in Guizhou, where meat was scarcer and more expensive. Consequently, many of our classmates took the opportunity, before the end of the internship, to purchase large quantities of pork from local markets in Zhuzhou's rural areas, which they then rendered into lard and pork cracklings to take back to Guiyang to supplement their diets. This became an additional benefit of our fieldwork experience. During the internship, we also took a weekend trip to Shaoshan to visit the birthplace of Chairman Mao Zedong, where we received an education in revolutionary traditions. In summary, this internship at the Zhuzhou Smelter was an invaluable experience for our class, broadening our horizons and significantly contributing to both our personal and professional growth.

(Ⅱ)

Regarding the "**Open-door Schooling**" (开 门 办 学) initiative, aside from the military training aspect which we were unable to conduct due to time or logistical constraints the school focused heavily on the practice of learning through work, given the practical nature of our major. This hands-on learning was prioritized as a way to improve students' technical skills. After returning from our internship at the Zhuzhou Smelter, the department organized another learning trip for the class to the analytical chemistry laboratory of the Guizhou Provincial Bureau of Geology and Mineral Resources. Following this, the department invited Engineer Ma from the central analysis lab of the Provincial Bureau of Geology to give lectures at the university, further enhancing our theoretical understanding of the subject. This combination of "going out and inviting in" lasted for more than a month and strengthened the connection between the university and the industrial sectors.

Since the academic program for worker-peasant-soldier students was only three years, and we enrolled in July 1972, we were scheduled to graduate and leave the university by July or August 1975. According to the university's arrangement, from April to July 1975, the final semester was designated for graduation internships. The university contacted relevant factories and research institutions in and around Guiyang to facilitate internships for the students. These institutions such as the Central Laboratory of the Institute of Geochemistry, Chinese Academy of Sciences in Guiyang, the Central Laboratory of the Provincial Bureau of Geology and Minerals, and the Chemical

Analysis Laboratory of the Provincial Metallurgical Design Institute were among the top places with well-equipped technical conditions for internships. In mid-April, I was fortunate to join nine other classmates, led by our chemistry department teacher, Saifeng Xue, for a graduation internship at the Central Analytical Laboratory of Guiyang Institute of Geochemistry, Chinese Academy of Sciences. The Guiyang Institute of Geochemistry, at that time, was a national-level research institution directly under the Chinese Academy of Sciences. It had over a dozen research departments, one of which was the Central Analytical Laboratory that provided services to researchers at the institute. The working conditions and equipment there were among the best of its kind. The Central Analytical Laboratory was divided into two sections: chemical analysis and instrumental analysis. The chemical analysis section had different groups, such as rock analysis, mineral analysis, and atomic absorption analysis. After arriving at the lab, I was assigned to the atomic absorption group for rock and mineral analysis, under the guidance of my supervisor, Teacher Anzhen Guo. My graduation project involved using atomic absorption spectroscopy to measure trace amounts of thallium in sulphide mineral samples.

Thallium is a dispersed element in the Earth's crust, meaning that it rarely occurs in its own mineral deposits but is instead found in small quantities scattered within rocks and certain sulphide minerals. The concentration of thallium in these mineral samples was extremely low, making accurate measurement a challenge. To address this issue, the lab's leadership tasked Teacher Guo and me with solving this difficult problem. The concentration of thallium in the samples was so low, approximately 1-2 ppm (micrograms per gram) of sample, that the detection limit of the atomic absorption spectrometer at the time, which was 3 ppm (micrograms), could not reliably measure it. To accurately measure the thallium, we had to increase the sample size and chemically pre-treat the samples to separate and enrich the trace amounts of thallium before measurement. With my supervisor's assistance, I started with chemical dissolution experiments and gradually worked through the necessary steps. After completing the experiments on chemical dissolution, I moved on to testing the conditions for separating and enriching trace thallium and for performing

1974.11.地质局马工程师
讲课结束时合影 (第三排右三为作者)

A photo of our class in November, 1974 (The third one, third row from right, is the author).

atomic absorption measurements. Although I encountered numerous failures during the complex and tedious experimental process, I eventually succeeded. After nearly three months of hard work, I completed my graduation thesis on the atomic absorption spectrometric determination of trace thallium in rock and mineral samples. At the end of my internship, I defended my thesis at the Central Analytical Laboratory, with several lab leaders and my supervisor in attendance. They expressed their satisfaction with my results. According to the university's and department's guidelines, chemistry students were expected to graduate if they could master chemical analysis techniques and complete production tasks satisfactorily, thereby becoming qualified chemical analysts. However, at the Central Analytical Laboratory of IGCAS, the expectations were higher. Instead of merely having us complete sample analysis tasks, the lab's leadership wanted us to develop new testing methods, honing our problem-solving skills. This raised the bar for our graduation internship, and the majority of my classmates at the lab successfully met the internship's requirements.

The author was defending his graduation thesis in the laboratory office at IGCAS in Guiyang, Guizhou in July, 1975.

After completing our three-month internships, we returned to the university, ready to face graduation and job assignments. In those days of the planned economy, graduates from universities and colleges were all assigned jobs by the state. According to the policy at the time, workerpeasant-soldier students were generally expected to return to the place they came from. For example, those who were recommended by factories would return to their original factories after graduation, while those from rural areas would go back to their respective counties, where the county's personnel bureau would assign them a job. However, the university and department still had some control over job assignments. Each year, the university could select 1–2 outstanding students from each class to stay on as teachers, and if the state urgently needed graduates in a particular field, the university would prioritize fulfilling those needs. Before my internship, the department had informed me that they were considering selecting one or two students from our class to remain at the university as teachers, and the likely candidates were me and Weiming Chen. Personally, I was content with the idea of staying at the university after graduation, as teaching at a university was an ideal and respectable career. Thus, I felt no anxiety about job placement and simply awaited the university's assignment notification in August. However, around mid-August, I received a phone call from Daxiu Shao, the head of the student affairs department, asking me to come to her office to discuss my job assignment. When I met with her, she explained:

瞻仰革命纪念地湖南第一师范

(左为作者右为徐渝春)

The author (left) and Yuchun classmate in Changsha, Hunan Province, China in September, 1974.

"Xiao Wu, we wanted to ask for your input on your job placement. Initially, both the department and university leadership had decided to keep you as a teacher. However, the personnel office from the Guiyang Institute of Geochemistry,

Chinese Academy of Sciences, has sent representatives to our university twice, specifically requesting you. When they first came before last week, we didn't agree, and I told them that you had already been assigned to stay at the university. But they came again this week and insisted on taking you. We want to know whether you would prefer to stay at the university or go to the Institute of Geochemistry. If you choose to go, we are willing to let you go to maintain a good relationship with the Guiyang Institute." I was surprised to hear that the Institute of Geochemistry had sent people to request me twice. While I had interned there for three months, I hadn't had any direct interaction with the institute's leadership, and I had no personal connections there too. So, I was taken aback. Knowing that the Institute of Geochemistry was a prestigious national research institution with better working conditions than the university, I replied without hesitation: "Teacher Shao, I was happy with the idea of staying at the university, but if the Guiyang Institute of Geochemistry is requesting me, I'll go to the Guiyang Institute of Geochemistry." Shao responded: "Alright, then. We'll assign you to the Guiyang Institute of Geochemistry. They are also requesting graduates from the chemistry, physics, and mathematics departments, but for your department, they specifically asked for you. It seems you did an outstanding job during your internship and brought honour to our university!" As we finished our conversation, Shao also mentioned: "By the way, a few weeks ago, we received a letter from your Puding County Party Committee Office, also asking for you. However, I turned them down, explaining that you were a chemistry graduate and that we had already decided to keep you at the university." And so, instead of becoming a university teacher as originally planned, I found myself on an unexpected path to the Chinese Academy of Sciences' Institute of Geochemistry. Additionally, I was surprised to learn that the Puding County Party Committee Office had also tried to recruit me. I wondered how they even knew my name, given that I had never worked at the county office or met any of its leaders. After much consideration, I speculated that perhaps during my time working at the commune office, I had written more than a dozen or so investigative reports on cases related to the "One Strike, Three Anti" campaign. When these reports were submitted to the Puding County Party Committee Office for review and filing, they might have caught the attention of some county leaders at that time.

In early September 1975, when I went to report to the Personnel Office of the Guiyang Institute of Geochemistry with my job assignment letter, I learned that besides me, two other classmates, Daonai Wang and Fuqing Sun, were also assigned to the institute. In addition, four students from the physics department (Jiahui You, Qinxian Wu, Mingzai Wang, and Yongming Li) and three from the mathematics department (Qiankai Zhang, Donghai Ning, and Jiaxing Liu) were also assigned to the institute, making a total of ten of us. Later, more students arrived from other universities, such as Guizhou Institute of Technology, Chengdu Institute of Geology, Peking University, Nanjing University, and the University of Science and Technology of China, bringing the total number of new recruits to about thirty. This was the first time since the Cultural Revolution began nine years earlier that the Institute of Geochemistry had brought in new personnel.

(Ⅲ)

We were the first batch of graduates from Guizhou University to report to the Institute of Geochemistry in early September. At the time, the Provincial Science and Technology Commission, following the province's directives, required our institute to send some of its staff to Zhenning County of Guizhou Province to participate in the Socialist Education Campaign. As a result, our group of new graduates was quickly put to work. In late September, the institute, led by Teacher Chenglin Xue and composed mostly of students from our batch at Guizhou University, sent a group of over ten people to Zhenning County's Chengguan Town to carry out the Socialist Education Campaign. Our group was divided into two teams of four or five people each, with one team stationed in Chengxi Brigade and the other in Chengnan Brigade. Initially, I was assigned to the Chengnan Brigade, but later, the team leader asked me to be the cook for the team, so I stayed behind and didn't go to the brigade. Our campaign team worked alongside local farmers during the day and held meetings with them in the evenings to study central government documents related to the Socialist Education

Campaign. This work lasted from late September 1975 until mid-March 1976, nearly six months in total. During that time, I cooked for my colleagues, honing my cooking skills. Whether it was steamed buns, dumplings, stirfried dishes, or other methods of cooking, I became quite proficient. Even though decades have passed, I can still confidently rely on my cooking skills today.

When the Socialist Education work concluded in late March 1976, Daonai Wang and I were assigned to the Central Analytical Laboratory at the Institute of Geochemistry. I was placed in the rock analysis group, while Daonai Wang joined the mineral analysis group. At that time, the head of the Central Analytical Laboratory was still the same, with Party Branch Secretary Ming Li and Deputy Director Yinzong Lu in charge, just as they had been during my internship. In a way, it felt like returning to a familiar workplace, as the two leaders were already well-acquainted with me, especially Secretary Li Ming, who had been one of my supervisors during my internship. I later learned that when the institute's personnel department went to Guizhou University to recruit students from the chemistry, physics, and mathematics departments, they specifically requested me, reportedly at the suggestion of the Central Analytical Laboratory. The Central Analytical Laboratory consisted of five groups: the rock analysis group, the mineral analysis group, the atomic absorption spectroscopy group, the X-ray fluorescence spectroscopy group, and the visible light spectroscopy group. The rock and mineral groups were focused on chemical analysis, while the other three were primarily instrument-based. However, even the instrumentbased groups, such as atomic absorption and X-ray fluorescence, still relied on chemical pretreatment of samples, making chemical analysis the foundation of all analytical techniques. For an analytical chemist, mastering chemical analysis skills was essential to ensuring accuracy in instrumental analysis. The rock analysis group, to which I was assigned, was the largest in the laboratory, with over ten members. This was because the Central Analytical Laboratory handled all the geological samples submitted by the institute's geochemical researchers, and the majority of those samples were rock samples, making for a heavy workload. The group leader, Chuanxian Ye, was a humorous man from Sichuan who had graduated from Yunnan University's chemistry department in 1963. Since I was a newcomer, the lab assigned me to work under Teacher Ye's guidance, and I could turn to him for help with any issues during my analysis work. Our group's responsibility was to analyze all the rock samples submitted by the institute's geologists. Every Monday morning, the group leader would distribute samples to the team members, with each batch typically consisting of around thirty samples. The time required to complete the analysis depended on the number of testing items needed and the complexity of the samples. Some tests could be completed in two or three days, while others took a week. As a newcomer, I was initially given only fifteen samples per batch, but after two or three weeks of practice, as I became more proficient, the number of samples was increased to thirty, matching the workload of the other team members. Rock sample analysis involved systematic chemical analysis, which included testing for twelve different elements or items, such as silicon, aluminum, calcium, magnesium, manganese, sodium, potassium, water content, and volatile components. Each result had to be accurate to two decimal places. Since it is a quantitative analysis, the total amount of all items in the analysis and test must be above 99.5% and below 101% to be qualified. If the total was less than 99% or greater than 101%, a retest was often necessary. To further test our skills and the accuracy of our analyses, the group leader would occasionally insert international standard samples into the batches. This made the work both challenging and highly demanding, requiring a high level of precision. Initially, I struggled to stay within the acceptable margin of error, but after two or three weeks of focused practice, my test results consistently met the required standards, and within two months, I could handle sample analysis independently.

When I joined the Institute of Geochemistry in the mid-1970s, there were three senior experts at the institute: Professor Guangchi Tu (涂光炽), who had graduated from the Southwest Associated University and returned to China from the U.S. in 1950, was the director of the institute and a renowned mineral geologist; Professor Chengji Guo (郭承基), who had studied in Japan for nearly ten years and returned to China in 1952, was a renowned rare and rare-earth element geologist; and Dongsheng Liu (刘东生), who had graduated from the Southwest Associated University's Geology and Geography Department in

1942, was a prominent environmental geologist known as the "**father of China's loess research**"(黄土研究之父). These three experts had made significant contributions to China's geological research and were highly respected in the academic community. Due to the guidance and support of these three senior experts, the academic atmosphere at the Institute of Geochemistry remained strong, even in the midst of the extreme leftist ideology that prevailed during the Cultural Revolution. At that time, the institute edited and published two national academic journals. One was a quarterly academic journal titled *Geochemistry*, while the other was a monthly literature review called *Geology and Geochemistry*. The institute's researchers frequently published papers in both these journals and in other national academic publications. The institute's library housed an extensive collection of professional books, journals, and magazines, not only in Chinese but also in various foreign languages. It was a place where researchers loved to spend time. Upon visiting the library, I realized why the Institute of Geochemistry had such a strong reputation and produced so many scientific achievements. It was largely due to the researchers' dedication and passion for their work, qualities I had never witnessed during my time at university. During working hours, the library was often full, with people quietly consulting research materials or reading professional journals. The library was always silent, with only the faint rustle of turning pages occasionally breaking the quiet. I was deeply moved by this display of commitment and felt fortunate to be working in such an environment.

As an analytical testing technician, I realized that I couldn't be satisfied with simply completing sample tests. I needed to master analytical chemistry skills and become proficient in foreign languages to quickly read foreign research papers, thus improving my research capabilities. In my spare time, I frequently visited the library to borrow English-language books on analytical chemistry, forcing myself to read English literature quickly and in large quantities. After two or three months of rigorous training, I became proficient in reading scientific English in my field. However, I didn't just want to read these articles; I also wanted to translate some of the more advanced and cuttingedge papers into Chinese to deepen my understanding and possibly publish them in Chinese journals to help others in the field. Reading and understanding English literature was one thing, but accurately translating it into Chinese was another challenge altogether, requiring not only strong foreign language skills but also a solid command of Chinese. Therefore, after I became proficient in reading English professional literature, I selected some excellent English articles to translate. Initially, the translations were slow, and the text often read awkwardly or clumsily, but after a period of practice, as my understanding of English grammar improved and my vocabulary grew, the process became smoother.

Another remarkable difference I noticed at the Institute of Geochemistry, compared to my university days, was that even though the Cultural Revolution hadn't yet fully ended, we occasionally received visits from foreign experts, and some of our researchers even traveled abroad. Whenever foreign experts visited, the institute would hold academic seminars. Out of curiosity, I attended one of these seminars in the No. 1 conference hall to see what it was like. The room was packed with researchers eager to hear the guest speaker, who delivered the talk in English. Despite my years of studying English, I couldn't understand a word! However, the translators at the seminar were all researchers from the institute. Seeing them converse with foreign experts and act as interpreters with ease left me deeply impressed and envious. I admired these colleagues, who not only published papers regularly but also spoke fluent foreign languages. As I became more familiar with the Institute of Geochemistry, I grew to love the place even more. At the same time, I realized how far I still had to go to become a competent researcher. Despite graduating from university, I felt there was still so much more to learn in this environment. Therefore, in addition to focusing on my daily work, I often used my free time to study foreign languages and professional literature.

(IV)

The Institute of Geochemistry, Chinese Academy of Sciences, was established in the spring of 1966 in Guiyang, in response to the central government's strategic directive to strengthen the development of the "*Third Front Construction*" (三线建设) and in line with the growing need for geochemical research. At that time, Moruo Guo, a famous Writer, Historian, Archaeologist, Thinker and Calligrapher in China, then   President of the Chinese Academy of Sciences, wrote an inscription for the institute's founding: *"Geochemistry is an emerging science. The establishment of a dedicated research institution in our country is a major achievement. I hope that it will make outstanding contributions to the study of the material composition, mineralization processes, and regularities of mineral formation, promoting the cause of socialist construction."*

The former President of CAS Moruo Guo's inscription for the establishment of IGCAS in spring of 1966.

The institute was formed from three primary sources: more than 400 personnel from the Beijing Institute of Geology of the Chinese Academy of Sciences; over 170 staff members from the Guiyang Institute of Chemistry, Chinese Academy of Sciences, which had been established in 1958; and more than 20 people from the Kunming Station of Beijing Institute of Geology, Chinese Academy of Sciences. Together, these three groups totalled over 600 employees, and the institute was located on Yangjiaba, Guanshui Road, adjacent to the Communist Party of Guizhou's provincial headquarters. From its founding until the mid-1990s, the Institute of Geochemistry was a specialized research institute directly under the Chinese Academy of

Sciences, primarily tasked with undertaking major theoretical research in geochemistry and conducting foundational research on the material composition, mineralization processes, and regularities of significant mineral resources to guide mineral exploration. During the planned economy era, the institute's research tasks were determined by national authorities and handed down through the Chinese Academy of Sciences, and the research funding was also allocated by the Academy. In 1975, in response to a severe shortage of high-quality iron ore resources in China, the government tasked several geological research units within the Chinese Academy of Sciences with conducting a nationwide search for rich iron ore deposits, a project commonly referred to as the "*Search for Rich Iron Ore Campaign* (富铁矿会战)." Our institute was one of the primary research units involved in this effort.

In early June of 1976, the leadership of the Central Analytical Laboratory decided to send me and Jinshou Yan from the atomic absorption group to Shanxi Province to conduct analysis and testing of geological samples for the institute's North Shanxi Iron Ore team. The sample testing was to be conducted at the Central Analytical Laboratory of the Taiyuan Iron and Steel Company in August and September. However, before heading to Taiyuan, Professor Qizhong Wen from the Quaternary Research Department invited Jinshou Yan and me to participate in a soil survey and analysis project at Dazhai Brigade in Shanxi's Xiyang County in July. Therefore, in mid-June, Qizhong Wen, Suhua Yu, Jinshou Yan, and I boarded a train and left Guiyang for Shanxi. As our train passed through Zhumadian in Henan Province, we noticed from the train windows that many telephone poles along the railway had bundles of some straw on top of their insulators. Curious, we pointed this out to one another when a nearby passenger quietly remarked: "Last summer (1975), Henan experienced catastrophic flooding after torrential rains, causing more than a dozen dams to collapse. The floodwaters inundated over a dozen counties, and many people died. But the authorities didn't allow anyone to talk about it." We then realized the gravity of the situation that the floodwaters had risen to such a height that they submerged the telephone poles, indicating the water was at least ten meters deep. Yet, such a significant disaster had never been reported on the national news or radio, leaving the public unaware of its occurrence. It became evident that during the Cultural Revolution, the media consistently reported only good news, omitting anything negative. After over two days of travel by train, we finally arrived at Dazhai Brigade in Xiyang County, Shanxi Province, and checked into the Dazhai Guesthouse. At the time, China was in the midst of a nationwide movement to *"Learn from Dazhai in Agriculture"* (农业学大寨), and people from all over the country were coming to Dazhai village for study tours. Although Dazhai village was only about ten kilometers from the county seat of Xiyang, the brigade had built an impressive guesthouse (essentially a hotel, although it was called a "guesthouse" at the time) to accommodate the many visiting delegations. After ten years of turmoil during the Cultural Revolution, life across China was extremely difficult. Grain, oil, and other foodstuffs were strictly rationed, and a large portion of people's daily food consisted of coarse grains. When we first arrived in Xiyang County, we stayed at the county government guesthouse for a day or two, but after moving to the Dazhai Guesthouse, we realized the food there was significantly better. At the county guesthouse, the staple foods were often cornmeal cakes and "minggedou" (a type of cornmeal lump), and it was rare to eat white flour buns. The breakfast millet porridge was almost just clear broth with only a few grains of millet, and the dishes were lacking in oil. However, at the Dazhai Guesthouse, there was much less coarse grain, and we frequently ate white flour buns along with meat. That's why Dazhai guesthouse always was full of guests almost every day, while the County Government guesthouse only had very few guests. We stayed at Dazhai for more than a week, during which we systematically sampled the different types of soil around the brigade and participated in harvesting wheat with the brigade members, as it was the height of the summer wheat harvest. During this time, we also wondered whether we might have a chance to meet Yonggui Chen (陈永贵), but Uncle Yonggui had long since been appointed Vice Premier of the State Council and was living in Beijing. The former brigade party secretary, Fenglian Guo (郭凤莲), had also been promoted to a leadership position in Xiyang County or higher, and the party secretary of Dazhai brigade had been replaced by the former women's director, Liying Song.

Although we were scientific researchers sent by the Chinese Academy of Sciences to work at Dazhai, we didn't get to meet Yonggui Chen or even Fenglian Guo. While we were collecting soil samples in Dazhai, we climbed the Tiger Head Mountain behind the village. Looking out from the mountain, we could see the vast terraces of Dazhai, nestled in the rocky hills of the Taihang Mountains. Through the hard work and meticulous efforts of the Dazhai people, the barren and rugged landscape had been transformed into layers of terraced fields. They had built reservoirs on the ridges to store water for irrigation, completely changing the previous reliance on rainfall. Seeing this, we couldn't help but admire the Dazhai people's determination and resourcefulness. We thought, if all of China's agriculture were like Dazhai's---combining hard work with ingenuity---the country's agricultural output could be dramatically improved, and the problem of feeding the population might be solved.

After spending about ten days at Dazhai and completing our soil sampling, we returned to Xiyang County and stayed at the county government guesthouse. There, we conducted soil analysis and testing at the County Land Bureau's laboratory. Around July 20, after completing the analysis of the Dazhai soil samples (which later led to one or two academic papers being published by Professor Qizhong Wen), Jinshou Yan and I left Xiyang and traveled to Taiyuan to join the research team working on the iron ore deposits in northern Shanxi. Professor Wen and Suhua Yu returned to Guiyang by train.

When we arrived in Taiyuan, the geological samples collected by the Shanxi North Iron Ore team had not yet arrived at the Taiyuan Iron and Steel Company's central laboratory, so Jinshou Yan and I had nothing to do for the time being. We took the opportunity to explore Taiyuan and its surrounding areas. After visiting several famous sites, including Jinci Temple, Shuangta Temple, and Yingze Park, on July 25, the party deputy secretary of our institute, Yunshan Chai, accompanied by Mingshan Mo, arrived in Taiyuan from Beijing in a Beijing Jeep sent by the institute. They were planning to visit the northern Shanxi Iron Ore team. We were all staying at the Taiyuan Steel Company Guesthouse at the time. Secretary Chai and the others decided to visit Wutai Mountain, located in northeastern Shanxi, on July 27 and asked if we would like to join them. Naturally, we eagerly agreed. We set off for Wutai Mountain early on the morning of July 27. The distance from Taiyuan to Wutai Mountain was about 200 kilometers, but since the roads at the time were all dirt and heavily eroded by summer rains, the journey took five or six hours, including a stop for lunch. We finally arrived at Wutai Mountain in the early afternoon. The Wutai Mountain temple complex, located in northeastern Shanxi Province, is considered the foremost of China's four sacred Buddhist Mountains (the other three being Mount Putuo in Zhejiang, Mount Jiuhua in Anhui, and Mount Emei in Sichuan). Wutai Mountain is dedicated to the Bodhisattva Manjusri, and its temples were first built during the Han Dynasty, flourishing during the Sui and Tang dynasties. By the Tang Dynasty, there were more than 300 temples at Wutai Mountain, with over 5,000 monks, making it a true centre of Buddhism. Although the temple complex had suffered some damage during the early years of the Cultural Revolution, the overall scale of the temples remained vast, and the atmosphere was solemn and sacred. The Foguang Temple and Nanchan Temple are two of the oldest surviving wooden structures in China. Although we were visiting during the Cultural Revolution, there were still a few monks residing at the temple, responsible for cleaning and protecting the temple property.

After finishing our tour in the late afternoon, the four of us drove to Wutai County and checked into the county guesthouse. Jinshou Yan and I planned to take a bus back to Taiyuan the next day, while Secretary Chai and Mingshan Mo were preparing to travel directly to northern Shanxi. The accommodations at the Wutai County Guesthouse were far from ideal. We stayed in basic one-story rooms, with three people sharing a large room. That night, I shared a room with Mingshan Mo and Secretary Yunshan Chai, while Jinshou Yan and the institute driver stayed in the room next door. In the middle of the night, I was suddenly awakened by the sound of our door frame rattling loudly. Thinking that it was Jinshou Yan knocking on the door to wake me up for the early bus to Taiyuan, I called out twice: "Teacher Yan, Teacher Yan! Are you knocking on the door?" but there was no response. Then, I heard someone outside shouting: "Earthquake! Earthquake! Everyone, get outside!" Upon hearing that, I immediately jumped out of bed and started putting on my clothes. At the same time, I saw Deputy Secretary Chai, who was sleeping beside me, jump out of bed completely naked, grab a large towel to wrap around his waist, and dash outside without a second thought. Once I had dressed and stepped outside, I saw that the guesthouse courtyard was filled with people, both men and women, many of them still in their underwear. The streetlights hanging from the eaves of the guesthouse were still swaying. People were anxiously discussing the situation, speculating that the earthquake must have been strong, though no one knew where it had occurred. After determining that there was no immediate danger, Secretary Chai returned inside to properly dress before coming back outside. Seeing the scene before me, I couldn't help but wonder why so many people had run outside without properly dressing. Didn't they feel embarrassed? Later, someone explained to me that in an emergency, such as an earthquake, where lives are at stake, survival is the top priority, and everything else becomes secondary. Secretary Chai and many others had rushed outside upon hearing the cry of "earthquake," demonstrating a textbook example of a classic survival response. After everyone returned to their rooms, it was already past 4 a.m. Most people were too shaken to sleep and spent the remaining hours chatting until dawn. After breakfast the next morning, Jinshou Yan and I caught the bus back to Taiyuan, while Secretary Chai and Mingshan Mo set off in the Beijing Jeep for northern Shanxi. When we arrived in Taiyuan, we learned that the earthquake had occurred in Tangshan City. The news broadcast on Central People's Radio reported that the epicentre was in Tangshan, with a magnitude of 7.8, and mentioned significant damage to buildings and casualties, though no specific numbers were provided. It wasn't until many years later that the full truth came to light. The Tangshan earthquake, which struck at 3:43 a.m. on July 28, 1976, had a magnitude exceeding 8, with a focal depth of 12 kilometers. The earthquake completely flattened the city of Tangshan, which had a population of over one million, and the death toll exceeded 240,000 people. The devastation and loss of life caused by the Tangshan earthquake were among the worst in history.

The earthquake in Tangshan also affected many cities in northern China, including Tianjin, Beijing, Shijiazhuang and Taiyuan. After the main shock, aftershocks continued, causing widespread panic throughout the region. Normal activities came to a halt, with earthquake prevention and disaster relief becoming the main focus. After the earthquake, most people were too afraid to sleep indoors, so they set up makeshift shelters in their courtyards and lived in them. In the aftermath, the central government issued an emergency notice, calling on the whole country to support Tangshan in its earthquake relief efforts. People who were on business trips to Beijing and nearby cities quickly returned to their home regions, and due to the need for earthquake relief, Taiyuan also requested that non-local personnel leave as soon as possible. Thus, Jinshou Yan and I had no choice but to take a train back to Guiyang at the end of July.

The year of 1976 was an extraordinary one in modern Chinese history, marked by a series of highly unusual and significant events. First, on March 8, 1976, a rare astronomical event occurred in Jilin Province, a meteor shower. At around 3 p.m. that day, a meteor weighing approximately 4 tons hurtled toward Earth at a speed of about 1,000 kilometers per hour and exploded 19 kilometers above the outskirts of Jilin City. The explosion created a meteor shower that spread over an area of about 500 square kilometers. The largest fragment weighed 1,770 kilograms, making it the largest known stony meteorite in the world. The vast distribution, the number of fragments, and the sheer scale of this meteor shower were unprecedented. The explosion was so powerful that it was comparable to a nuclear bomb, yet miraculously, not a single person or animal was injured, making it a global wonder. Second, in the same year, three of the most influential figures in modern Chinese history, Zedong Mao (毛泽东), Enlai Zhou (周恩来), and De Zhu (朱德) passed away within a few months. Premier Enlai Zhou died on January 5, Chairman of the National People's Congress De Zhu passed away on July 6, and Chairman of the Communist Party of China Zedong Mao died on September 9. The deaths of these three leaders had a profound impact on Chinese politics, particularly Zedong Mao's death, which marked the end of an era and significantly influenced the political direction of the country. In many ways, Mao's death paved the way for the later downfall of the "Gang of Four" and the end of the Cultural Revolution, which had lasted for ten years. Third, on April 5, 1976, during the Qingming Festival, more than one million people spontaneously gathered in Tiananmen Square to mourn

Premier Enlai Zhou and express their discontent with the "Gang of Four." This event became known as the *"Tiananmen Incident (天安门事件)"* or the *"April Fifth Movement (四.五运动)."* Fourth, on July 28, 1976, at 3 a.m., a devastating earthquake struck Tangshan, levelling the entire city of over one million people. The death toll reached more than 240,000, and the damage and devastation caused by the earthquake were unprecedented. Finally, on October 6, 1976, under the leadership of the newly appointed Chairman Guofeng Hua and with the assistance of veteran revolutionaries like Marshal Jianying Ye, the Central Committee successfully crushed the *"Gang of Four (四人帮)"*---Hongwen Wang, Chunqiao Zhang, Qing Jiang, and Wenyuan Yao---effectively ending the Cultural Revolution. This moment marked the beginning of a new chapter in Chinese history. In conclusion, 1976 was a truly unique year in modern Chinese history. Future historians will undoubtedly give it special attention in their accounts of this period.

(Ⅴ)

In early October 1976, after the "Gang of Four" was crushed, the ten-year Cultural Revolution officially came to an end, much to the relief of the entire nation. In July 1977, Xiaoping Deng (邓小平) made a political comeback and began overseeing the work of the State Council. After assuming leadership, Deng immediately launched a series of bold reforms. In July of that year, the Central Committee decided to abolish the practice of recommending students for university admission, which had been implemented during the Cultural Revolution, and instead reinstated the university entrance examination system, which had been suspended for 11 years. In October, the Ministry of Education also reinstated the system for recruiting graduate students. The restoration of both the university entrance exams and graduate school admissions in 1977 dramatically changed the fate of countless young people across China.

When I first heard the news in October about the Ministry of Education resuming graduate admissions, I didn't pay much attention, thinking it was mostly a matter for higher education institutions. However, by late January 1978, our institute received a document from the Chinese Academy of Sciences

(CAS), announcing that its various research institutes would also resume graduate admissions. The document listed the names of eligible supervisors and the number of students they would admit. At our Institute of Geochemistry, only three senior scientists, Guangchi Tu, Chengji Guo, and Dongsheng Liu, were qualified to supervise graduate students, and each was allowed to admit only one student. Guangchi Tu would recruit for the geochemistry of mineral deposits, Chengji Guo for analytical chemistry, and Dongsheng Liu for environmental geochemistry. The exam was scheduled for mid-May. The institute posted the admissions guidelines on the bulletin board and encouraged eligible researchers to apply. At the time, there were about 50 to 60 "worker-peasant-soldier" students like me who had been assigned to the institute after graduating from various colleges and universities. When most of them saw the admissions guidelines, they thought it was an unattainable goal. Many believed that doing a good job in their current positions was enough and had no aspirations of applying for graduate school. Most had a disinterested attitude, as if it had nothing to do with them. When I saw the admissions guidelines, I had a fierce internal debate. First, I considered that although we, the "worker-peasant-soldier" students, represented a new force in the institute, we had certain inherent deficiencies due to our background. Society often viewed us as having low competence and poor professional abilities. Even the more capable "worker-peasant-soldier" students who had done well in their studies were often looked at with suspicion, and promotions were frequently unfairly withheld. I thought to myself that I couldn't continue living and working in this shadow. Now that the opportunity to apply for graduate school had arrived, why not seize it and change my situation? However, I quickly realized that passing the entrance exams would be extremely difficult, as it would be a national competition with intense rivalry. Moreover, the preparation time was very short, only about three months from registration to the exam. As a result, I hesitated at first, wondering if I should even apply. What if I failed? Would it be embarrassing? But then I reasoned that since the supervisors were from our institute and the subject area was my field of study, I should at least give it a shot. Even if I didn't pass, I would still have my job at the institute, so I had nothing to lose. Once I made up my mind, I registered with the personnel department. In early February 1978, we received further instructions from the CAS, specifying the subjects and exact exam dates for each discipline. For analytical chemistry, the exam subjects were politics, a foreign language (either English or Russian), inorganic chemistry, and analytical chemistry. Politics and the foreign language would be national exams, while the basic subject and professional subject would be set by the institute and supervisors. The exam was scheduled for mid May. After deciding to apply for the exam, I felt an enormous amount of pressure. With only two or three months until the exam, I had to thoroughly review four subjects while also handling my daily analytical work. Time was very tight. This meant that my preparation could only be done in my spare time. For the next two or three months, I worked every day from Monday to Saturday (since we had a six-day work week at the time). Apart from my regular duties, I spent every evening and weekend studying for the exam. First, I systematically reviewed the theories in the textbooks for inorganic chemistry and analytical chemistry, going through each chapter and making sure I could fully understand and explain them. Then, I solved all the exercises in the textbooks, writing out the solutions in dedicated notebooks. For politics, I focused on key points related to major current events and political issues, summarizing and memorizing them. For English, I reviewed grammar systematically, practiced listening, and completed a large number of exercises, including multiple-choice questions on grammar and vocabulary, translation between Chinese and English, and so on. During these two or three months, I worked during the day and spent my evenings and weekends studying in my office (since my dormitory was shared with four or five people, making it hard to concentrate). At that time, only Jiahui You and I were "worker-peasant-soldier" students applying for graduate school, and his office was on the third floor of Building Three, next to mine. He had not been assigned a dormitory at the institute and was living with his parents outside the institute. Every night, we both studied diligently in our offices until one or two o'clock in the morning. Then, when we finally finished, he would ride his bike home.

That year, the renowned reputations of the three senior scientists at our Institute made the competition to become their graduate students extremely fierce. According to the admissions staff at the time, over 60 candidates from across the country applied to study under Professor Guangchi Tu, and more than 70 applied to Professor Chengji Guo. However, there was only one spot available for each of them, which shows how intense the competition was. In 1978, many scientific researchers at our institute were eager to apply for graduate school, with around 20 applicants overall. Most of these applicants were university graduates who had been assigned to work at the institute before the Cultural Revolution. Although the institute had received five or six dozen "worker-peasant-soldier" university graduates during the Cultural Revolution, none of them applied, except for me and Jiahui You, who also had graduated from Guizhou University in 1975 and were assigned to work with me in our institute. Jiahui You applied to the Beijing Institute of Computing Technology of CAS under Professor Qingshi Gao to study electronic computing, while I applied to Professor Chengji Guo in analytical chemistry. Many other applicants from our institute were pre-Cultural Revolution graduates who had relocated to Guiyang with the institute in 1966. Due to various factors, including geographical reasons, they hoped to leave Guiyang, so they applied to research institutes in Beijing, seeking to secure a *Beijing household registration (i.e., "Beijin hukou* (北 京 户 口)")*. In mid-May 1978, around 30 to 40 candidates from the Guiyang area, including us, took the entrance exams at Jiandao Street Primary School in Nanming District. The four exams were held over two consecutive days, with one subject in the morning and another in the afternoon. Since this was the first year that graduate admissions had resumed after the Cultural Revolution, candidates were allowed to bring foreign language dictionaries to the exam. After completing the exams, I wasn't particularly confident. While I felt that I had done reasonably well in politics, English, and analytical chemistry, I had serious doubts about inorganic chemistry. Why was I uncertain? The inorganic chemistry exam consisted of a single question: "Discuss the fundamental principles of chemical reactions." This question completely caught all the candidates off guard, as none of us had prepared for it. It was a challenging question that required a deep understanding of the mechanisms of chemical reactions. It wasn't something that could be directly found in textbooks.

Clearly, this question was designed by the examiner, likely the graduate supervisor, to test the candidate's depth of understanding based on years of scientific research experience. It was an exceptionally clever question. When I first saw that the exam consisted of only one question, like the other candidates, I was taken aback. At first, I didn't know w here to begin. After calming down, I started by thinking through the basic types of chemical reactions and then extrapolating those types to the fundamental nature of chemical reactions, such as the gain and loss of electrons, and electron transfer around the atomic nucleus. After writing continuously for over an hour, producing roughly 4,000 to 5,000 characters, I handed in the exam. Despite finishing, I wasn't confident at all, thinking that I would just leave it to fate.

As I mentioned earlier, there was a widespread prejudice at the time that all "worker-peasant-soldier" students were under-qualified and lacked real skills. Consequently, they were generally not highly regarded in the workplace and were often unfairly overlooked for promotions. This was one of the reasons I applied to graduate school to change my  status as a "worker-peasant-soldier" student by earning a graduate degree. When I applied for graduate school in 1978, people both inside and outside the institute who knew me didn't believe I could succeed. Some were even waiting for me to fail. For instance, there was another candidate for Professor Chengji Guo's program, a man named Xu, who had graduated also from the Department of Chemistry of Guizhou University in 1965 and was working at the chemical laboratory of the Provincial Metallurgical Design Institute. He had been the supervisor for some of my classmates during our graduation internships in 1975. Since the Metallurgical Design Institute was not far from the Geochemistry Institute, I had visited his lab to meet up with friends, and that's how I got to know him. In 1978, when the graduate admissions process resumed, Xu also applied to study under Professor Guo. Upon hearing that I had applied as well, he reportedly said to my classmates: "If Mingqing Wu can get accepted, then I certainly will too. And if I don't get in, there's no way he will either!" Clearly, Xu thought I had no chance and considered himself far more qualified. A few weeks after the exams, the results came out. Among the dozens of candidates applying to study under Professor Guo, a certain engineer named Zhang from the central analytical laboratory of Yunnan Tin Corporation in Gejiu, Yunnan Province, who had graduated before the Cultural Revolution, ranked first. I came in second, while Xu from the Metallurgical Design Institute placed somewhere below tenth. Since only the top two candidates were invited for interviews, Xu was naturally eliminated. After learning that I had placed second and was accepted, Xu reportedly told my classmates again: "Hmph! Mingqing Wu only got into Professor Guo's program because the graders at the institute must help him out. Otherwise, how could he have done better than me?" He insinuated that I must have received some kind of favouritism or backdoor help to get accepted. But the truth is, I was a newcomer at the institute, having only worked there for two or three years, and I had no personal connections with the senior staff or the professors. The exam papers were graded by a panel, and final rankings were based solely on the total scores from all four subjects. Any suggestion that I had used connections to pass the exam was simply groundless. Although the "workerpeasant-soldier" students recruited during the Cultural Revolution were, on the whole, a mixed group in terms of ability. However, there were also those who performed very well, and some were truly exceptional both in character and academic achievement. It's essential to evaluate people on an individual basis rather than make sweeping generalizations.

The two senior professors at the Geochemistry Institute had originally planned to each accept only one graduate student. After the entrance exams, they invited the top two candidates for an interview and would then select one based on the interview results. For Professor Chengji Guo's graduate program, the top two candidates were Zhang, an engineer from Yunnan Tin Company in Gejiu (who placed first), and myself (who placed second). However, due to the refusal of Yunnan Tin Company to release Zhang, he did not attend the interview. As a result, Tie Lin, a candidate further down the list, was brought in to replace

Zhang. Tie Lin was also a "worker-peasant-soldier" student who graduated from the Chemical Engineering Department of Guizhou Institute of Technology in 1975 and was assigned to work at the Chishui Natural Gas Fertilizer Plant in Guizhou. At the same time, Professor Guangchi Tu also conducted interviews with two candidates: Ying Li from Northwest University and Yunjin Tan from the Yichang Geological Institute in Hubei. After the interviews, all four of us were accepted. In late July of that year, we received our admission letters from the Chinese Academy of Sciences (CAS).

(VI)

In late August 1978, when the four of us newly admitted graduate students reported to the institute, we found that Professor Guo had suddenly gained another graduate student named Baoshan Zheng, a tall man. Originally, Baoshan Zheng had applied to study under Professor Dongsheng Liu. However, by the time Zheng was admitted, Professor Liu was preparing to transfer to the Beijing Institute of Geology, CAS, so before Professor Liu left for Beijing, he transferred his admitted graduate student, Baoshan Zheng, to Professor Guo. This brought the total number of graduate students in the Geochemistry Institute's 1978 cohort to five.

According to later public records, during the nationwide graduate admissions in 1978, only a few universities under the Ministry of Education, including Peking University, Tsinghua University, Fudan University, Zhejiang University, Nanjing University, Huazhong University of Science and Technology, and the University of Science and Technology of China (USTC), were authorized to admit graduate students, in addition to research institutes under CAS. That year, over 60,000 candidates applied to graduate programs across China, but only about 10,000 were admitted, with approximately 1,000 of them entering the CAS system. At our Geochemistry Institute, around 20 scientific staffs applied to graduate school in 1978, but only 10 were admitted. These included myself (Institute of Geochemistry), Jiahui You (Beijing Institute of Computing), Shihua Sun (Beijing Institute of Geology), Jie Yu (Beijing Institute of Geology), Ronghua Xu (Beijing Institute of Geology), Liu Zhang (Geological Institute of the Earthquake

Bureau), Yanchou Lu (Geological Institute of the Earthquake Bureau), Changsheng Li (Beijing Institute of Environmental Chemistry), Zhuocheng Liang (Beijing Institute of Geology), and Hongde Chen (later transferred from the Beijing Institute of Geology to the Geochemistry Institute). Among these 10, only Jiahui You and I were "worker-peasant-soldier" students who graduated in 1975; the others were pre-Cultural Revolution university graduates. Apart from me, the other nine were all accepted by CAS research institutes in Beijing, and after graduation, they remained in Beijing to work as they had hoped. Hongde Chen, after completing the basic courses for his

graduate studies at the Beijing Institute of Geology, transferred to Professor Guangchi Tu at the Institute of Geochemistry and stayed on to work in Guiyang after graduation. Jiahui You, after being accepted to graduate school, was sent by CAS's Beijing Institute of Computing to the University of Utah in the U.S. in 1980. He earned his PhD in 1985 and, in 1986, became a professor in the Department of Computer Science at the University of Alberta, Canada, where he remains a tenured professor today. Changsheng Li also went to study in the U.S. in the 1980s and stayed there to work.

According to the original plan, all CAS graduate students were supposed to go to the Beijing Graduate School of the University of Science and Technology of China (the predecessor of today's University of the Chinese Academy of Sciences) for one year of foundational coursework. However, due to delays in preparing the Beijing campus, classes wouldn't start until mid-October. At the Guiyang Institute of Geochemistry, Professor Guo wanted his students to start their studies as soon as possible and also required Tie Lin and me, both chemistry students, to take additional foundational courses in geology, petrology, and mineralogy. Therefore, the Personnel and Education Office of our institute decided that the three of us would report to USTC in Hefei, Anhui Province, in early September to start our coursework and attend geology classes in the Department of Geochemistry. Professor Guangchi Tu's two students, Ying Li and Yunjin Tan, would report to the Beijing campus in October to join other CAS students.

In early September 1978, the three of us arrived at USTC in Hefei and were placed into two graduate student classes alongside the university's own students. The graduate courses included three main subjects: Politics, English, and a second foreign language (the first cohort of 1978 graduate students were required to be proficient in two foreign languages by graduation). I chose Russian as my second language since I had studied it for six years in middle school and had a foundation in it.

The University of Science and Technology of China was founded in Beijing in 1958, and in the early 1970s, it was relocated to Hefei in Anhui Province in response to the national defence strategy. It was set up on the former campus of Hefei Normal University. However, due to the turmoil of the Cultural Revolution, USTC had made limited progress in Hefei. To accommodate the newly enrolled students of the 1977 and 1978 cohorts after the resumption of the national university entrance exam, the university constructed four five-story teaching buildings on former vegetable plots on the western side of the campus, which became known as the "Four Plaques."Since Hefei City, located south of the Huaihe River, is considered part of southern China according to state policy at the time. All public buildings of Southern China, including schools, were not equipped with heating or cooling systems. Winter temperatures in Hefei could drop below minus ten degrees Celsius, while summer temperatures, especially during the rainy season, often reached 36 to 37 degrees Celsius or higher. As a result, winters felt like icehouses, and summers like furnaces. Fortunately, before leaving for USTC, I borrowed a fur coat from the institute's logistics department. When it was too cold to stay in the classroom, I would wrap myself in the fur coat and sit on my bed with a blanket to study. In the hot, humid months of May and June, I tried to air out my fur coat in the sun to dry it, but instead of drying, more moisture appeared, and water droplets even formed on it.

1980.1.作者(右二)与小导师
王贤觉(左一)雷剑泉(右一)及
陈毓蔚赵___摄于青岛

A group photo of the author (the 2nd from the right) with instructors in Qingdao, Shandong, China in Jan., 1980.

I had to bring it back inside to dry it naturally. This was the typical climate of the rainy season in southern China, and for someone from the highlands of Yunnan-Guizhou Plateau, it felt like living in a steam room. At night, the oppressive heat made it impossible to close the doors and windows, so swarms of mosquitoes from the nearby fields would fly into the dormitory. After lights-out, the mosquitoes buzzed around the mosquito nets like a hive. In the morning, my arms and legs, pressed against the net, were covered in red welts from mosquito bites. Fortunately, I was young, and Hefei's abundant food supply at the time made life more tolerable. Eggs and pork were relatively cheap, and the school cafeteria served decent meals. For just ¥0.25 yuan, you could get a meat dish, and the ¥0.05 yuan soup often had egg or meat bits in it. So despite the tough conditions, we didn't feel like it was too hard to study. After a year of hard work, we successfully completed our graduate coursework at USTC in Hefei. In early August 1979, we returned to the

Institute of Geochemistry in Guiyang to begin preparing for the next phase of our graduate thesis work.

(VII)

My graduate supervisor, Professor Chengji Guo, was an academician of the Chinese Academy of Sciences and a renowned expert in rare and rare earth element mineral geology in China. He graduated from the Department of Geology at Peking University in 1943 and subsequently went to Japan to study at Kyoto University, where he pursued systematic studies in chemistry and analytical chemistry. Building on his solid foundation in chemistry in 1947, hebegan his graduate studies under the famous Japanese rare element geologist, Professor Jitaro Tagubo, at Kyoto University, focusing on the rare and rare earth element mineralogy and geology. After completing his doctoral degree in 1952, he returned to China with his Japanese wife and three children. With expertise in both geology and chemistry, Professor Guo was a true geochemist. Upon returning to China, he initially worked at the Ministry of Geology of the Central People's Government before transferring to the Beijing Institute of Geology, Chinese Academy of Sciences, in 1953. In 1955, Professor Guo led a team of researchers to explore rare element mineral resources in regions such as Shanxi and Inner Mongolia. After several years, they discovered many new deposits and minerals of rare elements across China. Based on  their research needs, Professor Guo established a new interdisciplinary field, mineral chemistry, which brought China's research in this domain to the forefront of the world stage.

The Baiyun Obo iron deposit in Baotou, Inner Mongolia, was first discovered by Daoheng Ding (丁道衡) in 1927. Through years of research, geologists determined that Baiyun Obo was a world-class, large-scale polymetallic deposit rich in rare earth elements, niobium, thorium, and other rare metals. In the late 1950s, Chinese geologists, led by Zuolin He, Qirui Peng, and Youdong Si, formed a joint research team with Soviet scientists, including Sokolov, Alexandrov, and Semyonov, to conduct comprehensive studies on the Baiyun Obo deposit. However, despite years of research, they were unable to fully understand the complex distribution, occurrence, and material composition of the rare and rare earth elements in the deposit. Consequently, when the Baotou Steel and Iron Company was constructed and went into production in the late 1950s, it lacked an economically viable and scientifically sound ore processing and metallurgical process. As a result, the rare earth elements and other rare metals in the iron ore were discarded with the slag, causing significant losses to the nation. To address this issue, the State Science and Technology Commission, the Ministry of Metallurgy, and the Chinese Academy of Sciences jointly commissioned a national-level research project. In 1962, Professor Chengji Guo was appointed to lead the project and, within two to three years, his team of young scientists solved many of the problems that had eluded both Chinese and Soviet scientists for years. The research report on the material composition of the Baiyun Obo iron deposit, which was later included in the *Compendium of Major Scientific and Technological Achievements* published by the State Science and Technology Commission in 1965, made significant contributions to the development of ore extraction, beneficiation, and smelting processes at Baotou Steel and Iron Company. This allowed for the recovery and utilization of rare earth elements and rare metals from the deposit, benefiting the nation greatly. For their work, Professor Guo and his team were commended by the State Science and Technology Commission, the Ministry of Metallurgy, and the Chinese Academy of Sciences. During his decades of research, Professor Guo also wrote and published a large number of academic papers and authored several theoretical monographs, including *Mineral Chemistry of Uranium, Mineral Chemistry of Radioactive Elements, Mineral Chemistry of Rare Earths* and *Mineral Chemistry of Rare Elements*. These achievements established his prestigious position and academic authority in the fields of geology and geochemistry in China.

Later, after over 30 years of research, Professor Guo and his team completed their study on the geochemistry, metallogenic mechanisms, and mineralization processes of the Baiyun Obo rare earth-niobium iron deposit in the mid-1980s. This major scientific achievement was awarded both the National Science Congress Achievement Award and the National Natural Science Award. In March 1981, Vice Premier Yi Fang, who also served as the Chairman of the State Science and Technology Commission and President of the Chinese Academy of Sciences, visited the Institute of Geochemistry in Guiyang. During his visit, he met with Professor Guo and the institute's scientific staff and praised Professor Guo for his significant contributions to the nation.

When Professor Guo worked at the Beijing Institute of Geology, he had already been training graduate students since the 1950s and had nurtured many specialists in rare and rare earth element mineral geochemistry for the country. When graduate admissions resumed after the Cultural Revolution, although the first batch of students was admitted for analytical chemistry, Professor Guo's intention was to train them in both chemistry and geology to become wellrounded geochemists. Therefore, as soon as we started our graduate studies, Professor Guo required us to focus on foundational courses in geology in addition to our graduate coursework. Before we began our graduate thesis research, Professor Guo raised the bar for us: our theses were not to be purely about analytical chemistry but needed to incorporate a geochemical topic. We were expected to apply our analytical chemistry skills to geological samples, obtain relevant data, and then analyze and discuss geochemical issues based on that data. In essence, our graduate theses were to cover two aspects: first, analytical chemistry, including method testing and sample analysis, and second, geochemical analysis and discussion using our collected data. To support me in this work, Professor Guo assigned me two advisors. One was Jianquan Lei, who guided me in conducting chemical experiments, and the other was Xianjue Wang, who supervised my geochemical research. Both advisors were key members of Professor Guo's research team and were instrumental in his work. My thesis topic, as set by Professor Guo, was: "Paper Chromatography Separation Technique for Trace Rare Earth Elements in Seafloor Sediments from the Taiwan Shallow and Their Geochemical Study."

A group photo of the Academician Chengji Guo's former graduate students in Oct., 2007 (The 2nd from Right is the author).

Rare earth elements (or rare earth metals) refer to the 15 lanthanide elements in the periodic table of elements, along with scandium and yttrium, for a total of 17 elements. These elements were first discovered as oxides in Sweden, appearing as earth-like materials and very rare, hence the name "rare earths." Rare earth metals are valuable strategic resources, often referred to as the "vitamins of industry"and the "mother of new materials." They are widely used in advanced technology fields and military applications. In metallurgy, adding certain rare earth elements into many metal materials can greatly enhance or alter their physical and chemical properties. For example, if adding some amount of neodymium to iron-based iron-boron magnets transforms them into neodymium-iron-boron magnets, which are tens of times more powerful than the original magnets. Currently, new functional materials such as permanent magnets, phosphors, hydrogen storage alloys, and catalysts developed from rare earths are indispensable raw materials for advanced manufacturing, new energy, and other high-tech industries. Additionally, rare earth elements are widely used in electronics, petrochemicals, metallurgy, machinery, light industry, environmental protection, and agriculture. China possesses the largest reserves of rare earth minerals in the world, making it crucial to strengthen basic and applied research on rare earth elements, both for theoretical and practical purposes.

A group photo of Academician Chengji Guo (the 5th person from the right in 2nd row) with staff of RE Research Dept. in April, 1980. (The 2nd person from the left in the 2nd row is the author).

Due to the similar chemical properties of rare earth elements, they often coexist in geological processes, making it challenging to separate and analyze individual elements in geological samples. This difficulty is particularly pronounced when dealing with rock samples containing extremely low concentrations of rare earth elements. In such cases, determining individual rare earth elements quantitatively was especially challenging given the equipment available at the time. Following my advisor's guidance, my thesis focused on analyzing seafloor sediments from the Taiwan Shallow. I used paper chromatography to separate 7-8 individual rare earth elements and then quantitatively measured them. After obtaining the experimental data, I studied and discussed the geochemical characteristics of rare earth elements in the Taiwan Shallow sediments. The most critical and challenging aspect of this work was the separation and determination of individual rare earth elements in the sediments. Under the guidance of Teacher Jianquan Lei, I dedicated a significant amount of time and effort to solving this experimental problem, often spending weekends and holidays in the lab. After nearly a year and a half of hard work, I successfully completed the experimental portion of my graduate thesis.

(VII)

In July 1981, after completing my experimental work, I finished my master's thesis, "A Study on the Geochemical Distribution of Rare Earth Elements in the Seafloor Sediments of the Taiwan Shallow," with the help of my geochemistry advisor, Teacher Xianjue Wang, using the data I obtained from my experiments. However, when Lin Tie and I submitted our completed theses to the education office of the institute, intending to apply for our master's thesis defence, we were met with rejection and obstruction by PXX, the head of the education department at the time. Her reason was that we had initially applied for the analytical chemistry major, and the Institute of Geochemistry did not have the authority to confer a master's degree in analytical chemistry. However, the fact was that when the decision to resume graduate admissions was made in October 1977, the issue of degree conferral was not on the agenda for the first batch of graduate students. In other words, when the 1978 cohort of graduate students was admitted, the criteria for admission were based on the academic level and reputation of the supervisors, not on whether they had the authority to grant degrees. As a result, the supervisors who received graduate admissions qualifications in the first batch were essentially the most renowned experts and scholars in their respective academic field nationwide, one could say they were all of academician status. Furthermore, our two graduate supervisors were leading experts in rare and rare earth element geochemistry in China. In 1980, both Professor Guo and Professor Tu were selected as Academician of the Chinese Academy of Sciences, and in 1981, they were appointed as the first doctoral supervisors by the State Council. Could it really be that Professor Guo, who was guiding us, was not qualified to confer a master's degree? Third, our master's theses were not purely analytical chemistry work; we used analytical chemistry methods to solve geochemical problems. What is geochemistry? Geochemistry is the application of chemical theories, methods, and techniques to the study of geological problems. In other words, geochemistry is an interdisciplinary field that bridges geology and chemistry.

Therefore, both in terms of the discipline's definition and our research content, our master's theses fully met the requirements for applying for a master's degree in geochemistry.Despite repeated negotiations by our advisor and two of our mentors with the education office, they were still met with flat rejection. The response from the education office was that if we wanted to apply for a Master of Science degree, we would have to contact an external research institution or university to apply for a master's thesis defence in analytical chemistry. Under these circumstances, our supervisor had no choice but to reach out to the Department of Chemistry at the University of Science and Technology of China (USTC), where Professor Guo had previously taught courses at USTC's Department of Geochemistry as a part-time professor in the late 1950s. He applied for us to either defend our theses at USTC or have them send someone to our Geochemistry Institute to conduct our defence. This would allow Lin Tie and me to apply for a Master of Science degree from USTC. In mid- November of that year, the Department of Chemistry at USTC sent Professor Maosen Zhang, the head of the department, and Associate Professor Fang Yin to the Institute of Geochemistry to oversee our thesis defences. Later, both Tie Lin and I received "excellent" evaluations and successfully passed our master's thesis defences. Early the following year, 1982, we were awarded Master of Science degrees from USTC. PXX from the education office attended our thesis defence at the time, but after the defence, when we both received "excellent" marks, she reportedly said to her staff: "Hmph! The two professors from USTC were just being irresponsible!" The implication was that the professors had given us undeservedly high marks. In contrast, after the defence, Professor Maosen Zhang from USTC's Department of Chemistry told Professor Guo: "Professor Guo, your two graduate students have done an extensive amount of work for their theses. Their workload exceeds that of many of our students at USTC, and the vast majority of their work pertains to geochemistry. They fully qualify to apply for a Master of Science degree at your institute and have no need to seek approval from an external institution." Many people, including Tie Lin and me, were puzzled by the difficult behaviour of the education office, particularly by PXX's rigidity, which left no room for flexibility. However, those who knew the internal situation well understood that PXX's behaviour was not merely an issue of inflexibility; there were deeper reasons. Put simply, if Professor Tu had been our advisor instead of Professor Guo, would she have dared to make things difficult for us? Even with a hundred opportunities, she would not have. Of course, PXX's obstruction in my case, whether it was in terms of promotions, career advancements, or overseas opportunities, was not the only time she created obstacles, nor would it be the last. There were even more "spectacular performances" to come.

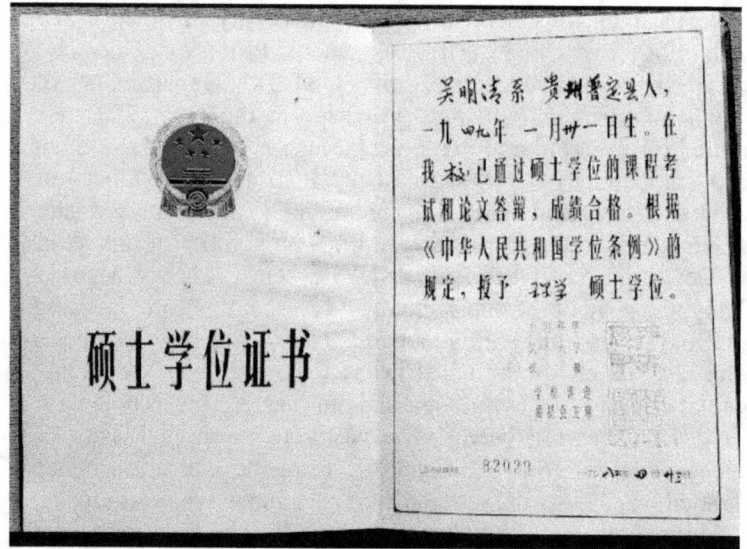

A photo of the author's Master Degree Certificate

Chapter 5   Sacrificing Dreams for Great Good

(I)

In November 1981, after graduating with my master's degree, both Tie Lin and I stayed at the institute to continue our work, joining our graduate advisor Professor Chengji Guo's Department of Rare Earth Element Geochemistry. At that time, Professor Guo was the director of the department, and the deputy director was Chuanxian Lin, who had graduated as one of Guo's students in the late 1950s. At that time, the Institute of Geochemistry had a total of thirteen research departments. Aside from our Rare Earth Elements Research department, there was also a Department of Rare Element Geochemistry. Before, these two departments were combined into one, collectively known as the Department of Rare Element Geochemistry (since rare earth elements are essentially a subset of rare elements). Before the Cultural Revolution, Professor Guo had been the director of this combined department. As the field of rare earth element geochemistry expanded, a portion of the research staff specializing in rare earth elements branched off to form the Department of Rare Earth Element Geochemistry, with Professor Guo serving as the director while also continuing as the director of the Department of Rare Element Geochemistry.

Since the 1960s, when these two departments were part of the Beijing Institute of Geology, their research strength and achievements in rare and rare earth elements were not only highly regarded within the entire institute but also throughout the national geological community. Even during the height of the Cultural Revolution, the Geochemistry Institute managed to organize and lead a national conference on rare and rare earth elements geology in December 1972, which was approved by the State Council and the Chinese Academy of Sciences. This event marked a historic moment as it was the first national academic conference hosted by a domestic research institute during the Cultural Revolution.

In October 1985, led by our Department of Rare Earth Element Geochemistry, the institute hosted the first National Symposium on Rare Earth Element Geochemistry in Ningbo, Zhejiang Province, where the Chinese Rare Earth Society was also established. Professor Guo was elected vice president of the society. These events highlight the significant position and influence of the Geochemistry Institute's rare and rare earth element research within the geological community of China. The remarkable research achievements in rare and rare earth elements were not only the result of the hard work and perseverance of the research staff but also owed much to the leadership and mentorship of scientists like Professor Chengji Guo. In a sense, Tie Lin and I were incredibly fortunate to have been admitted as the first post-Cultural Revolution graduate students under Professor Guo in 1978 and to have continued working under his guidance after graduation. We were genuinely delighted by this opportunity.

One afternoon in early January of 1982, just after completing my master's degree and before I had even had a chance to thoroughly consider my next steps in research, I received a notice from Lipu Shen, the party branch secretary of our research department, asking me to attend a branch meeting to discuss the re-election of the party branch leadership. For reasons unknown to me, either Lipu Shen was preparing to move back to Beijing (her husband, Ronghua Xu, had been accepted as a graduate student at the Beijing Institute of Geology in 1978 and had remained in Beijing after graduation) or she had simply grown tired of the position after many years, she proposed at the meeting that I take over as the party branch secretary. To my surprise, all the veteran party members present agreed with her proposal. The suddenness of this decision left me completely unprepared, and despite my repeated attempts to decline the offer, they insisted on pushing the role of party branch secretary onto me. After the meeting, the party branch submitted the election results to the institute's Party Committee, which surprisingly approved and endorsed the decision. At that moment, I truly felt like a duck being forced onto a perch without any say in the matter.

According to the administrative rank system within the Chinese Academy of Sciences (CAS), CAS is considered a ministerial-level unit, meaning that the directors and secretaries of its subordinate institutes hold equivalent ranks to bureau-level officials. Consequently, the administrative rank of heads and party branch secretaries of research departments is that of a department-level official. However, after the Cultural

Revolution, most of the research unit party secretaries were part-time positions held by scientific staffs who were also party members, with only a few exceptions where full-time party secretaries were appointed, usually doubling as deputy department heads. For those part-time party secretaries, though nominally department-level officials, they did not actually enjoy the benefits of that rank. In other words, being a part-time party secretary was merely an additional duty without any extra benefits.

A group photo of the staff from our REE Research Department in Dec., 1984. (The 3rd from the right in the 2nd row is the author).

Although I was a freshly graduated researcher, I had no room to negotiate in this situation, given that I had been a party member for nearly ten years. Fortunately, I had some experience from serving as the party branch secretary during my university days, so I reluctantly took on the responsibility. As party branch secretary, my first task was to focus on developing new party members. According to the records of our party branch, no new members had been developed in over a decade, since the Cultural Revolution had started. As a result, many in our research department held significant grievances against the previous secretary. In fact, before the Cultural Revolution, several senior scientific staffs of our department had submitted their applications to join the Party, but under the influence of the extreme leftist ideology at the time, these individuals were considered unsuitable due to issues with their family backgrounds or social connections. Consequently, their applications had been left unresolved for years. After taking over the party branch work, I made it a priority to understand the background and status of these senior staff members who had applied to join the Party. I found that they were not only key personnel in the research team but had also maintained a strong desire to join the Party for many years. I resolved to address their applications promptly. First, I gathered the applicants for a meeting, where we discussed their thoughts on joining the Party, as well as their motivations and urgency. I also assured them that the Party organization was always open to welcoming qualified individuals who were ready to join. Then I encouraged them to actively create favourable conditions, get closer to the Party organization, and strive to join the Party as soon as possible. The meeting left the participants visibly moved, and they enthusiastically expressed their determination to meet the necessary conditions to join the Party. Following the meeting, they all resubmitted their applications again. Within less than a year, our branch had successfully added three new members who had long been awaiting admission: one was the deputy head of the research department, Chuanxian Lin, who came from a capitalist family, and the other two, Xianjue Wang and Xueyuan Yu, were key personnel with minor "historical issues" in their family backgrounds. In the following years, 1984 and 1985, we added two more young members, further strengthening the party branch. This revitalized our research department, and the collective attitude of the team improved significantly. Senior members of our department commented on how the new party secretary brought a fresh, energetic perspective and promptly resolved the long-standing membership issues. In fact, the research work and the overall morale did improve notably. Starting in 1983, while actively applying for and undertaking research projects, our research department also began preparing for a national symposium on rare earth element geochemistry. Simultaneously, we collaborated on compiling the monograph *Rare Earth Element Geochemistry*, for which I was responsible for a chapter on the distribution of rare earth elements in the biosphere. When the book was published in early 1985, it received widespread acclaim from peers across the nation. In October 1985, under the leadership of our Geochemistry Institute, we hosted the first National Symposium on Rare Earth Element Geochemistry in Ningbo, Zhejiang Province, attracting hundreds of experts from across the country. At the conference, the Chinese Society of Rare Earth was officially established, with Academician Chengji Guo elected as vice president of the inaugural council.

(Ⅱ)

After completing my master's degree in July 1981, I continued working at the institute, taking on an important responsibility as an assistant to my advisor, Professor Chengji Guo, supporting him in his research projects. This meant helping him tackle the challenges and obstacles in his work, while also conducting my own research in sedimentary geochemistry. By the early 1980s, Professor Guo was already nearing seventy. While there were no formal retirement requirements for academicians (i.e. Academicians are not officially required to retire), Professor Guo was suffering from serious illnesses like coronary heart disease and emphysema. As a result, his work had shifted to a more reflective, indoor focus, summarizing his decades of research. His respiratory issues made him particularly sensitive to coal smoke, which was the main source of heating in Guiyang during winter. Given this, the city's air quality in winter was challenging for him. In 1981, the Guizhou Provincial Government, particularly Vice Governor Tianzhen Qin, became aware of Professor Guo's health issues and offered support. Initially, the province arranged for him and his wife to stay at the West Villa of Huaxi Park for nearly a year. Later, the Guizhou Provincial Science and Technology Commission helped them secure a small house in the provincial botanical garden. From 1982 onwards, the elderly couple moved into this house, away from the city's coal smoke environment. With his housing situation resolved, Professor Guo turned his attention to his long-held ambition: to compile and publish a comprehensive multi-volume academic work titled "The Geochemical Evolution of Rare Earth Elements", summarizing his decades of research. However, producing such an extensive book required both a vast amount of research material and a significant amount of funding for publication. In early 1983, I reported Professor Guo's request to the institute leadership. They agreed to assign someone from our research department to handle the task of collecting the necessary reference materials. However, they were unable to provide the required publication funding. The leadership suggested that Professor Guo apply for the "President's Fund," a special budget managed directly by the president of the Chinese Academy of Sciences, which was reserved for urgent or special projects. They thought this could be a potential source of support for the publication. When I reported this information to Professor Guo, he was thrilled and immediately said: "Mingqing, I haven't been feeling well lately. Do you think you could handle applying for the President's Fund on my behalf? Could you draft an application letter, and I'll take a look afterward?" At first, I thought that since I had found the funding source, Professor Guo would write the application himself. But to my surprise, he wanted me to write the letter for him. I knew this was a sign of his trust in me, but the responsibility felt overwhelming. I worried that if I failed, I wouldn't be able to bear the consequences. However, since Professor Guo had already made his request, I couldn't refuse. So, I reluctantly agreed. After receiving this task, I spent several days thinking it over. I wasn't very familiar with the format for applying to the President's Fund, so I decided to take a different approach: instead of writing a formal application, I would draft a direct letter to the academy's leadership. Once I felt prepared, I composed the letter in Professor Guo's voice and addressed it to Vice President Guangzhao Zhou, who was in charge of geosciences at the Chinese Academy of Sciences at the time. In the letter, I introduced Professor Guo's personal background and achievements, particularly emphasizing his contributions since returning to China in the early 1950s. These included solving key issues regarding the extraction and processing of the Baiyun Obo rare earth-niobium-iron deposit in Inner Mongolia, one of the world's largest of its kind. I also highlighted the importance of rare earth elements, especially those with unique properties and applications in high-tech industries, as strategic materials critical to technological development. Finally, I noted that Professor Guo had accumulated a vast amount of research data over the past three decades and that he wanted to use his remaining years to compile a large academic work. The letter concluded by requesting a grant from the President's Fund to support the publication of this work. After drafting and finalizing the letter, I took it to Professor Guo's home in the provincial botanical garden with a sense of trepidation, hoping he would personally revise it. To my surprise, after reading it, Professor Guo said: "Mingqing, this letter is excellent! I don't think it needs any changes. I'll sign it now, and you can send it off immediately." Hearing this, I felt a wave of relief, knowing that I had gained his approval. We sent the letter, but I still wasn't sure if it would work. However, about two months later, Professor Guo received a reply from Vice President Guangzhao Zhou. In his letter, Vice President Zhou thanked Professor Guo for his significant contributions to the nation's research on the Baiyun Obo deposit and expressed his support for helping senior scientists summarize their research achievements. He approved a grant of ¥50,000 yuan from the President's Fund to support the publication of Professor Guo's academic monograph. Professor Guo was overjoyed upon receiving the letter. To put this in perspective, in the early 1980s, ¥50,000 yuan was a substantial sum of money, especially since it came directly from a special fund overseen by the president of the Chinese Academy of Sciences. This gesture demonstrated how well the academy's leadership understood and valued Professor Guo's contributions, both before and after the Cultural Revolution, and reflected their care for senior scientists. Later, another vice president of the Chinese Academy of Sciences visited the Geochemistry Institute in Guiyang to inspect the work being done. When the leadership learned that there was still a shortfall in the funding for Professor Guo's book, they encouraged him to submit another report detailing the status of the publication. I helped Professor Guo write this second application again, and in early 1985, Vice President Zhou approved another ¥50,000 yuan again from the President's Fund. With a total of ¥100,000 yuan in funding secured, Professor Guo was able to focus on writing *The Geochemical Evolution of Rare Earth Elements*, which he worked on day and night starting in 1985. After seven or eight years of dedicated effort, the monumental 4-million-character work was finally published in five volumes by Guizhou People's

Publishing House in 1993. Professor Guo had realized his lifelong dream.

(Ⅲ)

Although I was a graduate student of Professor Chengji Guo, my research direction after graduation did not fully align with his field of expertise. After completing my master's degree, I continued to focus on the same area as my thesis, conducting research in marine sedimentary geochemistry. My master's thesis focused on the geochemistry of rare earth elements in the sediments of the Taiwan Shallow, with samples provided by the Qingdao Institute of Oceanology of the Chinese Academy of Sciences (CAS). This marked the beginning of a collaborative relationship between our institute and the Qingdao Institute of Oceanology, and Professor Yiyang Zhao from the Qingdao Institute of Oceanology served as one of the advisors for my master's thesis.

In October of 1983, the Qingdao Institute of Oceanology had a scientific expedition planned for the Okinawa Trough in the East China Sea. Professor Yiyang Zhao from the Institute's Geological Research Department wrote to me, asking if I would be interested in participating. The idea of a marine scientific expedition intrigued me, as I imagined it would be vastly different from land-based geological fieldwork. Eager to experience the work firsthand, I accepted the invitation. Along with me, Xiaoyue Xiao, a graduate from our institute and a student of Vice Director Ziyuan Ouyang, was also invited to join the expedition. His task was to collect cosmic dust on board for his graduate thesis.

The Qingdao Institute of Oceanology, Chinese Academy of Sciences, is the largest comprehensive marine research institute in China, with about 700 scientific personnel at the time. The institute operated a 4,000-ton research vessel called "Kexue Yihao" ("Science No. 1"), equipped with advanced marine research instruments, making it one of the largest and most advanced oceanographic research vessels in China at the time. The ship was capable of conducting comprehensive scientific expeditions in multiple disciplines, including marine biology, marine geology, physical oceanography, and marine chemistry.

1983.10.作者(左)与肖小月摄
于东海海洋科考船上

The author (left) and Xiaoyue Xiao on the marine research vessel in East Chin Sea in Oct., 1983.

It was also one of the few vessels in China capable of carrying out deep-sea expeditions. The decision to set sail in October was due to the relatively stable oceanic weather conditions during this season, with fewer tropical storms and typhoons, and more stable ocean currents---ideal conditions for marine research. By the time Xiaoyue Xiao and I arrived in Qingdao in late October, the crew and other expedition members had already boarded the ship half a day earlier. By the time we got on board, most of the best berths had already been taken, so Xiaoyue Xiao and I had to settle for cabins located closer to the engine room, where the noise was significantly louder. We joined a team of about 14 to 15 marine geologists on the expedition, including four or five graduate students from the Geological Research Department, such as Yongliang Yang (the son of our institute's former party secretary Jingren Yang), Shikui Zhai, and Jintu Wang. They were also on the expedition to collect geological samples for their theses, which were similar to the samples I needed, though our research objectives were different. As a result, our geological team was grouped together, while other teams focused on marine physics, chemistry, and biology, each with its own sampling methods and objectives. Unlike the others,

Xiaoyue Xiao's task of collecting cosmic dust was relatively simple. He merely placed a large, smooth plastic panel on a designated spot on the ship's top deck and waited for cosmic dust to naturally fall from space. He would collect the samples every 7 to 8 hours, making his job the easiest on board.

Our expedition vessel set sail from Qingdao at midday on a calm, sunny day in late October. The weather was perfect, and the sea was calm, so all the expedition members gathered on deck to wave goodbye to Qingdao. It was my first time aboard such a large vessel for a long-distance voyage, and I was thrilled. I couldn't contain my excitement, running from the bow of the ship, watching the waves part before us, to the top deck, where I gazed at the horizon, where the blue sky met the sea. Seagulls circled the ship, creating a picturesque scene that matched my elated mood. To our surprise, dinner that evening exceeded all expectations. The ship's meals included five or six different side dishes per meal, with meat, cabbage, tofu, fish, and shrimp. As for staple foods like rice and steamed buns, they were available in unlimited quantities. To top it all off, we didn't have to pay for food on the ship, which was an unexpected blessing considering that, in the early 1980s, food and other necessities were still rationed across China. However, our first challenge on board came when it was time to sleep. Our room, being near the engine room, was noisy beyond belief. Xiaoyue Xiao and I had to raise our voices significantly just to hear each other, and sleeping was even more difficult with the constant hum of the engine. I eventually managed to fall asleep by the early hours of the morning, but Xiaoyue Xiao couldn't sleep at all. We reported the issue to the expedition leader the next day, and after a couple of days, we were relocated to a room farther from the engine, where the noise was much more tolerable. This solved our sleeping problem. Our second challenge came in the form of seasickness. The "Kexue Yihao" had a maximum speed of 15 knots (about 30 kilometers per hour), and in calm waters, the ship was steady, with no noticeable swaying. The journey from Qingdao to the Okinawa Trough in the East China Sea was about 1,300 to 1,400 kilometers, taking over 40 hours. The first day was calm, but sometime during the night, I was jolted awake as the ship began to roll and sway. The next morning, when I looked out of the cabin window, I saw rough seas and dark clouds. The ship was now rocking so much that I had to hold on to the bed's handrails to keep myself steady. At breakfast, I noticed the dining hall was nearly empty, which I initially thought was because I had arrived late. By lunchtime, the situation hadn't changed. The kitchen staff explained that the rough seas had caused many of the crew to become seasick, and those who did come for food took it back to their cabins to eat. In the dining hall, the empty chairs slid back and forth across the floor as the ship swayed, but the tables were firmly bolted to the ground. The kitchen staff told me that under such conditions, it was mostly the veteran members of the expedition who came to the dining hall. They were seasoned sailors who could handle seven or eight-meter swells without issue. One of the kitchen workers asked if this was my first time on a ship, and when I said it was, he remarked that I didn't seem to suffer from seasickness too badly. I told him I could still manage to eat under the circumstances, though I couldn't eat too much. Unfortunately, Xiaoyue Xiao wasn't as lucky, and by lunchtime, he could barely eat anything. One of the veteran expedition members told me that the current seas were relatively mild and that during truly rough conditions, people couldn't even stand or sit without holding onto overhead handles and rings to avoid falling over. By that evening, the seas had calmed, and we all gradually fell asleep, finally getting some much-needed rest.

The Okinawa Trough is located on the edge of the continental shelf of the East China Sea, extending in a northeast-southwest direction for about 800 kilometers, with a width of approximately 300 kilometers. Our expedition started from the northern end of the trough, sampling at intervals of 40-50 kilometers by traversing the trough. The research vessel would cross the trough back and forth, ensuring that both the edges and the central areas of the trough were covered. The water depth in the trough generally ranges around 1,000 meters, with the deepest parts reaching over 2,000 meters. Our research vessel arrived at the northernmost sampling site of the Okinawa Trough around 3:00 a.m. on the third day. Once the ship anchored, floodlights illuminated the deck, and the research teams from different disciplines sprang into action. The marine chemists collected water samples from various depths, the marine physicists observed the ocean currents, and the marine biologists fished for plankton and benthic organisms in the seawater. As for the marine geologists, we prepared to collect two types of seafloor sediment samples: surface sediments and core sediments. Surface sediments were collected using a grab sampler, while core samples were obtained using a gravity corer. Both sampling tools were operated by shipboard machinery, and the experienced crew members were adept at handling these machines, while we younger members assisted as needed. The time required at each station depended on the difficulty of the sampling process. If everything went smoothly, a station could be completed in just over an hour, but if there were challenges or rough seas, we might have to repeat the sampling process two or three times, which could take more than two hours. After finishing work at one station, we would move to the next station about 40-50 kilometers away, which took about two hours of sailing. Our work followed a rotating schedule: we would rest in the cabin while the ship sailed to the next station, and once the ship reached the next site, we would immediately return to the deck to begin the next round of work. This cycle of two to three hours of work followed by two to three hours of rest continued for three to four days, sometimes up to five days, before we were allowed a full day of rest. Some might think this work schedule wasn't too exhausting, but that was far from the truth. With only two or three hours of rest between stations, it was nearly impossible to get proper sleep. After two or three days of this constant rotation, severe sleep deprivation set in, and we felt extremely fatigued. If the seas were rough, the constant swaying of the ship during work made us even more exhausted. Additionally, moving geological samples and tools, often weighing dozens of kilograms, required significant physical effort, making the work physically demanding. Without being young and strong, it would have been very difficult to handle this type of work. Clearly, the physical demands of marine geological research were much greater than those of land-based geological surveys. It became clear to us why the food on the ship was so plentiful and nutritious, it was essential to replenish the immense physical energy expended during these rigorous operations. Through this firsthand experience, we truly understood the challenges of marine geological expeditions.

After working at sea for about two weeks, just as everyone was feeling utterly exhausted and struggling to continue, the ship's weather forecast reported that a tropical storm in the Western Pacific was heading toward the Okinawa Trough. The captain immediately ordered all scientific operations to stop, and the vessel set full speed toward Zhoushan Archipelago to take shelter from the storm. This gave us a chance to rest and sleep without worry. The next morning, we awoke to the news from experienced crew members that we had arrived at Shenjiamen Port in the Zhoushan Archipelago. After disembarking, standing on solid ground felt completely different from being on the ship. After more than ten days at sea, even when the ship was stationary, it still felt as though the deck was constantly swaying beneath our feet. But now, standing on firm land, we could finally feel what it meant to be truly "grounded," and that sense of stability brought immense relief.

Shenjiamen Port is located on the southeastern side of Zhoushan Island in the Zhoushan Archipelago, facing the East China Sea and backed by the Qinglong and Beihu Mountains. It is a natural harbour and the largest fishing port in China, and one of the three largest fishing ports in the world (the other two being Bergen in Norway and Callao in Peru). Our research vessel needed to stay in Shenjiamen Port for two to three days to wait out the storm. Once ashore, a group of seven or eight of us young men from the marine geology team decided to visit the seafood market at the pier to buy some crabs. We bought about 20 to 30 pounds of large swimming crabs and brought them back to the ship, where the chef prepared them for us (at the time, the crabs cost ¥0.76 yuan per kg). That afternoon, our group of seven or eight young men feasted on crabs and beer, thoroughly enjoying a seafood banquet.

Shenjiamen Port is near the Putuo Mountain scenic area, and the next day, our geology team visited Putuo Mountain. Shenjiamen Port is in Putuo District, less than 10 kilometers from Putuo Mountain, separated by a stretch of water that we crossed by ferry. Putuo Mountain, though called a mountain, is actually a small island in the Zhoushan Archipelago, with an area of about 30 square kilometers. In the center of the island stands a mountain peak about 300 meters high, named Foding Mountain. Legend has it that Putuo Mountain is where the **Bodhisattva Guanyin** (观音菩萨) descended to enlighten the masses, earning it the nickname "**Buddhist Kingdom of the Sea and Sky** (海天佛国)." However, at the time, the island had few visitors. The reasons were twofold: first, China had only recently begun its reform and opening-up policies, and most people were still relatively poor, so tourism had not yet become popular. Second, Putuo Mountain was located in the remote Zhoushan Archipelago, making transportation very inconvenient. As a result, most of the visitors were locals. Due to the island's remoteness, lack of infrastructure, and poorly maintained temples, Putuo Mountain's facilities were far from meeting the expectations set by its reputation.

After staying in Shenjiamen Port for two to three days, the tropical storm in the Western Pacific subsided, and we returned to the Okinawa Trough to continue our work for another ten days. Finally, we completed the nearly monthlong marine geological expedition and safely returned to the Qingdao Oceanological Institute. After a few days of rest in Qingdao, I sorted through the 60 to 70 surface sediment samples we had collected from the Okinawa Trough. With these samples, Xiaoyue Xiao and I traveled back to Guiyang by train. Later, I conducted chemical composition, trace element, and rare earth element analyses and geochemical research on these samples, and eventually published two or three research papers in journals such as *Oceanologia et Limnologia Sinica* and *Geochimica*.

(IV)

My supervisor, Professor Chengji Guo, graduated from the Department of Geology at Peking University in 1943 and went to study at Kyoto University in Japan the same year, returning to China in 1952. During his time abroad, Professor Guo married a Japanese woman, who became a Chinese citizen upon their return and lived in China as a Japaneseborn Chinese. For over 30 years after their return, from the early 1950s to the early 1980s, Professor Guo had never revisited Japan. In the early 1980s, as China's scientific and technological fields gradually expanded due to reform and opening up, the Chinese Academy of Sciences (CAS) began to broaden its international academic exchanges by adopting a "send out" and "invite in" strategy. The "send out" part involved sending experienced senior experts who had previously studied abroad, as well as key academic personnel, to foreign institutions of authority for visits and exchanges, allowing them to learn advanced ideas while leveraging the relationships they had built during their studies for the benefit of Chinese research. The "invite in" part focused on bringing in authoritative experts and scholars from abroad to lecture and share their knowledge, thereby aligning China's scientific community with international standards. Professor Guo, having spent years studying in Japan and having made significant contributions to China's research in rare and rare earth elements, was naturally identified as a key candidate for international exchange. After applying to the CAS Bureau of International Cooperation and coordinating with relevant Japanese institutions, in April 1985, both Professor Guo and I received an invitation from the Japanese Society for the Promotion of Science (JSPS) to visit universities and research institutes in Japan for a month in late September 1985. After receiving the notice for the visit, we each received the official funds for clothing from our institute, applied for official passports from the Guiyang Public Security Bureau, and obtained Japanese visas through the CAS Bureau of International Cooperation. By July of that year, our visas were ready, and on around September 20, Professor Guo and I flew from Guiyang to Beijing. There, we picked up our passports and visas from the International Cooperation Bureau in CAS, where the bureau director personally met with us, gave us advice on our trip, and reminded us to stay safe. On the morning of September 25, around 11:00 a.m. (12:00 p.m. Tokyo time, as Japan is an hour ahead of Beijing), Professor Guo and I boarded an international large flight, Boeing 747, from Beijing and landed at Tokyo Narita Airport around 2:00 p.m. local time. After clearing customs, a representative from JSPS met us at the airport arrival and escorted us to our hotel in Tokyo that evening.

This was my first time traveling abroad, so upon arriving in Tokyo, everything seemed novel and exciting to me. The contrast between China and Japan was striking. Tokyo, as Japan's capital and its largest city, was also one of the world's most developed and populous international metropolises at the time. The city was filled with towering skyscrapers, yet the streets were relatively quiet, and the people moved quickly, without the leisurely pace often seen on Chinese streets. Tokyo's streets were also impeccably clean, with not a single piece of litter in sight. Pedestrians strictly followed traffic rules, stopping for red lights and crossing only when the light turned green. No one jaywalked when the light was red. In Japan, vehicles drive

The author visited Tokyo in Oct., 1985.

on the left side of the road, a rule likely adopted from British traffic laws when Japan first established its driving regulations. Tokyo's commercial districts were lined with specialized stores, which was something unheard of in 1980s China, where large stores sold a variety of goods. Japanese department stores, on the other hand, each specialized in a particular type of product. Before opening each morning, the store employees would line up in two neat rows at the entrance. As the doors opened and the first customers walked in, the employees on either side would bow deeply and greet them in soft voices, saying, "Irasshaimase" ("Welcome"). This is true even if only one customer enters the store. This welcoming ceremony lasted about ten minutes, and it was repeated every single day the store was open. Inside, the shelves were stocked with an overwhelming array of goods. For example, in electronics stores, televisions of all sizes, from small screens to massive 30-40 inch colour TVs, were neatly displayed, all from the same brand, creating an impressive and overwhelming sight. At that time, in mid-1980s China, black-and-white televisions had yet to become widespread, and owning a 12-15 inch black-and-white TV was already considered a luxury. Colour TVs were extremely rare and prohibitively expensive.

We planned to stay in Tokyo for four days, visiting two institutions. One was the Geological Survey of Japan (GSJ), located in Tsukuba near Tokyo, and the other was the University of Tokyo. On our second day in Tokyo, a representative from JSPS accompanied us to visit the GSJ in Tsukuba Science City. The Geological Survey of Japan was established in 1882 and was the only comprehensive geological research institution in the country, having already reached its centennial milestone by the time of our visit. Director Fujii of the GSJ gave us a detailed introduction to the institution's structure, its recent key projects, and its scientific achievements. We then toured the GSJ's Geological Museum, focusing on the fourth exhibition hall, which displayed a wide array of Japanese mineral and fossil specimens. In the afternoon, Professor Guo and Director Fujii exchanged insights on their respective research fields and findings. We also viewed a projected 3D geological map of the Japanese islands, showing fault lines and volcanic locations. That evening, Director Fujii hosted a banquet in our honour.

After returning to Tokyo, we spent the third day visiting the University of Tokyo's Department of Chemistry. Professor Akimasa Masuda, a renowned Japanese geochemist specializing in rare earth element geochemistry, welcomed us. His laboratory was equipped with advanced plasma mass spectrometry instruments, which allowed for the precise measurement of trace rare earth elements in geological samples. Due to this capability, Professor Masuda and his research team frequently published papers on rare earth element geochemistry in international academic journals, establishing a well-respected reputation in the field. Professor Guo and Professor Masuda discussed their research findings and explored potential scientific collaborations, including the joint training of graduate students and the possibility of sending visiting scholars to work in Professor Masuda's laboratory. After we returned to China, the institute leadership approved a proposal in 1987 to send Congqiang Liu, a master's graduate of Professor Guangzhi Tu, to Tokyo University's Department of Chemistry as a visiting scholar in Professor Masuda's lab. Congqiang Liu later became a PhD student there and, after earning his doctorate in 1993, worked as a researcher at RIKEN in Japan before returning to China in

1996. In 1997, he became the director of our institute, and in 2011, he was elected an Academician of the Chinese Academy of Sciences. He was one of the geochemists jointly cultivated by our institute and Tokyo University. During our visit to Professor Masuda's lab, there were initial discussions about sending me to pursue a PhD under his supervision, but this plan was later abandoned for various reasons, something I will explain later.

Our visit to Japan focused on visiting Professor Chengji Guo's alma mater, Kyoto University, where he had studied during his time in Japan. Kyoto, located in western Japan, is an ancient capital with a rich history and deep cultural heritage. Kyoto University is one of Japan's most prestigious universities, second only to the University of Tokyo. From 1943 to 1952, Professor Guo spent nine years studying at Kyoto University, where he not only gained knowledge but also found love. We planned to stay in Kyoto for two weeks, with the primary goals of visiting and lecturing at Kyoto University and allowing Professor Guo to reconnect with family and friends.

After our visit to the University of Tokyo, we took the Japanese Shinkansen bullet train from Tokyo to Kyoto, a distance of about 300 kilometers, which took approximately two hours. When we arrived at Kyoto Station at noon, we were warmly welcomed by representatives from Kyoto University, as well as Professor Guo's wife's older sister and younger brother (his brother-in-law). Upon hearing of Professor Guo's arrival in Kyoto, many of his former classmates from his time studying in Japan gathered from all over Japan to meet him. On the day of the reunion at Kyoto University Hall, more than twenty of Professor Guo's old classmates attended, the majority of whom were renowned professors at various universities in Japan, while others were senior executives at major Japanese corporations. The reunion of classmates after more than 30 years created an emotional and lively scene. The next day, when Professor Guo delivered a lecture at the auditorium of Kyoto University's Department of Geology and Mineralogy, the hall was packed. Originally he had spent nearly a decade studying in Japan and had married a Japanese woman, and was proficient in both Japanese and English, but Professor Guo insisted on delivering his lecture in Chinese out of respect for his homeland. To assist with the language barrier, a Chinese student named Xiao Zhang from the geology department was asked to serve as an interpreter.

However, Xiao Zhang had not been in Japan long enough to be fully fluent in Japanese, and he was unfamiliar with some of the specialized terms related to rare and rare earth elements. As a result, his translations were not ideal, and Professor Guo had to help correct certain Japanese words, occasionally lapsing into Japanese himself during the lecture, which caused bursts of laughter and applause from the audience.

The author (the left) and Prof. Guo (the right) visited Prof. Akimasa Masuda (the middle) at Tokyo University in Oct., 1985.

During the 1940s, when Professor Guo was studying in Japan, he lived for a time in the Kōkaryō dormitory near Kyoto University. Kōkaryō was a five-story dormitory made of gray brick and wood, rented by Kyoto University for Chinese students during World War II. In the early 1950s, the government of the Republic of China in Taiwan purchased the property. One evening after dinner, while walking with Professor Guo, he suggested that we visit the dormitory where he had once lived, and I readily agreed. As we walked, we arrived at Kōkaryō, but the building's exterior had become dilapidated over time, and it appeared quite rundown. Professor Guo was visibly moved by the sight. Inside, however, the facilities were still functional, and many Chinese students were living there. As we climbed the stairs, we happened to meet a fellow Shanxi native and an old classmate of Professor Guo's, named Hu, living in a single dorm room on the third floor. At first, Professor Guo was shocked and could hardly recognize his old friend, now an elderly man in his seventies with greying hair and a modest appearance. After a brief conversation, Professor Guo learned that his friend was still living alone, without family or property, and was residing in the dormitory under rather humble conditions, with furnishings that appeared to be salvaged from trash (it's common in Japan and the West countries for people to discard functional furniture at the end of the month, which others often collect and use). Seeing his friend's difficult living situation, Professor Guo refrained from asking further about his past, and we left Kōkaryō with heavy hearts.

Professor Guo met his Japanese wife during his time studying at Kyoto University. At that time, he lived in Kōkaryō, while his future wife's family ran a laundry shop nearby. Professor Guo frequently visited the laundry shop on weekends, and over time, he and his future wife became acquainted, their relationship blossomed, and by around 1947, they were married. His wife's original family name was Bayano, and after their marriage, Professor Guo gave her the Chinese name Xiujun Guo. In the summer of 2006, when I returned to China to visit family, I went to visit Mrs. Guo (Professor Guo had passed away by then). She fondly recalled their early days together, telling me that when Professor Guo first expressed his feelings for her, she had many reservations. She told him: "You are a great scholar, and I'm just a high school graduate. I'm afraid I'm not good enough for you!" But Professor Guo reassured her, saying, "The difference in education level is not a problem. As long as we love each other, that's all that matters. All you need to do is take care of the family and the children." They remained a devoted couple for 50 years, raising seven children (two sons and five daughters), all of whom Mrs. Guo single-handedly nurtured without ever seeking outside help. She truly was the epitome of a virtuous wife and mother.

Professor Guo was a scientist with a deep sense of patriotism. Despite spending nearly a decade studying in Japan and being a renowned expert in rare and rare earth element mineral geology, and having married a Japanese woman, he could have easily stayed in Japan to pursue an academic career. However, in the early 1950s, after completing his PhD, he made the resolute decision to return to China with his wife and children to contribute to the country's burgeoning rare and rare earth element geochemistry research. During our time in Japan, Professor Guo often spoke candidly with me during our walks. He confided that as he was nearing the completion of his PhD in Japan, several Japanese universities had offered him professorships, but he turned them all down. Professor Guo said two main reasons influenced his decision to return to China. "In Japan, when people talk about ancient China, they all speak with admiration," he said. "But when they talk about modern China, no one respects it." This was the first reason. The second reason was, "I specialize in rare and rare earth element mineral geochemistry, but Japan doesn't have these resources. China, however, is a resource-rich country when it comes to rare and rare earth elements. Only by returning to China could I truly make use of my knowledge." These heartfelt words reflected his genuine love for his country. However, after returning to China, Professor Guo faced unjust treatment during the Cultural Revolution, though he was later vindicated.

During our walks and conversations, Professor Guo never missed an opportunity to offer me earnest guidance. When discussing how to conduct scientific research, he said: "The most crucial thing in doing research is to fully immerse yourself in it. Don't think about anything else, your sole focus should be on your research topic. You must understand that there is no such thing as an eight-hour workday in scientific research. Once you dive into your research, you'll find that, apart from eating and sleeping, you're constantly thinking about your Project, how to conduct experiments to get accurate data, how to interpret the results, how to write the research report or academic paper. When you finally complete your research report or paper, the joy and sense of accomplishment you feel will be indescribable, that's when you experience the true pleasure of research!" When Professor Guo said this, I didn't understand it at all at first. he said: "When doing research, you shouldn't think about anything else except your topic." I thought, as ordinary people, how can we not think about our families, our meals, and daily necessities after work? It seemed impossible! However, later on, when I began to take on independent research projects, I realized that what Professor Guo had said was absolutely true. From choosing a research topic to writing the project proposal, and throughout the research process, you constantly think about how to overcome challenges, how to interpret experimental data, and how to write the research report or paper. It can get to the point where you almost forget to eat or sleep. It was then that I truly understood the depth of Professor Guo's advice!

Prof. Chengji Guo (the middle person in the front row) met with his former Japanese classmates in Kyoto University in Oct. 1985.
(The author is the first in the front left).

During our staying in Kyoto, besides visiting Kyoto University, we also visited Kyoto University of Education, Nara University of Education, Nara Women's University, and Osaka University. We reached an agreement with Kyoto University to expand academic exchange and collaboration. In the meantime, we toured several cultural and historical landmarks, including the Kyoto Imperial Palace (the former palace of the Japanese emperors during the Heian period), the monument dedicated to Premier Zhou Enlai's poem in Kyoto's Arashiyama (Zhou had written a poem titled "Arashiyama in the Rain" during his studies in Japan in 1919, and in 1979, Japanese friends raised funds to erect a monument with the poem inscribed in Arashiyama Park), and Nara Park. On October 25, 1985, after successfully completing our visit to Japan, we flew back to Beijing from Osaka.

The author (right) and Professor Guo photographed in front of Premier Zhou Enlai's poetry monument in Arashiyama, Kyoto, Japan in Oct., 1985.

Our trip to Japan was sponsored by the Japanese Society for the Promotion of Science (JSPS), which is similar to China's National Natural Science Foundation. The expenses for our visit were covered by JSPS, and the treatment we received was quite generous. Professor Guo was given the same living stipend as a professor, receiving ¥535,000 Japanese yen for one month, while I, classified at the lecturer level (since I was an assistant researcher at the institute, equivalent to a university lecturer or engineer), received ¥485,000 Japanese yen for the month. At that time, one US dollar was worth about ¥250 Japanese yen, so our monthly living expenses were around $2,000 US dollars each. Compared to Chinese scholars visiting Europe or the United States, the stipend provided by JSPS was among the highest.

(V)

During my visit to Japan in October 1985, Professor Guo had preliminarily arranged for me to study at Kyoto University or the University of Tokyo, with the plan for me to go to Japan for my Ph.D. studies either by the end of 1986 or early 1987. So, in February 1986, I enrolled in Chengdu Foreign Language Training Center of the Chinese Academy of Sciences to study English and began my language studies in early March. At the time, my English proficiency was fairly limited---reading and understanding professional literature posed no significant challenges, but my listening and speaking skills were still lacking. During my visit to Japan, my limited English skills significantly hindered my ability to communicate with Japanese colleagues. Upon returning to China, I realized that, as a researcher, I needed to improve my English listening and speaking abilities to a conversational level, even if I wasn't planning to go abroad. Therefore, upon arriving at the training centre, I was determined to make the most of this opportunity to elevate my English proficiency by one or two levels.

During my time studying English, it felt as if I had returned to school again. Every day, my schedule was packed with classes---listening, speaking, reading comprehension, and grammar. I had never before studied English so systematically. At the end of April, the centre was closed for the May 1st Labor Day holiday, which coincided with the weekend, so I took two extra days off to return to Guiyang and handle some work matters. Upon my return, I learned that the Institute's Party Committee had undergone a reelection, and I had been elected as a member of the Party Committee. The new Party Secretary was Zhengqiang Zhu, the new director was Xiande Xie, and the deputy directors were Ziyuan Ouyang and Yuwei Chen, with Jingrong Xu serving as the deputy Party secretary. The other committee members were Ziyuan Ouyang, Fuming Chen, Zhuocheng Liang, Jiatian Li, and myself. When Secretary Zhengqiang Zhu heard that I had returned from Chengdu, he called me to the Party Secretary's office. Secretary Zhu, in a serious tone, said: "Xiao Wu, I understand you are currently studying English in Chengdu and are planning to go to Japan for further studies later this year or early next year. However, the Institute's comrades trust you, and you've been elected as a member of the Party Committee. We are a permanent committee, and each of the nine members has specific responsibilities. If you go to Japan, you'll be away for at least four or five years. We have been grooming you as a successor, and we hope you won't disappoint our Institute's expectations." I replied: "Teacher Zhu, I am currently studying English. The plan to study in Japan is still in progress, and even if it's finalized, I'll still need to study Japanese for a period after my English studies. Tomorrow I will return to Chengdu and complete my English studies, after finishing my English studying and coming back I'll give you a formal response." After the May 1st Labour Day, I returned to Chengdu to continue my English studies for another two months and finished in mid-July, returning to Guiyang. After my return, Director Xiande Xie also had a conversation with me. Director Xie said: "Xiao Wu, the reason I called you today is to let you know that you were just elected to the Party Committee this year, which reflects the trust of the entire Institute. We hope you'll reconsider your plan to study in Japan. Could you give up this opportunity and perhaps go on a short-term visit instead? Secretary Zhu has already spoken to you. Since you are a permanent member of the Party Committee, if you leave, we will be one person short. We hope you'll give it serious thought." After hearing this and recalling Secretary Zhu's earlier conversation, I realized both leaders were asking me to give up my plans to study abroad and stay to work at the Institute. I thought to myself: "Am I being too difficult? Since both leaders have come to talk to me about giving up my plans, I should probably agree." I then told Director Xie: "Teacher Xie, since both of you have spoken with me and asked me to give up the plan to study in Japan, for the sake of the Institute's work, I'll give up the opportunity this time. But I have two requests: first, while serving on the Party Committee, I still want to continue my research work. If I meet the qualifications, my professional title should still be promoted accordingly. Second, if there are future opportunities for short-term overseas visits, such as a sixmonth or one-year term as a visiting scholar, the Institute should give me the opportunity. If the Institute can meet these two conditions, I'll give up this opportunity to study in Japan." Director Xie said: "There's no problem at all with your requests---the Institute can certainly accommodate them!" So, after getting a satisfactory answer from Director Xie, I gave up the opportunity to study in Japan that year and remained at the Institute. Although the two Institute leaders agreed readily at the time, with the opening of the Guangzhou branch of the Geochemistry Institute, both of them soon transferred to Guangzhou, and my requests were forgotten. Not only did I miss out on the opportunity to become a visiting scholar, but my promotion for a professional title was delayed several times. Of course, that's another story.

After joining the Party Committee, I was appointed as the youth committee member and secretary of the Institute's Youth League, overseeing all Youth League activities. I continued serving as the Branch Party Secretary of our research department, with my office remaining in the research department. My work arrangement was such that I would attend Party Committee meetings when called, but when the committee didn't need me, I focused on my research. In other words, besides my research duties, I was also handling three administrative roles: Party Committee work, Youth League work, and my responsibilities as the research department's branch Party secretary. For many people, managing these three administrative tasks would be more than enough, but I also had to balance my research tasks. I could have chosen to fully commit to administrative work, seek closer ties with leadership, and potentially advance my political career, which might have even led to a leadership role at the Institute, since the director and secretary positions were equivalent to senior government roles. However, I had no interest in politics or leadership--my sole focus was on developing my scientific career. My supervisor was a renowned scientist, and I aspired only to become a research professor like my supervisor, with no interest in holding any official title. So, despite the heavy workload on both the administrative and research sides, I took on all the responsibilities.

Once I became involved in the Party Committee's work, I quickly realized just how time-consuming it was. Since the Institute followed a system where the director was responsible under the Party Committee's leadership, most administrative tasks had to be discussed and approved by the Party Committee before being implemented. Moreover, the Party Committee itself had numerous responsibilities, such as Party organization development, political education for all employees, and studying and implementing the policies of the central and local Party authorities. As a result, the Party Committee held meetings at least once or twice a week, sometimes lasting an entire day, and other times only two or three hours. As for my responsibilities as the research department's branch Party secretary, those were mostly administrative. At that time, China had a six-day workweek, with Saturday mornings dedicated to political study sessions led by Party branches. These sessions were a mandatory part of every week across the country, with Saturday afternoons reserved for cleaning the workplace. Sunday was the only day off. In contrast, the Youth League work was more flexible. My main task was to oversee the activities of the dozen or so Youth League branch secretaries, giving them autonomy in organizing events without micromanaging. Altogether, these administrative tasks took up more than half of my time and energy, leaving my research work to become a secondary focus. To make up for this, especially after I was assigned full-time to the Party Office in 1989, I dedicated my evenings, weekends, and holidays to my research. Typically, after dinner on weekdays, I would watch the 7:00–7:30 p.m. CCTV news, then head to my professional office to work on my research---whether it was organizing geological samples, reviewing scientific literature, analyzing experimental data, or writing academic papers. I would usually work for four hours each evening, leaving the office around 11:30 p.m. to head home, wash up, and sleep by midnight. In the morning, I'd wake up at 7:00 a.m. and listen to Voice of America to improve my English listening skills. Even on Sundays, I often spent time in the lab or office. This personal schedule, which I started in the latter half of 1986, continued until I went abroad in the mid-1990s. As a result, from 1986 to 1995, I hardly watched any television shows or movies. It was this work ethic, this tireless spirit of taking advantage of every available moment that allowed me to handle both administrative and research work effectively. Even after being assigned to the Party Office in 1989 as the chief, I was still able to produce high-quality research papers, publishing at least one or two papers every year or two in reputable academic journals.

Chapter 6   Surveys in Northwestern China

(I)

By 1986, my research on the sedimentary geochemistry in the Okinawa Trough on the East China Sea continental shelf had come to an end. In 1987, I was invited by Professor Zhonggang Wang from our research department to join him on a geological field investigation to Xinjiang, focused on granite. This was an opportunity I gladly accepted. First, Xinjiang is not only vast in territory but also rich in mineral resources, making it a dream destination for anyone conducting geological research. Second, since I had a background in chemistry and had studied geology after starting graduate school, I was still considered a latecomer to the field and had very limited experience in fieldwork. I was eager to learn from the geological experts in our institute. Therefore, when Professor Wang asked if I would be willing to go, I agreed without hesitation.

Mr. Zhonggang Wang, while only in his third year at Nanjing University in 1954, was required to graduate early due to the country's urgent need for geological specialists. Since the mid-1950s, he had been working closely with my advisor, Professor Chengji Guo, on research related to the giant Bayun Obo rare-earth iron ore deposit in Inner Mongolia. He was one of Professor Guo's key assistants and a core member of the research team, with a wealth of experience in fieldwork and vast knowledge. Thus, I was eager to learn from him about the intricacies of geological fieldwork.

At that time, our institute was tasked with a national project called the "305 Project," which involved comprehensive geological, geophysical, and geochemical research to accelerate the identification of Xinjiang's mineral resources. Mr. Zhonggang Wang was responsible for the geochemical study of granite formations in northern Xinjiang under this project. According to his plan, the first geological field survey was scheduled for August to October of 1987, followed by a supplementary investigation from July to September of 1988. We carried out both investigations as planned, and each had its own thrilling moments. Although more than thirty years have passed, many scenes from those expeditions remain vivid in my memory.

The author with his wife and daughter visited Tianchi Lake in Urumqi, Xingjiang, China in Aug., 1987.

For the first field geological expedition in the summer and autumn of 1987, the original plan was to set out in mid August. However, due to some matters related to his daughter's university admission, Professor Wang needed to stay behind and would join us later in Xinjiang. He asked me, along with Zhensheng Dong, Jie Zhang, and our driver Yanhua Jiang, to depart first and meet in mid-August at the Xinjiang branch of the Chinese Academy of Sciences (CAS) guesthouse in Urumqi. At that time, my daughter was six and a half years old and scheduled to start first grade of elementary school on September 1st. My wife also had an aunt who worked in Hami, Xinjiang, so I decided to take advantage of the summer vacation to bring my family on a trip. We would first visit Beijing, and then take a train from there to Xinjiang to visit my wife's aunt and explore. In late July, we left Guiyang by train, heading for Beijing. After arriving in Beijing, we visited several famous landmarks, including the Forbidden City, the Summer Palace, the Great Wall at Badaling, and the Ming Tombs Reservoir. Then we took a direct express train from Beijing to Urumqi, stopping in Hami along the way. My wife had not seen her third aunt in over twenty years, so this family reunion was especially heartwarming. We stayed in Hami for a week, after which we took a train to Urumqi. In Urumqi, we toured attractions like the Tianchi Lake and various city landmarks. By mid-August, my wife and daughter returned to Hami by train, and then made their way back to Guiyang by train again at the end of the month, while I stayed in Urumqi to meet up with the other members of our field expedition.

In our geological field investigation team, there were four members: our team leader Zhonggang Wang, and the team members Zhensheng Dong, Jie Zhang, and myself. Mr. Dong was an experienced geologist who had graduated from the Beijing Institute of Geology in the mid-1960s, and Jie Zhang was a graduate student whom Professor Wang had recruited in 1986. We had an eight-seater Beijing Jeep, and our driver was a young woman from our institute's driver team named Yanhua Jiang. Originally, team leader Professor Zhonggang Wang planned to arrive in Xinjiang in mid-August, but he had to delay his trip to handle some personal matters related to his daughter's education after she failed the college entrance exam. By late August, the three of us decided to begin our fieldwork in the eastern Xinjiang region, focusing on the amazonite granite around Hami and Xingxingxia area. After conducting field research in the Xingxingxia region for a few days, we decided to take a detour to visit Dunhuang in Gansu Province, which was only about 300 kilometers away. After returning to Urumqi from Dunhuang in mid-September, we were still waiting for Professor Wang to arrive, with nothing to do but rest at the guesthouse of the Xinjiang branch of the Chinese Academy of Sciences.

Finally, on September 30, our long wait ended when Professor Wang arrived. The next day, October 1st, we took a break for National Day. On October 2, our field team set off for Altay. According to the plan, our target was the Late Hercynian granite in the mountains of Hemu Township, Burqin County, near the China-Mongolia border in northern Altay. We arrived in Altay City that evening and stayed at the Altay region guesthouse. The next day, we headed to Burqin and checked into the county government guesthouse, preparing to head into the mountains on October 4. From Burqin to Hemu Village in Hemu Township, it was about 270-280 kilometers, but local people told us the road was rough, mostly dirt and stone, and it would take an entire day by car. They also warned us that by early October, it might already be snowing in the mountains, and even if we

1987.8.新疆哈密星星峡大白石头泉考察天河石花岗岩

The author conducted a field survey of amazonite granite in Xingxingxia, Hami, Xingjiang, China in Aug 1987.

managed to get in, we might not be able to get out due to the snow making the roads impassable. Despite the warnings, Professor Wang insisted that since we had come all the way to Xinjiang, we should push ahead and at least take a look. So, after breakfast on the morning of October 4, we set out. It was a clear day, but once we left the county and entered the mountainous area, the road condition was indeed very bad. We frequently had to stop the jeep to clear rocks or water puddles from the road, and at times, we had to get out and help push the vehicle. As a result, we could only manage about 30-40 kilometers per hour. By late afternoon, around 3 or 4 p.m., the sky began to darken, and we had only covered about 170-180 kilometers, with another 100 kilometers to go before reaching Hemu. At that point, we spotted a caravanserai (horse and mule station) near a bend in the road. We decided to stop there for the night. Upon inquiring, we found out that the station did offer lodging, so we settled in.

When we asked what food was available, the host said they only had potatoes and "baursak." None of us knew what "baursak" was, and someone speculated it might be a local dish of lamb or beef, since the host family was Kazakh. After about 40-50 minutes, the host brought out our meal: a large bowl of partially cooked potato slices boiled in lamb fat, and a bundle of cold, hard, diamond-shaped dough pieces fried in lamb fat, wrapped in an old and rather dirty white cloth. It turned out that this was the baursak, a staple of Kazakh shepherds. We had no choice but to accept the local fare, especially since we hadn't eaten since breakfast. Even though Xinjiang's lamb doesn't have a strong gamey flavour, for us southerners, the taste of lamb fat in the potatoes was overwhelming, especially once the dish cooled and the flavour intensified. However, the baursak, being dry, didn't taste as strongly of lamb fat, even though it wasn't very fresh. Despite this, we were cold and hungry, and we devoured most of the potatoes and quite a few pieces of baursak in no time. After dinner, Professor Wang called the host over to settle the bill. The total cost for the five of us was ¥10 yuan for the meal (¥2 yuan per person). The host asked if we wanted breakfast the next morning, and we agreed, so he collected another ¥10 yuan for breakfast again. After dinner, the host wrapped up the leftover baursak in the same cloth, tied it up, and hung it from the ceiling above the dining table, explaining that it was to keep the mice from eating it. Then we asked where we would be sleeping, and the host informed us that they only had one large room for five or six people, with no private rooms. The cost for the room was ¥5 yuan per person per night. Since we had a female driver, we discussed the sleeping arrangements. Driver Xiao Jiang (Yanhua Jiang) said: "Let's all stay in the same room for the night. Even if there were private rooms available, I wouldn't dare sleep alone out here in the wilderness!" So, that night, all of us slept fully clothed in the same room. In the middle of the night, someone peeked out the window and shouted: "Oh no! It's snowing outside!" This woke everyone up, and we rushed to look outside. Sure enough, heavy snow was falling, covering the mountains and ground in white. Professor Wang exclaimed: "It seems we're out of luck this time! We'd better leave first thing in the morning, or we might really get stuck here!" The next morning, after a quick breakfast of potatoes and baursak, we hurriedly set off in the snow. The roads in the Altay Mountains are mostly black mud, and while passable in dry weather, they become extremely slippery when it rains or snows. Our driver, Xiao Hua (as we affectionately called Yanhua Jiang), was still a novice with only three years of driving experience, and she struggled to navigate the slippery roads. The jeep often got stuck in the mud or blocked by rocks, and we had to frequently get out to help clear obstacles or push the vehicle. As we descended to lower elevations, the snow turned to rain, and we stumbled and slid our way through the mud for eight or nine exhausting hours before finally reaching Burqin County Town around 4 or 5 p.m. By the time we arrived at the county guesthouse, we were all completely drenched and covered in mud, looking like a group of mud-coated monkeys. Fortunately, we could finally take a hot shower and change into clean clothes at the guesthouse.

The field geological investigation work in the Altay region of Northern Xinjiang was no longer feasible, but Professor Zhonggang Wang believed that the situation in the Western Tianshan area might be better. So, after leaving the Altar region, we decided to head southwest through Fuhai, Karamay, Kuitun, Wusu, and Jinghe, and then across the Guozigou Valley toward Yining City (伊宁市). However, by mid-October, the Yili region had already experienced heavy snowfall. Our vehicle got stuck in Guozigou for four to five hours due to snow blocking the road, and we arrived late in the capital city of the Yili (伊犁) region, Yining City (伊宁市). After resting for two days in Yining, we drove to Xinyuan County for fieldwork. Unfortunately, it was also snowing heavily there, and the mountains were covered in a blanket of white. Despite the challenging conditions, we decided to proceed with the planned work in the mountains. However, once we were on the mountain, the granite outcrops were completely covered by snow, so we had to use geological hammers to scrape away the snow just to collect a few granite samples. Although we were technically a geological field team, our personal equipment was quite rudimentary. We had no specialized work clothes or climbing boots for the mountains. Each of us was only equipped with a geological bag, a hammer, a compass, and a sun hat. Since we had left Guiyang in the summer, we were dressed for the warmer seasons, wearing light clothing and sneakers. By the time we arrived in Northern Xinjiang, it was already winter, and our outfits were neither warm nor waterproof. In the mountains, it snowed continuously, and once we descended, the snow turned to rain. After just half a day of work, we were soaked to the skin. Faced with such harsh weather conditions, Professor Wang had no choice but to call off the fieldwork and drive back to Yining City. On the way back, around three or four o'clock in the afternoon, we encountered an incident on the road. A large truck carrying coal was driving ahead of us, and it seemed that the driver had spotted our young and attractive woman driver, Xiao Hua, in his rearview mirror. Perhaps wanting to play a prank or for some other reason, he began driving in the middle of the road at a slow speed of 30-40 km/h, preventing us from overtaking. Even though Xiao Hua honked repeatedly, the truck driver ignored her, refusing to give us the way. After a long day in the field, cold, wet, and hungry, we were eager to pass the coal truck and get back to the guesthouse for rest and food. When the truck finally moved slightly to the left, leaving just enough space on the right, Xiao Hua attempted to overtake it. However, just as our car was parallel to the truck, the truck driver suddenly accelerated and swerved to the right, causing our jeep's side mirror to be knocked off by the truck's body. We were forced to stop and pick up the shattered mirror from the ground, cursing our bad luck. Since trying to overtake on the right was technically a traffic violation, we couldn't report the incident to the police station, as the fault lay with our driver. So, we grudgingly followed the coal truck for another half an hour at a snail's pace until it finally turned off onto another road, allowing us to speed up. Based on our past experiences, we had always found people in Xinjiang to be warm and hospitable, especially when they saw we were visitors from inland China. During our earlier fieldwork in Hami of Eastern Xingjiang, for example, when our vehicle broke down, local drivers would often stop to help us with repairs. However, this particular truck driver seemed to be the exception. As the saying goes: "In a forest full of trees, you'll find all kinds of birds."

After spending two more days resting in Yining, we drove back to Urumqi. By then, it was late October, but Professor Wang was still reluctant to call it quits. He was determined not to return to Guiyang empty-handed after coming all the way to Xinjiang. So, he decided to head to the Eastern Tianshan region in Hami area for further exploration. We spent another ten days traveling through places like Barkol, Mulei, and Qitai in Eastern Xinjiang, but no matter where we went, it snowed everywhere. We couldn't gather any ideal geological samples, and the entire experience was physically exhausting. By middle November 1987, after having explored the Altay region in the north and both the Eastern and Western Tianshan mountains, Professor Wang finally accepted that the weather conditions were simply too harsh for fieldwork. He decided it was time to end the expedition and plan for the following year. By the time we returned to Guiyang, it was already late November.

During that month-long period from early October to middle November, we endured harsh conditions with snow and wind while traveling across Northern Xinjiang, covering thousands of kilometers from north to south, and from west to east. Due to the late season, our fieldwork results were poor, and the entire experience was extremely tiring. To make matters worse, our driver, Xiao Hua, was inexperienced and lacked knowledge about vehicle maintenance. Whenever the car encountered minor issues, she didn't know how to handle them. In particular, the vehicle's tires, which had inner tubes, frequently got punctured while driving on the rugged mountain roads. Replacing or repairing the inner tubes wasn't just a technical task, but also required considerable physical effort. Since Xiao Hua didn't have the strength to manage it, the task of changing and fixing tires naturally fell on the male members of the team. One of the biggest challenges we faced was inflating the tires after repairing the inner tubes. Without a proper air pump, we were left with only a hand pump meant for inflating basketballs. Every time we had to inflate a tire, the four of us would take turns, each pumping 1,000 to 2,000 strokes before switching off. To fully inflate a single tire, it took at least 25 to 30 minutes of continuous effort. Tire punctures occurred about once every three to five days, and by the end of the expedition, after countless tire changes and repairs, each of us had become an expert in tire repair, able to complete the task in just 30 to 40 minutes from start to finish.

(II)

Given the lessons learned from the 1987 fieldwork experience, Professor Zhonggang Wang was much more cautious when planning the 1988 summer field expedition, particularly regarding timing and the choice of driver. First, he scheduled the expedition to begin in early July, and second, he selected an experienced driver, Chengjun Wei, to handle the driving. The high summer temperatures in July and August were the best time for fieldwork in the mountainous Altay region of Xinjiang. Unlike last year, when the late start and reliance on a young, less experienced female driver caused numerous difficulties, this year's expedition was expected to go more smoothly due to the earlier start and the skilled driver.

In early July 1988, our team of four (Professor Zhonggang Wang, Zhensheng Dong, driver Wei, and myself) set off from Guiyang. We first flew to Beijing for some administrative matters, and then continued on to Xinjiang, arriving in Urumqi by mid-July. Since the Xinjiang branch of the Chinese Academy of Sciences in Urumqi served as a logistical base for field expeditions, the vehicle we used for fieldwork had been stored in the branch's garage since the previous autumn. Once we arrived, Wei retrieved the car, performed a few minor repairs, and we were ready to begin our work.

In mid-July, we arrived in Altay and met another fieldwork team from the isotope geochemistry research department, led by Aiqin Hu, also from our institute. Professor Wang decided that our two teams should combine forces for a few days to conduct joint fieldwork in the area around Altay City. With the combined teams, we now had eight or nine people and two vehicles, including four senior geologists and three young researchers like myself. This presented a great opportunity for us younger team members to learn from the experienced geologists. Whenever we encountered an interesting rock during our fieldwork, we would pick it up and ask the senior geologists to identify it. For example, we asked about the differences between granitic gneiss and biotite granite, or how to distinguish metamorphic rocks from plagiogranites. The veteran geologists were always patient and took the time to explain these concepts to us. During our downtime, we also chatted with our driver, Mr. Wei. We asked him why, during last year's expedition, we frequently experienced flat tires, whereas this year, under his driving, such incidents were much less frequent. Mr. Wei explained: "Fieldwork involves driving on mountain roads, which are generally in poor condition. This requires the driver to adjust the vehicle's speed and choose the best path based on the road conditions, avoiding potholes and rocks as much as possible to reduce the risk of a flat tire. Additionally, the driver should always carry at least two spare tires and a pump. If a flat does occur, we can simply swap the tire and keep moving, saving a lot of time. At the end of each day, I also inspect the vehicle thoroughly, and if I spot any issues or potential problems, I take the car to a repair shop for maintenance, ensuring it's always in good working condition." It was clear from this experience that having a seasoned driver was essential for a successful field expedition. With Wei's expertise, the fieldwork proceeded much more smoothly and with fewer interruptions.

After about a week of joint fieldwork around Altay City, our teams parted ways. According to Professor Wang's plan, our primary objective for this year was to study the Hercynian granite in the Kanas region near Hemu Township in the northern Altay Mountains. One morning in late July, we departed from Buerjin County and reached the village of Hemu by the end of the day without any issues. Hemu is the most remote township in Buerjin County, Altay, Xinjiang. Despite being the location of the township government, Hemu village was quite small at that time, with only about 20 to 30 households. The residents of Hemu village were mostly Tuvans, an ethnic group of Mongolian descent. Legend has it that the Tuvans in Hemu are a remnant of Genghis Khan's westward expedition. For generations, they have lived as hunters and herders. Their homes were typically built by stacking logs with a diameter of about 30 to 40 cm. Although these log houses appeared primitive, they were sturdy and well-insulated, keeping warm in the winter and cool in the summer. Some of these structures could last for centuries without rotting. Hemu village was situated in a broad river valley at the foot of the Altai Mountains, with the snowcapped peaks clearly visible to the north. The Hemu River, formed by meltwater from the mountain snow, flowed quietly past the village. The area surrounding the village, within a radius of about two or three kilometers, was mostly grassland, which then transitioned into dense virgin forests. Our fieldwork target was the ancient granite exposed in the ridges of the Altai Mountains upstream along the Hemu River.

Now, Hemu Village is a renowned tourist destination both domestically and internationally. However, in the 1980s, not only was it unknown in China, but even within Xinjiang, few people had heard of it. Back then, most people only knew of Kanas Lake, largely due to the widespread rumours of giant red fish sightings there. These tales sparked curiosity, and many would drive to Kanas Lake in the summer, hoping to catch a glimpse of the famous big red fish. Since Hemu Village was only about more than ten kilometers from Kanas Lake, visitors to the lake would often stop by Hemu out of convenience. Once they arrived, they were struck by the untouched natural beauty and unique cultural scenery of the village, realizing it was a rare gem for tourists. Word quickly spread, and before long, visitors flocked to Hemu, regardless of whether they spotted the red fish at Kanas Lake. The idea was: "Since we've come all this way to Kanas, why not explore Hemu too?" Eventually, as more and more people visited Hemu, it gained recognition. Later, the local government improved the infrastructure, making travel to Kanas and Hemu much easier, and the village's fame only grew. Hemu Village has since become a key highlight on Xinjiang's tourism map.

We arrived at Hemu Village in the afternoon around 3 or 4 p.m. After settling in at a local villager's home near the township office, we still had plenty of daylight left. Professor Zhonggang Wang wasted no time and headed straight to the township office to inquire about hiring a guide to take us into the mountains. Not long after, Professor Wang returned, reporting that the township chief wasn't there, as he had gone to a meeting in the county. The township staff further explained that most of the young and able-bodied men from the village had gone up into the mountains to cut grass for winter livestock feed due to the good weather. With no one familiar with the area available to guide us, Professor Wang sought advice from Zhensheng Dong and me. He said: "The township staff said the chief is away and may not return for some time. Even if he comes back, it might still be difficult to find us a guide. It wasn't easy for us to get here, and sitting around waiting doesn't seem like a good plan. I suggest we head into the mountains on our own, following the Hemu River until we reach the granite outcrops. What do you think?" Being new to fieldwork, I had no particular suggestions, so Professor Wang turned to Mr. Zhensheng Dong for his opinion. Mr. Dong said: "The weather's been great, and there's no point in waiting if we can't find a guide. Hence, I agreed with you. Let's go into the mountains ourselves." Professor Wang said: "That's great! Then. No need to wait for the township chief. Tomorrow morning, we'll head into the mountains on our own." With that decision made, we prepared for the journey.

The next morning, after breakfast, we packed up. Knowing the journey might take longer than expected, Professor Wang advised me to bring cooking gear and food in case we had to spend the night in the mountains. I packed a large field bag with a cooking pot, some dried noodles, half a bottle of soy sauce, some salt, a few cans of luncheon meat, and matches. Before leaving, I borrowed an axe from our host, just in case, and made sure to pack my personal field equipment: a geological hammer, compass, flashlight, and other essentials. Since there was a simple village road that extended three to four kilometers to the edge of the forest behind the village, our driver, Mr. Wei, drove us to the end of the road at the forest's edge. As we parted ways, Wei jokingly said: "Make sure you're back early tomorrow. I'll have dinner ready for you guys!" We waved goodbye, promising, "See you tomorrow!" and then set off on foot into the forest.

After entering the primeval forest, we discovered a narrow winding path along the Hemu River. So, we followed this trail deeper into the forest. Shortly after entering, we immediately felt mosquitoes biting us. I said: "Huh! That's strange! How can there be mosquitoes biting in broad daylight?" Professor Wang explained: "Back when we were working on pegmatite in Koktokay (which is in Fuyun County, Altay Prefecture, Xinjiang), we also noticed that even during the day, there were many mosquitoes in the woods, and their bites were particularly fierce. I'm afraid we're going to be bitten by mosquitoes today in this forest too!" At first, there were not many mosquitoes, but as we ventured deeper into the forest, their numbers began to grow. These mosquitoes were generally twice the size of the ones we see in the interior south regions, with long legs and antennae, and their bodies were marked with grey-black or grey-white spots. We called them "flower mosquitoes," something we had rarely seen in southern China. These mosquitoes seemed to be fearless. Once they landed on our faces or hands, they wouldn't budge even when we tried to shoo them away, and their bites were painful. The deeper we went into the mountains, the more numerous the mosquitoes became, swarming us like a disturbed hornet's nest. To prevent being bitten, we wore canvas geology hats on our heads, canvas gloves on our hands, and carried washcloths in one hand to brush away the mosquitoes, while holding a branch with leaves in the other hand, swatting the mosquitoes around our heads and faces in turns. When the three of us entered the forest, they let me walk at the front, Mr. Dong stayed in the middle, and Professor Wang brought up the rear. I thought they might have arranged this way to take care of me as a novice, so I took the lead without hesitation. After walking for about one or two hours, the narrow path became increasingly indistinct. Without pushing aside the brambles and examining the path carefully, it felt like there was no way forward. To scout the way, despite being bitten badly by mosquitoes, I switched the branch in my right hand, previously used for swatting mosquitoes, to a wooden stick. I used it to sweep the dew off the shrubs on both sides of the path while pushing aside the thorny bushes to check the trail carefully. In this way, I thought, even if we encountered snakes or other wild animals, they would hear the noise and slip away beforehand, making our journey safer. I had heard that the mountains of Xinjiang were home to many venomous snakes, and their venom was so potent that they could kill a horse. Therefore, in such a primeval forest, one must be extra cautious. Usually, we talk about the idiom "Beating the grass to scare the snake," today we were putting it into practice. However, the biggest threat we faced today remains mosquito bites. Because there were too many mosquitoes, it didn't take long before fresh red bloodstains started appearing on the washcloth used to swat them. These were from mosquitoes that had fully sucked blood from our faces or necks and were then squashed by the cloth. The mosquitoes' blood stained the towel. What made these mosquitoes particularly dangerous was that, even though we wore hats and gloves, and kept waving our hands to brush them off, they still managed to land on our heads or gloves and bite through the fabric, making our hands and scalps ache. In this gruelling and extreme situation, we pressed on with sheer willpower, trekking for nearly ten hours without stopping to rest. Around 6 or 7 pm in the evening, we finally reached a small patch of open ground by the Hemu River, about the size of two or three basketball courts. In the center of the grassland, there was a fire pit that seemed to have been used not long ago, suggesting someone had camped there before. Since the sun had not yet fully set, we could see that the granite outcrops of the Altai Mountain range were still several dozen kilometers away. We decided to set up camp there for the night. If we continued, we might face more mosquitoes as it got dark, and we would have trouble finding our way. Thus, Professor Wang, our team leader, suggested, "Let's pitch a tent here and camp for the night."

Once we stopped on the open ground by the river, the axe borrowed from the local villagers came in handy. I used it to chop down some small tree trunks to build a frame for a makeshift shelter, then gathered pine branches to cover the top, and laid a bed of dried pine needles and grass on the ground. Our makeshift camp was ready. While I was setting up the shelter, Professor Wang and Dong collected a large pile of dry wood and twigs from the forest, which I split into two or three-foot-long firewood logs. Professor Wang and Dong then lit a large fire at the entrance of the shelter. To ward off wild animals and to keep warm, we needed to keep the bonfire burning all night. Worried that we might run out of firewood, I went back into the forest to gather more dry trees, chopped them into shorter pieces, and stacked them beside the shelter entrance. When we first lit the fire, the smoke was so thick that it drove away all the mosquitoes and insects. Once the fire was roaring, the number of mosquitoes around us noticeably decreased. However, the most embarrassing thing that day was when we had to relieve ourselves. It was nearly impossible to manage---one hand holding a branch to swat the mosquitoes around the head and face, while the other hand was busy fending off the ones biting around the waist and below. We could only finish quickly and clumsily, and the awkwardness was indescribable. Not long after, Dong finished cooking some noodles, and the three of us enjoyed the meal with canned luncheon meat, chatting and laughing. This dinner felt especially satisfying, as we were all exhausted and starving after a whole day in the forest. After dinner, we sat around the fire, casually chatting. Only then did we notice that all three of us had large red and itchy mosquito bites on our faces, necks, and hands. Perhaps my skin was better back then because I only had some small, itchy red bumps that disappeared in a few days. When it was time to sleep, I lay down near the fire pit at the entrance of the shelter, while Professor Wang and Dong slept inside. Since we didn't have sleeping gear, we lay fully dressed on the pine needles and dry grass, wrapping our heads and feet tightly with towels and clothes to protect against the mosquitoes; otherwise, it would have been impossible to sleep. Lying by the entrance, I had the extra duty of getting up occasionally to add firewood to the fire pit to keep the fire from dying out. Around midnight, I was awakened by a faint noise outside the shelter. After getting up, I realized that the fire pit was almost out of wood, so I quickly woke them up, and while adding more wood, I told them there seemed to be some animal activity around us. We all rushed out of the shelter, grabbed our flashlights, and shined them wildly around the area while shouting loudly, our voices echoing throughout the valley.

The next morning, after we got up, the fire was still burning. We reheated the leftover noodles from the previous night, quickly ate breakfast, and prepared to set off again. Looking at the granite outcrops in the distance, Professor Wang suddenly said: "It looks like we've only covered atmost thirty kilometers yesterday. That outcrop seems still several dozens of kilometers away. Even if we walk for another day, I'm not sure we'll reach it. Besides, the path is becoming hard to follow, and the mosquitoes are overwhelming. I suggest we stop advancing today and look for some large boulders by the river to collect samples and head back." Dong and I were overjoyed to hear this and agreed: "Yes, let's do that! The forest path is really too tough!" So, we split up along the river, collecting over twenty samples, which we loaded into my large geology bag.

On the way back, we faced the same difficulties. My bag, which already contained cooking utensils, food, and other items, now weighed over forty pounds with the added granite samples. But since I was young and had grown up doing farm work in the countryside, I was used to carrying heavy loads and didn't feel particularly tired. As I kept the lead, occasionally, I would walk fast enough to pull ahead of them, so sometimes I would stop to wait for them by the side of the trail. In the afternoon, hunger began to set in, so I would stop from time to time to eat wild berries along the roadside. Finally, around four or five o'clock in the afternoon, we emerged from the forest and reached the open fields at the edge. Hemu Village was in sight, but by then, the sky had become overcast, and a strong wind began whipping through the landscape---clearly, a storm was coming. We were still three or four kilometers from the village. I quickened my pace, breaking into a jog, hoping to reach the village before the rain hit. Unfortunately, the storm arrived faster than expected, and when I was about one kilometer from the village, the downpour began. Glancing back, I saw the others were about 500 meters behind me. By the time I reached our lodgings at the villager's house, I was completely drenched. A short while later, they arrived, equally soaked to the bone.

When the three of us finally made it back to our lodgings in Hemu, we were greeted by the delicious aroma of food coming from the kitchen. It turned out that our driver, Mr. Wei, had prepared a pot of chicken soup. We asked where he had gotten the chicken, and he replied: "I knew you guys would be exhausted after your trip into the mountains, so I bought two old hens from a local family to make chicken soup. I also picked up a few bottles of beer from the small shop near the township office so we can celebrate when you get back." Mr. Wei also shared some news from the day we had been away. He said: "The township chief returned from his meeting in the county yesterday afternoon. When he heard that you had already gone into the mountains, he asked me if you had taken a guide and mosquito nets. I told him you hadn't, and he said, 'Oh no! That's dangerous! There are black bears in the mountains, and hunters set bear traps up there. Without a guide, if someone accidentally steps on one of those traps, it could break their leg. Also, the mosquitoes in the forest are vicious; without nets, they could bite someone to death. You should never go into the mountains without a guide and proper mosquito protection---it's extremely risky!'" Hearing Wei recount the township chief's words, the three of us couldn't help but feel a sense of fear and relief. Thankfully, we had made the smart decision to turn back halfway. If we had continued wandering in the forest for another three or four days, who knows what could have happened? After we changed into dry clothes and freshened up, we sat down to enjoy Wei's delicious chicken soup and beer. Between the four of us, we devoured nearly both chickens, thoroughly enjoying our feast. Later that evening, as we reflected on our adventure, Professor Zhonggang Wang remarked: "Xiao Wu, I didn't realize you had such strong survival skills! It seems you're quite suited for fieldwork." I responded: "Professor Wang, I've been used to climbing mountains and trekking through forests since I was a kid---this was nothing!" Professor Wang nodded thoughtfully and said: "Honestly, this was a very dangerous trip. We completely underestimated how many mosquitoes there would be, and the township chief's warning about the bear traps made it even scarier. We were lucky we turned back when we did. If we had kept going, who knows what might have happened in that forest? In fact, even if I had left ¥500 yuan back at our campsite, I wouldn't dare go back to retrieve it!" Professor Wang's sentiment was heartfelt, especially considering that at the time, a researcher's monthly salary was less than ¥200 yuan, so ¥500 yuan was no small amount. After reflecting on the risks we had faced over the past couple of days, Professor Wang decided we deserved some compensation for our hard work. As the team leader, he gave each of us ¥60 yuan as a bonus.

(Ⅲ)

After completing our fieldwork at Hemu in the Altai Mountains, it was already late August. We then moved on to the eastern part of Altay, around Fuyun and Qinghe counties, to continue our research. One afternoon, around August 25, the three of us were conducting fieldwork in the mountains of Fuyun County, as usual, with me leading the way. We were walking along a sloped hillside, intending to cross a small stream and head toward a granite outcrop on the opposite ridge. The vegetation on both sides of the stream was lush, with grass over half a meter tall. By this point, my sneakers had been worn smooth from all the hiking. As I lifted my right foot to leap across the stream, I landed on a steep stone slab hidden by the tall grass. My right foot slipped the moment it touched the slab, and I slid one to two meters down the incline. As I fell, my right hand instinctively reached out to brace myself. In that moment,

I heard a sharp "crack," and an intense pain shot through my wrist. Soon after, the injured area began to swell. Seeing this, Professor Wang hurried over and asked: "Xiao Wu, are you okay? How's your hand?" Though my wrist was swollen and painful, I didn't think it was too serious at the time. I assumed I had simply strained a tendon when I braced myself against the stone, so I replied: "I'm fine! I think probably just sprained it---it'll get better in a few days." That evening, when we returned to our lodgings in Beitun, the pain in my wrist had become so severe that my right hand even could no longer hold chopsticks to eat dinner. Initially, I planned to visit the local hospital the next morning, but as luck would have it, there was a small clinic nearby that specialized in treating injuries from falls. After dinner, I decided to go check it out. When I entered the clinic, I noticed that the doctor spoke with a Sichuan accent, so I started chatting with him in our hometown dialect. As soon as he learned that I was from Guizhou and was in Xinjiang for geological fieldwork, the atmosphere became friendlier. The doctor, surnamed Chen, was in his fifties and had been practicing medicine in Xinjiang for over a decade. After asking about my injury and examining my swollen wrist, he concluded that it wasn't a fracture but likely a sprain. He prepared some fresh herbs, mashed them into a paste, and applied it to the swollen area before wrapping it with a bandage. He also tied a sling to support my arm. Finally, he gave me a prescription for herbal medicine to soak in alcohol, which he said would be effective in treating my injury. After all this, Dr. Chen only charged me ¥10 yuan for the treatment. Later, when we returned to Guiyang, I got the herbal medicine, made the tincture, and it worked remarkably well. After injuring my wrist, Professor Wang asked if I wanted to rest at the guesthouse for a few days. I declined, as our field team only had three members, and I didn't want to leave the team short-handed. Since we had a car, we were always on the move, one day in this county, and possibly in another the next. Although I couldn't do much with my injured hand, I didn't want to stay behind, so I continued to accompany Professor Wang and Dong on our fieldwork. While I couldn't contribute much, being together as a team kept things lively.

At the end of August, we drove to the city of Karamay, a new city in northern Xinjiang that had grown because of the oil industry. Though Karamay was relatively small, with a population of only a few hundred thousand, the city was wellplanned, with uniform buildings and very clean streets. Even the public restrooms were different from those in other cities, giving the city a refreshing and unique vibe. This level of organization and cleanliness wasn't seen in any other city in Xinjiang. After we arrived, Professor Zhonggang Wang decided that we would rest for two days. During the break, I decided to visit the Karamay People's Hospital to consult an orthopaedic doctor. Although the herbal treatments from Dr. Chen in Beitun had helped a little, the pain in my right wrist had not subsided. At the hospital, the orthopaedic doctor took an X-ray, and the image revealed that I had a distal radial fracture in my wrist, with a crack clearly visible, two or three centimetres long. No wonder the pain hadn't subsided---it was indeed a bone fracture. The doctor immediately set my wrist in a cast and prescribed me some painkillers. He instructed me to return to the hospital in two weeks to have the cast removed. I explained to the doctor that we were conducting geological fieldwork in Xinjiang and would likely be in another location two weeks later, making it difficult to return. The doctor said: "You can have the cast removed at any other hospital, or even do it yourself, as long as you're careful not to re-injure the area." He also advised me that after the cast was removed, I shouldn't lift heavy objects with my right hand until the fracture was fully healed and recommended a gradual rehabilitation process.

In early September, we arrived in the Ili region (伊犁地区). Even though it was autumn, the weather was perfect, with sunny days and temperatures in the mid-20s Celsius. The area was filled with the fragrance of ripe fruits, making our fieldwork especially pleasant. Everywhere we went, the skies were clear and crisp, and the mountains were full of wild fruit such as apples, apricots, and pears. We picked and ate the fruits from the trees wherever we went. By mid-September, we had successfully completed our fieldwork in Ili. Upon returning to Urumqi, I went to the hospital to have my wrist cast removed, and by the end of September, we had returned to Guiyang. Recovering from my wrist fracture in Xinjiang was a long process. In the first few years after the injury, I couldn't lift anything heavy with my right hand. Even carrying slightly heavy items would cause pain. Additionally, my wrist would ache a day or two before any major changes in the weather, such as when it had been sunny for a while and was about to rain. It took almost ten years for my wrist to fully recover, allowing me to lift heavy objects without pain.

Our geological fieldwork in Xinjiang spanned the summers of 1987 and 1988, and we traversed nearly every county in northern Xinjiang. There were many interesting experiences, but due to space limitations, I've only recounted a few notable moments. Overall, Xinjiang left me with the impression that it is vast and beautiful. With an area of 1.6 million square kilometers, it accounts for one-sixth of China's landmass and is the largest province in the country. There's a saying, "You don't know how big China is until you visit Xinjiang," and it's only after being there that you truly understand what it means for a country to be vast and resource-rich. Xinjiang is a treasure trove, abundant in oil, natural gas, and many other mineral resources. It's a truly wonderful place, and we must thank our ancestors, particularly General Zongtang Zuo, for ensuring that such a precious land remained part of China.

(IV)

In the first half of 1988, before embarking on our fieldwork in Xinjiang, I had collaborated with Professor Qizhong Wen from the Quaternary Research Department to write a grant proposal for the National Natural Science Foundation of China. The project was titled "A Comparative Study of the Chemical Compositions of the Malan Loess in the Middle Reaches of the Yellow River and the Crustal Clark Values." Since I had never independently researched loess before, I wasn't confident about leading the application, so we submitted the proposal with Professor Wen as the primary applicant and myself as the second. We submitted the proposal through the institute's science and technology office to the National Natural Science Foundation. Professor Wen was a seasoned expert in Quaternary research and loess studies, having studied under the father of Chinese loess research, Dongsheng Liu, in the 1960s. Thanks to Professor Wen's expertise, our proposal was approved later that year, with a funding allocation of ¥70,000 yuan for research spanning three years, from early 1989 to the end of 1991.

According to the project timeline, we were scheduled to begin fieldwork on the loess in early 1989. So, in late April of that year, Professor Wen and I began planning for fieldwork on the Loess Plateau in northwestern China. Our research plan started in the Lanzhou area of Gansu Province, with the aim of conducting six or seven large cross-sections from west to east across the Loess Plateau. We intended to collect samples from various points across the plateau, stretching eastward to the mid-western regions of Shanxi Province. In mid-May, a team of four, including Professor Wen and me, flew to Beijing, intending to finalize our plans before heading to Lanzhou, Gansu. At that time, Beijing was in the midst of the student protests in Tiananmen Square, sparked by the death of Yaobang Hu (胡耀邦), who was the former General Secretary of Chinese Communist Party Committee. Students were holding sit-ins and demonstrations, and the protests had spread to various sectors of society, including some government staffs who joined the students' movement. The streets near Tiananmen Square were often packed with crowds supporting the students' cause. However, we were preoccupied with our upcoming fieldwork and didn't have the time or focus to observe the movement closely. After two or three days in Beijing, we boarded a train bound for Lanzhou, Gansu Province.

We arrived in Lanzhou around May 20, 1989. By this time, our institute's driver, Mr. Su Tian, had also arrived in Lanzhou with our vehicle, as we had previously arranged to meet him at the guesthouse of the Chinese Academy of Sciences' Lanzhou Branch around this date. The day after our arrival, we officially began our fieldwork. On the first day, we departed from Lanzhou, heading south through Dongxiang, Linxia, and into Hezuo before reaching Min County, where we stayed overnight at the Min County guesthouse. Every 25 to 30 kilometers along the county road, we stopped to collect a 600 to 700-gram sample of loess from the surrounding terrain. Our sampling process adhered to strict requirements and standards. We did not collect surface soil or deep layers of buried loess; instead, we specifically sampled the loess located 30 to 40 centimeters below the surface, known as Malan Loess. Our first day's work covered a small cross-section from north to south. On the second day, we traveled north from Min County to Weiyuan, then eastward to Longxi, before heading north again through Dingxi and Huining. We continued northeast into the southern part of Ningxia's Xihaigu region (i.e., Xiji County, Haiyuan County, and Guyuan County were abbreviated Xihaigu region), an area known for its poverty. Compared to Gansu's Dingxi region, however, the natural environment in Xihaigu region was relatively better. Dingxi suffered from a severe lack of water, with no rivers in the area, making access to drinking water for both people and livestock extremely difficult. The Dingxi Loess Plateau was also mostly barren, with little vegetation. When our vehicle drove along the roads, the dust it kicked up would rise 20 or 30 meters into the air and linger for 10 to 20 minutes before settling. The local residents relied entirely on rainwater stored in cisterns for drinking. Water was so scarce that the same water used for washing one's face in the morning was saved for washing feet in the evening, and then used again to water the livestock. For the locals, water was truly "as precious as oil."

Occasionally, we saw wheat growing in the fields, but the crops were stunted, standing only about a foot tall, with short, thin heads of grain. It was clear that the harvest would be meagre. In our view, Gansu's Dingxi region was one of the most impoverished areas in northwestern China. While passing through Huining County, we stayed at the county government's guesthouse for one night. Huining is historically significant as the site where

the three main forces of the Red Army met during the Long March, and the town has a towering monument commemorating this event. One would expect such a place to receive substantial government support and development, but at the time, the town didn't even have running water. The guesthouse had to rely on horse-drawn carts to fetch water from far away, and the water available for washing was murky and yellow. As for the Xi (Xiji), Hai (Haiyuan), and Gu (Guyuan) regions of Ningxia, the altitude is relatively high, but the natural landscape is much better compared to Dingxi in Gansu. Although Xihaigu is a mountainous area, trees and grass can grow on the mountain tops, and where there is grass, there can be grazing. Thus, the local people's living conditions do not appear to be particularly impoverished. As we continued driving northward from Xihaigu, the altitude gradually decreased. By the time we reached Tongxin County, the area had completely transformed into a plain. If we were to continue north, we would reach the regions of Wuzhong and Yinchuan in Ningxia. This area is a Yellow River floodplain formed by sediment deposited by the river's waters. With the Yin Mountains to the north acting as a natural barrier, the climate here is mild, and the soil is fertile, making it a uniquely prosperous land in the northwest, often referred to as the **"A Little Jiangnan beyond the Great Wall** (塞北的小江南)."** We stayed one night at the guesthouse of the Tongxin County Government and conducted sampling surveys the following day. There were vast farmlands here, with the wheat growing tall and robust. If a person stepped into the fields, it would be almost impossible to see them among the wheat stalks. At that time, our field investigation in Ningxia stopped at Tongxin County because if we were to go further north to places like Zhongwei, the loess there would no longer be entirely aeolian (wind-blown) in origin but would mainly be fluvial. That is to say, the loess north of Tongxin County is not predominantly transported by wind but is more likely formed by sediment deposited by the Yellow River. This fluvial loess clearly falls outside the scope of our research, as our focus is on aeolian Malan Loess.

After concluding our investigation in Tongxin County, we drove south into the Liupan Mountains, located on the border between Ningxia and Gansu. The Liupan Mountains gained fame due to a poem written by Chairman Mao during the Long March when the Red Army crossed the mountains. We had initially imagined that this area, located deep in the northwest, would be barren and desolate. However, upon entering the

Liupan Mountains, we were greeted by vast expanses of pristine forests, which left us perplexed. We wondered how such rich vegetation could exist in the typically arid and rain-deprived Loess Plateau region. Sensing our confusion, Professor Qizhong Wen, a seasoned researcher of the Quaternary period's paleoenvironment and paleoclimate, explained that the Liupan Mountains are located in a transitional zone between the temperate and semi-arid regions. The area benefits from a mix of continental and maritime monsoon climate influences, resulting in significantly higher rainfall compared to surrounding regions, with annual precipitation reaching 600-700 mm. This abundant rainfall has allowed the Liupan Mountains to become an ecological "island" in the region, preserving their ancient forest cover. Professor Wen also noted that the Liupan Mountains held strategic importance throughout history, serving as a key point along the eastern route of the ancient Silk Road. The area's cool and pleasant climate during the summer months earned it the nickname "the green pearl of the Loess Plateau." Historical records also show that Genghis Khan once stationed his troops here to rest and regroup during his western campaigns and eventually passed away in this region.

After leaving the Liupan Mountains, we entered Gansu's Qingyang region. Located on the eastern edge of Gansu Province, Qingyang is also known as "Longdong (陇东)" (Eastern Gansu). It is home to the largest loess plateau in the region, the Dongzhi Plateau (董志塬), which is considered the world's largest and most intact loess plateau. With its vast area and thick loess layers, the plateau has earned the title "The First Loess Plateau under Heaven." In addition, the Ziwuling secondary forest in the Qingyang region, covering over four million acres, is the largest water-conservation forest on the Loess Plateau, often referred to as the "natural reservoir" of the region. The area's flat terrain, fertile soil, and abundant resources have made it Gansu's grain basket since ancient times.

After completing our loess research in the Qingyang region of Gansu, we continued south, passing through Heshui and Ning County, eventually crossing into Shaanxi Province to conduct further investigations in Changwu, Binxian, and Qianxian. This region is densely populated and known for its thriving agriculture and industry, traditionally referred to as the "*Eight*

Hundred Li of Qin Chuan" (八百里秦川) (Qin Plain). The Qin Plain, also known as the **Guanzhong Plain** (关中平原), is an alluvial plain formed by sediment deposited by the Wei River. The region's mild climate and fertile soil made it a critical agricultural base for the rise of the Qin civilization and the eventual unification of China by Qin Shi Huang (秦始皇). The name *"Eight Hundred Li of Qin Chuan"* originated from this. As such, it is also regarded as one of the cradles of Chinese civilization.

After finishing our investigations along the Binxian, Qianxian, Liquan, and Xianyang counties, we continued north, passing through Jingyang, Sanyuan, and Tongchuan, before arriving in Yijun, Huangling, Luochuan, and Yan'an. While in Huangling County, we stayed at the local government guesthouse for a night and took the opportunity to visit the nearby *Mausoleum of the Yellow Emperor* (黄帝陵). The Yellow Emperor, along with the *Yan Emperor* (炎帝), is considered one of the founding ancestors of the Chinese people, which is why the Chinese often refer to themselves as the *descendants of Yan and Huang* (炎黄子孙). It is said that before the reign of the Yellow Emperor, the land was ruled by the Yan Emperor. However, *Chiyou* (蚩尤), the leader of the Jiuli tribe, sought to overthrow the Yan Emperor and take his place. As a result, the Yan Emperor allied with the Yellow Emperor to resist Chiyou. The two sides eventually fought a decisive battle at Zhuolu, where Chiyou was defeated and killed. Afterwards, the Yellow Emperor became the supreme leader of the Hua tribe, leading the Huaxia (华夏) people out of the barbaric era and into the age of civilization. After the Yellow Emperor's death, a mausoleum was built for him on Qiaoshan Mountain, north of Huangling County in Shaanxi Province, along with a temple for worship. The Yellow Emperor's Mausoleum is located on the mountainside of Qiaoshan Mount, about one kilometer north of the county town, with its back against Qiaoshan and facing southeast. The Ju River surrounds the foot of the mountain on three sides. Legend has it that the Yellow Emperor ascended to heaven upon his death, and this mausoleum serves only as a symbolic tomb for his clothing and belongings. The mausoleum is grand and imposing (standing 3.6 meters high, with a circumference of 48 meters), earning the title of the *"First Mausoleum Under Heaven* (天下第一陵)." Surrounding the tomb are tens of thousands of ancient cypress trees, which have stood guard for thousands of years. Among them is a cypress said to have been planted by the Yellow Emperor himself, which is over five thousand years old and is honoured as the *"Father of the World's Cypress Trees"* (世界柏树之父). Every year during the Qingming Festival, the state holds a public memorial ceremony at the mausoleum, attracting Chinese people from all over the country and around the world to pay their respects and offer tributes.

After visiting Huangling County, we headed north to neighboring Luochuan County, where we stayed for a day due to the well-preserved loess sections in the area. The geological

The author (left) with Prof. Qizhong Wen (right) photographed in front of the cypress tree planted by the Yellow Emperor at the Yellow Emperor's Mausoleum in Huangling County at Shaanxi Province in Jun., 1989.

heritage site at Heimu Valley in Luochuan County is a remarkable product of both internal and external geological forces over time, documenting the earth's crustal evolution, tectonic movements, and geomorphological changes over the past 2.4 million years of the Quaternary period. The loess sections in Heimu Valley are fully exposed, stable, and easily distinguishable, making the area an ideal site for studying the paleoenvironment, paleoclimate, and significant geological events of the Quaternary period. Although our main focus was on Malan Loess, we couldn't resist visiting and carefully examining the famous loess sections in Luochuan.

Loess landscapes are shaped by long-term geological erosion. Loess is a yellowish, homogeneous, soil-like deposit, and vast expanses of loess have been formed by winddeposited dust over the past two million years, transported from the deserts and Gobi regions in the northwest. Luochuan is home to expansive loess plateaus. Over time, water erosion has carved the plateaus into a landscape of countless valleys, creating a rugged and fragmented terrain. This ongoing process of landslides, collapses, and sedimentation has given rise to the unique loess landscape we

The author took a photo in front of the Yellow River Bridge in Tongguang, Shaanxi Province in June, 1989.

see today. When we arrived at Heimu Valley in Luochuan, the loess profile was indeed a spectacular sight. The area boasted a complete exposure of ancient loess and paleosol layers, along with an array of geological features such as loess landslides, collapses, loess cliffs, sinkholes, natural bridges, columns, and walls. The scenic and geological significance of the site was so impressive that it has since been designated a national loess geological park.

After leaving Luochuan County and continuing north, we arrived in the Yan'an region, and naturally, we couldn't miss the opportunity to tour this historically significant city. Yan'an, the revolutionary base of the Chinese Communist Party after the Long March, served as the headquarters of the Central Committee and the capital of the ShaanxiGansu-Ningxia Border Region from 1937 to 1947. Yan'an is home to many revolutionary landmarks, including the old sites of the CPC Central Committee at Fenghuang Mountain, Yangjialing, Zaoyuan, and the Military Commission at Wangjiaping. On the second day, we visited the revolutionary sites at Yangjialing,

Zaoyuan, and Wangjiaping, and we took some photos by the Yan River. After our tour of Yan'an, we traveled north through Ansai, continuing our sampling investigations in Jingbian and Hengshan. From Hengshan, we headed east to Mizhi, then south through Suide, Qingjian, Yanchuan, and Yanchang, collecting samples along the way before arriving in Yichuan. Regarding the counties in northern Shaanxi, there is a well-known local saying that reflects their unique characteristics: "Qingjian's stone slabs, Wayaobu's coal, Mizhi's beauties, and Suide's strong men." It means that Qingjian County is known for its high-quality stone slabs, Wayaobu for its coal, Mizhi for its beautiful women, and Suide for its tall, handsome men. While we neither had the time nor the interest to verify these claims, legend has it that Diao Chan, one of the Four Great Beauties of ancient China, was from Mizhi County. This suggests that there may be some truth to the local saying.

After completing our investigations in Yanchuan and Yanchang counties, we crossed the Yellow River from Yichuan to Jixian in Shanxi. On the way, we visited the Hukou Waterfall on the Yellow River. The Yellow River forms the border between Shanxi and Shaanxi, and after flowing south from Inner Mongolia, it takes a sudden turn into the Shanxi-Shaanxi Grand Canyon. Here, the river, which is over 500 meters wide, is compressed between the canyon's cliffs, narrowing to just 30 meters across. The water plunges down a 50-meter drop, surging and roaring as it crashes through the narrow gorge. The waterfall is aptly named "**Hukou** (壶口)" (meaning "mouth of the teapot") due to its resemblance to water pouring from a giant teapot. **The Hukou Waterfall** (壶口瀑布) is approximately 30 meters wide and 50 meters high, and, along with the **Huangguoshu Waterfall** (黄果树瀑布) in Guizhou, is one of China's most famous waterfalls. When we visited in mid-June, the Yellow River was in flood season, and the waterfall was especially magnificent. After crossing the Hukou Waterfall into Shanxi Province, we traveled from Jixian through Daning to Xixian, and continued north to Jiaokou. From Jiaokou, we headed east to Lingshi County, then south to Huozhou, Hongtong, and finally arrived in Linfen. Continuing southward, we reached Houma and Yuncheng before concluding our investigation in Sanmenxia (三门峡). After finishing our work in Shanxi, we crossed the Yellow River from Sanmenxia into Tongguan, returning once again to Shaanxi Province. At this point, after nearly a month and a half of arduous travel through the provinces of Gansu, Ningxia, Shaanxi, and Shanxi, covering approximately 3,000 kilometers by car, we successfully completed our planned geological survey of the Loess Plateau.

(V)

Upon arriving in Huayin County, Shaanxi Province, that afternoon, our geological survey team decided to relax a bit. We agreed to take on an exciting challenge: climbing Mount Huashan at night. After enjoying a meal of Shaanxi's famous dish, "yangrou paomo" (mutton stew with flatbread) in Huayin City, we drove straight to the foot of Mount Huashan. We checked into a guesthouse at the base of the mountain, leaving our driver, Mr. Su Tian, who had difficulty walking, behind at the guesthouse to wait for us the next day. Around 8:00 p.m., I, along with Professor Qizhong Wen, Jimin Sun, and Wancai Huang, set off on the mountain path to begin our night climb. Some might ask: "Why climb Mount Huashan at night? Isn't mountain climbing usually done during the day? Wouldn't it be dangerous climbing at night without being able to see the paths or the scenery?" The choice to climb Mount Huashan at night was actually quite logical for several reasons. First, because of Mount Huashan's unique granite landscape, its steep trails can be unbearably hot and difficult under the scorching sun during the day, making the climb gruelling. At night, the temperature is much cooler, making the ascent more comfortable. Second, while you miss out on the stunning daytime views, you also avoid seeing the steep and daunting trails, which helps reduce fear and anxiety during the climb, allowing for a more relaxed experience. Third, many people climb at night to reach the summit in time to witness the sunrise, which is one of the most famous and breathtaking views on the top of Mount Huashan. At that time, there was no cable car to reach the summit as there is now. Visitors had no choice but to rely on their own two feet to climb up and down. Since we had just spent over a month conducting field investigation across the Loess Plateau and we were still in good physical condition, we were confident in our ability to tackle the night climb.

Mount Huashan is famously known for its dangerous and steep paths. As the saying goes: "*There is only one way up Mount Huashan from ancient to now*"(自古华山一条路). We scrambled up, using both hands and feet to make our way forward. The first major challenge we encountered was the "**Thousand-Foot Precipice** (千尺幢)". This is a narrow, steep path carved into a nearly vertical rock face, consisting of several hundred stone steps that ancient builders created to allow travellers to ascend. Though it was nighttime, and we couldn't see much of the trail, the steepness of the mountain was palpable---it felt like a 70-

degree incline. The path was barely wide enough for a person's foot, but thankfully, iron chains were installed on both sides for safety. After carefully navigating the precarious steps of the "Thousand-Foot Precipice," the path became somewhat easier, leading us to the second major obstacle: the **Hundred-Foot Gorge** (百尺峡)." This is a dangerous spot because it's dark and you can't see anything at night. However, the gorge, when we saw it during the daytime descent, was revealed to be two towering rock walls that almost touch, with a couple of enormous boulders wedged between them. Ancient workers carved a narrow passage under the boulders, which visitors must squeeze through to continue their ascent. Passing under these boulders, known as the "**Scary Stones** (惊心石)," gave us an eerie feeling in broad daylight, as we feared they could fall at any moment. At night, however, we were oblivious to the danger. We then tackled several more famous challenges, such as the "**Heavenly Stairs** (天梯)" and "**Canglong Ridge** (苍龙岭)." Especially climbing the "Heavenly Stairs" left a particularly deep impression on me. I still vividly remember it: a nearly vertical cliff face, with only a narrow, hanging iron chain ladder for climbers to ascend or descend. Although the cliff was only about more than ten meters high, the abyss below made the climb extremely perilous. Climbers had to concentrate fully, gripping the chain with their backs to the void, while those descending had to slowly lower themselves step by step without looking down. After conquering the "Heavenly Stairs" and crossing Canglong Ridge, we finally reached the summit of West Peak at around 12:30 a.m. We spent the night at a guesthouse at the top of West Peak, along with five or six other climbers, all of whom had agreed to watch the sunrise together the next morning. At around 5 a.m., just as the sky began to lighten, we all gathered on the rocks at the top of West Peak, eagerly awaiting the sunrise. However, after half an hour of waiting, it became clear that the overcast weather would obscure the sunrise, and although the sky brightened, we never saw the sun break through the clouds. Slightly disappointed, we returned to the guesthouse for breakfast before deciding to explore West Peak.

Mount Huashan, also known as Taihua Mountain, is one of China's Five Great Mountains (the others being Mount Taishan in the east, Mount Hengshan in the south, Mount Hengshan in the north, and Mount Songshan in the centre). Of the five, Mount Huashan is renowned for being the steepest and most dangerous, earning it the title of "the most perilous mountain under heaven." The Mount Huashan has five major peaks: East, West, South, North, and Central, all of which are connected by narrow paths. West Peak is particularly famous for its massive, lotus-shaped rocks, which give it the alternate name "Lotus Peak". From the summit of West Peak, the panoramic view is spectacular. Waves of clouds seem to roll across the horizon, mountains and valleys stretch endlessly into the distance, and standing atop the peak feels like being transported to an ethereal realm. West Peak is also home to numerous cultural and historical sites, such as Cuiyun Palace, Lotus Cave, the Giant Spirit Foot, and Axe-Cleft Rock, where the legend of Chenxiang cleaving the mountain to rescue his mother in the tale of "**The Lotus Lantern** (宝莲灯)" is said to have taken place. There are also countless inscriptions carved into the cliffs, showcasing a variety of calligraphic styles, from regular script to cursive and seal script. After exploring West Peak, we headed toward South Peak, which, at an elevation of 2,154.9 meters, is the highest point on Mount Huashan. Known as the "First Peak of Mount Huashan," Upon reaching the summit of the South Peak, one feels as if the heavens are within arm's reach, and it seems almost possible to pluck the stars by hand. Gazing around, one sees the mountains rolling endlessly in a vast expanse of green; the Yellow and Wei Rivers meander like thin threads; and all the magnificent landscapes unfold before the eyes. This awe-inspiring grandeur of Mount Huashan truly reveals its towering and majestic grandeur, offering an experience as if one is standing on the threshold of the heavens, treading upon floating clouds. It evokes the sentiment of "After seeing Mount Huashan, no other mountains are worth viewing."

Due to time constraints, after visiting West and South Peaks, we decided to descend the mountain. People often say: "Going up is easy, coming down is hard," and this is especially true on Mount Huashan. It's not just about physical exhaustion after the climb---many of the paths are so steep that the descent is far more difficult and requires even more caution. With narrow steps carved into vertical cliffs and sheer drops just beyond the trail, the challenge of descending was much greater than the climb. Each step put tremendous pressure on our knees, and for someone like me, who had injured my knee running in my middle school days, the descent was quite painful. As we made our way down, we encountered several labourers, some carrying or hauling dozens of kilograms of supplies up the mountain. Watching them sweat and struggle up the cliffside, we realized that our difficulties as tourists paled in comparison. These labourers, driven by necessity, risked their lives to carry heavy loads up the treacherous paths for their livelihood. Seeing their determination gave us a renewed appreciation for how fortunate we were by comparison.

After finishing our climb of Mount Huashan, we drove to Xi'an (西安), marking the end of our geological survey of the Loess Plateau. We spent a few days in Xi'an, visiting historical sites such as **the Banpo Neolithic Village** (半坡遗址), the **Terracotta Army** (兵马俑), and the Mausoleum of the **First Qin Emperor** (秦始皇陵). Finally, in late July, we took the train back to Guiyang, concluding our trip.

Chapter 7   Reaping What You Sow

(I)

While studying in the Chemistry Department at Guizhou University, I remember hearing in my third year that one of our professors had recently published a paper in the "Journal of Chemistry". At the time, I thought to myself: "That's impressive! A professor publishing in such a prestigious journal!" I greatly admired that achievement. After I started working at a national research institute, where we had access to a library filled with both domestic and international journals, I often saw colleagues publishing research papers in two national academic journals our institute produced: *Geochemistry* and *Geology and Geochemistry*. Additionally, many researchers frequently published in other relevant journals across China. During my graduate studies, my supervisor, Professor Chengji Guo, was a renowned expert in rare and rare earth element mineral geology. Before the Cultural Revolution, he had already published numerous academic papers and authored seven or eight scholarly books, establishing himself as a highly productive scientist. Working in such an academic environment at the Institute of Geochemistry, with my mentor as a role model, I was constantly motivated. From the time I started graduate school, I set my goal: to work hard in scientific research and strive to publish as many high-quality papers as possible. However, conducting scientific research is no simple task. First, you need a solid foundation in theoretical knowledge in your field. Second, you must fully understand the current state of research in your area, both domestically and internationally, as well as its development trends, so that you can identify new problems and growth points. Moreover, you need to find effective methods and approaches to solve these problems. For instance, if you're conducting research in geochemistry---a relatively new interdisciplinary field combining geology and chemistry---you need a strong foundation in geology, petrology, mineralogy, and palaeontology, as well as knowledge of various branches of chemistry, such as inorganic chemistry, organic chemistry, and physical chemistry. Lacking knowledge in either geology or chemistry would make it nearly impossible to conduct geochemical research.

My graduate advisor, Professor Chengji Guo, was a prime example of integrating geology and chemistry. He studied geology as an undergraduate at Peking University and later pursued four years of chemistry at Kyoto University in Japan. Under the tutelage of renowned Japanese geologist, Prof. Masutaro Takubo, he focused on rare and rare-earth element mineral geochemistry. As a result, Professor Guo excelled in both geology and chemistry, making him a true geochemist. Recognizing the importance of chemistry in geochemical research, when he resumed mentoring graduate students after the Cultural Revolution, he first selected students with a background in analytical chemistry, intending to rigorously train them to become qualified geochemistry specialists.

My own master's thesis combined two areas: analytical chemistry and geochemistry. In analytical chemistry, I worked on separating and testing trace rare earth elements in seafloor sediments using paper chromatography. In geochemistry, I explored the distribution characteristics and material sources of rare earth elements in the sediments of the Taiwan Shallow. During the 1960s and 70s, determining trace individual rare earth elements in rock and mineral samples was still a challenging task. The 15 lanthanide elements of the rare earth group are like 15 identical twins, they not only look alike but also share similar chemical properties and tendencies, often appearing together in geological processes. Thus, separating and identifying each individual element is highly difficult. Back in the 60s and 70s, the common approach was to first enrich the total rare earth content using chemical separation, followed by separating the individual rare earth elements using ion-exchange methods. Finally, each element was tested using X-ray fluorescence spectroscopy. In contrast, my thesis adopted a simpler method---paper chromatography---to separate the individual rare earth elements, followed by spectrophotometry for testing. Although this method could only separate 7 to 8 individual rare earth elements, it was more convenient and cost-effective compared to traditional techniques. However, because the process was still quite challenging, it took me about a year and a half in the lab to complete the experiments. After finishing the analytical chemistry experiments, I organized the data and provided geochemical interpretations, which formed the basis for my conclusions and eventual research paper. Between 1983 and 1986, I summarized my master's thesis work into two or three academic papers, which were later published in *Geochemistry* and in proceedings from relevant national academic conferences.

After completing my master's degree in 1981, my research gradually transitioned from pure analytical chemistry to geochemistry. This meant I began participating in fieldwork, gaining an understanding of geological samples, their field conditions, and sampling techniques. Following fieldwork, samples were sent to various laboratories for testing as per the research plan. Once the experimental data were gathered, I analyzed and interpreted the results geochemically. In October 1983, I collaborated with Professor Yiyang Zhao from the Qingdao Institute of Oceanology, Chinese Academy of Sciences, joining their marine geological survey of the Okinawa Trough in the East China Sea. We analyzed the geochemistry of major chemical compositions, rare earth elements, and trace elements in the collected sediment samples. This collaboration resulted in three co-authored research papers, one of which was presented at the Third Sino-Soviet Symposium on Geology, Geophysics, Geochemistry, and Mineral Resources of Pacific Marginal Seas held in Vladivostok, Soviet Union, in October 1989. There, we engaged in academic exchanges with international colleagues.

(II)

In early 1989, around February, Professor Yiyang Zhao from the Qingdao Institute of Oceanology, Chinese Academy of Sciences wrote to inform me that a joint academic conference between Chinese and Soviet marine geological research institutions would be held in Vladivostok (formerly Haishenwai 海参崴), Soviet Union, in late September of that year. He asked if I would like to attend and interested, he advised, I should quickly write a detailed abstract of about 2,000 to 3,000 words in both Chinese and English and send it to the Geological Research Department at the Qingdao Institute of Oceanology by mid-April. The abstract would then be compiled by the Chinese organizing committee and submitted to the Soviet Pacific Ocean Institute for printing. This academic conference was led by the Soviet Pacific Ocean Institute, with the Chinese Academy of

Sciences' Qingdao Institute of Oceanology representing the Chinese side. This was the third such joint Sino-Soviet conference, as the previous two had already been held with positive results on both sides. The hosting venue alternated between the two countries, with the first held in Vladivostok and the second in Qingdao. This third conference would return to Vladivostok. Since I had never been to the Soviet Union, I was excited about the opportunity and immediately wrote back to Professor Zhao, expressing my willingness to attend. By March, I submitted my abstract in both languages to the Chinese organizing committee at the Qingdao Institute. The title of my paper was: "The Major Chemical Composition Characteristics of the Sediments in the Okinawa Trough and Their Geological Significance." In late July, upon returning from a field survey of the Loess Plateau, I received an official invitation from the Chinese organizing committee for the Sino-Soviet academic conference. The letter stated that the Third Sino-Soviet Symposium on Marine Geology, Geophysics, Geochemistry, and Mineral Resources in the Pacific Marginal Seas would be held from September 26 to September 30, 1989, in Vladivostok, Soviet Union. The notice instructed attendees to prepare by obtaining personal passports and formal attire (suits) for the conference. At the time, Chinese citizens visiting the Soviet Union only needed a passport, without requiring an entry visa. Since my official passport from my 1985 visit to Japan was still valid, I didn't need to apply for a new one. In late August, I received a final notice from the Chinese organizing committee, reminding us to assemble at the Chinese Academy of Sciences' guesthouse in Beijing on September 22 and depart for the Soviet Union on September 23.

After taking the train from Guiyang to Beijing on September 21, I reported to the Chinese organizing committee for the Sino-Soviet academic conference. Our delegation included participants from both the Chinese Academy of Sciences and the State Oceanic Administration. Specifically, there were seven people from the Qingdao Institute of Oceanology, three from the South China Sea Institute of Oceanology, two from Shandong University of Oceanology, one from the Second Institute of Oceanology in Hangzhou, one from the Marine Division of the CAS Resource and Environmental Bureau, and myself from the

Institute of Geochemistry. In total, our Chinese delegation had 15 members. On the evening of September 23, at around 8:00 p.m., our group of 15 boarded a direct train from Beijing to Mudanjiang, Heilongjiang Province, arriving the following morning at 9:00 a.m. on September 24. Traveling from Mudanjiang to Vladivostok was not particularly convenient at that time, requiring a transfer in Suifenhe. After having breakfast and lunch combined in Mudanjiang, we took a train to Suifenhe (about 160 kilometers away), which has since been upgraded to city status and is a significant border town in Heilongjiang Province. From Suifenhe, we transferred to a cross-border train to Grodekovo, a small town on the Soviet side (a distance of just 27 kilometers). By the time we arrived at Grodekovo, it was already past 3:00 p.m. Fortunately, the Soviet organizing committee had sent a bus to pick us up at the Grodekovo train station. After clearing customs, we boarded the bus directly. From Grodekovo to Vladivostok was still over 200 kilometers, but by around 6:30 p.m., we finally reached our destination--- the Pacific Grand Hotel in Vladivostok, where the Sino-Soviet marine academic conference was to be held.

The third Sino-Soviet Symposium on Marine Sciences in the Pacific Marginal Seas had registration on the 25th and officially commenced on the 26th. After registering in the morning on the 25th, and with no other obligations, Professor Yiyang Zhao from the Qingdao Institute of Oceanology invited me and a few others to take a stroll around the city. Vladivostok, formerly known as Haishenwai (海参崴), is the largest port city in the Russian Far East, located at the southern tip of the Amur Peninsula. During the Qing Dynasty, Haishenwai was part of Chinese territory, under the jurisdiction of the Jilin General. On November 14, 1860, Russia forced the Qing government to sign the **Treaty of Beijing** (中俄北京条约), ceding the land east of the Ussuri River, including Haishenwai, to Russia. The Russians then renamed the city Vladivostok, meaning "**Rule the East** (统治东方)" in Russian. Vladivostok holds significant strategic importance as a natural ice-free port, serving as a crucial outlet for Soviet access to the Pacific Ocean and as the home of the Soviet Pacific Fleet. The city is also home to the Far Eastern Branch of the Siberian Division of the Soviet Academy of

Sciences, the Pacific Oceanological Institute, and Far Eastern Federal University. As we wandered aimlessly around the streets of Vladivostok, we came across a bronze statue of a Russian soldier on horseback standing in an open area, with the large numbers "1860" displayed prominently beside it. Someone in our group, familiar with history, quietly remarked: "You see, Haishenwai used to be our Chinese territory, but in 1860, the Russians took it. After the Russians arrived, they drove out all the Chinese who lived here, and those who refused to leave were killed. That's why you won't see any Chinese people here today." Another person added: "Yes, this is what happens when a country becomes weak. The late Qing Dynasty was already so corrupt and decayed that it could do nothing but surrender to foreign powers." Seeing the statue and the inscription, we all felt a bit uncomfortable, and no one had much to say after that. We visited several shops as we strolled down the streets, noticing that the goods in Soviet stores were not particularly abundant and often lacked variety. The clothes on display were not only monotonous in style but also drab in colour. Perhaps because Russians tend to be tall and burly, the clothes were all oversized. Many items looked rough and bulky. The furniture sold in the stores, such as tables and chairs, had disproportionately large legs, making them appear somewhat ungainly. The food section was dominated by items that suited the Russian palate, such as rye bread (black bread), with few fresh vegetables on offer. There were, however, plenty of potatoes and salted, roasted salmon. At the time, the Soviet Union was a global superpower competing with the United States, with a formidable heavy industry and military complex. However, the Soviet government had always placed less emphasis on the civilian economy, which is why their light industry lagged significantly behind. As a result, the goods in Soviet stores were not only monotonous but often gave the impression of being "clumsy, oversized, coarse, and dull"---from rough designs to crude workmanship. Even the doors, windows, and sanitary facilities in our "high-end" hotel, the Pacific Hotel, appeared rather awkward and cumbersome.

After registering, we received the conference schedule and learned that the conference would last five days. Apart from the opening ceremony on September 26, when the meals were provided, we had to purchase our own food for the remaining four days at the hotel's cafeteria. To cover these expenses, the Soviet organizing committee gave each participant five rubles per day, for a total of 20 rubles. In the late 1980s, the ruble was

The 3rd Sino-Soviet Marine Symposium was held in Vladivostok, Soviet Union (The 3rd person from the right in the front row is the author) in September 1989.

valued higher than the US dollar, with one ruble worth about $1.5 US dollars, or about ¥8-9 Chinese yuan. This meant we were given the equivalent of over ¥40 Chinese yuan per day. A typical breakfast---consisting of black bread, porridge, and milk---cost about one ruble. Lunch and dinner, each around two rubles, mainly featured black bread as the staple food. Rice was rare, and if you arrived late, there would be none left. The rye bread was usually large and thickly sliced. Since it was our first time eating Russian food, many of us tried black bread along with jam or fish roe. However, the bread's coarse texture was hard to enjoy. Freshly baked rye bread was passable, but once it hardened, it became nearly impossible to eat. On the third evening, I saw that they were serving roasted maruha (salmon, with red meat after roasting), so I spent two to three rubles on a roughly one-pound fish. Unfortunately, it was extremely salty, and the flesh was so tough it couldn't be easily torn apart. I ended up taking a long time to finish it and had to drink a lot of water afterward.

During the conference, we also visited the Soviet Pacific Oceanological Institute located in Vladivostok. One afternoon, all participants were taken by boat to the institute's marine experimental base outside Vladivostok Harbour, where we were treated to a seafood banquet, which served as the institute's formal dinner reception. The banquet featured various seafood dishes, including prawns, sea crabs, sea snails, king crabs, and many other marine products whose names I couldn't even identify. After the opening ceremony on the first day, the conference began with a keynote speech by the director of the Pacific Oceanological Institute from the Soviet side. From the second day onwards, the conference split into specialized groups for marine geology, geophysics, geochemistry, and other disciplines for detailed academic exchanges. On the third day, I presented my paper on "The Major Chemical Composition Characteristics of the Sediments in the Okinawa Trough and Their Geological Significance" in the geochemistry session. The conference concluded on September 30. On the morning of October 1, the Soviet organizing committee once again provided a bus to take our Chinese delegation back to the border town of Grodekovo. October 1 was China's National Day, and upon arriving in Grodekovo at noon, we found the locals celebrating our National Day as well. With a few hours to spare before our train to Suifenhe, we wandered around Grodekovo and visited a small park where we saw the Soviet celebration activities for China's National Day. Around 3:00 p.m., we boarded the train to Suifenhe, and later that evening, we took another train back to Mudanjiang.

After our group returned to Mudanjiang City from the conference in the Soviet Union, the delegation disbanded, with everyone going their separate ways. Most of the other participants planned to take the train back to Beijing, but since I was busy with work at my institute, I wanted to fly back to Beijing to return to Guiyang as soon as possible. On the morning of October 2, I woke up early and headed straight to the Mudanjiang Civil Aviation ticket office to purchase a same-day flight to Beijing. It was still early, around 7 a.m., and the streets were mostly empty. As I walked along the left side of the street, a man on a bicycle suddenly rode past me. The man, who appeared to be riding against traffic, seemed to be scanning the street for potential targets. Just as he passed me, something wrapped in a handkerchief fell from the back of his bike. I stopped and was about to shout: "Hey! Comrade, you dropped something!" when a young man, probably in his twenties, suddenly appeared behind me. He quickly picked up the handkerchief-wrapped bundle and said to me: "Don't say anything! Let's see what's inside." As he untied the handkerchief, I saw that inside was a red square jewelry box. Before opening the box, the young man said again: "Let's see what's written inside!" Immediately, I became suspicious. How could he know there was something written inside the box before even opening it? This guy must be part of a scam! When the young man opened the box, there was indeed a piece of paper along with a gold ring. He held the note up to my face, and I saw it read: "Manager Zhang, I just got back from Shenzhen last night. I bought you this gold ring for ¥3,000 yuan. Please accept it. Xiao Li." The young man quickly turned to me and said: "Don't speak out, let's split this, just the two of us!" At that moment, I fully realized what was happening. This young man and the guy on the bike were clearly working together in an elaborate scam, and the gold ring in the box was undoubtedly fake. I didn't even bother responding to him. I simply said: "Take it with you and go away! I don't want any of it," and walked away quickly toward the Civil Aviation ticket office. Had I been tempted by the thought of free money and agreed to split the "loot" with the young man, he would have undoubtedly given me the fake gold ring and asked for ¥1,500 yuan in cash. And if I refused, he might have tried to rob me, knowing I was an outsider. At the time, I was carrying a bag that contained two to three thousand Chinese yuan in cash, so things could have turned out much worse. So why was I able to recognize the scam so quickly? It's because I had heard a similar story a couple of years earlier during a trip to Xinjiang for field investigation. In the summer of 1987, when we were conducting a geological field survey in Xinjiang, several other research institutes from Beijing were also there working on the same national "305 Project." One afternoon, a young driver from the Beijing Institute of the Remote Sensing at the Chinese Academy of Sciences went out to stroll around Urumqi City on his own. He was carrying a small black purse on his wrist, containing several thousand Chinese yuan. As he walked down the street, he suddenly heard someone shout behind him: "Hey! My friend, did you drop your wallet?" He turned around to find three young Uyghur men standing behind him, one of whom was holding a wallet he had just "found" on the ground. The driver completely knew the wallet wasn't his, but for some reason, he said: "Oh, yes, yes, that's my wallet. Thank you!" The Uyghur man opened the wallet, which contained a small amount of money, and handed it to the driver. Just as the driver was about to leave, the Uyghur men surrounded him and said: "Hey, brother, we found your wallet, you should reward us!" The driver responded: "There's not much money in this wallet. How should I reward you?" The men insisted: "Even if there's not much money, we still found it for you. You should give us some money." But the driver refused to give those anythings. The several Uyghur men then jostled him into a nearby alley, where they took the small purse he had been carrying, and within minutes, the group of men disappeared. The driver reported the robbery to the nearest police station, but the officers told him: "Without any leads, your case will be hard to solve." As far as I know, that case was never resolved, and the driver lost several thousands of Chinese yuan. The story of the driver being scammed and robbed in Urumqi spread widely among our colleagues at the Chinese Academy of Sciences who were working in Xinjiang at the time. After hearing about the driver's mistake, I kept it in my mind, which helped me quickly recognize the scam I encountered in Mudanjiang city. The young man realized I wasn't falling for their trick and left with the jewelry box in hand and went quickly away.

After returning to Beijing, I immediately tried to book a flight back to Guiyang, but tickets were scarce, and the earliest available flight was three or four days later. I figured that I could take a train and arrive in Guiyang sooner, so I went to Beijing West Railway Station and bought a ticket for the 8 p.m. express train to Kunming, which would pass through Guiyang. I boarded the train that night, and it arrived in Guiyang at around 6 a.m. on the third day. However, another strange incident occurred when I arrived in Guiyang. The train arrived at Guiyang Station at 5:40 a.m., and the Guiyang's sky was still dark. After leaving the train station, I walked down Zunyi Road, heading toward the intersection by the Service Building to catch a minibus back to my institute. It was just getting light, and the streets were mostly empty. As I walked, a man on a bicycle suddenly sped past me, and once again, something wrapped in newspaper fell from the back of his bike. Recognizing the scam from my experience in Mudanjiang, I didn't bother shouting: "Hey, you dropped something!" Instead, I wanted to see if someone would come to pick it up. Sure enough, a young man rushed over, grabbed the newspaper-wrapped bundle, and said to me: "Don't say anything! Let's see what it is, and we'll split it." At that moment, I immediately switched to speaking in Guiyang dialect and firmly said: "You've got to be kidding! I'm a local here in Guiyang, and you're trying to pull this scam on me? I've seen this trick plenty of times. Get lost!" The young man, realizing I was a local and not an outsider, slinked away with the bundle. These were the only two times in my life that I've encountered such scams, and they happened just days apart--one in the northeast and the other in the southwest. Although these two locations were more than 3,000 kilometers apart, the scams were almost identical. From these experiences, I learned two valuable lessons: First, never be tempted by something that seems like easy money, and second, always be cautious and alert when traveling. Scammers have countless tricks up their sleeves, and it only takes a moment of inattention to fall for their schemes.

Another of my research projects was the geochemical study of Chinese loess. In the first half of 1988, I co-authored a proposal with Professor Qizhong Wen from the Quaternary Research Department at our institute. The project, titled "A Comparative Study of the Average Chemical Compositions of Chinese Loess and the Crustal Clarke Value", was successfully granted ¥70,000 yuan from the National Natural Science Foundation of China (NSFC). During our research, we found that the average chemical compositions of loess closely resembled the Clarke values of the Earth's crust, further confirming the close relationship between the material source of loess and crustal materials. By the end of 1991, after completing this NSFC-funded project, we had written and published five scientific papers, and our research results were awarded the second prize for scientific achievements in Guangdong Province (through a submission by Professor Qizhong Wen at the Guangzhou Institute of Geochemistry).

(Ⅲ)

Professor Ziyuan Ouyang (欧阳自远) was the deputy director and a member of the Party Committee of our institute's third leadership team at that time. He is a renowned astrochemist and geochemist in China, the chief scientist of China's lunar

exploration program, an academician of the Chinese Academy of Sciences (CAS), and is affectionately known as the "Father of China's Lunar Exploration." Mr. Ouyang graduated with distinction from Beijing Institute of Geology (now Chinese University of Geosciences) in 1956. After graduation, he stayed at the university to pursue a postgraduate degree under Soviet experts. When Sino-Soviet relations deteriorated, he studied under Professor Guangchi Tu, a famous ore deposit geologist at the Beijing Institute of Geology, CAS, specializing in mineral deposit studies. After graduating in 1960, Ouyang became a pioneer in China's research on extraterrestrial materials, including meteorites, cosmic dust, and lunar rocks, as well as comparative planetary studies. In the 1970s and 1980s, Ouyang led systematic research on the Jilin meteorite shower and the lunar samples gifted to China by the United States' Apollo mission, producing a series of significant scientific breakthroughs. In the mid-1990s, based on years of experience in astrochemical research, Mr. Ouyang keenly perceived the strategic importance of China developing its lunar exploration program. Hence, he was the first to propose the "Lunar Exploration Engineering Project" (i.e., "Chang'e Lunar landing Program") to CAS, the State Science and Technology Commission, and other relevant national bodies. After rigorous scientific evaluation for several years, the project was finally approved by the State Council of China in the early 2000s, with Ziyuan Ouyang appointed as the project's chief scientist. His advocacy and leadership led to the implementation of China's series of Chang'e lunar missions and subsequent space exploration projects, earning him the title "Father of China's Lunar Exploration." Mr. Ziyuan Ouyang was one of the mentors I admired most at our institute, apart from two other esteemed elders, Professors Tu and Guo. Not only was Ouyang a scholar of immense knowledge and academic accomplishment, but he was also approachable and deeply respected by all staff in our Guiyang institute. Between 1986 and 1990, we both served on the institute's Party Committee, so we had frequent work-related interactions. Given his extensive network of connections outside the institute, I often sought his assistance when applying for external research projects.

The first project I worked on during the summer of 1988 was one I secured through Professor Ziyuan Ouyang. It was from the Open Laboratory at the Lanzhou Institute of Geology, CAS, and involved using chemical thermodynamics to study the mineral compositions of fossilized marine shells. This project required knowledge of chemical thermodynamics, stratigraphy and paleontology, inorganic chemistry, and mineralogy. During my study of the rare earth element distribution patterns in marine shell fossils, I found that the mineral composition of these fossils was predominantly calcium-based. Older fossils generally consisted of calcium phosphate, while in younger fossils, calcium carbonate gradually replaced calcium phosphate. Interestingly, between the two polymorphs of calcium carbonate, calcite and aragonite, calcite minerals formed first, followed by aragonite---a curious phenomenon. Although the biomineralization of marine shells may differ from inorganic chemical processes, the mineral compositions and structures they produce are fundamentally the same. Thus, the biomineralization of marine shells should also follow the universal principles of chemical thermodynamics. To investigate this, we used thermodynamic principles to calculate the activity-pH relationships of phosphates and carbonates in marine shell fossils. The results were satisfactory, and we used the thermodynamic data to plot activity-pH diagrams for these minerals. Based on these diagrams, we conducted a qualitative analysis of the paleooceanic pH conditions corresponding to different fossil mineral compositions. Our findings suggested that during the late Proterozoic era (approximately 500 million years ago), when calcium phosphate shells were prevalent, oceanic pH values were likely close to 6. By the Paleozoic era (approximately 500–300 million years ago), when calcium carbonate shells dominated, the pH of ocean waters had likely risen to around 6.45 or higher. When this paper was completed, it earned the approval of Ziyuan Ouyang, and it was later published in the *Journal of Sedimentology* in 1991.

Another project I undertook in the second half of 1988, also coordinated through Professor Ouyang, was a collaborative research effort with the Nanjing Institute of Geology and Palaeontology, CAS, focusing on the rare earth element (REE) geochemistry of marine shell fossils from the Xinjiang region. In the early 1980s, during a stratigraphic and paleontological investigation of the western margin of the Tarim Basin in Xinjiang, Professor Xiu Lan and her team from the Nanjing Institute collected a set of well-preserved marine shell fossils from Late Cretaceous to early Tertiary marine strata. They hoped that we could study these fossils from a REE geochemical perspective to provide valuable insights into the region's paleo-oceanic environment. Given that marine shell fossils form in ancient oceanic settings and that cerium (Ce), a REE, can exist in both trivalent and tetravalent states, we hypothesized that the REE patterns in these ancient oceans shell fossils could help explore the redox conditions of At the time, a few international researchers had already begun exploring this area. We obtained these fossil samples from the Nanjing Institute, carefully prepared them, and then used the neutron activation analysis equipment at the Beijing Institute of High Energy Physics, Chinese Academy of Sciences, to measure the concentration of individual REEs in these fossils. Our analysis revealed significant cerium depletion in samples from two stratigraphic layers. It is well known that cerium, being a variable valence element, behaves differently under oxidizing and reducing conditions. In an oxidizing environment, trivalent cerium (Ce^{3+}) readily oxidizes to tetravalent cerium (Ce^{4+}), which precipitates out as it is adsorbed onto colloidal iron and manganese oxides. This leads to cerium depletion in seawater and enrichment in ferromanganese nodules. Under reducing conditions, however, dissolved iron and manganese oxides release Ce^{4+}, which is reduced back to Ce^{3+} and reenters the water column, eliminating cerium depletion and sometimes even resulting in local cerium enrichment. The degree of cerium anomaly in a solution thus directly reflects the redox conditions of the environment. Based on these findings, we concluded that cerium could serve as a

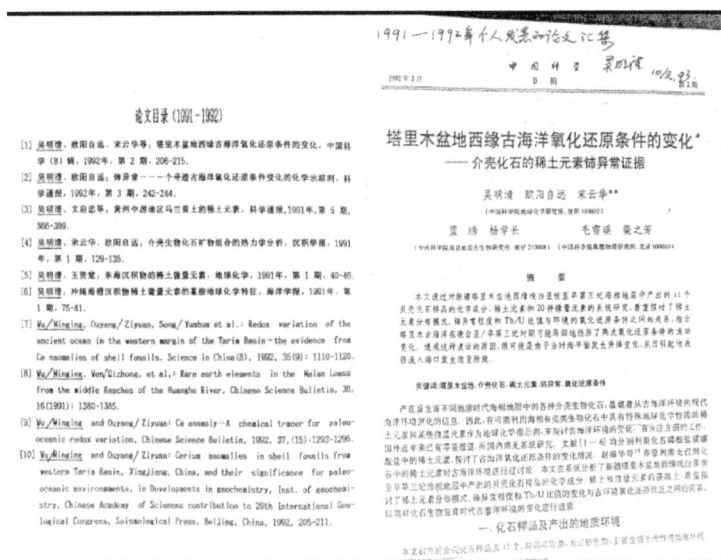

The list of academic papers published by the author from 1991 to 1992.

reliable geochemical tracer for studying ancient oceanic redox conditions. We inferred that the ancient ocean in the western margin of the Tarim Basin had experienced two significant redox fluctuations. Our conclusions aligned closely with those derived from the stratigraphic and paleontological studies conducted by the Nanjing Institute. Since this was a novel research finding---unprecedented in China and rarely seen internationally---we wrote two scientific papers on this topic, which were published in 1992 in two of China's top academic journals: *Science in China (Series B)* and *Chinese Science Bulletin.* These publications attracted attention from both domestic and international scholars.

In my daily research, I always placed great emphasis on reading and summarizing findings, often utilizing weekends and holidays to study professional literature and write. After being transferred to work in the institute's Party Committee office in

1989, I spent my days at the office from Monday to Friday, and every evening from 7:30 p.m. onwards, I would work on my scientific research in my office for about four hours---this was my routine, day after day, for several years. Starting in 1988, I

made it a point to write and submit at least one or two research papers annually to relevant academic journals. By what I consider sheer luck, in 1991 and 1992, I managed to publish ten academic papers as the first author, both in Chinese and English, within these two years. This set a new record at our institute for the most first-author academic papers published in two consecutive years and earned me the title of the top researcher at the institute, despite my primary role being in administrative duties. As a result, I was awarded the institute's research paper prize for two consecutive years, which amounted to ¥2,000 yuan annually (at the time, the institute offered a ¥400-yuan reward for each paper published in a top-tier journal). In October 1993, due to my outstanding research achievements, I was recommended by the institute's academic committee and approved by the Chinese Academy of Sciences as a Young and Middle-aged Expert with Outstanding Contributions, granting me a special government allowance from the State Council. In 1994 and 1996, I went on to win two provincial and ministerial-level second prizes for scientific and technological achievements, as well as two first prizes for scientific achievements at the institute level.

(IV)

Around early March 1990, one morning, Deputy Director of our Institute Hongsen Xie, who was in charge of the institute's daily operations, came to the Party Committee office to see me. He said: "Xiao Wu, the Science Press is preparing to publish the **Biographical Dictionary of Contemporary Chinese Scientists**, and two or three months ago, they sent us a letter requesting submissions. They asked our institute to write a 4,000 to 5,000-word biography for each of our two senior academicians. Ziyuan Ouyang has already written Academician Guangzi Tu's biography, but no one has written Academician Chengji Guo's biography yet. I've already asked several of Guo's former colleagues from the Rare Earth Department, but they all said they couldn't do it. Now, I can only turn to you. What do you think?" When I heard it was about writing a biography for Academician Guo, I knew it would be a daunting task for me. So I replied to Director Xie: "Director Xie, I don't think I'm up to this. You know, I've only known Academician Guo for over a decade, and I'm not familiar with his research work and contributions before the Cultural Revolution. Since his major scientific achievements were made before that time, it would be more appropriate to ask one of his old colleagues from the Rare Earth Department to write this." Director Xie responded: "Xiao Wu, it's not that I didn't try asking them---I did already, but they all said they couldn't write it. I'm left with no choice but to ask you to take it on. The deadline is approaching, so you'll need to start as soon as possible." Given the situation Director Xie described, it seemed I had no choice but to accept the task. Reluctantly, I agreed. At the time, Academician Guo had already gone to Beijing to attend the National People's Political Consultative Conference (he served as a member of the Sixth and Seventh National Committees of the CPPCC from 1980 to 1990). I said to Director Xie: "Director Xie, since Academician Guo is in Beijing, I'll wait until he returns to the institute to interview him and gather some information before I start writing. Does that sound okay?" Director Xie replied: "That's fine. I'll send a letter to Science Press on behalf of the institute, asking them for a two to three-month extension on the deadline."Looking back, there were two things I hadn't anticipated about this situation: first, that no one was willing to write a biography for such a renowned figure as Academician Guo, one of the two founding academicians of the institute; and second, that Director Xie would assign this task to me, leaving me completely unprepared. The reality was that starting in 1988, nearly all of Academician Guo's old colleagues from the Rare Earth Department had relocated to the Guangzhou branch, leaving only a few people, including Guo, in Guiyang. Perhaps that's why Director Xie couldn't find anyone else suitable for the job.

After attending the National Committee session in mid March, Academician Guo stayed in Beijing for over a month to gather materials for writing his academic monograph. In early May, when he flew back to Guiyang, Director Xie and I went to Guiyang Airport to pick him up. On the way back, Director Xie told him about the request from Science Press to contribute biographies of both Tu and Guo to the *Biographical Dictionary of Contemporary Chinese Scientists* and mentioned that I had been assigned to write Guo's biography. So, I said to Academician Guo: "Sir, after you've had a few days to rest, I'd like to interview you to gather some information about your research work before the Cultural Revolution. Once I have that, I can start writing your biography. Does that sound good?" To my surprise, Professor Guo responded: "Mingqing, there's nothing much to take with you about writing the biography. You can just write it yourself." I had hoped that by interviewing him after his meetings, I could gather some useful material and insights to aid in writing the biography, but since he declined, I had no choice but to collect all the materials myself. Over the next few days, I went to the institute's library to look up all the academic papers Professor Guo had published in geoscience journals before the Cultural Revolution, made copies of them, and borrowed his pre-1966 academic monographs to read and summarize. I took detailed notes on key points, carefully constructed an outline, and after two or three weeks, I completed a 4,000 to 5,000-word draft biography. I then spent additional time revising and refining it. After finalizing the draft, I enclosed it in a large envelope along with a letter and asked Mrs. Guo, who was going into town from the provincial botanical garden to do some shopping, to deliver it to Academician Guo for review. A week later, when Mrs. Guo came back down the mountain, she returned the envelope to me. I assumed that Academician Guo had made revisions to the draft. However, when I opened it, I found a letter from him. The letter began with: "Mingqing, thank you for your hard work! I've finished reading the draft you wrote for my biography, and it's excellent! There's nothing I feel needs changing. You can submit it to the institute and send it to Science

Press as it is. Thank you very much!" Ever since I handed in the draft to Academician Guo, I had been worried that he might not be satisfied with it and would ask me to rewrite or make significant changes, leaving me feeling anxious. After reading his letter, I finally felt a sense of relief, knowing that my work had been fully approved. After the institute submitted the draft to Science Press, Guo's biography, along with Tu's, was published in the fourth volume of the *Biographical Dictionary of Contemporary Chinese Scientists* by Science Press in 1991. This volume was released and distributed both domestically and internationally. Consequently, much of the biographical information about Chengji Guo found in search engines like Baidu or in other encyclopedias and dictionaries of Chinese scientists is based on this biography from Science Press.

(V)

In April 1990, during the Party Committee's re-election (which occurs every four years), I was re-elected as a committee member and continued to serve as the chief of the Party Committee Office. At that time, there were only three staff members in the Party Committee Office, including myself. Our office's responsibilities included carrying out tasks assigned by the Party Committee, managing ideological and political education for all Party members and staffs of our Institute, preparing various reports for the Party Committee, overseeing Party organization development, and handling Youth League matters, among other duties. The workload was extensive, so we were always busy. As a Party Committee member and the chief of the Party Committee Office, in addition to attending Party Committee meetings, I often needed to write various reports for Party Committee and represented the Party Committee at various external meetings or handled related tasks with higher-level Party and government departments. Towards the end of each year, I was also responsible for drafting various summary reports and ensuring they were submitted on time to the Party Committee and relevant departments. I estimated that I wrote at least a dozen reports of various sizes each year in the name of the Party Committee Office. During major political campaigns or holiday celebrations, the office staff would be even busier, and we often had to enlist help from staff in other offices.

However, there were occasional lulls in the office. Even when there was little to do, I never used office hours to read professional books or work on my scientific research, instead spending my time drinking tea or reading the newspaper. I believed that one should focus on the job at hand, and I was adamant about not engaging in personal or unrelated work during office hours. However, since I was reluctant to abandon my professional research while being primarily involved in Party and administrative work, I squeezed in time for my research during weekends, holidays, and evenings. As the saying goes: "No pain, No Gain!" Despite the demanding workload in the Party Committee Office, I was able to achieve significant results in my research over the years.

Although my scientific research work has never been interrupted, and I have consistently published research papers, I was treated unfairly in the evaluation of my professional title. According to the institute's conventions and regulations, if one's scientific achievements or results reach a certain level, it generally takes five years to advance one level in professional titles. In other words, from Assistant Researcher (equivalent to Lecturer or Engineer) to Associate Researcher (Associate Professor), or from Associate Researcher to Researcher (Professor), it usually takes five years if everything goes smoothly. I graduated with my master's degree in 1981, and in 1983, I was designated as an Assistant Researcher. By 1988, I should have been promoted to Associate Researcher. However, when it came time for promotion evaluations in 1988 and 1989, and I inquired about my promotion to Associate Researcher with the personnel department oh the Institute, PXX, who made things difficult for me when I was applying for a master degree, from the HR office said that there were limited spots for the promotion, and many senior colleagues who graduated earlier than I had still not been promoted. She asked me to wait for another one or two years. Her dismissive response was clear to me---she intended to treat me the same as those worker-peasant-soldier students who hadn't qualified for graduate school. With just one sentence, she inexplicably delayed my promotion for several years. Finally, in 1991, when the personnel department could no longer ignore the fact that my scientific research achievements were widely recognized in the institute, they reluctantly allowed me to apply for the Associate Researcher position, and I was successfully promoted that year.

In terms of my character and conduct, many people believe that I am not suited for administrative work in China, where networking and interpersonal relations are highly valued. Firstly, I tend to be straightforward in speech and action, preferring to get directly to the point without any unnecessary detours. I don't engage in manipulative tactics, and I sometimes unintentionally offend people without realizing it. Secondly, I dislike and avoid flattering or currying favour with leaders. I refuse to engage in insincere praise or sycophantic behaviour. If I were ever required to say something insincere in front of a leader, I would feel uncomfortable and awkward. Whenever I see someone trying to win favour with the leadership through flattery, I avoid them out of disdain. Consequently, apart from normal workrelated interactions, I seldom engage with leaders socially. Thirdly, after I joined the Party Committee, whenever employees occasionally raised issues about the institute's administrative management on their way to or from work and asked me to convey their opinions at Party Committee meetings, I always relayed their concerns without hesitation. I believed that if people trusted me enough to share their concerns, failing to pass them along would betray their expectations. Naturally, this approach was appreciated by the staff, but it gradually led to friction with certain leaders, particularly LXX, the Deputy Director and Party Committee member responsible for administrative work. LXX frequently talked about Marxism-Leninism, earning him the nickname "Lee Marx," but in reality, he was a selfish and power-hungry individual. To be fair, since LXX became Deputy Director in the mid-1980s, there were widespread complaints from staff of our institute about the administrative department he oversaw, especially concerning housing and construction projects. Around 1990, the chief of the Administrative Department was arrested by the Guiyang Public Security Bureau after being reported for accepting bribes during the bidding process for construction projects. As a result, LXX's administrative management was in complete disarray. Strangely, after the Party Committee elections in 1990, LXX was promoted from Deputy Director and Party Committee member to Party Secretary, and his wife, PXX, held a key position in the HR department, overseeing education and personnel matters. She had also obstructed and complicated my application for a master's degree and my promotion to Associate Researcher. According to the Communist Party's rules and principles for grassroots organizations, if both husband and wife work at the same unit, one of them cannot hold a top leadership position while the other is in charge of critical areas like personnel or finance. This is to prevent corruption or abuse of power. However, this rule was blatantly ignored at our institute under LXX's leadership. After the former HR Chief, Kewen Zhang, transferred to the Guangzhou branch in 1988-89, the institute initially appointed Xuejun Xiao as the new HR Chief. Mr. Xuejun Xiao, who had been one of the leaders in the publications group, was known for his integrity, dedication, and strong work ethic. He was also an elected Party Committee member after the 1990 election, making him the ideal candidate for the HR Chief position. After taking over the HR department, Xuejun Xiao worked diligently to address practical issues such as staff members being separated from their families, earning the trust and respect of the institute's employees. However, despite Xuejun Xiao's qualifications and positive influence, he was eventually marginalized by LXX. By late 1993, Lee had managed to remove Xuejun Xiao from the HR Department of our Institute and assigned him to a position at the Guizhou Provincial Poverty Alleviation Office. After pushing Xuejun Xiao out, Lee promoted his wife, PXX, to the HR Chief position, giving her complete control over the institute's personnel, education, and foreign affairs for seven or eight years, without even appointing a deputy. Such blatant violations of organizational principles were unprecedented in the institute's history and rare even in society at large.

To be fair, the individual members of the Party Committee elected in 1990 were highly qualified. Among the committee members were Zhenmin Gao, Pingqiu Fu, Baogui Zgang, Xuejun Xiao, Mingqing Wu, and Ruizhong Hu. With the exception of newcomer Ruizhong Hu, the others---Zhenmin Gao, Baogui Zhang, Xuejun Xiao, and Pingqiu Fu---were long-time colleagues with strong technical expertise and reputations for integrity and fairness. They enjoyed broad support and high regard among the institute's staff. However, due to LXX's unethical behaviour and the manipulation of the HR department by his wife, PXX, these honest and capable individuals were gradually sidelined. By 1993, Mr. Xuejun Xiao had been forced out of the HR department and the Party Committee, leaving PXX to dominate the HR office of our Institute.

After I was re-elected to the Party Committee in 1990, LXX and his wife, PXX, attempted to groom a workerpeasant-soldier student working in the Discipline Inspection Committee to replace me in the Party Committee Office, aiming to push me out. In reality, I didn't want to stay in the Party Committee Office long-term, as my passion lay in scientific research, and I also hoped for the opportunity to study abroad. However, neither LXX nor his wife could find a legitimate reason to remove me from the Party Committee Office, and I was reluctant to leave without a better option. According to the institute's scientific reform policy, the salaries and benefits of those engaged in frontline research or technical development were to be covered by their project funds, while those in administrative roles were paid through the institute's general management budget. Without my own research project or funding, returning to the research department would have meant relying on someone else's project, which would only be possible if someone was willing to take me in. Given that I had been working in the Party Committee Office for years and had not yet secured a significant research project, I hesitated to leave my administrative position.

Regarding the possibility of studying abroad, I had previously approached PXX, who was in charge of foreign affairs and education in the HR department. In 1990, before the Party Committee re-election, I visited PXX and reminded her that the former institute's Director and Party Secretary from 1986 had promised me a short-term overseas study opportunity if I gave up the chance to study in Japan and stayed to work in the Party Committee. I asked her if the HR department had any plans regarding this promise. PXX immediately rejected me, saying she had never heard of such an arrangement and claimed that the institute didn't have any overseas opportunities at the moment. Even if there were, she said, with so many graduate students now, I would be far down the list. At last she told me: "Whoever promised you that, you should go ask them for it!" Her response implied that even if there were study abroad opportunities, I would not be considered. Of course, this outcome was not surprising to me, I had anticipated it all along.

Just when Lee XX and his wife, PXX, were racking their brains trying to figure out how to get me out of the Party Committee Office, the Bureau of International Cooperation of the Chinese Academy of Sciences issued a directive in the spring of 1992. It requested that research institutes select some mid-level management staff for English training in Beijing, in order to supply personnel to China's foreign embassies and consulates. After receiving the document, the institute's personnel office quickly informed me and asked if I was willing to go. For many years, I had been dreaming that if I had the opportunity to study abroad, it would be beneficial for my professional work and personal development, but I had never had such an opportunity. When I heard the news, I thought that working as a diplomat abroad could also be a good choice, so at the end of March 1992, Xuejun Xiao and I both signed up to go to Beijing for English training (Xiao also wanted to leave due to being sidelined by PXX after taking up a position in the personnel office). After completing three months of English training in mid-July, we were told to return to our respective institutes and await further instructions, but there was no follow-up. Of the more than 20 people who went for language training across the entire Chinese Academy of Sciences, only five were reportedly sent abroad. Time came to earl 1993, relevant departments in Guizhou Province issued a directive again, asking our institute to select a mid-level management cadre (department-level) to serve as Deputy County Mayor for Science and Technology in Qingzhen County, Guizhou Province, for a term of three years. During the tenure, the individual's treatment at the institute would remain unchanged, and they would also receive a salary from the county. When the institute received the notification, the personnel office once again approached me and asked if I was willing to go. I thought to myself, while working in the Party Committee Office, I could still use evenings and weekends to continue my research. However, if I were to serve as the Deputy County Mayor for Science and Technology in Qingzhen County, although the financial benefits would be attractive (as I would receive a dual salary), I would have to give up my beloved scientific research entirely (as I would no longer have time in the evenings or weekends to work on research). This was clearly not what I wanted, so I politely declined. These two incidents made it even clearer to me that Lee and his wife truly didn't want me to stay in the Party Committee Office for long (likely fearing that I might become a threat to them after they retired). Working in such a hostile environment naturally made me unhappy, and I began to seriously consider finding a way out as soon as possible.

(VI)

Confucius said: "At thirty, I stood firm; at forty, I had no doubts; at fifty, I knew my destiny." By 1993, I was already in my forties, well past the age of confusion. By this time, I had come to realize that I could no longer continue working in the Party Committee Office indefinitely, I needed to plan for my future. Since joining the Party Committee and the Party Committee Office in 1986, although I had managed to achieve good results in my scientific research while fulfilling my administrative duties, I had invested a great deal of energy and sacrificed a lot of my personal time. I was fully aware that one's energy and time are limited, and it would be impossible to maintain this dual role over the long term without risking my health or compromising the quality of my research. I realized that if I left the Party Committee Office and focused solely on research, I would likely achieve even greater breakthroughs and have more room for development in my scientific career. However, the immediate priority was to secure a major research project before leaving the Party Committee Office, so that I could devote myself entirely to it without any concerns. After careful consideration, I set a clear goal and resolved to identify new research topics by analyzing recent scientific achievements and discovering new problems or areas for growth.

Among the 5-6 research papers I published between 1991 and 1992, the most significant one used rare earth element (REE) cerium anomalies in marine shell fossils to explore the redox conditions of ancient marine environments, yielding promising results. This work was pioneering in China, and only a few studies abroad had touched on the topic, with no systematic research yet conducted. I decided to further pursue this line of inquiry by continuing to explore ancient marine environments using rare earth elements, so I began reading extensively from relevant domestic and foreign literature. Through this research, I noticed that a few international scholars had already started studying rare earth and trace elements in the Cretaceous-Tertiary (K/T) boundary strata, aiming to investigate the causes of the mass extinction event that wiped out the dinosaurs, and they had achieved significant results. Inspired by this, I thought about several well-preserved Permian-Triassic (P/T) boundary sections in South China, which could serve as excellent research subjects. By studying the unique geochemical behaviour of rare earth elements in these P/T boundary strata, I could potentially explore the ancient marine environments and investigate the causes of the mass extinction at the end of the Permian. This kind of research had never been done in China, and even internationally, no reports had surfaced yet. As a result, in May 1993, I drafted a proposal titled "Geochemical Study of Rare Earth and Trace Elements in the Permian-Triassic (P/T) Boundary Sections in South China: Implications for the Mass Extinction Event" and submitted it to the National Natural Science Foundation of China through the institute's Science and Technology Department. In June 1993, I also learned that the Academy's Education Bureau had a scholarship program for studying abroad, so I prepared another application for the CAS Education Bureau's study abroad funding program and submitted it.

Before proceeding, there's an important thing to explain what is meant by a mass extinction event, and specifically, what is the Permian-Triassic (P/T) extinction event? Through research, scientists have found that since the advent of life on Earth, there have been five major mass extinction events throughout geological history. These five events occurred approximately 440 million years ago at the end of the Ordovician period, 350 million years ago at the end of the Carboniferous period, 250 million years ago at the end of the Permian period, 200 million years ago at the end of the Triassic period, and 65 million years ago at the end of the Cretaceous period. During each of these catastrophic geological events, the vast majority of life on Earth was nearly wiped out. Among them, the Permian-Triassic (P/T) extinction event that occurred 250 million years ago was the most significant. According to statistics, around 96% of all species on Earth went extinct during this period. Various hypotheses have been proposed to explain the causes of this extinction, such as climate disasters, undersea volcanic eruptions, or asteroid impacts, but none have yet been confirmed with reliable evidence or reached a consensus. Because the Permian-Triassic extinction was the largest of the five extinction events, it has attracted particular attention from scientists. I considered that there are several most well-preserved Permian-Triassic (P/T) boundary sections in southern China, providing unique material conditions for Chinese scientists to study this largest extinction event. Although these sections have attracted the attention of numerous geologists and paleontologists both domestically and internationally, no studies have yet been reported, either in China or abroad, that use the unique geochemical properties of rare earth elements to explore the paleoceanic environment at that time and investigate the causes of the end-Permian mass extinction event. Therefore, I chose the project titled "Geochemical Study of Rare Earth and Trace Elements in the Permian-Triassic (P/T) Boundary Sections in Southern China: Implications for the Mass Extinction Event," intending to use the unique geochemical properties of rare earth elements to explore the ancient marine environment at the end of the Permian and, hopefully, to provide some basis for investigating the causes of this extinction event.

A Group photo of the International Symposium on Datebase to Sedimentology in Chengdu, China, in July, 1994 (The 5th person from the left in 2nd row is the author).

Although both of my grant applications had been submitted, I was uncertain whether they would be approved. However, I thought to myself, if even one of these two grants was approved, I would announce my departure from the Party Committee Office in 1994 and would not participate in the next election for the Party Committee. While I eagerly awaited news about the approval of my grant applications, like waiting for the stars and the moon, I received notifications in mid-September 1993 from the National Natural Science Foundation of China (NSFC) and the CAS Education Bureau informing me that both grants had been approved. The NSFC granted me ¥70,000 yuan for a research project with a three-year execution period, while the CAS Education Bureau granted me a six-month senior visiting scholar position in North America (either the U.S. or Canada) with a funding allowance of $5,000 USD. This meant that, during my visit abroad, in addition to a monthly living stipend from the Chinese embassy or consulate, I would receive an additional $5,000 USD, providing a doubleliving allowance, a treatment more generous than that of ordinary government-sponsored scholars or students. Upon learning that both grants were approved, I breathed a huge sigh of relief. I felt that my hard work over the past few years had finally paid off. I now had my own research projects and, at last, a chance to study abroad, this opportunity that I had earned through my own research efforts, not through anyone's favour. The excitement and joy I felt at the time were indescribable. Additionally, I wasn't sure if any other scientists from our institute had successfully applied for a CAS overseas study grant after me, but I certainly hadn't heard of anyone else before me. Therefore, it's safe to say that I was likely the first person in the institute's history to successfully obtain a study abroad grant from the Education Bureau of the Chinese Academy of Sciences.

Numerous examples throughout history show that success is rarely accidental but is the inevitable result of hard work. In other words, no one succeeds by chance; behind every success lies untold effort and hardship. Imagine if, after joining the Party Committee in 1986, I had only focused on "holding office" and coasted in my research, without delving into my field or maintaining my language skills, simply seeking a comfortable life. Within three to five years, I would have likely ended up like some other scientific personnel in management roles, with my research career abandoned. If that had happened, how could I have stood up to certain individuals' malice or suppression within the institute? Therefore, it is no exaggeration to say that during my eight years in the Party Committee and Party Committee Office, I not only fulfilled my responsibilities in party and administrative management but also achieved remarkable success in my part-time research work through perseverance and hard work. Otherwise, I would not have been able to independently secure two national-level grants after spending seven to eight years in party work. Moreover, the research projects I applied for were not imagined out of thin air; they were derived from years of scientific work and built upon previous research achievements, while also drawing on the advanced ideas of my international peers. The challenges I faced during this process were beyond the understanding of outsiders. This demonstrates that while hard work does not always guarantee success, without hard work, success is impossible. Thus, behind every success lies perseverance, and every moment of glory in front of others is accompanied by countless untold hardships. The saying, "You reap what you sow," is indeed true.

Chapter 8   A Narrow Escape During Lap Chole

(I)

In mid-September 1993, shortly after I officially received the news that both my National Natural Science Foundation project and my Chinese Academy of Sciences study abroad grant had been approved, I informed the senior leaders and other Party Committee members at the institute that, starting from January 1, 1994, I would step down from the Party Committee Office to focus entirely on my research project. I also let them know that I would not be running for re-election in the Party Committee elections in early 1994. The senior leader(Lee) appeared very pleased on the surface, but upon learning that I had not only secured the National Natural Science Foundation project but had also obtained the CAS study abroad grant, what he truly felt was probably only known to him.

From the beginning of 1994, I started planning how to carry out my National Natural Science Foundation research project. The title of my project was "Geochemical Study of Rare Earth and Trace Elements in the PermianTriassic Boundary Sections in Southern China and Its Implications for the Mass Extinction Event." The project consisted of two main parts: one related to geological work and the other to analytical testing. The success of the project hinged on two key factors: the proper selection of geological sections and the precise sampling of the boundary sections. If the geological sections were poorly chosen or if the sampling from the boundary sections was imprecise, the reliability of the subsequent analytical testing data would be greatly compromised. Therefore, even during the project proposal phase, I had given careful consideration to the composition of the research team. I specifically invited experienced geological personnel from our institute to join the team. Given that the geological sections for this study were primarily located in Guizhou, I also invited Dequan Zhou, a geological engineer from the Regional Geological Survey Team of the Guizhou Geological Bureau, to be part of the team. This team composition ensured the quality and smooth execution of the geological work for our research project. As for the analytical testing of the geological samples for the project, since I had a six-month study abroad grant, I planned to take the collected samples abroad. By fully utilizing the advanced analytical equipment and facilities available in foreign laboratories, I aimed to obtain more accurate analytical data, which would, in turn, lend greater authority to the research results.

While planning how to conduct my National Natural Science Foundation of China (NNSFC) project, I spent a significant amount of time in the institute's library, reading a large number of foreign academic papers in my field, particularly keeping an eye on any relevant articles from the United States and Canada. Whenever I found papers related to the geochemistry of rare earth elements in stratigraphic boundaries (regardless of the geological period), and the author was a professor or scientist from an university or research institution in the US or Canada, I would immediately note down the author's contact information. I then wrote letters to these professors or scientists to introduce myself, explaining that I had a six-month government-funded visiting scholar program and was planning to bring my own

research project and samples to their laboratory without requiring them to cover my living expenses. Not long after, in the latest issue of *Geology* (1994), I found an article on organic carbon isotope studies related to the Permian-Triassic (P/T) mass extinction event in British Columbia, Canada. The first author was named Kun Wang, which led me to speculate that he might be Chinese. I promptly wrote him a letter, introducing the research content of my NNSFC project in detail and informing him of my study abroad grant, asking if his institution would be willing to host me. At the same time, I found that Professor Wright of Columbia University's Geology Department was also conducting research on the geochemistry of trace elements in P/T boundary sections, so I wrote to him as well. About a month and a half later, I received a reply from Kun Wang in Canada. He informed me that he was indeed a Chinese student, his Chinese name being Wang Kun, and that he had graduated from Peking University's Geology Department. He went to Canada for studies in 1988 and completed his PhD at the University of Alberta in 1994. He was currently working as a postdoctoral fellow at the Geological Survey of Canada (GSC). Kun Wang expressed interest in my project and said that both he and his supervisor (a research professor at GSC) were keen to collaborate and welcomed me to join their team at GSC. A week or two later, I also received a reply from Professor Wright at Columbia University. He also expressed interest in collaborating and asked me to send him a letter of recommendation. After carefully weighing the options between the two institutions, I decided that working at the Geological Survey of Canada might be easier with a fellow Chinese researcher on the team. Given that my spoken English was not very strong at the time, I was concerned that adapting to communication in the US might be more challenging. Therefore, I politely declined Professor Wright's offer and focused on finalizing arrangements with the Geological Survey of Canada. Subsequently, I exchanged several letters with Kun Wang and his postdoctoral supervisor, Professor Wayne Goodfellow, sending them my English CV along with recommendation letters from Academician Ziyuan Ouyang and my supervisor, Academician Chengji Guo. Meanwhile, I continued to work closely with the project team, conducting fieldwork at stratigraphic sections, while patiently waiting for the official invitation from the Geological Survey of Canada.

The NNSFC project focused on studying the geological boundary sections related to the Permian- Triassic (P/T) mass extinction event in South China, with key stratigraphic sections located in Guizhou, Sichuan, Hubei, and Zhejiang provinces. Guizhou had three well-preserved sections: one in Zunyi's Gaoqiao, one in Dulaying near Guiyang, and another in Lekang, Wangmo County. In Sichuan, Hubei, and Zhejiang, each had one well-preserved section: i.e., the Shangsi section in Guangyuan, Sichuan Province; the Huangshi section in Hubei Province; and the Meishan section in Changxing County, Zhejiang Province.

Of these, the Meishan section in Changxing was the well-studied and widely known, with numerous Chinese and foreign scholars, including those from the Nanjing Institute of Geology and Palaeontology and China University of Geosciences, conducting extensive paleontological research. It had also been recommended as the global reference section for the Permian-Triassic boundary by the international stratigraphic community. As a result, our project team selected these sections as the primary research targets.

The author (right) and Professor Junya Nan (left) conducted a field investigation at the P/T Section of Gaojiao, Zunyi, Guizhou Province in July 1994.

Starting in May 1994, our team, consisting of Junya Nan, Changhe Ma, Dequan Zhou, and myself, began conducting field surveys and sample collection at the Gaoqiao section in Zunyi, Guizhou. Due to the project's high precision requirements for boundary identification and sampling, each section required at least a week to complete. After completing work at the Gaoqiao section, we moved on to the Dulaying section near Guiyang, and finally to the Lekang section in Wangmo County, southern Guizhou. Along the way, we also surveyed a Devonian-Carboniferous boundary section in Muhua Township, Changshun County, collecting systematic samples. After concluding these surveys, we visited Triassic stratigraphic sections in Ziyun County of Guizhou Province in September 1994. Due to the heavy workload and time constraints that year, we postponed work at the Huangshi section in Hubei and the Meishan section in Zhejiang to the following spring. After returning to the institute, we were faced with the large task of processing hundreds of geological samples. As the project leader, I had to personally oversee every aspect of the work. Months of fieldwork and extensive sample processing had taken a significant toll on my physical and mental energy, and by the end of the year, I was feeling thoroughly exhausted.

(II)

Around mid-November 1994, while I was still busy processing samples in the lab, I received the official invitation letter from Director Duke of the Geological Survey of Canada (GSC). The letter stated that GSC was delighted to welcome me and hoped I could arrive in Canada in April 1995. I was overjoyed by the news and knew I had to speed up my sample processing and other preparations for going abroad.

On the morning of November 24, I had my usual breakfast---two bowls of egg-fried rice, which I've loved since my childhood---and then headed to my office to continue sorting geological samples and handling business. By the afternoon, I began to feel tightness all over my body and a general sense of discomfort. Even though I had no appetite, I forced myself to eat a little at dinner. However, by 9 p.m., I started feeling a dull pain in my upper right abdomenth at extended to my back, along with increasing tightness. The discomfort was unbearable, so I decided to head to bed early, thinking that maybe a good night's sleep would help me feel better by the morning. Unfortunately, once I lay down, the pain in my upper right abdomen only intensified. I tossed and turned in bed, trying to find a more comfortable position, but no matter how I shifted, the pain worsened. At this point, I realized it was probably a gallbladder attack because, during a routine body checkup in the fall of 1991, I had been diagnosed with gallstones. I had also heard from others about the severe pain associated with gallbladder inflammation. Still, I thought I might be able to tough it out until morning before heading to the hospital. However, by around 1:00 a.m., the pain had become excruciating, radiating to my back, and I was drenched in sweat, groaning in agony. Seeing my condition, my wife asked in alarm: "What's going on with you? Why does it hurt so much?" "I think it's a gallbladder attack!" I replied. "Then let's get you to the hospital for emergency care right away!" she insisted. "Yes. I can't take it anymore. Let's go!" I said, in too much pain to argue. At that time, taxis weren't available, and public transportation had long since stopped running in the middle of the night. Fortunately, we lived not too far from the Guizhou Provincial People's Hospital, so my wife accompanied me on foot to the emergency room. The on-duty doctor asked about my symptoms, and I explained that I had been diagnosed with gallstones three or four years ago during a routine checkup, but I had never experienced any discomfort until now. I told him that I had eaten two bowls of egg-fried rice for breakfast in this morning, felt unwell in the afternoon, and then developed severe pain in my upper right abdomen in the evening, which radiated to my back. After hearing my description and considering my symptoms, the doctor diagnosed me with gallbladder inflammation caused by gallstones and said I needed a pain-relief injection. The doctor promptly prescribed me an injection of Demerol, and within ten minutes of receiving the shot, I felt the pain in my upper right abdomen gradually subside. After about half an hour, the pain had disappeared completely. To be safe, my wife and I waited in the emergency room for another hour, but since the pain didn't return, we thanked the doctor and walked back home. By that time, it was around 3 or 4 a.m. already.

I slept through the rest of the night and woke up around 9:00 a.m. the next morning, managing to eat a little breakfast. However, by mid-morning, the pain in my upper right abdomen started to return, and by 11:00 a.m., it had become unbearable again, just like the night before. My wife and I rushed back to the emergency room at the Provincial Hospital. I asked the doctor for another injection of Demerol, but the doctor replied: "You can't have another painkiller injection again. Demerol can become addictive if used too much. Your gallbladder inflammation is very severe now; you'll need to be admitted to the hospital for treatment." That morning, after completing the necessary paperwork, I was admitted to the surgical ward on the eighth floor of the hospital's surgical building. Later that day, the surgical team performed an ultrasound, confirming that my gallbladder inflammation was indeed very severe. The ultrasound showed that my gallbladder had swollen to the size of an egg, with a stone about two centimeters in diameter inside it. The doctor explained that based on my current condition, I needed to stay in the hospital for intravenous treatment to reduce the inflammation. Once the inflammation subsided, I would need surgery to remove the gallbladder. I knew I had a lot of preparation works to make before going abroad, but now that I was in the hospital, there was nothing I could do but follow the doctor's orders. Since I had no choice, I accepted my situation and focused on getting well.

(III)

From the day I was admitted on November 25, the hospital administered daily intravenous treatments to reduce the inflammation (usually one or two IV bottles in the morning and another one or two in the afternoon). The doctors explained that after the inflammation was under control, they would perform surgery to remove both the gallbladder and the stones, permanently resolving the problem. They told me that simply removing the stones wouldn't solve the issue because new stones could eventually form, causing the inflammation to flare up again. Therefore, in cases of gallbladder inflammation caused by gallstones, the typical treatment was to remove the gallbladder entirely after the inflammation subsided. I asked how long it would take for the inflammation to go down. The doctor said that in most cases, the inflammation would subside after about a week of IV treatments, but given the severity of my condition, it would likely take at least two weeks. Thus, the plan was to administer IV treatments for about two weeks, after which I would undergo surgery to remove the gallbladder.

I've always been in relatively good health and rarely get sick, so this was my first time being hospitalized and needing surgery. I had often heard from friends and family that when undergoing surgery, it's best to ask a friend or acquaintance to find a familiar surgeon. This way, the surgeon may be more meticulous and responsible during the operation, leading to a better outcome. With that advice in mind, we managed to find Dr. Fang, the deputy chief surgeon in the surgical department of the Provincial Hospital, through a friend. He would be the lead surgeon for my operation. During my hospital stay for IV treatments to reduce inflammation, Dr. Fang often visited my room to chat with me. Through our mutual friend, he learned that I was a former member of the party committee and the head of the party office at the Geochemistry Institute, and that I was planning to go abroad as a visiting scholar the following year. This made Dr. Fang particularly warm and friendly, and we found we had many

1994.8.贵州紫云县野外考察

The author conducted a field geological investigation in Ziyun County, Guizhou, China in Aug., 1994.

common topics of conversation, making our chats quite enjoyable. In the mid-1990s, the typical gallbladder removal surgery was the traditional open surgery, which took about an hour and a half and was considered a relatively minor procedure. Initially, Dr. Fang also suggested that I undergo the standard open surgery. However, one day during our conversation, Dr. Fang mentioned laparoscopic surgery for gallbladder removal and said: "Xiao Wu, you seem to be in good health and are very busy with work. I'm considering performing a laparoscopic surgery to remove your gallbladder. What do you think?" I asked him what laparoscopic surgery was, and he explained: "Laparoscopic surgery is a new technique that has been developed in recent years. It doesn't require an incision; we just use lasers to make a few small holes in your abdomen and insert a probe to guide the surgery by watching it on a monitor. The advantages are that the incisions are small, and recovery is quick. For example, if we perform the surgery today, you could be out of bed tomorrow and discharged the day after." He went on to say: "We recently brought this new technique to our hospital from Shanghai. Just two weeks ago, I performed laparoscopic surgery on a woman in her sixties, and she was discharged by the third day. She recovered very well. Since you're younger and in good health, you should recover even faster, allowing you to return to work quickly." After hearing all the benefits of laparoscopic surgery, I thought, why not go for it? Moreover, my general attitude was to trust the professional's judgment, so I readily agreed to Dr. Fang's suggestion for laparoscopic gallbladder removal. I said to Dr. Fang: "Okay, I trust you." Dr. Fang concluded: "Alright then, it's settled. You've been in the hospital since the 25th, and after two weeks of IV treatment, by December 8th, your gallbladder inflammation should be fully under control. We'll perform the laparoscopic surgery then."

On the morning of December 8, around 8:00 a.m., a nurse came to inform me that it was time to go to the 13th-floor operating room for my surgery. She asked if I could walk on my own or if I needed a stretcher. I figured I wasn't so weak that I couldn't walk, so I said I could take the elevator to the operating room. I made my way to the 13th-floor surgical ward on foot and found several young female nurses preparing for the operation. Upon my arrival, one of the nurses asked me to remove my hospital gown and lie down on the operating table, which resembled a hospital bed. Two young nurses approached me, noticed I was still wearing my shorts, and, with a smile, asked: "Mr. Wu, we'll need to take off your shorts now. Is that alright?" Feeling slightly embarrassed, I replied: "No problem, go ahead. It's fine." (Once you're in a hospital, any sense of personal privacy or dignity becomes irrelevant, and you just simply follow the doctors' and nurses' instructions.) A slightly older woman, probably the anesthesiologist, said: "You'll be under general anesthesia for this surgery. Normally, the anesthetic is injected into the spine, but we'll just add it to your IV fluids this time. It's much less painful than a spinal injection.""That's great! Thank you!" I responded. A nurse had already inserted an IV line into my right ankle and started the infusion. I glanced at the clock on the wall: it was about 8:50 a.m. I lay quietly on the operating table and quickly drifted off to sleep.

I don't know how long I was unconscious, but at some point, I vaguely felt a burning sensation on my abdomen, like something was being welded onto a steel plate. But the feeling quickly subsided. After a while, in a dreamlike state, I suddenly heard a muffled male voice say: "Oh no! His gallbladder is as big and hard as an egg. How are we going to get it out?" And then I lost awareness again. I don't know how much time had passed, but suddenly I had the sensation of my body, which had been lying flat, slowly rising into the air. It felt like I was ascending faster and higher. When I opened my eyes, I saw countless bright, shining stars arranged in a very orderly manner, like the atomic lattice structures we learned about in chemistry class. The light from these stars was incredibly strong and dazzling, and I felt as if I were one of these stars. I wondered: "What's happening? Am I not going to make it? Have I reached the edge of the solar system? How are there so many bright stars in the sky?" A heavy feeling settled in my heart. Again, I have no idea how much time passed, but suddenly I felt as light as a feather, slowly descending back to the ground. I thought: "Oh! Maybe I've been saved? It seems like I've returned to Earth," and I felt a sense of relief. Sometime later, I heard a female voice ask: "What time is it?" Another woman responded: "It's 12:30 p.m." By this time, I was fully conscious and thought to myself: "Wasn't the surgery supposed to last just over an hour? Why has it been more than three hours?" I began to feel the doctor stitching up my abdomen, and it was quite painful as the thread tugged tightly at my skin. Realizing I had undergone open surgery, I pushed the oxygen mask off my face with my right hand (my left arm was strapped with a blood pressure cuff and couldn't move) and shouted: "Doctor, please give me more anesthesia! I'm in a lot of pain!" The surgeon replied: "Almost done! Just hang in there a little longer, we're stitching the third layer now!" A nurse added: "Hurry! He's waking up!" I asked: "Wasn't this supposed to be laparoscopic surgery? Why am I being stitched up?" I think it was Dr. Fang who replied: "Oh boy! This surgery gave us quite the challenge!" implying that they had run into some major difficulties during the operation. I gritted my teeth and endured the pain for another half hour as they finished stitching me up. By around 1:00 p.m., the surgery was finally over. On the third day after my surgery, the head nurse, Xiao Zhang, who had been present throughout the entire procedure, explained to me in detail what had happened during the operation. She started by saying: "Mr. Wu, your surgery was extremely dangerous! We almost lost you." I asked her what had gone wrong, and she explained: "At first, Dr. Fang did attempt to perform the laparoscopic gallbladder removal. In laparoscopic surgery, four small incisions are made using a laser beam---two near the chest, one near the navel, and one in the upper right side of the abdomen near the liver. After making the incisions, two probes equipped with cameras are inserted into the abdominal cavity, and the surgery is conducted by watching the operation on a monitor. However, since the inflammation in your gallbladder hadn't completely subsided, it was still as large as an egg---red, swollen, and quite hard. Despite Dr. Fang's efforts to enlarge the small incisions, which were only about a centimeter in diameter, he couldn't take the gallbladder out to cut. Dr. Fang tried again and again, but with no any success. He was growing increasingly frustrated and at one point even said: 'His gallbladder is so hard. How are we supposed to get it out?' After multiple attempts and still no progress, things took a turn for the worse. Somehow, either Dr. Fang's assistant accidentally punctured an internal artery with one of the probes while maneuvering inside the abdominal cavity, or something else went wrong. The result was immediate internal bleeding. Dr.

Fang realized the situation was critical and urgently tried to stop the bleeding while directing others to suction the blood out. But because the incisions were so small and the blood was gushing so fast, it was impossible to see the exact location of the bleeding inside the cavity, making it difficult to control. As the bleeding continued, your blood pressure, which was being monitored throughout the operation, plummeted suddenly to 40-50/80-90 mmHg, and it was still dropping. If the bleeding couldn't be stopped soon, your life would be in serious danger. Dr. Fang, clearly stressed by the situation, exclaimed, 'Damn it! Is this surgery really going to fail today? And this was supposed to be for a friend!' Finally, after a series of emergency interventions, the bleeding was controlled, and Dr. Fang breathed a sigh of relief. Although the bleeding had been stopped, it became necessary to perform a blood transfusion. According to hospital regulations at the time, if an employee needed a transfusion, their work unit was required to provide a blood donation certificate before the hospital would proceed with the transfusion. Otherwise, the patient's family would have to find a donor or purchase blood. Fortunately, the Geochemistry Institute organized annual blood donations, so the institute's medical office had the necessary certificate. In emergency situations, however, the hospital could start the transfusion as long as the family provided a deposit. Dr. Fang arranged for someone to call the institute's medical office to bring the donation certificate, while asking my family to provide a ¥300-yuan deposit. The hospital then administered over 2,000 milliliters of plasma. Once your blood pressure stabilized, Dr. Fang had no choice but to proceed with the second option: the traditional open surgery. During the open surgery, it was discovered that although your body frame wasn't particularly large, your chest cavity was quite broad, which caused your liver to sit higher than usual. Dr. Fang made an incision along the edge of your ribs, which ended up being about 20 centimeters long (Note: the length of the scar, even after 20-30 years, is not much different than it was right after the surgery). Once the incision was made, the gallbladder could easily be removed along with part of the liver, and the gallbladder was finally cut out. Because of the internal bleeding, the emergency measures, the transfusion, and then the need to switch to the traditional surgery, your operation ended up taking the equivalent time of two or three similar surgeries. Fortunately, we managed to save you, and the surgery was ultimately a success." The head nurse emphasized repeatedly: "Mr. Wu, your surgery was incredibly risky! Luckily, Dr. Fang had enough experience and stayed calm when things went wrong. Otherwise, the consequences could have been disastrous."During my recovery, Dr. Fang visited me in the hospital to chat. When we discussed the surgery, Dr. Fang admitted that the failure of the laparoscopic surgery was due to an error in judgment on his part---he had underestimated my condition and let experience bias his decision. He explained: "Typically, when patients with gallbladder inflammation are hospitalized and given IV antibiotics, the inflammation subsides in three to five days, or at most a week. Once the inflammation is gone, the gallbladder softens, making it easy to remove through the small incisions made during laparoscopic surgery. Normally, we don't even do a follow-up ultrasound to check if the inflammation has subsided before proceeding with surgery." "In your case, you had been hospitalized for two weeks and had been receiving antibiotics for that entire time. I never expected that your inflammation would still be so severe. Cases like yours are very rare. Since the inflammation hadn't gone down, it was impossible to remove the gallbladder using laparoscopic surgery." Dr. Fang concluded: "This was a case of me relying too much on past experience, and it nearly cost us dearly. In the future, we'll have to make sure to do an ultrasound before laparoscopic surgery to avoid situations like yours." With a smile, he added: "But you're lucky---you survived this, so you're bound to have good fortune in the future!" I replied: "I'm just an ordinary guy, so I don't know about future fortune. If there's any good luck coming my way, it's thanks to you! If you hadn't been the one doing the surgery, I might not have made it off that operating table." Dr. Fang laughed and said: "No, no! It was your own good luck." When discussing post-operative recovery, I asked Dr. Fang if there were any dietary restrictions I needed to follow. He said: "No restrictions at all. I've always believed that after surgery, patients should eat whatever they feel like. If you want some chicken soup, have your wife make some for you---it'll help with your recovery!" Encouraged by his advice, my wife bought an old hen the next day and made chicken soup. Within two days, I had finished the entire pot of soup, both broth and meat. For the past 20 to 30 years since the surgery, I've eaten whatever I wanted---chicken, duck, fish, and meat---and never had any digestive issues.

After the surgery, around 2:00 p.m. that same day, my wife arranged a meal at a small restaurant near the Provincial Hospital to thank the medical team. Since she didn't know all the staff involved in the surgery, she asked the head nurse to gather everyone who had participated. Unfortunately, not all of the nurses were informed or perhaps some didn't hear the invitation, because three days after

手术27年后的疤痕(2022.3.)

the surgery, a nurse roughly replaced my drainage tube, causing me significant pain. I later realized that perhaps she wasn't invited to the meal, as the nurses who had previously changed my tube had been much gentler. After I mentioned this to the head nurse, she realized her oversight and said: "Oh, that's right! I didn't see her at the restaurant. I looked for her but couldn't find her before the meal." Thankfully, no such incidents occurred again. After a week in the hospital, my stitches were removed on December 15, and I was discharged that afternoon.

In reflecting on why my gallbladder surgery went so wrong---almost costing me my life---I believe that beyond Dr. Fang's admission of overconfidence, the main reason was that the Provincial Hospital had just introduced laparoscopic surgery from Shanghai. The surgeons were still in the early stages of mastering the technique and lacked experience in handling unexpected complications. In a way, I had become something of a test case for this new procedure. If I had undergone traditional open surgery from the start, none of this would have happened. Additionally, since the surgery, I often experienced vivid dreams where I could fly. In these dreams, I would leap lightly off the ground and soar 20 or 30 meters into the air, where I could either hover or walk freely in the sky. If I wanted to come back down,

I could easily descend to the ground. These dreams usually took place in the area around the Provincial Hospital and felt incredibly surreal, as if I were walking on clouds. This flying dream recurred several times in the first year or two after the surgery.

Chapter 9   Visiting Canada and New Success

(I)

After undergoing the gallbladder removal surgery on December 8, 1994, at Guizhou Provincial People's Hospital, I was fortunate to have survived despite the unexpected complications that nearly cost me my life on the operating table. This was a blessing in disguise, and I felt immense relief. However, after enduring such a health ordeal, my once robust body had shed 10 to 20 pounds following my discharge from the hospital. While I felt lighter and quicker on my feet, a glance in the mirror revealed a pale face and a weakened figure. Upon returning home on December 15, my initial plan was to rest for a while and regain my strength before resuming work. However, the sight of the invitation letter from the Geological Survey of Canada (GSC), which requested my presence in April 1995, rekindled a sense of urgency within me. I began to calculate what tasks I needed to tackle immediately. First, I needed to write back to the GSC, informing them that I had been hospitalized and had undergone surgery, and that it might be difficult for me to make it to Canada by April. However, I would strive to travel as soon as possible. Second, I had to quickly apply for a personal passport and prepare to travel to Beijing after the New Year to handle the necessary procedures at the Chinese Academy of Sciences (CAS) Education Bureau and apply for a Canadian visa. Third, while waiting for my visa, I planned to prepare for my trip, complete the preparation of geological samples for Canada, and hopefully visit the boundary sections in Huangshi, Hubei, and Meishan, Changxing County, Zhejiang to collect additional samples. After outlining my plan in my mind, I rested for only two or three days after being discharged from the hospital. I first wrote a reply to the GSC around December 20. Then, after obtaining a letter of introduction from my institute, I headed to the Guiyang Public Security Bureau to apply for my personal passport. About a week later, just before the New Year, I received my passport.

On January 7, 1995, shortly after the New Year, I donned a black wool coat and carried a small bag containing various documents and personal items needed for the Canadian visa application. I boarded a flight to Beijing to handle my outbound travel procedures with the Chinese Academy of Sciences. After arriving at Beijing Capital Airport that afternoon, I took a taxi into the city and stayed at the CAS guesthouse in Sanlihe. Since January 7 was a Saturday, I rested the following day, and on Monday, January 9, at around 9:00 a.m., I went to the CAS Education Bureau's Study Abroad Department, where I was received by Director Yuan. I handed over the invitation letter from the GSC director, along with the approval documents for my study abroad fund, and explained that I had already coordinated with my Canadian counterparts and was now at the stage of handling travel procedures. I added that the Canadian side was expecting me to arrive in April. Director Yuan carefully reviewed the documents and then asked: "Have you taken the EPT (English Proficiency Test)?" He informed me that passing the EPT was a prerequisite for handling overseas travel procedures. I explained: "I haven't taken the EPT because I've been too busy with my fieldwork and geological surveys. I also just had surgery a few weeks ago, and now the Canadian professor is urging me to arrive by April, so there's no time to take the test." After listening to my explanation, Director Yuan repeatedly reviewed the invitation letter sent by the Director of the Geological Survey of Canada. He then glanced at my surgical wound, still wrapped in gauze, and perhaps seeing my poor physical condition yet making the effort to travel to Beijing, and not wanting to delay my scheduled trip to Canada, he reluctantly said: "Well, your case is a special situation, so let's handle it with special measures. Since you don't have time to take the EPT, I will arrange for you to take an oral exam at the Foreign Language Training Center of the Graduate School of USTC in Beijing. If you pass the oral exam, I'll proceed with your visa application." I quickly responded: "That's great! Thank you very much, Director Yuan!" Director Yuan then asked for my room number at the guesthouse and suggested I go back to rest while he made the arrangements. He would call the guesthouse to inform me when to go to the Graduate School of USTC for the oral exam. After returning to the guesthouse, around 3:00 p.m. that same afternoon, the receptionist came to my room and told me to go to the front desk to take a call (at that time, there were no telephones installed in the guest rooms). When I got to the front desk and picked up the phone, it was Director Yuan from the Study Abroad Department of the CAS's Education Bureau. He informed me that the arrangement for the oral exam at the Foreign Language Training Center Office of the Graduate School of USTC was finalized, and I should go there at 9:30 a.m. the next day to meet Chief Wang, who would be expecting me. Before ending the call, Director Yuan also mentioned that the Graduate School of USTC is located within the compound of the Beijing Institute of High Energy Physics, Chinese Academy of Sciences, on Yuquan Road, and gave me detailed directions on how to get there by subway.

The next morning, after breakfast, I left the guesthouse at around 8:30 a.m. and walked to the Muxidi subway station. It was rush hour, and the subway was packed. Holding my small black bag to protect my surgical wound, I did my best to avoid being jostled by the crowd. Despite my efforts, people inevitably bumped into me, aggravating the pain from my wound. At one point, I exclaimed: "Please don't push me, my wound has been hit!" A passenger next to me noticed the look of pain on my face and he promptly announced: "There's a fellow passenger here who has an injury. Please don't crowd him; everyone, please make a little space." The surrounding passengers then automatically cleared a bit of room. At this moment, a passenger by the window offered me his seat. Only after I sat down did I finally feel at ease. Fortunately, I only had to ride for four stops, and after getting off at Yuquan Road, I asked for directions to the Beijing Institute of High Energy Physics of CAS and finally, I safely arrived at the Graduate School located within the grounds of the Institute of High Energy Physics of CAS.

After inquiring within the compound of the Beijing Institute of High Energy Physics, I learned that the Foreign Language Training Center Office of the USTC Graduate School was located on the second floor of one of the buildings. When I found Chief Wang of the Foreign Language Training Center, she immediately knew I was the person from the CAS's Study Abroad Department who had called to schedule the oral exam. She asked: "Are you Mr. Wu here for the oral exam?" I replied: "Yes, that's right." She then asked: "Which country are you planning to go to? When are you leaving, and how long will you stay?" I answered: "I'm planning to go to Canada. The collaborating professor on the Canadian side requested that I arrive by April. I'll be there as a visiting scholar for six months." Chief Wang said: "You can rest in this office for a while. I'll go find two other foreign language teachers, and we'll conduct your oral exam together, okay?" I said: "Sure, I'll wait here." Although I agreed verbally, I couldn't help feeling a bit nervous at the thought of facing two more teachers during the oral exam. Not long after, Chief Wang returned with a young Chinese female teacher and a young foreign man. She introduced them to me: the Chinese teacher's surname was Zhang, and the foreign teacher's name was Michael, from Canada. When Michael learned that I was preparing to go to Canada as a visiting scholar, he was very pleased and asked: "Which city and university are you going to?" I told him I would be going to the Geological Survey of Canada in Ottawa. I asked Michael which city he was from in Canada, and he said he was from Toronto. He also mentioned that Toronto and Ottawa are both in Ontario Province and not too far from each other. This back-and-forth exchange naturally brought me closer to the three teachers.

After the introductions, Chief Wang said: "Let's officially start the oral exam now. First, Mr. Wu, please introduce yourself in English, covering your personal background, education, and work experience. After your self-introduction, the teachers will ask you some questions, and the final part will be reading comprehension and answering questions." Thus, the oral exam officially began. I first introduced myself in English, stating my name, where I was from, my workplace, the universities I attended for undergraduate and graduate studies, my fields of study at each level, and what research I have been engaged in over the years. This detailed self-introduction took about twenty minutes. Then, the three teachers each asked me a few questions, such as how many family members I had, where my hometown was, and what my parents did for a living. When they noticed my pale complexion and weak physical state, Chief Wang, in particular, expressed concern and asked about my health condition. I explained to them about the cholecystitis surgery I had undergone a month ago. Some medical terms I didn't know how to express in English, so Chief Wang helped translate them. After explaining my condition, I showed them the surgical wound. The three teachers were quite moved by my dedication, knowing that I had traveled to Beijing for work only two or three weeks after being discharged from the hospital. After the Q&A session, Chief Wang took out a printed English article (double-sided) and handed it to me, saying: "Mr. Wu, the final part of the oral exam is reading comprehension. Please take 5 to 10 minutes to read this article and then answer the questions at the end." Then she and the other two teachers left the room. I looked at the article she gave me---it was a popular science piece on environmental protection, with a dozen multiple-choice questions (A, B, C, D) at the end. The content was not difficult, and since environmental issues were within my area of expertise, I finished reading the article and answering the questions in no time.

About seven or eight minutes later, Chief Wang returned and asked if I had completed it. I said I had, and handed the paper to her. Chief Wang said: "Please rest here for a while. We teachers will discuss your performance and then let you know the results." I replied: "Okay." About ten minutes later, Chief Wang came back and said: "Mr. Wu, congratulations! You have passed the oral exam. You can go back to the guesthouse and rest. I'll call Director Yuan at the Study Abroad Department of the Education Bureau and let him know that you've passed your English oral exam!" I thanked Chief Wang and left the Foreign Language Training Center Office of the USTC's Graduate School, then took the subway back to the CAS's guesthouse. By the time I got back, it was already past 11:30 a.m., and with the morning rush hour over, the subway was relatively empty. I felt very relaxed and happy during the ride.

The next morning, a little past nine o'clock, I went to the Study Abroad Department of the Education Bureau of CAS again. When Director Yuan saw me, he quickly said: "Mr. Mingqing Wu, Chief Wang from the Foreign Language Training Center of USTC Graduate School has called me and said that you've passed the oral exam. Now we can proceed with your application for a visa to study in Canada." He then handed me a checklist of the documents needed to apply for a Canadian student visa. The list included my passport, the invitation letter from the Canadian side, notarized copies of my degree certificates, a notarized document for my date of birth, notarized professional qualifications, and so on. After I submitted all the required documents, Director Yuan said: "Now you can return to Guiyang and wait for further notice. I estimate that we will have news about the visa approval by March or April. Once it's ready, we'll either send you a letter or call you, and you can come back to Beijing to pick up your passport and visa, and then book your flight to Canada." After hearing this, I bid farewell to Director Yuan, and the following day, I took a flight back to Guiyang with peace of mind.

Here, I must mention that although I suffered a severe illness and nearly lost my life during the surgery, it turned out to be a blessing in disguise. If I hadn't fallen ill and undergone surgery, my government-sponsored overseas trip might not have been as early or as smooth. At that time, the policy for government-sponsored scholars required that all visiting scholars first pass an English Proficiency Test (EPT) before they could go abroad. Those who didn't pass the EPT couldn't proceed with their travel arrangements. I heard from people at my institute that the EPT was similar to the TOEFL exam and was quite challenging for those with average English proficiency. Many people had to take the test two or three times before passing. Given my English level at the time, if I had taken the EPT without preparation, I might not have passed on the first try. Moreover, with my busy work schedule and the Canadian professor urging me to go as soon as possible, I didn't have the time to undergo English training. Even if I had, it would have taken at least three to five months, which would have delayed my Canadian professor's research timeline. However, due to my illness and surgery, and with the Canadian Geological Survey requesting my swift arrival, the CAS Education Bureau had to handle the situation flexibly, allowing me to pass with just an oral English test. I'm not sure if my case was unique in the CAS Education Bureau's handling of language requirements for visiting scholars, but it was certainly a rare exception.

After returning to Guiyang from Beijing, although I was still physically weak, there were many tasks to complete before leaving the country, so I had to muster the strength to return to work. In 1994, I had conducted extensive fieldwork in Guizhou, collecting geological samples from four boundary sections (three from the Permian-Triassic and one from the Devonian-Carboniferous boundary), totalling over 200 samples. These samples needed to be sorted out meticulously. Some had to be sent to the lab for thin-section preparation and mineral combination identification, while others needed to be sent to the Guizhou Provincial Geological Survey for fossil identification. All the samples had to be packed and prepared for shipment to Canada. Additionally, I had to redraw the geological profiles based on the sampling locations. While these tasks seemed trivial, they were actually quite time-consuming, and it took me over a month, until late February, to complete everything. Meanwhile, the GSC cooperative professor wrote me to inquire about my health and asked when I could arrive in Canada. I replied that I was recovering and working on my visa application, aiming to reach Canada by mid-to-late May. Kun Wang who was a postdoctoral student of my cooperative professor in GSC also wrote to inform me that he already had the geological samples from the Huangshi section of Hubei, so I only needed to collect additional samples from the Meishan section in Changxing County, Zhejiang Province. In early February, I wrote to Professor Chuzhen Chen of the Nanjing Institute of Geology and Paleontology of the Chinese Academy of Sciences (with whom I had co-authored a paper on the Permian-Triassic boundary in Tibet in 1992-1993) to ask if he could accompany me to the Meishan section for sampling. He answered me and agreed. In mid-March 1995, I traveled to Nanjing by train, and from there, Professor Chen and I took a long-distance bus to Changxing County in Zhejiang Province. We spent three days collecting nearly 40-50 samples from the Meishan section. I returned to Guiyang with the samples in late March.

In mid-April, I received a notification from the CAS Education Bureau's Study Abroad Department that my Canadian visa had been approved and that I should go to Beijing to collect my passport and visa and book a one-way ticket to Canada. I immediately flew to Beijing, retrieved my passport and visa, and booked a flight to Canada for May 31. After returning to Guiyang, I arranged for the shipment of my geological samples to Canada. Since I had over 200 samples, packed into three large wooden crates weighing about 70-80 kilograms, I opted for sea freight to save costs. Sea freight would take more than a month to reach Canada but was much cheaper, costing only about more than ¥300 yuan, compared to nearly ¥3,000 yuan for air freight.

Once everything was ready, I flew to Beijing in late May, and on May 31, I boarded an international flight from Beijing to Vancouver, officially beginning my journey to Canada.

(II)

On the afternoon of May 31, 1995, I flew from Beijing Capital Airport to Vancouver, Canada's west coast, and then took a connecting flight that evening to Ottawa, Canada's capital, arriving around 10:00 p.m. I was greeted at the airport by Kun Wang, a Chinese student. Since Kun Wang was doing his postdoctoral work under the same professor with whom I would be collaborating, and we had exchanged several letters since mid-1994, we had become good friends despite meeting in person for the first time. Kun Wang not only picked me up at the airport but also helped me find accommodation in Ottawa and assisted with all the necessary procedures upon arrival. Without his help, it would have been much more difficult as a first-time visitor to a foreign country, especially with my limited language skills. Even now, I remain deeply grateful to Kun Wang for his assistance. The next morning after I arrived in Ottawa, Kun Wang first took me to Chinatown to get familiar with the shopping areas, then to the Chinese Embassy's Education Department to complete my registration and receive my first month's living allowance of $700 CAD. At that time, there were two levels of government-sponsored scholars: regular visiting scholars, who typically stayed for one year and received a monthly allowance of $510 CAD, and senior visiting scholars, who typically stayed for six months and received a monthly allowance of $700 CAD. Since I held the title of associate researcher, I was classified as a senior visiting scholar and received $700 CAD per month. Additionally, as I was funded by the CAS Education Bureau's scholarship, I was entitled to an additional $5,000 USD, with $2,500 USD paid upon arrival and the remaining $2,500 USD disbursed before my return to China. As a result, my financial support as a visiting scholar was considerably higher than that of most other scholars.

In early June, after arranging my basic needs for food, shelter, and transportation in Ottawa, Kun Wang introduced me to Duke, the Director of the Geological Survey of Canada and then to Professor Wayne Goodfellow, my collaborator at the GSC. We discussed my work plan during my stay. Professor Wayne Goodfellow was Wang's postdoctoral supervisor at the Geological Survey of Canada and a leading expert in marine hydrothermal deposit geochemistry and stable isotope geochemistry. He was also a senior scientist at the Geological Survey of Canada and an adjunct professor at the University of Ottawa. The Survey's director had appointed him as my collaborator. According to Professor Goodfellow, my tasks during my visit included three main objectives: conducting organic carbon isotope analysis on my more than 200 geological samples from the Permian-Triassic boundary sections in South China, performing trace rare earth element and platinum group element analysis using ICP-MS, and, if time permitted, conducting oxygen and sulphur stable isotope analysis on the same samples. In short, during my six-month stay, Professor Goodfellow expected me to complete at least the first two complex analytical tasks. Shortly after outlining my work plan, Professor Goodfellow left in mid-June for a marine geological survey in the Pacific Ocean.

Photographed by the author in front of the entrance to the Geological Survey of Canada, Ottawa, Ontario in Jan., 1996.

.

According to the arrangements made by my collaborating professor, the first laboratory task I was assigned was to extract enough organic carbon (i.e., kerogen), from the 200+ sedimentary rock samples I had brought from China, for carbon isotope analysis. Kerogen refers to the dispersed organic matter in sedimentary rocks that is neither soluble in alkali nor in organic solvents and is chemically stable. It is the residue formed after millions of years of complex biochemical and chemical changes undergone by organic matter during sedimentation. This dispersed residue is called kerogen, and it represents the bulk of the organic matter in sedimentary rocks (accounting for about 80-90%). Therefore, if kerogen can be extracted from sedimentary rock and its carbon isotope composition accurately measured, we can indirectly determine the organic carbon isotope composition of the sedimentary organic matter from the geological period in which the kerogen's parent rock was deposited. This offers significant insight into studying and understanding ancient marine productivity and paleoenvironmental conditions. At that time, this was an innovative research area in international geochemistry. For this reason, Professor Goodfellow and Kun Wang wanted to collaborate with me using the geological samples from the Permian-Triassic extinction event boundary sections in China to study organic carbon isotopes, aiming to provide insights into the causes of the global mass extinction event at the end of the Permian. Extracting kerogen from sedimentary rock samples through chemical treatment is an extremely complex laboratory procedure, one I had never encountered in my previous chemical analysis work. The Canadian Geological Survey only had one person who could perform this task, but he had retired before my arrival, leaving his laboratory empty. My collaborating professor arranged for me to work in this lab. To help me quickly master the process of extracting kerogen from sedimentary rock samples using chemical methods, the professor requested that the retired expert come back to the lab through the Geological Survey's HR department to teach me the extraction process. One morning in early June, the elderly expert returned to the lab as scheduled. He briefly explained the experimental procedure and handed me a handwritten three-page document outlining the steps. After about two hours in the lab, he left, and I never saw him again. It seemed that his teaching was limited to just this; whether I could successfully master the process and extract kerogen from the geological samples was now entirely up to me. After the expert left, I carefully reviewed the hand-written procedure. The process was not only lengthy but also quite difficult, requiring extensive use of highly corrosive solutions such as hydrochloric acid and hydrofluoric acid. Any carelessness could result in a safety hazard. I was told that Professor Goodfellow had previously asked some of his PhD students and postdocs to perform this experiment, but none were able to handle it. Therefore, I figured that the professor was also unsure whether I could succeed. Although my undergraduate degree was in analytical chemistry, and I had worked for three years in the central analysis lab at the Geochemistry Institute, and had also spent over a year conducting experiments for my master's thesis, I had never done such a complex and lengthy experiment as extracting kerogen from sedimentary rock. To be honest, I wasn't very confident either.

In mid-June 1995, the three crates of geological samples I had shipped from China finally arrived at the Canadian Geological Survey. I first took all the samples to the sample preparation workshop, where each sample was ground to 200 mesh, and then set aside portions from each sample for the kerogen extraction experiment. The chemical process for separating and purifying kerogen from sedimentary rock samples involved first using hydrofluoric acid to remove silicates, then using hydrochloric acid to remove carbonates, followed by heavy liquid flotation and centrifugation to eliminate other insoluble minerals. The end result was relatively pure kerogen. Since the kerogen content in sedimentary rock is very low, the only way to extract enough for carbon isotope analysis was to increase the sample size. I weighed around 100 grams of each sample, and for those with especially low organic content, I weighed up to 150-200 grams. Processing such large quantities of rock required multiple rounds of treatment with large amounts of hydrochloric and hydrofluoric acids. It took a full two days to complete the entire process, from weighing the samples to drying the purified kerogen. After two batches of trials, I became proficient with the procedure in about a week. I gradually increased the number of samples processed per batch from 10 to 15-20 samples. In mid-July, when I informed Kun Wang of my success in the kerogen extraction experiment, he was very pleased and immediately emailed Professor Goodfellow to report the good news. According to Kun Wang, the professor was delighted upon hearing of my success. About a week later, Kun Wang invited me to a Moroccan buffet restaurant in Ottawa's Little Italy street to celebrate. He told me that Professor Goodfellow had been so pleased with the success of my experiment that he had asked Kun Wang to take me out to dinner as a reward. Kun Wang also invited the former director of the Geological Survey, who had been retired for many years, to join us. That afternoon, the three of us enjoyed a lively meal, chatting and laughing for two or three hours. This showed just how important my success in extracting kerogen from the sedimentary rock samples was to Professor Goodfellow. After about two more months of intense work, by mid-September, I had completed the kerogen extraction from all the geological samples I had brought from China. The kerogen samples were then sent to the appropriate laboratory for carbon isotope analysis, delivered by Kun Wang.

The original term of my visiting scholar program was set for six months, from June 1, 1995, to December 1, 1995. By mid-September, I had just completed the first of the three tasks assigned by my collaborating professor, which involved the chemical pre-treatment for carbon isotope analysis--namely, the extraction of kerogen from the geological samples. If I didn't extend my visit, I would only be able to complete two tasks at most, leaving no time for summarizing the results or drafting academic papers. Considering the need for a complete research plan and scientific work, I began discussing an extension with my collaborating professor in late September. I requested a six-month extension to my visit to the Geological Survey of Canada and asked if he could provide funding for my living expenses during the extended period. According to the Chinese government's regulations for visiting scholars, once the six-month period is over, the Chinese Embassy no longer provides a stipend, and any extended stay must be self-funded. After discussions, Professor Goodfellow agreed to extend my visit by six months and provided me with $3,000 CAD living expenses. By mid-November, I had successfully obtained a six-month visa extension from Canadian immigration authorities, and I had also completed the formalities for the extension with the Chinese

Embassy in Canada (this allowed my home institution to continue paying my salary during the extended stay).

The author participated in travel against Quebec independence in Ottawa, Ontario, Canada in Oct. 31, 1995.

With the visa extension and formalities in place, I felt at ease and was determined to complete my research work during the extension and deliver satisfactory results. From October to December 1995, I focused on the plasma mass spectrometry (ICP-MS) analysis of 15 rare earth elements (REE) and platinum group elements (PGEs) in the geological samples I had brought from China. Because the concentrations of REE and PGE in these geological samples were extremely low, I first had to chemically pre-treat the samples to enrich the target elements, which would increase the sensitivity and accuracy of the instrumental tests. Over a span of two months, I successfully completed the chemical pre-treatment and ICP-MS analysis of over 200 geological samples from China, obtaining a large amount of valuable REE and PGE data. This work was highly praised by Professor Gregoire, the head of the chemistry lab at the Geological Survey of Canada.

The author is working in the ICP-MS laboratory in Geological
Survey of Canada in Ottawa, Ontario, Canada in November, 1995.

After celebrating New Year's Day 1996, I began my final task,
as arranged by my collaborating professor, at the Stable Isotope
Laboratory in the Department of Geology at the University of
Ottawa, where I performed oxygen and sulphur isotope analysis
on my geological samples. I had never worked with stable
isotopes such as oxygen and sulphur before, as isotope work was
outside my usual field of expertise, making this another
completely new task for me. Around January 5th, I visited the
Stable Isotope Laboratory at the University of Ottawa and met
with the lab head, Dr. Pierre Schenkyn. Dr. Schenkyn provided
me with a written procedure for the isotope analysis and had a
lab technician demonstrate how to prepare and load samples into
the instrument. After two or three days of practice, I fully
grasped the methods for analyzing oxygen and sulphur isotopes
in geological samples. January and February were the coldest
months in Ottawa, with daytime temperatures often hovering
around -20 degrees Celsius. The University of Ottawa was about
5 kilometers from my residence, and while there was a direct bus
route, purchasing a monthly bus pass cost around $60 CAD, and
individual tickets were two to three dollars each trip. To save
money and keep fit, I chose to walk to and from the university
every day. My gallbladder surgery had been just a year earlier,

and my energy levels hadn't fully recovered. Despite wearing a down coat, a hat, and gloves, experiencing such extreme cold for the first time in my life was a real challenge. By the time I reached the lab, I was often drenched in sweat, with even my down coat soaked through. Walking home after work was no different. I followed this routine for two months, commuting daily between my residence and the University of Ottawa. By the end of February 1996, I had completed the oxygen and sulphur isotope analysis on all the geological samples I had brought with me. Dr. Schenkyn, the head of the Stable Isotope Lab at the University of Ottawa, gave me an "excellent" evaluation for my work at their lab. By this point, I had successfully completed all three laboratory tasks assigned to me by my collaborating professor. The next step would be to summarize the results and proceed to write academic papers based on the research findings.

The author was working in the Stable Isotope Lab of the Dept. of Geology at the University of Ottawa, Canada in Feb., 1996.

(IV)

By the end of February 1996, I had completed all the laboratory work on the 200+ geological samples I had brought from China. In nine months of intensive laboratory work, I had gathered a vast amount of valuable data, covering four key areas: organic carbon isotope geochemistry, trace rare earth element geochemistry, platinum group element geochemistry, and oxygen-sulfur isotope geochemistry. Using this data and material, I could potentially write at least 3-4 high-quality scientific papers. In fact, the research output I completed in less than a year abroad would have taken two to three years to finish in China. This starkly demonstrated the higher efficiency of working abroad, a fact not easily comparable to domestic conditions. My collaborating professor was also very pleased with the progress of my laboratory work. The next step was to organize the data, review the literature, and start writing papers, all of which needed to be completed before the end of May, as my visiting term was set to conclude on May 31st, and I was scheduled to return to China in early June. This meant I only had three months to finish summarizing the project.

After discussing the matter with my collaborating professor, we agreed that although the project encompassed several aspects---organic carbon isotope geochemistry, trace rare earth and platinum group element geochemistry, and oxygen-sulfur isotope geochemistry---organic carbon isotope geochemistry was the core and most critical component. Therefore, the professor requested that I focus on summarizing and writing a report or paper on the organic carbon isotope geochemistry findings, while leaving the other aspects to be addressed later. With this in mind, I began organizing the data while diving into the specialized library at the Geological Survey of Canada. I reviewed a large amount of literature related to my research field and made photocopies of any relevant documents for future reference. After two to three weeks of intense reading, I had thoroughly familiarized myself with all the foreign literature pertinent to the project. By that time, I had also completed organizing the data and had created a series of charts and graphs based on the results, laying the foundation for writing the research report and papers. The final step was to write the scientific paper in English---an entirely new challenge for me. In the past, I had published around 20-30 academic papers, most of which were in Chinese. Even for the few English versions that had been published, they were usually translated from the Chinese version by the journal editors, and I had only written the English abstracts. This time, however, I had to write a full-length scientific paper in English for the first time. To ensure a smooth writing process, I applied the approach I had used in the past: first, I drafted the research paper in Chinese. After multiple rounds of revisions, I finalized the Chinese version and then translated it into English. After two to three weeks of drafting and

revision, I finally produced a Chinese manuscript of about 14,000–15,000 words. The title of the paper was "The Organic Carbon Isotope Record of the Permian-Triassic Boundary Mass Extinction Event in South China." Based on this draft, I spent another two weeks translating and finalizing the English version, which was completed by early May 1996. When I handed the printed and finalized English manuscript to Professor Goodfellow for review, he said: "Leave the manuscript here, and I'll take a look. Let's discuss it in a couple of days." I replied: "Alright." About two or three days later, Professor Goodfellow called me to his office. As soon as I reached the doorway, he enthusiastically greeted me with a handshake and said: "Dr. Wu, please come in! Have a seat! I've finished reading your paper, and it's very well-written. With some minor revisions, I believe it could be submitted to some leading international journals in our field." I thanked him, and he continued: "Dr. Wu, when we have our casual conversations, your spoken English doesn't seem very fluent, but your written English is quite impressive! I'm curious---do you find speaking English or writing it more difficult?" I replied: "For me, spoken English is more challenging." He said: "Ah, that's not too hard to fix. If you live in an English-speaking environment for an extended period, and keep practicing, I'm sure you'll soon be able to communicate freely in English." I responded: "That would certainly be great if I had such an opportunity!" Professor Goodfellow then added: "You've been here for a year, and your scientific work has been outstanding. Every laboratory task you were assigned was completed exceptionally well, especially the kerogen extraction experiment---it was brilliantly done! I've had postdocs and PhD students try to perform that task before, but none of them succeeded. It's clear to me that your abilities and skills are on par with my top students, if not better!" Embarrassed, I thanked him repeatedly. It was clear that after a year of work at the Geological Survey of Canada and after submitting my research paper, Professor Goodfellow was extremely satisfied with my contributions, and I had finally earned his full recognition. It's worth noting that from the very beginning, when I first contacted the Geological Survey of Canada, I had submitted my resume in English, so Professor Goodfellow should be fully aware that my highest academic degree was a master's. However, since I started working with him at the Geological Survey of Canada, he had consistently referred to me as "Dr. Wu." At first, I felt somewhat uncomfortable with this, but I came to believe that, on the one hand, it might have been out of respect for my professional title as an associate research professor, and on the other hand, it could have reflected his acknowledgment of my scientific competence and capabilities.

As my year-long visiting scholar program was drawing to a close, the Chinese Embassy's Education Department in Canada required all scholars to submit a recommendation letter or work assessment written by their collaborating professor at the end of their visit. This was to ensure that the visiting scholars had successfully completed their research plans. In late May 1996, I asked Professor Goodfellow to write a recommendation letter for me, and he readily agreed, saying: "No problem. Come by tomorrow to pick it up." The next day, when I went to his office, Professor Goodfellow greeted me warmly, saying: "Dr. Wu, I've written your recommendation letter and printed three copies. Take a look and see if you're happy with them." I thanked him repeatedly and reviewed the letter carefully, feeling quite pleased with its content. The letter was divided into two main parts. In the first part, Professor Goodfellow provided a detailed summary of the research project I had completed during my year at the Geological Survey of Canada, highlighting the significance of the results and affirming that the collaboration had yielded satisfactory outcomes. The second part was an overall evaluation of my scientific capabilities, where he wrote: "Dr. Wu has proved to be a capable, dedicated and highly cooperative fellow research scientist during his stay at the Geological Survey of Canada. He has mastered several specialized analytical techniques and contributed significantly to joint research on the cause and consequences of mass biological extinctions." The letter was signed by Dr. Wayne Goodfellow, Senior Scientist at the Geological Survey of Canada and Adjunct Professor of the Department of Geology at University of Ottawa.

Later in May, another collaborating professor, Conrad Gregoire, the head of the Analytical Chemistry Laboratory at the Geological Survey of Canada, also wrote me a recommendation letter. He, too, gave me high praise for my work. In his letter, Professor Gregory wrote: "Dr. Wu impressed me with his ability to quickly learn a difficult procedure related to a field outside his own area of training. He was an extremely hard and diligent worker who didn't get discouraged, even when there were challenges to overcome. Dr. Wu is an affable person, capable of getting along will with others and is a team player. It has been a pleasure to have worked with him during his stay in Canada." The letter was signed by Dr. Conrad Gregoire, Head of the Analytical Chemistry Laboratory at the Geological Survey of Canada and Adjunct Professor of the Department of Chemistry at Carleton University. Here, it is important to note

that, in Western societies, especially in the scientific community, earning recognition or praise from fellow experts is no easy feat. If you lack genuine ability and merely talk the talk or engage in superficial efforts, it is impossible to earn such commendations. Western scientists do not hand out praise lightly unless you demonstrate real talent and produce outstanding results. Otherwise, there's nothing to talk about.

In early June 1996, later when I submitted the two recommendation letters from my professors to the Chinese Embassy's Education Department as part of my final report on the visiting scholar program, Counsellor Wang, the head of the Education Department, carefully read the letters. After carefully reading Counsellor Wang was visibly pleased and waved my recommendation letters around, saying to the other visiting scholars and staff present: "Please take a look at the letters Professor Wu's supervisors wrote for him. His work at the Geological Survey of Canada has been excellent! I've been working at the Education Department for many years, and I've never seen a reference letter as glowing as this!" Then, turning to me, he said: "Mr. Wu, your Canadian collaborate professors have given you very high praise! You've brought honour to our Chinese visiting scholars!" His words made me feel quite embarrassed, and I could only humbly reply: "I don't think it's anything special; I just worked hard and completed some lab tasks." After completing the program, I returned to Beijing in mid-June 1996. Upon arrival, I reported to the Study Abroad Department of the Education Bureau at the Chinese Academy of Sciences (CAS) to confirm that I had completed my public-funded visiting scholar program and returned on schedule. In addition to submitting a final report summarizing my work in Canada, I also submitted copies of the two recommendation letters from my collaborative professors. The Study Abroad Department of CAS expressed their approval and praise for my work.

To be fair, my year as a visiting scholar at the Geological Survey of Canada was not without its challenges. On the contrary, I faced several significant difficulties, three of which were particularly challenging. The first difficulty I encountered was my physical condition. When I arrived in Canada in late May 1995, it had only been six months since I had undergone gallbladder surgery, and my body was still quite weak. I had rented a room on the outskirts of Ottawa, about 5 kilometers from the Geological Survey of Canada, and there was no public transportation available in the area at that time. I had to either walk or ride a bicycle to commute to work every day. Walking 10 kilometers daily, round-trip, was obviously unrealistic for someone who had just had surgery. So, I bought a second-hand bicycle for $50 CAD and committed to cycling to work every day. Additionally, to consciously strengthen my body and improve my physical fitness, I swam for an hour at the free swimming pool in the basement of my apartment building every evening after dinner. I maintained this routine almost daily. After about three months of cycling to work and swimming daily, I had basically regained my pre-surgery level of health, which provided the physical foundation I needed to complete the high-intensity laboratory work.

The second major challenge I encountered was the extremely lengthy and complex process of extracting kerogen from sedimentary rock samples. The entire experiment took two full days to complete, and I had no specific guidance or assistance---everything had to be figured out on my own. While the Geological Survey did bring back the retired expert who had previously specialized in kerogen extraction, he only spent about two hours in the lab before leaving me with a handwritten experimental procedure. After receiving this handwritten document, I had to translate it into Chinese as best as I could (since the cursive handwriting in English was difficult to decipher), and then follow the experimental steps one by one, gradually figuring out the process on my own. After a week of trial and error, I finally succeeded in extracting kerogen from the sedimentary rock samples. This success was undoubtedly due to my prior experience working in the central analysis lab at the Geochemistry Institute of the Chinese Academy of Sciences, where I honed my skills in rock chemical analysis. Without such a solid foundation in chemical analysis theory and practical skills, it would have been incredibly difficult for anyone unfamiliar with chemical techniques and English scientific literature to quickly master this complex process. The same applied to the plasma mass spectrometry analysis of trace rare earth and platinum group elements, as well as the oxygen and sulphur isotope analysis---these were also entirely new to me. However, thanks to my strong background in chemical analysis and my patient, meticulous work ethic, I was able to overcome these challenges and achieve success in all of them. Kun Wang later told me that Professor Goodfellow held such a high opinion of my work at the Geological Survey of Canada because, over the course of the year, he saw that I was highly dedicated to my research, with a solid academic foundation, a clear mind, and highly specialized skills in chemical analysis. No matter how complex the laboratory work was, I was able to handle it competently and complete it successfully, which is quite rare among geochemistry researchers and something he greatly admired. Many of his PhD students and postdocs, having come from a geology background, lacked a strong foundation in chemistry and were unfamiliar with analytical chemistry. When they entered the lab and saw highly corrosive reagents like nitric acid, hydrofluoric acid, and caustic soda, they were often scared, which is why most of them were unable to handle the lab work.

The third major challenge I faced was the language barrier, specifically in spoken English communication and writing scientific papers in English. Like many Chinese, I had a solid grasp of grammar and reading comprehension, but speaking and writing in English were my weaknesses. When I first arrived at the Geological Survey of Canada, communicating with Westerners in English was quite difficult. Before the teachers who had taught us spoken English back in China had never been abroad, and their pronunciation wasn't accurate, which affected ours. As a result, even simple English words or sentences often caused misunderstandings. Not only did we struggle to understand native English speakers, but they also had trouble understanding us, making verbal communication very challenging. Since I worked alone in a lab, I had no opportunities to practice spoken English during work hours. After work, I returned to my apartment and mostly interacted with other Chinese people, so my English speaking skills made no progress after six months. To improve my English listening and speaking skills, I made friends with local Christian church members, using their attempts to evangelize as an opportunity to practice. However, having grown up in an atheist society, I found it hard to take an interest in their discussions of "God" or "the Lord," and after a while, I stopped going to church, citing my busy work schedule. Still, my interactions with the church members helped me gradually become more familiar with the local English language and expressions. As for writing in English, I relied on the skills I had developed in translating scientific papers from Chinese to English and in technical writing during my time at the Institute of Geochemistry. In the end, I was able to overcome this challenge as well. As the saying goes: "It's easy to stay comfortable at home, but stepping outside presents difficulties everywhere." There are always challenges when you're abroad; it all depends on your attitude toward them. But to overcome difficulties, you must have the confidence and the necessary tools to do so.

(V)

Shortly after I arrived in Canada, around July or August 1995, the International Geological Correlation Program (IGCP) under the International Union of Geological Sciences (IUGS) was planning a global research project titled "Response of the Ocean/Atmosphere System to Past Global Changes." One of the key areas of this project was studying the causes of the global mass extinction event that occurred approximately 250 million years ago during the PermianTriassic (P/T) period, known as the IGCP 386 project. At the time, the project leader and secretary was Professor H. H. Geldsetzer from the Calgary Section of the Geological Survey of Canada. Because southern China is home to several wellpreserved and internationally renowned Permian-Triassic (P/ T) boundary sections, where evidence of the mass extinction event can be studied (the same sections I was researching for my National Natural Science Foundation project), Professor Geldsetzer was looking for a suitable Chinese scientist to collaborate on the IGCP 386 project. At the same time, Professor Geldsetzer had co-authored a research paper with Kun Wang, published in early 1994 in *Geology*, on the Permian-Triassic boundary section in British Columbia, Canada. He was also a colleague and close friend of my collaborating professor, Wayne Goodfellow. After I began working at the Geological Survey of Canada, Kun Wang told Professor Geldsetzer about me and my work. Over time, Kun Wang kept Professor Geldsetzer informed about my laboratory work and the progress of my research program. By late May 1996, when my visit to Canada was nearing its end, Professor Geldsetzer had learned from Kun Wang and Professor Goodfellow that I had completed the organic carbon isotope, trace rare earth and platinum group elements, and oxygen and sulphur isotope analyses for over 200 geological samples from several Permian-Triassic boundary sections in China. These analyses had yielded a wealth of valuable data, and the organic carbon isotope research had produced significant results, which I had compiled into a research paper. Professor Geldsetzer then sent me an email requesting the English manuscript of my paper titled "Organic Carbon Isotope Record of Permian-Triassic Boundary Mass Extinction Events in Southern China", and mentioned that the IGCP 386 project might invite me to participate in their international research collaboration. He asked if I would be interested in joining the project. Naturally, I was thrilled to receive this news. I mailed him the manuscript and replied via email, expressing my strong interest in joining the IGCP386 project. In his reply, Professor Geldsetzer explained that the international collaboration for the IGCP 386 project was still in the early stages, with coordination and negotiations ongoing with several other countries. He assured me that once the details were finalized by the IUGS, he would notify me immediately. He also suggested that after returning to China, I begin preparing for the IGCP 386 project, including identifying potential institutions and researchers within China who could participate in the collaboration.

After my returning to China in mid-June 1996, I met with members of my National Natural Science Foundation research team, including Professor Junya Nan and Dr. Weidong Yang, to discuss the preliminary information regarding Professor

Geldsetzer's invitation for me to participate in the IGCP 386 project. We tentatively decided that Professor Junya Nan and Dr. Weidong Yang from our Geochemistry Institute would serve as the primary members of the IGCP 386 China team. At the same time, I reached out to several other researchers via letters, including Researcher Zhifang Chai from the Neutron Activation Analysis Laboratory of the Beijing Institute of High Energy Physics, CAS, Researcher Jinshi Chen from the Carbon Isotope Analysis Laboratory at the Beijing Institute of Geology, CAS, and Researcher Qiang Ji from the Institute of Geology at the Chinese Academy of Geological Sciences. I inquired whether they were interested in participating in the upcoming IGCP 386 project. All of them responded positively.

With these institutions and researchers tentatively confirmed, in early August 1996, I wrote to Professor Geldsetzer at the Calgary section of the Geological Survey of Canada, providing details of the preparations I had made after returning to China regarding the proposed IGCP 386 project. This included information about the Chinese institutions and researchers planning to participate. I also suggested that, if the IGCP 386 International Team agreed, the Chinese team could be based at our Institute of Geochemistry, Chinese Academy of Sciences, with the team leader and deputy leaders coming from our project group. In late August, I received a reply from Professor Geldsetzer, who accepted my proposal. He agreed that the Institute of Geochemistry would serve as the official representative for the IGCP 386 project in China and confirmed that I would serve as the leader of the Chinese team, with Professor Junya Nan and Dr. Weidong Yang as deputy leaders. In his letter, Professor Geldsetzer also mentioned that, in addition to receiving my response, he had also received feedback

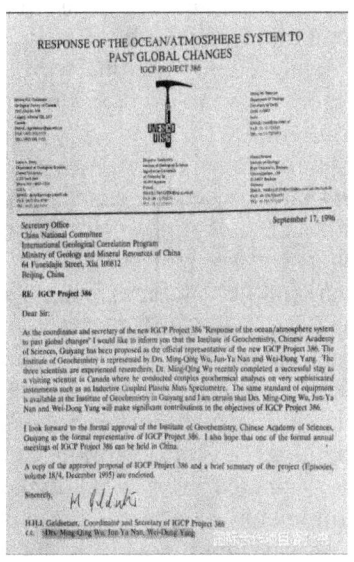

from Dr. Kun Wang after his visit to our institute. Wang had praised the advanced analytical instruments and equipment at our Geochemistry Institute, expressing confidence that we were fully capable of undertaking the IGCP 386 research. As it turned out, after my return to China in mid-June 1996, Kun Wang visited our institute for academic exchange while on his summer vacation in July. During his visit, Kun Wang gave a presentation on using organic carbon isotopes to study ancient marine environments, which was met with great enthusiasm from the scientific community at our institute. After the presentation, Academician Ziyuan Ouyang remarked: "Kun Wang's talk was excellent! This is the kind of high-level academic lecture we need. Some of the previous professors we invited weren't nearly as impressive." After Kun Wang returned to Canada in mid August, he apparently provided a detailed report of his visit to Professor Geldsetzer, which undoubtedly played a significant role in helping us secure the IGCP 386 project. In mid-September 1996, the IGCP 386 international team sent an official letter to China's Ministry of Geology and Mineral Resources, notifying the ministry's International Commission on Stratigraphy (ICS) in China that the Institute of Geochemistry, Chinese Academy of Sciences, had been designated as the official representative of the IGCP 386 project, titled "Response of the Ocean/Atmosphere System to Past Global Changes." The letter also announced that Dr. Mingqing Wu, Professor Junya Nan, and Dr. Weidong Yang had been appointed as members of the IGCP 386 China team, with Dr. Mingqing Wu serving as the team leader and Professors Junya Nan and Weidong Yang as deputy leaders. The letter emphasized that these three scientists were highly experienced researchers, noting that Dr. Wu had just completed a year of work in Canada as a visiting scientist, where he conducted a series of complex analyses using some advanced equipments such as plasma mass spectrometers. The letter also expressed confidence in their ability to make significant contributions to the IGCP 386 collaborative research. At the same time, Professor Geldsetzer sent me a letter notifying me that our institute had been officially designated as China's representative for the IGCP 386 project, along with a copy of the formal project agreement. In late September, when I presented this official documentation to Academician Ziyuan Ouyang, he remarked: "Xiao Wu, you've done an excellent job! Not only have you secured the IGCP 386 project, but you're also the team leader for China. I also secured an IGCP 386 project, but we're only participating as a supporting institution." He looked at me with a sense of approval.

After receiving the official confirmation from the IGCP 386 international team in late September 1996, our team, including Professors Junya Nan and Weidong Yang, immediately began preparations for the project. To secure funding, I submitted a key project funding application titled "Geochemical Records and Paleoceanographic Environment of Global Mass Extinction Events in the Paleozoic" to the Bureau of Natural and Social Coordination of the Chinese Academy of Sciences in late September 1996. We applied for a grant of ¥400,000 yuan and planned to apply for additional funding from the National Natural Science Foundation of China in the first half of 1997. Once we secured sufficient funding, our project team would officially launch the IGCP 386 international collaborative project in 1997.

Chapter 10   Oppressed and Thinking of Leaving

(I)

In mid-June 1996, after completing my a-year-long visiting scholar program at the Geological Survey of Canada, I returned to China as scheduled. By mid-September of the same year, I had formally secured the IGCP 386 international cooperation project commissioned by the International Union of Geological Sciences, and I was appointed as the leader of the Chinese team for this project. This was an unprecedented occurrence at the Institute of Geochemistry. Those at the institute who heard about it were astonished. Some remarked: "Mingqing Wu has worked in the institute's Party Committee and Party Committee Office for so many years, always seeming ordinary. But wow! After leaving the Party Committee Office and working abroad for a year, he managed to bring back an international cooperation project. His professional and scientific abilities are truly impressive!" As a result, many believed my opportunity to shine had arrived. At the time, I thought similarly. Having left the Party Committee two years earlier, I was finally free from the entanglements of administrative duties. Now, returning from abroad with an international cooperation project in hand, I was determined to focus fully on this project and devote myself entirely to scientific research. However, as the saying goes: "The tree wishes to remain still, but the wind does not stop." After I returned to the institute, some of the heads of the management department were unhappy. They heard that I was doing very well in Canada and brought back an international collaborative project from abroad. They thought, that I had left the Party Committee, my professional business had developed quite well and there was nothing wrong with me politically. They worried that after they retired, I might rise again in the future and that would be detrimental to them. So they began using their power to suppress me in various ways, obstructing and undermining me step by step in matters of promotions and other opportunities.

The first instance of suppression was stripping me of the eligibility to apply for promotion to researcher (i.e., research Professor title). In September 1996, the institute planned to promote a batch of researchers. According to the usual practice of promoting every five years, those who had been promoted to associate researchers in 1991 were eligible this time, which should have included me based on both my qualifications and years of service. However, the institute's personnel office deliberately set up barriers to exclude me alone from being eligible to apply. In mid-August 1996, the personnel office posted a notice in the institute's bulletin board, stating: "In accordance with relevant instructions from higher authorities and following the established practice of applying new methods for new people and old methods for old people, all university graduates before the Cultural Revolution and associate researchers promoted before 1992 are eligible to apply for researcher promotion this time. However, university graduates during the Cultural Revolution, even if promoted to associate researcher before 1992, are not eligible to apply for promotion this time. By order of the Personnel Office of the Institute of Geochemistry, August x, 1996." According to this notice, my colleague and classmate Baoshan Zheng and I, who were students of the same supervisor and graduated in the same year, both promoted to associate researcher before 1992, were treated differently. Since Mr. Zheng entered university before the Cultural Revolution, he was eligible to apply, but I, who entered university during the Cultural Revolution, was not. At the time, the Institute of Geochemistry had two or three dozen students who graduated during the Cultural Revolution. Among those promoted to associate researcher before 1992 and who had also completed graduate studies, I was the only one at the institute. This notification, invoking "instructions from higher authorities" and following "established practices," was clearly fabricated to target and exclude me. When this notice was posted, many who knew the background expressed their dissatisfaction on my behalf. Some said: "Look, this notice from the personnel department is obviously designed to exclude Wu Mingqing from applying for researcher promotion. These people are truly malicious!" A few colleagues even suggested: "Mr. Wu, this notice is absurdly unfair. Why don't you go and argue your case with the personnel office?" When I first saw the notice, I was indeed angry. But after calming down, I realized that arguing with such malicious people would lead nowhere. Confrontation would only make me more upset, and there was no point in it. So, I told those who sympathized with me: "Is there any point in reasoning with them? They hold the power and can do whatever they want. But I believe they can block me for a while, but not forever. Let's wait and see." Some colleagues even remarked indignantly: "Hmph! Xiao Wu, they only dare to bully you because you are a student of Professor Guo. If you were a student of Professor Tu, do you think they would dare? They wouldn't even have time to praise you!"

It is no exaggeration to say that PXX, the head of the personnel department, has consistently used her authority over professional titles to selectively hinder and suppress certain researchers at the institute. However, when it came to her husband, LXX, she had no qualms about breaking the rules. LXX, who held an administrative leadership position at the institute, enjoyed the benefits of his role without having independently undertaken any research projects or published first-author papers in top journals. Yet, PXX shamelessly pushed for her husband to be promoted to the rank of researcher. When LXX's first review for researcher was unsuccessful, PXX arranged for a new panel of reviewers, making sure they gave her husband a smooth path to promotion. This is a prime example of how LXX and PXX exploited their power for personal gain at the Institute of Geochemistry.

The second instance of suppression was PXX attempt to confiscate my personal passport. After I returned from Canada in mid-June 1996, I occasionally needed to send and receive faxes related to international cooperation using the institute's fax machine. Between July and August 1996, Professor Geldsetzer, the head of the IGCP 386 project, proposed that I return to Canada in the first half of 1997 to collaborate on a short-term experimental project involving kerogen extraction for about six months, after which I would return to China to continue leading the Chinese team of the IGCP 386 project. When PXX learned of this, she became fixated on preventing me from going abroad again and concocted a plan to confiscate my personal passport. Thus, the personnel department, under the guise of the foreign affairs group, posted a notice on the bulletin board stating: "In accordance with instructions from higher authorities, all public-funded returning scholars must submit their official passports to the personnel office's foreign affairs group within three months of returning. This is mandatory. By order of the Personnel Department's Foreign Affairs Group, September x, 1996." This ridiculous notice clearly showed that this conniving woman had no understanding of, or blatantly disregarded, national policies. First, since the early 1980s, the relevant national departments had never issued any instructions requiring public-funded returning scholars to submit their passports to the foreign affairs department. Second, in 1993, the Ministry of Public Security adjusted the policy on passport issuance, stipulating that public-funded scholars staying abroad for over six months (including six months) would be issued personal passports rather than official passports. Furthermore, personal passports are citizens' private identification documents, and aside from specific regulations for certain officials or some special occupations, personal passports should be kept and used by individuals. From this, it was obvious that this notice was also aimed specifically at me, just as the earlier notice about the researcher promotion was, but without directly naming me (since I was the only public-funded returning scholar at the institute in June and July that year). When I saw the notice, I found it both infuriating and absurd. Wanting to expose PXX's ignorance, I took my personal passport to the personnel department office the next day, found PXX in front of several of her colleagues, and said: "Head PXX, it seems your notice doesn't apply to me! I am a public-funded returning scholar for sure, but you should look carefully, I hold a personal passport, not an official one! I'm afraid you have no right to confiscate my personal passport, do you?" Seeing the passport's cover, she awkwardly replied: "Hmm, that's strange! In the past, all public-funded scholars were issued official passports. How come they're issuing personal passports now?" She was left with no choice but to act helpless. I knew the policies well, but instead of explaining, I deliberately said: "I don't know why the Public Security Bureau issued me a personal passport either. You should go to the Guiyang Public Security Bureau to ask them if they made a mistake!" With that, I left the personnel office.

The third incident was withholding my Scientific Research Start-Up Funds for Returned Scholar. In the mid-1990s, the Ministry of Education issued a specific policy stating that any scholar who had been abroad for more than six months (including six months) was eligible to apply for a CNY ¥20,000 yuan research start-up fund from the Ministry of Education, through their home institution. This policy was something I was informed about by the Chinese Embassy's Education Department in Canada when my visiting scholar program was coming to an end. The intent was to support returned scholars in starting their research work. Upon my return to the Institute of Geochemistry in mid-June 1996, I promptly submitted my application to the Ministry of Education's Department for Returned Scholars through the institute's personnel department. By around November 1996, a few staff members in the personnel department informed me that my ¥20,000 yuan research start-up fund had apparently been approved. One afternoon, I went to the personnel office and asked the head: "Head PXX, I've heard that my ¥20,000 yuan research start-up fund from the Ministry of Education has been approved. I'd like to claim it to start my next phase of research." She immediately replied: "No, not yet! It's still early for yours, and it might not be approved until next year." I responded: "But someone mentioned that it had already been approved. Why are you now saying it hasn't?" "Who said that? They must be mistaken. Wait a few more months, and if it gets approved, we'll notify you," she answered. Hearing this, I didn't argue further and left the office, albeit feeling frustrated. However, the personnel office never contacted me again, and by February 1997, before I left the institute for another trip abroad, I still hadn't received the ¥20,000 yuan start-up funding. It was clear that the personnel department had withheld the money. Whether or not this sum ended up in PXX's personal pocket remains known only to her. Although the institutes under the Chinese Academy of Sciences (CAS) are generally considered "cleaner" than local government administrative departments, the fact that PXX had control over personnel and financial matters for over a decade at the Institute of Geochemistry created opportunities for corruption. It is not impossible that embezzlement occurred. As such, it might be necessary for the relevant disciplinary and auditing bodies to investigate the financial records of the personnel and education department at that time to check for any potential corruption resulting from the abuse of power.

PXX of the personnel department of our institute is from Sichuan, and she and her husband, LXX, were originally from the same hometown. After graduating from university in the late 1960s, she was initially assigned to work in Heilongjiang Province. After marrying Lee, she transferred to the Institute of

Geochemistry in the late 1970s, starting as a general staff member in the personnel department. Over time, as senior staff retired or transferred, she rose to become deputy head and later head of the personnel department. Later LXX, her husband, put her in charge of all personnel, education, and foreign affairs matters at the institute. As a result, she was referred to by some as "Head P" and by others as "Principal P" (since she also oversaw graduate education), consolidating considerable power. In 1986, I joined the Party Committee of the institute and worked alongside her husband (LXX), who at the time was the deputy director and a member of the Party Committee. In 1990, her husband, LXX, had become the Party Secretary. If her actions to suppress me in 1996, as the personnel head, were due to the differences between me and her husband when we worked together in the Party Committee, it would be more understandable. However, her attempts to make life difficult for me and another student, Lin Tie, of Professor Guo during our degree conferral process back in 1981, long before I was even acquainted with her or her husband, suggest a deeper, more puzzling motive. In the late 1970s, I was a newcomer at the institute, with no personal connection to either of them, i.e., PXX and her husband LXX both, let alone any animosity. However, after two notable incidents involving the two senior professors, i.e., Professor Tu and Professor Guo, at the institute, I occasionally overheard speculation that there seemed to be tension between the two senior scientists. In October 1978, when the Chinese Society of Mineralogy, Petrology, and Geochemistry was founded, Professor Guo was originally recommended by our Institute's Party Committee to serve as vice-president. However, the conference secretariat unexpectedly removed Mr. Guo's name from the candidate list just before the election, causing Mr. Guo to miss even a regular membership on the society's council. The second incident occurred in 1980 when the Chinese Academy of Sciences (CAS) was selecting new academicians. The institute and the geochemistry society both did not recommend Professor Guo, and he was ultimately elected thanks to strong backing from the Chinese Society of Geology and personal involvement from then Vice Premier Yi Fang, who was also the president of CAS at the time. However, according to insiders, these incidents were unrelated to Professor Tu (Guo's peer), as the two professors had no personal grudge. It was believed that certain individuals, sycophants in Professor Tu's circle, intentionally played one professor against the other. Nevertheless, after these events, some opportunistic individuals at the institute began to treat the two professors and their students differently. For instance, graduates of Professor Tu's group were swiftly arranged for publicly funded overseas study opportunities, while those of Professor Guo faced difficulties obtaining the same opportunities. Head P of the personnel department, clearly one of these opportunistic individuals, took advantage of this situation, explaining her long-standing hostility toward me. Some openly said to me at the Institute: "Xiao Wu, over the years, you've followed the wrong mentor. With your qualifications, abilities, and expertise, if you were Professor Tu's student, not only would they never dare bully you, but you'd likely have been made deputy director or deputy Party secretary when the leadership reshuffle happened in 1990." To this, I could only respond helplessly: "Please don't say that. I'm not that kind of person, and I've never had such ambitions."

(Ⅱ)

When a person encounters one or two instances of unjust treatment at work, it is already frustrating enough. However, I had endured many such experiences over the years, and all of them came from the institute's personnel department that wielded the most power. For anyone repeatedly facing such issues, the natural reaction is to consider leaving the organization. As the saying goes: "If you can't win, why stay? There are other places that will appreciate you." By August and September of 1996, I had made up my mind: I had to find a way to leave the Institute of Geochemistry. Coincidentally, that year the State Ministry of Personnel issued a directive allowing returned scholars to move freely across China's research institutions. This meant that scholars like me could move to first-tier cities like Beijing and Shanghai, as long as a receiving institution with a matching specialization was willing to accept us. Family members would also be allowed to relocate without any residency restrictions. Given this new policy, I thought I'd try to transfer to a CAS institute in Beijing, where there were several institutes aligned with my specialization. Moreover, I had returned from abroad with an international cooperation project in hand. If I could find a familiar contact in Beijing to receive me, the process would be smoother.

At the time, I thought of Dr. Congqiang Liu, who had just returned from studying in Japan. Liu had completed his master's at our institute in 1987 before pursuing his PhD at the University of Tokyo, returning to China in early 1996. Instead of returning to our institute in Guiyang, he had stayed in Beijing Institute of Geophysics, CAS. When he came back to Guiyang for a visit in

A group photo of Professor Guo (the middle person in front row) with his staff of REE Research Department in Nov, 1985.(The author is the 3rd person from the right in the front row).

August, I met him at the institute and told him all about the IGCP 386 international cooperation project I had brought back from Canada. He expressed strong interest in the project and said we could potentially work together. To make the move to Beijing, I needed to secure a receiving institution, and this required knowing the right people and handling the process in person. I also had other important business to attend to in Beijing: first, to apply for a second Canadian visa at the Canadian Embassy; second, to coordinate with the Ministry of Geology and Mineral Resources about the IGCP 386 project; and third, to consult the

Ministry of Personnel about the specific policies on scholar relocation. So, in late September 1996, I flew to Beijing. The day after my arrival in Beijing, I first visited the Ministry of Personnel to inquire about the policies for returned scholars. There, I met with the head of the department responsible for managing technical professionals. I specifically asked about family relocation and was told that returned scholars could move their families with them to Beijing or Shanghai, provided that the receiving institution's specialization matched and there was a need for them. With this confirmation, I immediately called Dr. Congqiang Liu and informed him that I was in Beijing and would like to meet. He said: "No problem. Let's meet at the entrance to the Institute of Geophysics tomorrow at noon. I'll treat you to lunch!" The next day at noon, we met as planned at the entrance to the Institute of Geophysics and then walked to a nearby restaurant to chat over lunch. During lunch, I said to Mr. Congqiang Liu: "Congqiang, how are things at the Institute of Geophysics? Do you need people? If you do, I can transfer here. The Ministry of Personnel has a policy that allows returning scholars to relocate nationwide. Then we could work together on research projects." Mr. Congqiang Liu replied: "I'm not sure what the situation will be here. Right now, I only have an office and no staff. I don't have any projects or funding either. If my position here becomes stable, I'll definitely need people, and getting you transferred wouldn't be a problem. But the reality is, I don't even know how long I'll stay here, or if I'll be able to stay at all." Upon hearing this, I felt quite disappointed. My initial plan had been to transfer to Liu's institute if he needed staff. That way, I could leave the challenging environment at the Institute of Geochemistry, relocate to Beijing, and collaborate with a good friend on research---hitting three goals with one move. But now, hearing that Liu not only didn't need staff but was unsure of his own future, I was caught off guard by how uncertain the situation had become.

Originally, my plan was that if I could transfer to Beijing, there would be many logistical matters to handle---my job transfer, arranging work, relocating my wife and child's household registration, and finding a school for my child. Each of these issues would require time and effort to resolve. I had thought that if I could make the transfer, I would first settle in Liu's institute, then focus on setting up the international cooperation project I brought back from Canada, and temporarily put off going to work with Professor Geldsetzer at the Geological Survey of Canada. But now, since transferring to Beijing was no longer an option and there was no other suitable destination, I decided to take Geldsetzer's invitation letter and apply for a Canadian visa. I would aim to go to Canada for a few months in the first half of the year and then reassess the situation when I returned. With this decision made, after parting with Congqiang Liu at lunch, I went straight to the Canadian Embassy in Beijing with my visa application documents. At around 2:00 p.m., I arrived at the embassy and submitted my application materials. The consular officer asked me: "Would you prefer your passport and visa to be mailed or collected in person?" I responded: "I'll come to collect them." The officer said: "Please leave your contact details, and we will notify you when your passport and visa are ready for collection." After submitting the visa application, I went to the office of the International Commission on Stratigraphy of the Ministry of Geology and Mineral Resources in Xicheng District, Beijing, to submit the letter of appointment for the IGCP 386 international cooperation project. Once all the tasks were completed in Beijing, I flew back to Guiyang.

(Ⅲ)

In late December 1996, I received a notification from the Canadian Embassy in Beijing that my visa had been approved and was ready for collection. I immediately flew to Beijing, picked up my passport and visa from the embassy, and booked my flight to Canada for mid-February 1997. After returning to Guiyang, I wrote to Professor Geldsetzer at the Calgary Section of Geological Survey of Canada, informing him that my visa had been approved and that I would arrive in mid-February to work with him for six months. However, after sending the letter, I didn't hear back from him for nearly three months, right up until I was preparing to leave in mid-February. Since I had other preparations to focus on, I didn't dwell too much on the lack of response.

By January 1997, I had heard that my supervisor, Professor Guo, had been hospitalized and was gravely ill, having been in the Guizhou Provincial People's Hospital for over a month. It had been a long time since I last saw him, so I made a point to visit him before leaving the country. Sometime around late January, I went to see Professor Guo in the VIP ward at the provincial hospital. At first glance, I noticed that he had become much older and frailer. I remembered that his birthday was on January 21, 1917, meaning he had just turned 80 that year. When he saw me, he was overjoyed. In our conversation, Professor Guo was still deeply concerned about his special rare-earth geochemistry research project. He repeatedly told me that once he recovered, he wanted us to apply for a larger research project together. I stayed with him for over two hours, chatting the whole time during the day. Before I left, Professor Guo unexpectedly brought up his thoughts about what would happen after his death, asking for my advice. He said that after he passed, his biggest concern would be for his wife, Mrs. Guo. She had devoted her life to their family and had never worked, so she had no retirement pension. He was worried that after he passed, she would be left without financial security. I reassured him, saying, "Mr. Guo, you and Mrs. Guo have seven children. If each of them contributed ¥100 yuan to your wife a month, that would give Mrs. Guo ¥700 yuan monthly, which should be enough for her living expenses." Professor Guo responded: "But can each of them afford to give ¥100 yuan a month?" I said: "That shouldn't be a problem, right?" But he replied: "Their salaries aren't very high. I think this might be difficult for them." His deep love for Mrs. Guo was evident, and even at his advanced age, he was still thinking about his children's well-being too. Truly, it was a reflection of a parent's selfless heart. Although he had been hospitalized for over a month, he still appeared to be in relatively good spirits. I thought he might be discharged, just as he had been in the past. So I encouraged him, saying: "Mr. Guo, I'll definitely visit you when I return from my trip abroad. Please rest and focus on recovering." With that, I bade farewell to Professor Guo. Unfortunately, when I left China in mid-February 1997, Professor Guo passed away shortly afterward. That visit to the hospital became my final farewell to him.

On February 9th, 1997, which was the Chinese Lunar New Year's Eve, I prepared for my international flight scheduled for February 13. After celebrating the New Year, my wife and I took the train from Guiyang to Beijing on the first day of the Lunar New Year (February 10). Before leaving, I didn't inform the institute's leadership but mentioned my departure to a few colleagues on the Party Committee and spoke to my project team members, Junya Nan and Weidong Yang, asking them to handle any communications related to the international cooperation project while I was away. After arriving in Beijing on February 12, we stayed at the Chinese Academy of Sciences guesthouse in Sanlihe. That evening, I happened to meet Director Hongsen Xie from our Institute of Geochemistry at the guesthouse, and I briefly informed him of my plans to go abroad. Director Xie said: "That's great, Xiao Wu! If you have the opportunity, go for it!" On the afternoon of February 13, I boarded an international flight from Beijing to Canada, while that evening, my wife returned to Guiyang on a train to Kunming.

Later, I heard that on February 13th, the very day I flew from Beijing to Canada, my supervisor, Professor Guo, passed away. Since I had always been responsible for handling most of Professor Guo's affairs at the institute, after his passing, the higher-ups, LXX, at the institute were searching for me everywhere to deal with the funeral arrangements. Naturally, he couldn't find me. Early on the morning of February 14th, LXX even went to my house looking for me. My daughter happened to be home, and LXX asked her: "Is your dad home? Where did he go?" My daughter, not knowing how to lie, replied: "My dad went to Beijing and left for abroad." Upon hearing this, LXX was furious, and he stormed back to the institute, angrily proclaiming: "This Mingqing Wu is really outrageous! He left the country without even informing anyone at the institute." For some time afterward, I heard that this guy, LXX, repeatedly mentioned my "unauthorized departure" at various meetings, almost as if he was accusing me of "defecting." Additionally, it was said that he kept pressing at Party Committee meetings to find out who had "illegally stamped" and approved my exit procedures. In reality, this guy, much like his wife, was a government official who was not only incompetent but also ignorant of national policies. First of all, it wasn't my first time going abroad, which required any sort of official stamp for approval. Secondly, if I had a letter of invitation and a Canadian travel visa, I was free to leave the country. Did holding a personal visa still require the approval of the institute? This clearly showed that this guy was nothing but an empty suit.

(IV)

On February 13th, 1997, after flying from Beijing to Canada, I arrived in Ottawa to find it still covered in snow. That winter in Ottawa was exceptionally cold, and the snowfall was unusually heavy. After returning, a friend helped me settle back into the small shared apartment at 448 Cambridge Street, where I had previously stayed. This apartment had long been a popular residence for Chinese students and visiting scholars. The landlord, Mr. Pei, was a native of Shandong, originally from Taiwan. Though the twostory building was neither spacious nor particularly clean, it was well-equipped and reasonably priced. Additionally, its proximity to Chinatown and the university, as well as convenient public transportation, made it a favourite among Chinese students and scholars. I had stayed there for over six months during my previous visit, so I was considered an "old tenant." Upon returning, I found that most of the tenants were still there, and though a few new faces had moved in, we were all from mainland China, so it didn't take long for everyone to become acquainted.

Upon returning to Ottawa, I immediately got in touch with Kun Wang and prepared to reach out to Professor Geldsetzer about when to start work. Kun Wang came to see me the very next day after hearing I had returned. As soon as we met, he said: "Mr. Wu, you probably don't know yet, but Professor Geldsetzer has passed away from liver cancer!" I was shocked and replied: "How could that be? When I left last June, he was perfectly fine! How did he pass away so quickly?" Wang continued: "It was only in early October last year that he was diagnosed with liver cancer, but by then, it was already terminal. He didn't even undergo surgery, and within three months of hospitalization, he passed away. He died just after the New Year of 1997." I sighed heavily and said: "Wow, that's really unfortunate. How could he pass away in just two or three months? So what's going to happen to our project now?" Wang replied: "We don't know what's going to happen. I'm not sure who's going to take over IGCP 386, and with Geldsetzer gone, our project might be in jeopardy." Hearing this, I felt uncertain about my prospects in Canada. After Kun Wang left, I fell into deep thought: What should I do next? Should I immediately pack up and head back to China? But I had only just arrived, and if I returned so soon, how would I explain it to the people at the institute? Yet when I recalled all the difficulties and oppression I had faced at the institute in recent years, I felt a surge of anger. Now that I had left, there was no turning back. No matter how challenging it might be, I resolved to find a way to stay. The most pressing issue now was to settle down, sort out my status, and find a job. Fortunately, I still had several thousand dollars left from my time as a visiting scholar, so I wasn't too worried about my immediate living expenses. As for the international cooperation project, with Geldsetzer gone, I decided to let it go for now and see how Junya Nan and Weidong Yang back in China were handling things.

About three or four months later, around June 1997, I received a letter from Professor Junya Nan, a member of the project team in China. Inside was another letter in English--Mr. Nan had forwarded it to me. It turned out to be from Professor Harald Strauss at the Institute of Geology, RuhrUniversity Bochum in Germany, who was writing on behalf of the IGCP 386 international project team. Since they didn't know I had come to Canada, they had sent the letter to my former address at the Institute of Geochemistry in Guiyang. In the letter, Professor Strauss explained that after Professor Geldsetzer passed away in January 1997, the IGCP 386 international cooperation project team had sent two or three letters to me in China. One letter informed me of the change in project leadership, while another requested a report on China's project plans for 1997. However, months had passed without any response from the Chinese team, and they were unsure of our situation. To avoid delaying the project's progress, the IGCP 386 international project leadership team had consulted with the Ministry of Geology and Mineral Resources in China. Apparently, the ministry had always been dissatisfied with the fact that our institute, the Institute of Geochemistry at the Chinese Academy of Sciences, had secured the IGCP 386 project. As a result, they suggested transferring the project to China University of Geosciences in Wuhan, which led to Professor Hongfu Yin at CUG being appointed to take over full responsibility for the project. Upon reading the letters from Professor Strauss and Junya Nan, I realized what had happened. After I left China in midFebruary 1997, the IGCP 386 international cooperation project team had sent two or three letters to the institute, which Weidong Yang, as a project team member, had received. However, Mr. Yang had neither informed Mr. Junya Nan nor forwarded the letters to me in Canada. He hadn't even replied on behalf of the Chinese team to Professor Strauss. As a result, we lost our leadership role in the IGCP 386 international cooperation project in China. When Professor Nan finally discovered that Yang had been holding onto the letters, he confronted him, but by then, it was too late to reverse the situation. Upon receiving this bad news, I became even more determined to stay in Canada. Based on later information, it became clear that China University of Geosciences in Wuhan didn't achieve particularly notable results with the IGCP 386 project, and the project wasn't renewed as scheduled. If our Institute of Geochemistry had continued to lead the project without any mishaps, I believe we would have made significant breakthroughs, especially since IGCP 386 project was centered on geochemical research---a field in which our institute excelled with our advanced research methods and equipment. In contrast, China University of Geosciences specialized in stratigraphy and paleontology, areas in which they were strong, but their geochemistry capabilities were lacking.

On the other hand, the fact that Weidong Yang, a member of our project team, received several letters from the IGCP 386 international cooperation project leader addressed to me but neither informed Professor Junya Nan nor forwarded the letters to me in Canada, does have its reasons and context. It turns out that his position at the institute was also unexpectedly difficult at the time, and in retrospect, we can't place all the blame on him. Based on what I later learned, after I left for Canada in February 1997, Weidong Yang, as one of the leaders of the Chinese team for the IGCP 386 international cooperation project, was implicated because of his association with me. He, too, faced baseless exclusion and suppression by LXX and his wife, PXX, at the Institute of Geochemistry. Weidong Yang had earned his PhD from Chengdu Institute of Geology in 1989 and joined the Institute of Geochemistry the same year as a postdoc, becoming a permanent member of our institute in 1991. He was a Party member, had strong professional abilities, and was considered a promising young researcher---one of the key successors being groomed at the institute. By 1995, he had already been appointed as Assistant Director of the institute and Head of the Scientific

Research Office of our Institute. However, because he also served as the Deputy Head of the Chinese team for the IGCP 386 international cooperation project, which I had brought back from abroad, he inexplicably became the target of exclusion and suppression by Lee and his wife. Within less than two years, Yang was abruptly removed from his positions as Assistant Director and Head of the Research Office, and as it became increasingly difficult for him to continue working at the institute, Yang began considering a bold plan in 1998---to leave the institute and travel across the country by bicycle for on-site geological surveys. Unfortunately, his journey ended prematurely, and he returned without completing his goal. After 2000, facing no other options, Yang used a three-month stint abroad as a visiting scholar to settle in Vancouver, Canada, for good. While Professor Junya Nan was also a key member of our international cooperation project team, he escaped the persecution that befell Weidong Yang and me. This was likely because Professor Nan was a long-standing employee at the institute, a regular worker without any official titles or authority, which shielded him from LXX and his wife's attacks. To this day, when veteran colleagues at the institute recall how the couple unjustly targeted me and Weidong Yang, they can't help but express their sympathy and dismay. Everyone agrees that this couple was not only incompetent but also manipulative, using their positions to suppress talented young scientists, forcing them to leave the country. Their malice seemed to know no bounds.

In reality, Weidong Yang and I were far from the only ones at the Institute of Geochemistry who faced such oppression from LXX and his wife, PXX, at our institute. Over PXX one or two decades of monopolizing control over personnel, education, and foreign affairs, it wasn't uncommon for her to make life difficult for students of other mentors---only sparing a select few whom she dared not challenge. For those students whose words or actions didn't align with her desires, they could expect trouble when it came to getting degrees, promotions, or public funding for overseas studies. Therefore, during the 1980s and 1990s, many graduate students at the Institute of Geochemistry were subjected to her unreasonable treatment. Among the nearly one hundred students who remained abroad, quite a few had experienced some degree of oppression or hardship at her hands.

Chapter 11   Building a New Life Abroad

(I)

When I returned to Ottawa, Canada, in mid-February 1997, I came with high hopes. However, upon landing, I received the devastating news of my international collaboration project leader's death. It felt like a heavy blow, shattering my hopes of continuing my research work and indicating that my second visit to Canada was now filled with uncertainty. I knew very well that without the support of the international project, I had lost my foundation in Canada, and it also meant cutting off any easy route to return to China. It was clear that I had no other option but to find a way to stay in Canada. However, when I calmed down and thought about the road ahead, I realized it was full of uncertainties. First, if I were to stay in Canada long-term, I would need to apply for skilled immigration. Second, even if I succeeded in immigrating, I had heard that it was difficult to find a job in my field in Canada. This meant that I might have to change careers and start over. Furthermore, I had also heard that Canada had strict age limits for skilled immigrants. Being in my mid-ages, I had no idea if I could successfully immigrate. So, I decided to consult with a local Chinese friend to learn more about skilled immigration and seek advice. I thought of Mr. Shubang Zhou from the Chinese Christian Union Church.

Back in 1995-1996, when I was working as a visiting scientist at the Geological Survey of Canada, I once met Mr. Zhou while shopping at a Chinese store in Chinatown. He had immigrated to Canada from Guangzhou in the late 1970s and served at the Chinese Christian Union Church on weekends. He had invited me to join their activities, and since I didn't have any friends or acquaintances in Ottawa and felt lonely on weekends, I occasionally went to the church for some of their events. Over time, we became friends. One weekend, I went to see Mr. Zhou and shared my situation and thoughts about immigrating, hoping to get his advice. Mr. Zhou said: "Based on what you've told me, it seems like you've done pretty well in China! You've made quite a few achievements in your research, and you performed excellently at the Geological Survey of Canada, with high praise from your supervisor. I also understand the difficulties and

The Parliament Building in Ottawa, Canada.

circumstances you've faced in China. In recent years, many middle-aged people from China have immigrated for similar reasons---they had no choice but to leave. But I must warn you, immigrating is a tough road, especially for someone of your age. You need to think this through carefully!" Mr. Zhou explained that Canada was indeed a country highly sought after by new immigrants. It is vast, rich in resources, politically stable, and its people are friendly. There is free healthcare for everyone and 12 years of free compulsory education, with excellent benefits for the elderly and children. Living here is particularly beneficial for the education of your children and future generations. Some jokingly say that Canada is a paradise for the elderly and children, but middleaged people face a tough struggle here. Due to the small population, the job market isn't as favourable, especially for new immigrants from countries like China, with different cultural and linguistic backgrounds. Many immigrants with excellent professional qualifications find it difficult to secure work in their fields and have to change careers or go back to school for another degree. He pointed out that for someone my age, going back to school for a degree without sufficient financial support wasn't realistic. So, if I wanted to immigrate, I had to be mentally prepared to switch careers and endure hardship. He also mentioned that while interpersonal relationships in Western societies are relatively simple, and you don't need to rely on connections to deal with government offices, the first few years for new immigrants can be extremely challenging. However, after seven or eight years, or a decade of hard work, most Chinese immigrants manage to build comfortable lives, including owning homes, and their next generation won't have to endure the same struggles. When it came to the specifics of how to apply for skilled immigration, Mr. Zhou advised me to consult an immigration lawyer or hire one directly. This would make the process more straightforward and give me a better chance of success.

After carefully listening to Mr. Zhou's detailed explanation and analysis, I spent several days reflecting on the situation, repeatedly pondering the question: "Should I stay or go back?" For several days, I was torn and couldn't decide. After all, I had worked at the Institute of Geochemistry, the Chinese Academy of Sciences, for more than twenty years, achieved the title of associate researcher (associate professor), and even though I had been suppressed, I figured it wouldn't be too difficult to be promoted to full researcher (professor) within a year or two. Staying in Canada would mean giving up everything I had built in China, starting from scratch, and it would also mean leaving behind my wife and daughter. This thought weighed heavily on me and made me hesitant. But then, I would remember the ugly faces of Lee and his wife at the institute, and the thought of returning to that environment made me reconsider. This internal conflict plagued me for days, to the point where I couldn't eat or sleep properly, and I felt completely lost. In the end, I decided to leave it to fate and use a random method to determine my future. I took a sheet of A4 paper and cut it into eight small strips. On four strips, I wrote "Go back," and on the other four, I wrote "Stay." I rolled each strip into a small ball and placed them in a jar. I shook the jar thoroughly and then randomly picked one ball using chopsticks. I decided that if I drew "Go back" three out of four times, I would return to China; if I drew "Stay" three times, I would stay in Canada. As fate would have it, I drew "Stay" three times out of four. That's when I finally made up my mind to stay in Canada. Had I not used this method, I don't know how much longer I would have agonized over this decision. Once I made the decision to stay, I felt much more at peace. I realized that with my project leader in Canada now gone, going back to China would only subject me to more humiliation and suppression. I reasoned that it was better to figure out how to stay in Canada. Even if things got tough here, I had been through worse hardships during my youth and the Cultural Revolution, so I was confident I could endure. At worst, even if I couldn't find a job in my field, I would take any other work available. I was willing to sacrifice my career to give the next generation a chance at a better, freer life. After all, I had had enough of the backstabbing, exhausting life of always having to please others. I didn't want my children to go through the same struggles. As long as I could live peacefully and comfortably, far away from that toxic environment, I would be satisfied. With that resolve, I decided to give it everything I had.

When I applied for immigration, I heard from a friend that for skilled immigration applicants, the immigration office scores them based on various criteria. If you're over 45 years old, you lose the points for age, and the older you are, the harder it becomes to immigrate. Since Mr. Shubang Zhou suggested that I should consult a lawyer, I found a Chinese immigration lawyer named David Shen on Bank Street in Ottawa through an ad in a Chinese-language newspaper. Mr. Shen, a young and handsome man from Beijing, had come to Canada to study and settled down after graduating. He was friendly and down- to-earth. After I consulted him about skilled immigration, he noted that although I was older, my qualifications---education, degrees, and work experience---were excellent. When he saw the two reference letters from the two professors I had worked with at the Geological Survey of Canada, he immediately said that, based on his experience, someone like me, despite my age, should have no problem getting approved. With that assurance, I handed over all the necessary documents for my immigration application and entrusted him with handling it. Perhaps my qualifications were indeed good, and the strong recommendations from the professors certainly helped. My application was approved without even needing an interview, and the process took only about four months. However, the situation for my wife and daughter was delayed due to medical examination issues. The problem started when the Canadian Embassy in Beijing sent their medical forms to Guiyang, requiring them to undergo physical exams at Guiyang Medical University. After they completed the exams and sent the forms back to the embassy, the response came that the forms were improperly filled out, and they needed to retake the physical exams. After the second round of exams, the embassy indicated that one of my daughter's results was unsatisfactory. With all this back-andforth, over a year passed. Finally, in the second half of 1998, the Canadian Embassy sent a third set of medical forms, instructing them to go to West China Medical University in Chengdu for their exams. After this third examination, everything was fine, and both my wife and daughter passed. In May 1999, they finally received their immigration visas. In late July 1999, my wife and daughter flew to Canada, and our family was finally reunited in Ottawa, marking the beginning of our new life as immigrants.

The author and his wife in the front of the Civilization Museum in Gatineau, Quebec Province, Canada in Jun., 2000.

(Ⅱ)

Even though Canada is one of the most sought-after destinations for immigrants, before finishing my visiting scholar program and returning to China, I never considered immigrating to Canada. It was only after returning to China and facing continuous suppression from those in power that I developed the desire to leave the Institute of Geochemistry. When I came back to Canada for the second time, I encountered the unfortunate death of my international project leader and the transfer of the project to another institution. After much consideration, despite being nearly fifty, I decided to immigrate to Canada---and to my surprise, I was successful.

Naturally, I was thrilled when my immigration application was approved. Finally, I had a legal status that allowed me to stay in Canada long-term. However, finding a job turned out to be much more difficult than I had anticipated. I thought back to my time working at the Geological Survey of Canada as a visiting scientist and how well I had collaborated with the two professors there. I hoped that I could reach out to them to see if they had any work or needed help or to explore the possibility of joining them at the Geological Survey of Canada. After meeting with them, I learned that neither professor had any projects or work available, and they were unable to assist me. Moreover, due to the global economic crisis in 1997, Canada's economy was in bad shape. Many companies were laying off employees, and even government departments, including the Geological Survey of Canada, were downsizing. Dr. Kun Wang, who had been doing postdoctoral research at the Geological Survey of Canada during my time there in 1995-1996, told me that he had been trying to get a permanent position at the Geological Survey of Canada for three years. Despite his exceptional qualifications and academic prowess, the Geological Survey of Canada wasn't hiring, and even he couldn't secure a position. In terms of academic credentials, Kun Wang was outstanding among his peers. During his PhD studies, he had already published an academic paper in *Science*, one of the world's top journals, and during his postdoctoral period, he continued publishing some papers in *Geology*. His supervisor at the Geological Survey of Canada greatly valued him and hoped to keep him on after his postdoc ended. Kun Wang told me that after three years at the

Geological Survey of Canada, he had become well-acquainted with the management---from the director to HR and various research department heads. The director had even told him privately that if the hiring freeze lifted and there was only one position available, it would go to him. However, from 1997 to 1999, Wang waited in vain for the government to resume hiring. By early 2000, seeing no prospects, he had no choice but to return to China with his family.

This experience showed me that even someone as talented as Kun Wang faced difficulties, so my own chances of securing a professional job in Canada were slim. Back in those days, it wasn't just Canada where it was difficult to find work in geological fields---this was the case in the U.S. and many other Western countries as well. Not only were geologyrelated jobs hard to come by, but jobs in many other professional fields were equally scarce. The one exception was the field of computer science and information system technology, which was in high demand. As a result, many young immigrants who couldn't find jobs in their fields went back to university to pursue master's degrees in computer science, then re-entered the workforce upon graduation. I was told that among the dozens of graduate students from our Institute of Geochemistry studying abroad in the U.S. and Canada, only a small number were still working in geology or geochemistry field. The majority had already switched fields. For me, the situation was even more challenging. First, I had no background in computer science, and second, I was older, making it unrealistic for me to return to university for a degree in that field. Since getting into the Geological Survey of Canada was out of the question, and finding work in geology or geochemistry seemed nearly impossible, I wondered if perhaps finding a job in chemistry might be easier. So, I began searching online for job postings at factories, mines, and environmental chemistry labs around Ottawa. I tailored and printed dozens of resumes and sent them to these laboratories, hoping to land a position in a chemistry lab. However, despite sending out all those resumes, I heard nothing---like throwing stones into the sea, I received no feedback for months.

Next, I thought, since I couldn't find a job in my field, I would try to find any general job to cover my living expenses. But even general jobs were hard to come by. In Canada, finding a job often requires two things: connections and experience. Unfortunately, I had neither. With the tough economic climate, unemployment was high, and the competition for jobs was fierce. For example, if a restaurant posted a job opening for one or two kitchen helpers, 20 to 30 people would show up to apply, and they usually preferred candidates with prior experience. For a newcomer like me, it was nearly impossible to get hired.

Photographed by the author with his wife and daughter in Huaxi Park, Guiyand, Guizhou, China in June, 1994.

One morning, I saw an ad in a local English-language newspaper for a mushroom farm located about 20 kilometers south of Ottawa that was hiring mushroom pickers. The farm was quite far, and there was no public transportation to get there. While I was fretting over how to get to the interview, a Western friend of mine named Porter offered to drive me there during his lunch break. I also brought my old bicycle, which we loaded into the trunk of his car, thinking I would ride it back afterward. Porter dropped me off at the farm and immediately returned to work. When I arrived, the ad said they were hiring four people, but more than 20 people showed up to apply, most of them middle-aged women in their 40s and 50s who had previously worked at the mushroom farm. The interview process was simple: one by one, we met with the hiring manager, who told us to wait for a phone call. By the time the interviews ended, it was already after 4 p.m., and I had to ride my bike back.

However, my bike tires were quite worn out, and while it was fine for short rides in the city, the rough gravel roads were too much for it. After riding for a while, the tires started leaking air. Luckily, there were gas stations every 3 to 5 kilometers along the way, and each one had a coin-operated air pump. I spent 25 cents at each stop to refill the tires. But after riding another few kilometers, the tires finally gave out completely, leaving me no choice but to push the bike the rest of the way home. And, as I expected, I never heard back from the mushroom farm. Months passed, and I continued my gruelling job search. By late August 1997, one of my roommates, Puqun Li, a fellow student who had just returned from visiting his family in China over the summer, mentioned something during a chat. He asked: "Mr. Wu, would you be interested in a dishwashing job at Carleton University's cafeteria?" He said that he had a Canadian friend who worked there, and the cafeteria was hiring dishwashers for the new school year. If I was interested, he could put in a word for me with his friend. Desperate for work, I jumped at the opportunity. In early September, when the new semester began, I started working at Carleton University's cafeteria.

Carleton University is a research university in Ottawa known for its programs in journalism, economics, public administration, and computer science. At the time, the university had over 10,000 students, but only about 700 to 800 lived in the campus dormitories. The cafeteria provided meals (lunch and dinner) for these dorm students daily, and during mealtimes, the cafeteria's kitchen staff had to wash and sanitize a large number of plates, bowls, cups, and utensils. To say the job was exhausting is an understatement---without good physical strength, it would be impossible to keep up. Some might think that dishwashing is just about standing at the sink, rinsing dishes one by one. But that's a major misconception. In a cafeteria that serves 700 to 800, or even more than 1,000 people, dishwashing has long since become an industrial process. The whole operation was divided into several stages, with each person responsible for one task. All the stages were interconnected by machines, much like an assembly line in a factory. To be more specific, the system consisted of a dishwashing machine that automatically washed and steam-sterilized the dishes, along with a conveyor belt that sorted the various items. After students finished their meals, the

The author and his daughter were reading book at home in Jun. 1987.

trays loaded with dishes, cups, and cutlery were brought to the back of the kitchen. The trays were placed on a conveyor belt, which had three stations: one for sorting cutlery, one for cups, and one for sorting plates, bowls, and removing leftover food. Each station was manned by one person. The dishwasher had two stations: one for loading the dirty dishes and another one for receiving and sorting the clean, sterilized dishes. These two stations were also manned by one person each. In total, the process had five steps, handled by five workers. Except for the first station, where cutlery was sorted, all other stations were fast-paced and physically demanding, especially the two stations at the dishwasher. Working near the high-temperature steam was hot and tiring, and after just 30 minutes, you'd be drenched in sweat. The work was done in rotation, so everyone got a turn at each station. Since it was an assembly line, timing and cooperation were critical---if one station made a mistake, the whole line had to stop, disrupting the workflow and affecting the quality of the work. It took about two to three weeks of training and hands-on practice before I could handle all the tasks.

The school cafeteria usually starts serving lunch to students at 11:00 a.m., with lunch service ending around 2:00 p.m. Then, dinner service begins at 4:00 p.m. and finishes around 6:00 p.m. Our dishwashing shift would start around 11:30 a.m., after the first wave of students had finished their lunch, and would last until about 2:30 p.m. After finishing the dishwashing, we'd finally have our lunch, followed by a one hour break. At 4:00 p.m., dinner service would begin, and our evening dishwashing shift would start again. We'd usually finish around 7:00 p.m., and after having our own dinner, we would head home, usually not arriving until after 8:00 p.m. In total, we worked about six hours a day, eating two meals in the cafeteria. Although this job

wasn't great, and the pay wasn't high (based on Ontario's minimum wage), the meals were a real perk. The cafeteria offered all sorts of Western foods like steaks, hamburgers, sandwiches, and various desserts. You could take as much as you wanted, with each meal costing just 50 cents. Back then, we were young with hearty appetites, so we'd easily eat two or three large steaks and at least two hamburgers per meal. During the three months I worked in the Carleton University cafeteria, my total living expenses probably didn't even reach 200 Canadian dollars.

In mid-December of 1997, during a weekend when I visited the Chinese Christian Fellowship with some friends, a Chinese friend mentioned that a high-tech company in Ottawa was hiring. He had been working there for over a month, so I asked him for the company's contact information and planned to apply.

(Ⅲ)

In mid-December of 1997, after hearing about the job opening at a high-tech company, I decided to visit the company on Monday after the weekend. The company was called JDS Uniphase, a high-tech company located in the western suburbs of Ottawa, specializing in manufacturing fiber-optic communication components. Although fiber-optic communications had nothing to do with my field of geochemistry, I had heard they were hiring across all professional fields, so I didn't hesitate to apply. After filling out my resume, the HR department told me to come back in two days for a test. Two days later, I arrived at JDS Uniphase around 2:00 p.m. for the test, along with about 20 other candidates. Most were new immigrants from Eastern Europe, the Middle East, and Southeast Asia, with only a few Canadians. We were seated, and HR handed out test papers. The test consisted of six questions spread over two pages, mostly high school level math problems, with one hour allotted to complete it. I finished in about 30 minutes, but many others were still working by the time the hour ended, and they reluctantly handed in their papers when the HR staff called time. Before we left, HR told us to await further notice for interviews. Shortly after New Years Day in 1998, around January 4th, I received a call asking me to come in for an interview the next morning at 10:00 a.m. The next day, I arrived at the company and was interviewed by John Smit, the manager of the kitting room in the technical services department. He explained that the department required higher qualifications and told me that I had done well on the test. He asked about my education (I told him I only had a university degree) and offered me a position in his department. He then explained the main tasks of the kitting department: (1) Testing and classifying the optical and electrical parameters of the fiber optic components produced by the company. (2) Based on the design drawings provided by the optical communication engineers, we were to gather and prepare all necessary components. (3) Distributing the prepared components to the assembly line workers and providing replacements for any faulty or damaged components during the assembly process. Regarding pay, the starting wage for assembly line workers was $9 CAD per hour, while the starting wage in our department was $13 CAD per hour (at that time, Ontario's minimum wage was $6.85CAD per hour). The work was organized in three shifts: the morning shift from 7:00 a.m. to 3:00 p.m., the afternoon shift from 3:00 p.m. to 11:00 p.m., and the night shift from 11:00 p.m. to 7:00 a.m. the next day. There was one dollar 1 hourly premium for the afternoon shift and two dollars 1 hour for the night shift. After the interview, I officially started working at JDS Uniphase on January 11, 1998, choosing the afternoon shift from 3:00 p.m. to 11:00 p.m. So, my wage was $14 CAD per hour in the beginning.

At the late stage of 1990s, fiber-optic communication technology was rapidly developing across Europe and North America. Major companies like Cisco and Lucent in the U.S., Nortel in Canada, and Alcatel in France emerged as giants in the telecom industry, requiring vast amounts of fiber-optic communication components. JDS Uniphase, a small company founded in Ottawa in the mid-1980s to produce these components, quickly expanded. When I joined the company in early 1998, there were just over 1,000 employees, but by the end of 1999 and into early 2000, the workforce had exploded to more than 20,000, with the company growing 10 to 20 times its original size. At the time, JDS Uniphase even established branches in the U.S., Europe, and Xiamen, China, becoming a multinational corporation. The company's stock split three times in 1999, and many engineers and senior employees saw their stock holdings exceed CAD one million. From 1999 to 2001, JDS Uniphase continued its rapid expansion, hiring a large number of new immigrants each year to work on the production lines. Many Chinese immigrants who had just arrived in Canada found jobs at JDS Uniphase within a week of landing. Although the pay wasn't high, the company provided a lifeline for new immigrants, helping them adjust to Canadian society and the job market. It's no exaggeration to say that almost every Chinese immigrant who arrived in Ottawa between 1999 and 2001 worked at JDS at some point. Therefore, in Ottawa's Chinese community, everyone knew about JDS very well.

(IV)

At the end of July 1999, my wife and daughter arrived in Ottawa, and our family was finally reunited. The days of longing for each other were over. To prepare for their arrival, I had rented a two-bedroom apartment and spent around $1,500 CAD on a 37-inch Panasonic TV and a Sanyo stereo system. The apartment had just been freshly painted, and the whole place exuded a joyful atmosphere.

My wife and daughter arrived in Ottawa at the end of July, right in the middle of the golden season of the Canadian summer. On the weekends, I drove them to explore Ottawa's Chinatown and the Parliament Hill area. Once they had settled in, I took them on trips in different seasons to help them get acquainted with Ottawa and its surroundings. Although Ottawa is Canada's capital, the population isn't very large, around 700,000 to 800,000 at the time, making it the fourth-largest city in Canada. While the population is small, the city itself is quite large, stretching about 50 kilometers from east to west and 30 kilometers from north to south (not counting the sparsely populated outskirts). The Ottawa River lies to the north, with the city of Gatineau in Quebec on the other side, where Parliament Hill, the iconic Parliament buildings, stand tall along the riverbank. The Rideau Canal flows through the southern part of the city, often filled with luxurious yachts in the summer, and in winter, it turns into an ideal natural ice-skating rink. Canada offers stunning natural beauty year-round: in spring, Ottawa is full of blooming flowers, with the Tulip Festival drawing large crowds in May; in summer, the city is lush with greenery and flowers adorning every corner; in fall, the trees are ablaze with red maple leaves, and the air is filled with the scent of ripe fruits; in winter, despite the snow and ice, it's a paradise for winter sports enthusiasts, with the annual Winterlude festival in February. After my wife and daughter arrived, I drove them to see Niagara Falls and Old Quebec City during the summer, took them to Gatineau Park in the fall to admire the red leaves, visited Ottawa's Winterlude in the winter, and enjoyed the blooming tulips during the Tulip Festival in the spring.

As for Canada's social environment, it's peaceful and safe. You never see homes with burglar bars or security doors, and shopping centers have large, spotless glass windows. Petty theft is nearly non-existent, and serious crimes are rare. Canada, as a developed Western country, is rich in resources, with stable prices and a relaxed, harmonious lifestyle. After less than a year, my wife and daughter had fully adapted to Ottawa's lifestyle, experienced Canada's four-season beauty, and appreciated the city's cultural environment. Even though they were in a foreign land, they grew to love it here.

The most pressing issue for my daughter, Xia Wu, after arriving was her education. Before coming to Canada, she had just graduated from Guiyang No. 1 High School and had taken the national university entrance exam in early June, scoring high enough for admission to a top university in China. After arriving in Canada, we suggested she repeat one year of high school in

Ottawa to improve her English, and then apply to university in 2000, which she agreed to. To attend high school in Ottawa, she first had to undergo a placement assessment by the city's school board. One afternoon, we took her to the school board's assessment office. After submitting all the necessary documents regarding her academic records, a female teacher took her to another room for a math assessment. After about half an hour,

The author visited the Ottawa Tulip Festival in May, 2001.

the teacher brought her back and called me into the office. She told me: "Mr. Wu, your daughter's English is excellent. Her listening and speaking skills are solid, and her pronunciation is very good. She should have no problem attending high school here." Since the teacher had taken my daughter for a math assessment, but kept talking about her English abilities, I started to wonder if my daughter hadn't done well in math test. So, I asked the teacher: "Excuse me, but how did my daughter do in the math assessment?" The teacher immediately replied: "Excellent! Her math skills are far beyond the level of our high school students here, and I've reviewed her high school transcripts already---her grades are outstanding. If it weren't for the need to improve her English, she could go straight to university!" Hearing this, I was greatly relieved.

My daughter Xia Wu was born in January 1981, so she had just turned 18 in 1999, and had just graduated from high school in China. If she hadn't come to Canada, she would have started university in China that year. Xia Wu had always been a smart and lovable child, and very diligent and responsible in her studies. From elementary school to high school, she consistently ranked among the top students in her class and never caused her parents any worry about her academic performance. After the school board's evaluation, she was admitted to Grade 13 at Glebe Collegiate Institute, one of the top high schools in Ottawa. After a year of study, she achieved an average of over 95% in all her subjects, and in June 2000, she was accepted into both Carleton University and the University of Toronto. She ultimately chose to study electrical engineering at the University of Toronto, one of Canada's leading universities. During her time there, she received scholarships every year and graduated successfully in 2004. Now, my daughter's family is settled in Toronto, where she has not only achieved professional success but also has a thriving family with three children (two boys and a girl), and the eldest of whom is already 15 years old and in high school already.

After my wife arrived in Canada, although life here was worry-free, we came empty-handed. I was the only one working, bringing in about CAD 3,000–4,000 a month. While my daughter was attending high school with no financial burden, my wife felt bored staying at home. Just two or three weeks after arriving, she started talking about wanting to find a job. However, not knowing any English was a significant barrier. Even if she wanted to find a job at a Chinese shop in Chinatown, the chances were slim since many shop owners preferred to hire undocumented workers to save on labor costs. Fortunately, there was a government-run immigration school next to where we lived, offering free English classes to new immigrants. So, my wife began attending classes five days a week, learning English from scratch--starting with the alphabet, ABCD. After only a month or two, she found a job through a friend's introduction at a small print shop run by a Pakistani family, working as a bookbinding assistant. Since she had to work during the day, she switched to taking evening English classes at the immigrant school. By this time, my wife was almost fifty years old, and without any prior English knowledge, she had to start from zero. However, through sheer determination, she dedicated nearly all her spare time to learning English, going through two or three electronic dictionaries in the process. In a relatively short period, she gained enough language proficiency to manage daily conversations. Over the past two decades, from the time she started working until her retirement, she always worked in English-speaking environments at Western companies. Remarkably, after just three years of living in Ottawa, she successfully passed the English citizenship test and became a Canadian citizen in 2002. Even though she is now retired and older, she still continues to study English from time to time.

The author with his wife and daughter visited the Ottawa Winterlude Festival in Ottawa, Ontario, Canada in February, 2000.

(V)

People watching the TV program "Animal World" are often captivated by the stunning footage while also marvelling at how constant competition defines the animal kingdom. Humans, as intelligent beings within the animal world, face similar competition in the workplace. Particularly in a multicultural country like Canada, employees in any given company may come from various ethnic backgrounds, with Canadians sometimes being the minority, and immigrants making up the majority of the workforce. As a result, workplace competition can occur not only between different ethnic groups but also within the same community.

In the technical services department at JDS, where I worked, the team grew from just over 20 people when I joined in early 1998 to around 70 or 80 by the end of 1999. Our team included about 10 Filipinos, 12 or 13 Chinese, 15 or 16 Eastern Europeans, more than a dozen people from the Middle East and Africa, and around 20 people from India, Pakistan, Bangladesh, and Vietnam. The team was split into three shifts---morning, afternoon, and night---each with over 20 people. Since we were part of the technical services department, the manager, Mr. John Smit, was Canadian and had high educational requirements for his employees. When I first joined, except for a few Filipinos with lower educational backgrounds, most of the employees from various countries had at least a university degree, and several even held master's degrees. As the company continued to grow, Mr. Smit was promoted to a higher position as department director, and from the second half of 1999, our department manager became a Filipino woman named Alma. In Canada, small immigrant communities like those from the Philippines or Vietnam tend to stick together and support each other. If one of their own is in a leadership position, they often give special attention to others from their community. However, larger immigrant groups, such as our Chinese, are often fragmented. In fact, it's well-known that Chinese immigrants are notorious for infighting. There's a common saying in overseas workplaces: "One Chinese is a dragon; three Chinese became worms," meaning that when three Chinese people work together, constant internal conflicts render them ineffective. After Alma, a Filipino, became our manager, the dynamics in our department started to change. Despite the department's technical nature and higher educational requirements (along with a correspondingly higher starting salary compared to other departments), more and more Filipinos with only high school or even lower education levels began to join. Over time, many of these Filipino employees were promoted to positions like team leader or coordinator, overseeing the morning, afternoon, and night shifts. By the time our department had grown to about 80 people, there were more than 20 or so people on each shift, which was further divided into two groups. Each shift had one team leader and two coordinators. Out of the three team leaders, two were Filipino, and out of the six coordinators, four were Filipino. In other words, two-thirds of the leadership roles in our department were held by Filipinos, which was an incredibly disproportionate situation. To make matters worse, once Filipinos gained control of most leadership positions, there was a noticeable bias in how tasks were assigned, performance was evaluated, promotions were made, and raises were given---always favouring Filipino employees or those close to them, while others were often sidelined or treated unfairly.

Following that, two or three more incidents occurred in our shift. At that time, there was an engineer in our shift (the one I was part of) named Gang Wu, a fellow Chinese. He graduated from Chengdu Institute of Telecommunication Engineering in Sichuan Province, China and after studying optoelectronics in Canada, he graduated with a master's degree in 1995 and was hired by JDS as an optoelectronic communications engineer. Mr. Gang Wu had formal training, and there was no doubt about his technical skills. However, for some reason, he developed significant conflicts with our Filipino department manager over work-related issues. When Gang Wu assigned tasks to us, the Filipino team-leader, whose name is Nonito, in our shift would constantly find fault with him. Sometimes, we couldn't stand it and would argue with the Filipino leads in defence of Gang Wu. But not long after, Gang Wu was transferred out of our department, and the Filipinos became even more complacent.

The second incident occurred around August 1999. An employee named Lao Zhang, who had just joined our shift that fall, was assigned to work in the same group as me. The Filipino Teamleader Nonito asked me to work with him and show him the ropes. Lao Zhang had graduated from a university physics department in China, and it didn't take him long to become familiar with the job. However, he had two bad habits: first, he liked to smoke, and second, he often acted sarcastically towards the Filipino leads, which made them dislike him, though they couldn't do much about it. One evening, during a break around

9 p.m. (at JDS, we had a 15-minute-break every two hours), Lao Zhang either forgot the time or deliberately went somewhere to smoke and didn't return to work for over 15 minutes after the break ended. The Filipino Teamleader Nonito came over and asked me: "Where's Mr. Zhang? Why isn't he back at work after more than 20 minutes?" I told him I didn't know. When Lao Zhang returned, I warned him that our head had been looking for him and that he should be more mindful of his breaks. Lao Zhang dismissively replied: "Who cares? What's he going to do about it?" Not long after, Nonito, who was our Teamleader, confronted Lao Zhang. Before Nonito saying anything, Lao Zhang, with his broken English, said: "Somebody told me that are you looking for me? What do you want?" He intended to ask politely why the lead was looking for him, but his poor English and tone made it come across as: "Someone said you were looking for me? What do you want?" As soon as Lao Zhang opened his mouth, I thought, "This is bad, the Filipino guy is going to lose it." And sure enough, Nonito, who was our Teamleader, immediately told Lao Zhang: "Come with me!" and then took him away. I'm not sure what they discussed, but shortly after, the Filipino Teamleader Nonito returned with Lao Zhang, along with the Filipino department manager Alma. They went to Lao Zhang's workstation, asked him to pack up his things, and told him to leave. In other words, the department manager used this opportunity to fire Lao Zhang on the spot.

Ironically, this event ended up being a blessing in disguise for Lao Zhang. Two or three months later, Lao Zhang reappeared at JDS in a different department, this time as a shiny, newly hired engineer. When we inquired further, we found out that after being fired, Lao Zhang had discovered that JDS was hiring fiber optic communication engineers, so he applied for the position. Although Lao Zhang wasn't formally trained in telecommunications, his background in physics and the experience he gained working in our department helped him pass the interview smoothly and get hired as a fiber optics engineer. Even though the Filipinos in our department saw Lao Zhang with his engineer badge, they didn't know what had happened. Given their poor reputation within the company, they didn't dare say anything. I suspect Lao Zhang omitted his short stint in our department from his resume when he reapplied for the job.

Otherwise, the HR department would have likely consulted with the Filipino manager and the teamleader, who certainly wouldn't have given him a good recommendation. However, due to Lao Zhang's relatively short tenure and low seniority, he was among the first to be laid off during JDS's initial wave of layoffs in 2001.

The fact that Lao Zhang was fired for returning late from a break by just 10 or 20 minutes clearly felt like they were bullying the Chinese workers. As a result, not only the Chinese but also employees from other ethnic groups in our department began to express growing dissatisfaction with the Filipinos' heavy-handed management style. Meanwhile, the Filipino leads increasingly showed their disdain for certain members of our team. This led to unfair treatment in work assignments, performance evaluations, promotions, and salary raises. By April 2000, more than a dozen employees from our shift, fed up with the situation, jointly wrote a letter to the company's HR department, detailing the various unreasonable practices in our department, accusing the Filipinos of racial discrimination. However, when the HR department convened a meeting to discuss the issues raised, instead of addressing them or offering solutions, they downplayed the situation, arguing that the Filipinos had been promoted because they had been with the company longer, and they completely ignored the concerns about the Filipinos' education levels or qualifications. After that, nothing changed. If anything, those of us who had complained faced even more frequent instances of unfair treatment in terms of promotions and salary increases. The Filipino manager and leads especially singled me out, knowing that I had the highest education level among those who had raised the complaints. I had also defended the Chinese engineers who had been forced out, including Lao Zhang. While they didn't dare openly confront me, they engaged in subtle sabotage, trying to damage my reputation and block my chances for promotion.

First, they started making an issue of my age, suspecting that I had falsified it. On my first day at the company in early 1998, I reported to the Filipino female supervisor in our department, who handed me an employee registration form to fill out. The form was very simple, requiring basic details like name, gender, date of birth, home address, phone number, and education level. After filling it out, I handed it back to her. However, about half an hour later, the Filipino supervisor came back to me with the same form and said: "Mr. Wu, it seems there's a mistake on your form. HR wants you to fill it out again." I was taken aback, thinking the form was so simple---how could I have made a mistake? But then I realized she might be doubting my age. Back when I was working as a visiting scholar at the Geological Survey of Canada, I was already 46 or 47, but many of the Canadians I worked with thought I looked like I was in my 30s and refused to believe I was in my 40s. I figured the Filipino supervisor must have seen my birthdate, January 31, 1949, and, thinking I didn't look like I was in my 50s, assumed I had entered it incorrectly, which is why she asked me to fill it out again. In reality, my official age is a year younger than my actual age---I was actually born in January 1948. But there had been an error when I first started school, and that mistake had stuck ever since. The two incidents of filling out the registration form were long past, and I didn't give them much thought, certainly not enough to remember them. However, it seems the Filipinos did take it seriously.

One evening in June or July 2000, during a break time while our group was having dinner together (there were about 10 of us), the Filipino Coordinator, whose name is Ronier, suddenly asked me: "Mr. Wu, how old are you this year?" I replied: "I'm 51." The Filipino Coordinator Ronier responded: "No, no! You can't be that old." I laughed and asked him: "Well, how old do you think I am?" He said: "You look about 35 or 36, maybe 37 at most." I said: "Do I really look that young? Besides, if someone is older, they would only claim to be younger. But if someone is young, they would never claim to be older---it's just not how people usually think!" Then Ronier asked again: "Are you a refugee?" Ah, now I understood. Since some refugees from certain countries like Vietnam, Laos, and the Middle East, upon arriving in Canada, would destroy all their personal identification and then fabricate their age, education, and other details. The Philippines thought I might be a refugee who had come illegally and was lying about my identity. I firmly replied: "What do you mean refugee? I'm a legal immigrant, and we don't have refugees from China!" The Filipino Coordinator Ronier then asked: "Where were you before you came to work at JDS?" I said: "Before I came here, I was in China. I only came to Canada in February 1997 and started working at JDS in January 1998. Is there a problem with that?" After I responded, the Filipino coordinator went silent, but the whole exchange made everyone at the table uncomfortable, and the conversation ended on an awkward note.

Why did they ask if I was a refugee? It turns out that during the summer of 1999, a ship carrying illegal immigrants from the Caribbean Sea was intercepted by the Canadian Coast Guard off the coast of Vancouver. Many of the passengers were Chinese, and the story was heavily reported in the Canadian media, such as TV, Radio, and newspaper, making it widely known across the country. The Filipinos likely thought I might be one of those illegal immigrants who had destroyed their identification and fabricated their age, education, and work history. Despite my clear statement that I was a legal immigrant, the Filipinos never believe me and instead spread rumours that I was an illegal immigrant. Some even speculated that I might have connections to an underground organization, otherwise, how could I have successfully entered Canada? Even a few Chinese colleagues in our department added fuel to the fire. As a result, in August 2000, the Immigration Canada sent me a letter requesting certified documents to verify my date of birth, to confirm that I hadn't falsified it. I promptly sent them the certified copies as requested.

Then in February 2001, the company was hiring two chemical engineers (since their operations involved the use of various chemical reagents and solvents like adhesives and organic solvents), and I saw this as a great opportunity. If I could get the job, not only would I be working in my field, but I could also escape the drama with the Filipinos---two birds with one stone. So, I submitted my application to HR, and I passed the interview. However, when HR sought feedback from our department, my Filipino Teamleader Nonito claimed that he had once seen me use my work computer to send an email to China related to company business. As a result, the company's security department launched an investigation, asking if this was true. I firmly denied it, explaining that while I occasionally used the work computer to send personal emails, none of them ever involved company business. The security team didn't seem fully convinced, so they took my work computer away for about a week to inspect it. When they returned it, they didn't say anything further. Later, a few Chinese colleagues told HR that when I worked in China, I was not only a member of the Communist Party but also a department-level official and had even received national-level awards. (Since we often talked about our past experiences in China during breaks, most of us knew each other's backgrounds.) As a result, HR sent someone to interview me about my work experience in China. I truthfully explained my time working at the Chinese Academy of Sciences' Institute of Geochemistry and provided some related documents. After hearing my explanation and reviewing the documents, the HR officer said: "Wow, I didn't expect that you'd already achieved so much in China and held such a high position. Why would you want to immigrate to Canada?" Of course, I couldn't outright say that I had been treated unfairly in China, so I simply told them that during my time as a visiting scholar at the Geological Survey of Canada, I had been deeply attracted to Canada's natural beauty and cultural environment, which led me to decide to immigrate. I knew that no matter how I explained it, they wouldn't fully understand China's cultural and political context, so they were obviously skeptical of my story and even suspected at one point that I might be a spy sent from China. For a while after that, I noticed that my e-mails were behaving strangely, and some letters from China had clearly been opened and inspected. After all this, my application for the chemical engineer position was naturally unsuccessful.

(VI)

As the saying goes: "All good things must come to an end." The rise and fall of JDS Uniphase (JDS) Optical Communications Company is a perfect example. Starting in 1999, JDS experienced a rapid surge in business, like a rollercoaster soaring upward. The company's workforce grew from just over 1,000 employees in early 1998 to over 20,000 by the year 2000. To accommodate this vast workforce and expand production, the company leased numerous high-rise buildings in the suburbs of Ottawa to serve as production facilities for fiber optic communication components. In early 2000, the company also invested heavily in constructing a massive one-million-square-foot facility on Marivale Road in the southern outskirts of Ottawa, aiming to replace the dozens of leased buildings and reduce production costs. However, as fate would have it, by the time the new building was nearing completion in the second half of 2001, the fiberoptic communication industry had begun to experience a downturn due to oversupply. The company not only stopped hiring but also began laying off employees. Many new hires, who had barely warmed their seats, were suddenly and unexpectedly laid off and sent home. JDS followed the typical practice of laying off employees with the shortest tenure first, gradually moving toward those with longer tenure. Those of us who had joined the company in 1997 and 1998, while not yet facing immediate risk of being sent home, all felt uncertain about how long we could continue working there. But the good times didn't last long. In October 2002, after almost five years at JDS, I, too, was laid off. By the second half of 2003, after the massive layoffs that reduced JDS from a nearly 30,000-employee global company to a mere 300strong R&D team, the company sold off its one-millionsquare-foot facility to the Royal Canadian Mounted Police. The once-flourishing JDS Optical Communications Company had faded into history.

After leaving the company, I was already in my fifties and once again faced the challenge of finding a job. Although the economy in Canada had improved somewhat in the early 2000s, aside from the fields of computer science and information technology, finding a professional job in other fields remained quite difficult. After receiving unemployment insurance for a few months, I started searching for jobs online in early 2003. My undergraduate degree was in analytical chemistry, and I had also studied geological geochemistry in graduate school. Although jobs in geological geochemistry were scarce, I thought perhaps it would be easier to find work in a chemical analysis lab. After some online searching, I found that there was an environmental chemistry laboratory in Calgary, Alberta, hiring. Calgary was located in western Canada, over 4,000 kilometers away from Ottawa, but I figured that since it was a professional job, the distance was worth it. So, in late January 2003, I flew to Calgary for an interview, which went smoothly, and I was hired on the spot.

The environmental chemistry lab was located at the intersection of 51st Avenue and 12th Street in Calgary, and it had around 40 to 50 employees. The lab's operations were divided into two main sections: chemical analysis and instrumental analysis. Chemical analysis was further split into two laboratories: one focused on testing environmental samples such as air, rainwater, groundwater, and wastewater, while the other focused on soil chemical analysis. I was assigned to the soil chemical analysis group, which was looking for additional personnel due to the agricultural activity in the Calgary area. Every spring, before sowing, local farmers would collect and send soil samples to the lab for analysis to assess the soil's fertility and determine which nutrients needed to be supplemented. In the soil chemistry analysis group, there were about 20 people, with eight or nine of us being new hires. Most of the newcomers were locals from Calgary, and four of them were Chinese immigrants who had arrived around 2000. Their backgrounds were in analytical chemistry or petrochemical engineering. The soil samples sent by farmers were mainly tested for the three major nutrients essential for soil fertility---nitrogen, phosphorus, and potassium---along with trace elements like copper, zinc, manganese, and molybdenum, which are essential for plants, and heavy metal pollutants such as lead, cadmium, mercury, and arsenic. Each of us was assigned a batch of samples daily, typically between 20 and 30 samples. First, we selected the appropriate analysis method for the test, performed the chemical pretreatment of the samples, separated and concentrated the components to be measured, and then used techniques such as spectrophotometry, atomic absorption, or plasma emission spectroscopy to determine the concentrations. These methods were ones I had learned in university, and after working in the chemical analysis lab at the Institute of Geochemistry for three years, I was thoroughly familiar with them. As a result, analyzing 20 to 30 soil samples a day was easy for me, but for others (especially the Canadians), the workload was exhausting.

Although this was considered professional work, the pay during the probationary period was not high---$16 CAD per hour, with a monthly salary of around $3,000 CAD. During the interview, the company had informed us that the probationary period would last six months, after which they would formally hire some of the new employees. Everyone worked hard, hoping to be hired as permanent employees at the end of the probation period, as that would raise the hourly wage to $20 CAD, bringing the monthly salary to about $4,000 CAD, which was considered quite well at the time.

In late July 2003, after the probationary period ended, the company only hired three out of the nine new employees in the soil chemistry analysis group. One was a Canadian, one was Polish, and one was Chinese. The low selection rate surprised and disappointed everyone, especially since those hired weren't necessarily the most capable among us, but they were skilled at building relationships with the lab supervisors. I later heard that the lab preferred to hire fewer permanent employees to cut costs, as the workload for soil analysis was only heavy for a few months of the year. After July, the workload would drop, and the lab found it more economical to hire seasonal workers each year than to keep a large team of full-time employees. I had been considering moving my family to Calgary if I was hired permanently, as it was relatively close to Vancouver and would make trips to China more convenient. But with no permanent job, and my wife living alone in Ottawa while my daughter was still studying at the University of Toronto, I flew back to Ottawa in late July 2003.

(VII)

Before I left Calgary, the boss of the Calgary Environmental Lab told me that their company was part of a chain spread across Canada, with its headquarters in Calgary but also having branches in other provinces, including one lab in Ottawa. He said if I wanted to work at the Ottawa lab, they could recommend me. I didn't want to miss this opportunity, so I asked the Calgary boss to write down the address and phone number of the Ottawa lab. After returning to Ottawa in August 2003, I immediately contacted the lab. The lab was located near 1500 Marivale Road. When I found it, the lab manager told me it was a small facility with only about a dozen employees, and their soil chemistry analysis work had already concluded for the year, so they didn't need any new staff. However, if I was still interested, they said they would call me around March or April of the following year when they needed people for soil chemistry analysis. Learning that they only hired seasonal workers, I left my contact details and departed.

Next, I sent out several resumes to environmental chemistry labs in the Ottawa area. One of the labs that specialized in water chemistry analysis contacted me for an interview. Although I hadn't done specialized work in water chemistry before, I had a solid foundation in analytical chemistry and was familiar with the methods. The interview went well, and they offered me a six-month trial position with an hourly wage of $15 CAD. Although the salary wasn't ideal, with no better options at the time, I accepted the job. Around October 2003, I also applied for a position at a lab in New Jersey, USA, run by my old friend and colleague Fangling Deng, but ultimately, I didn't take the job. Fangling Deng had been assigned to the Institute of Geochemistry after graduating from Chengdu Institute of Geology in 1976. He became a graduate student in 1979, and during his time at the institute, we were not only neighbours but also good friends. In early 1989, he was sent to the Scripps Institution of Oceanography in California as a visiting scholar and later stayed in the U.S., where he and his old friend Li Yu cofounded a small chemical company in New Jersey that produced pregnancy test reagents. When we reconnected in 2003, he suggested that I work with him, believing that if we joined forces, the business would grow significantly. In October 2003, I went to visit Fangling to discuss the opportunity, and although everything seemed settled, my wife didn't want to move to the U.S., and with my daughter still studying at the University of Toronto, I didn't want to live apart from them again, so I passed on the opportunity to work in the U.S.

Having decided against going to the U.S., I continued working at the water chemistry lab in Ottawa. At the time, my wife was still working at the small print shop run by the Pakistani family, and my daughter was attending university in Toronto. Our household income was around $5,000 CAD per month (I made over $3,000, and my wife earned over $2,000), so financially, we were comfortable. However, after living in one place for a long time, as is typical in Chinese culture, you eventually feel the need to have your own house. Only when you own your home does it truly feel like you have a place to call your own. Renting forever felt unsatisfactory, and on top of that, many of the Chinese friends who had come to Ottawa with us had already bought houses, yet we were still renting, which felt somewhat inadequate. But given our monthly income, it was clear that buying a decent house still required some financial stretching.

One day, I went to Ottawa Airport to pick up a friend visiting from China. At the airport exit, I happened to run into an old colleague from JDS, a man from Yugoslavia, who was driving a taxi at the time. We struck up a conversation, and after catching up on each other's work situations, I asked him how much he earned driving a taxi. Although he didn't give me an exact number, he said the income was quite good. I then asked if driving a taxi was more profitable than working at JDS, and he replied that it was much higher. When we worked at JDS, we could make around $3,000 CAD a month, so when he said, "much higher," I figured it must be at least $4,000 to $5,000 CAD a month. He asked about my income, and I told him it was about the same as when I worked at JDS. He suggested I switch to driving taxis, saying the job was flexible, with no fixed hours---when to start and when to finish was entirely up to yourself. He also said airport taxi business was stable, though the job was somewhat tiring, it was lucrative. I then asked how I could get a taxi driver's license, and he explained that as long as I had an Ontario G driver's license, the next step was to take an English test at Algonquin College. Once I passed the test, I could sign up for a three-week taxi driver training program, and after completing the training program and passing the exam, I could go to the city government to get a taxi driver license. This Yugoslavian friend had also studied chemistry. After being laid off from JDS, he started driving a taxi and said he had already bought a 200-300 square meter house.

After I got home, I thought about it for a few days. I was already over fifty, and I wouldn't be able to work for many more years. Earning just over $3,000 a month, I didn't know how many years it would take to save up for a decent 200-square-meter house, which at the time cost around $300,000 to $400,000 CAD. I figured that I should pursue any work that allowed me to make money quickly. So I decided to give taxi driving a try and see how much I could earn. I could still keep working at the water chemistry lab since my Yugoslavian friend said driving a taxi could be done on weekends or in the evenings. Once I made up my mind, I visited Algonquin College the next day after work, found the office for the taxi driver training program, and asked for details. The staff told me there would be an English exam for the taxi driver license training program the next evening at 8 p.m., and if I passed, I could join the training program. If I failed, I would have to take an English language course first. Although I had no idea how difficult the test would be and had no time to prepare, I decided to give it a shot.

The following Wednesday, I took the English exam at Algonquin College and passed with a score of over 70. After that, I attended the three-week taxi driver training program. After passing the exam, I went to the city government to get my taxi driver's license. With this license, I was now legally permitted to drive a taxi. In Canada, no matter what kind of work you do, you need a license---whether it's driving a taxi, working as an electrician, a chef, or a barber, you must go through training and get certified before you can start working. If you work without a license and get caught by the government, you could face heavy fines. This is one of the key differences between Western countries with strong legal frameworks and developing nations like China, where if you have the skills, you can do the job without worrying about certification.

In mid-April 2005, after obtaining my taxi license, I found a business partner in the airport taxi fleet through a friend's introduction. The arrangement was that he would drive during the day, and I would drive at night. He worked from morning until 5 p.m., and I would take over from 5 p.m. until midnight. On weekends, I would drive on Saturdays, and he would take Sundays, which suited my schedule well since I was still working at the water chemistry lab from Monday to Friday. My plan was to work hard, earn as much as possible, and save up for a house as soon as possible. At the time, Ottawa Airport had a total of 120 taxicabs, with most of them having two drivers. Some drivers had the same shift arrangement as I did, with one driving during the day and the other at night, while others alternated driving every other day. Once I started driving a taxi, I realized the business was different from what I had imagined. Most of the earnings were in cash, and the income was indeed much better than what I earned at the lab. If you drove during the day, there was a morning peak from around 7 a.m. to 10 a.m. Ottawa, being Canada's capital, had many people flying in for business with the federal government in the morning and flying out in the afternoon or evening. During the morning rush, many passengers lined up for taxis, and taxis returning from the city to the airport would immediately have to head back into the city. After dropping passengers in the city, they'd return to the airport again, repeating the cycle, sometimes barely able to keep up with the demand. The airport is about 12 to 13 kilometers from downtown Ottawa, so each round trip took only about 30 to 40 minutes. On a busy morning, a taxi could make three or four trips into the city, and by the end of the morning rush, a driver could easily have transported passengers for 5 to 6 trips. At the time, the average fare from the airport to the city was around $30 CAD per trip. There was also an afternoon rush, starting around 4:30 p.m., where taxis would be busy again until about 6:30 to 7:00 p.m. during this time, picking up travellers arriving for business or locals returning from trips. Then, around 11:30 p.m., there was another peak again. By that time, many taxi drivers had finished their shifts and gone home already, leaving fewer taxicabs available. Meanwhile, two or three large flights from Vancouver or Toronto would land, bringing in many passengers. This busy period usually lasted from 11 p.m. until around 1:00 a.m. Because of this predictable and consistent flow of passengers, business at Ottawa Airport taxis was booming. Many people who completed their taxi driver training and obtained licenses found it difficult to find a partner in the airport taxi fleet due to the high demand. The income from driving a taxi was ideal, and since I was already in my 50s and juggling two jobs was exhausting, I knew my body couldn't handle it for the long term. After over a year, I eventually quit my job at the water chemistry lab.

(VIII)

As a professional, before I used to know very little about the taxi industry and even had some misconceptions. First, many people think of taxi driving as a service job, assuming that it might carry a lower social status. This, however, is more of a societal mindset issue. In Western societies, people's attitudes are quite different from those in the East. In the West, there's no stigma attached to different jobs. As long as someone is working and supporting themselves, their job is considered respectable.

Furthermore, even members of the upper class would never look down on service workers. In fact, at times, they actively participate in service roles to understand the hard work involved. For example, during special events like Christmas or disability receptions organized by city halls, municipal officials, including mayors, often join the ranks of service workers to serve tea and food. They don't feel inferior in these situations; instead, they find it meaningful. Second, many people believe that taxi driving is hard work and that the income may not match the effort put in. However, the taxi management model abroad is entirely different from that in China. In China, taxi license plates are mostly owned by companies, and the companies take the majority of the earnings, leaving drivers with a smaller share. Abroad, most taxi license plates are owned by the drivers themselves, with taxi companies playing only a management role. Drivers pay the company a fixed management and insurance fees, but most of the income goes to the driver. In this way, it can be said that until you're in the industry, you don't know how it works. While driving a taxi is hard work, especially due to long hours, the income is substantial. Moreover, taxi drivers control their schedules entirely. The longer they work, the more they earn. Conversely, if they want to work less, their earnings will naturally decrease. The third misconception is that taxi drivers might not be well-educated. While it's true that many older taxi drivers who have been in the business for decades may have lower education levels, they often own the taxi license plates. Most of these old drivers are from the Middle East, having immigrated to Canada during the conflicts in the 1960s and 1970s. At that time, the city government didn't have well-established taxi management regulations, and the taxi industry was just starting, so the requirements for drivers were lower. Citizens who wanted to drive a taxi could get a license plate after passing the standard driving test and paying a small fee. However, most of these old drivers have retired, and they've sold or leased their license plates to the next generation of drivers. Since the 1990s, the government has introduced stricter taxi management regulations, significantly raising the entry requirements and improving the education level of taxi drivers. According to city regulations, taxi driver's licenses must be renewed yearly, and drivers must provide a criminal background check every two years. As new immigrants from Eastern Europe, India, Pakistan, Bangladesh, and other South Asian countries have increasingly entered the workforce, many highly educated individuals have joined the taxi industry. It's not uncommon for taxi drivers in Canada to hold university degrees, and some even have master or doctoral degrees. This phenomenon is not unique to Canada but can be seen across major cities in Western countries.

It should be said that although driving a taxi has relatively flexible working hours and relatively higher income, it is indeed a very hard job. If a taxicab is shared by two drivers, taking turns behind the wheel, the workload is relatively manageable. However, if one driver is responsible for a single cab, the burden is significantly heavier. Additionally, winter is typically the peak season for taxi business in Ottawa, as the long, cold winter drives more people to take taxis. But the winter weather also brings hazardous road conditions, and during snowstorms, traffic accidents become more frequent. During my years driving a taxi, I personally witnessed several severe accidents involving taxi drivers. I also had my own share of accidents, flipping my car into a roadside ditch two or three times during snowy nights and being hit by other drivers on a few occasions. Fortunately, I was never injured in any of these incidents. If I had to sum up the differences between working in Canada and China, it would be with this phrase: "In Canada, the body may be tired, but the mind is at ease; in China, the mind is tired, even if the body is not." When your body is tired, a good night's sleep can solve the problem. But when your mind is weary, no amount of sleep will help, and it can severely affect your rest. For this reason, I'd rather have physical exhaustion with peace of mind than mental fatigue, even if it means the work is easier. Despite the hardships, after several years of hard work, I was able to help fund my daughter and son-in-law's entrepreneurial venture in 2007 and, in 2009, finally bought a two-story, 200-square-meter house with a double garage through a loan. This fulfilled my long-held dream of homeownership.

(IX)

From 2010, as Ottawa Airport continued to expand, more tourists and business travelers began visiting the city, and the demand for airport taxis grew year by year. In contrast, the city's taxi fleet was massive, and the differences in business between city taxis and airport taxis became increasingly pronounced. As a result, the black-market value of Ottawa airport taxi license plate soared. By 2013, the price of an Ottawa airport taxi license plate had skyrocketed from around $250,000 CAD just two or three years earlier to between $370,000 and $400,000 CAD. At the same time, a city taxi license plate was only worth about $250,000 CAD. City taxi drivers had long been dissatisfied with the city government's regulation prohibiting city taxis from picking up passengers at the airport. As they watched airport taxi drivers' incomes grow, their dissatisfaction increased, and they began petitioning the government to change this policy.

In 2014, the long-serving CEO of Ottawa Airport retired due to age, and the airport authorities appointed a new CEO. The new CEO immediately implemented a new revenuegenerating rule, requiring airport taxi drivers to pay a $5 CAD entry fee for every trip they picked up. This rule sparked outrage among the airport taxi drivers. Following the new rule, drivers picking up an average of 8 to 10 trips of passengers per day would have to pay $40 to $50 CAD in entry fees daily, amounting to $1,200 to $1,500 CAD per month per driver. For individual drivers, this was a significant sum. Thus, starting in August 2015, Ottawa airport taxi drivers began a collective strike that lasted a full year. Although the strike received strong support from the Canadian Auto Workers Union, which had hundreds of thousands of members, it was unable to change the decision made by the airport authorities. Meanwhile, the strike was not supported by the city's taxi companies and drivers. On the contrary, city taxi companies actively supported the airport's decision and organized city taxis to go to the airport to pick up passengers during the strike. As a result, the strike not only failed to overturn the airport's decision but also prompted the Ottawa city government to revamp its outdated taxi management model. The city decided to no longer maintain a separate airport taxi fleet. Instead, any taxi licensed by the city government could pick up passengers at the airport as long as they adhered to pay the $5 CAD entry fee rule. In August 2016, recognizing that the strike had been ineffective, the Canadian Auto Workers Union decided to end the Ottawa airport taxi drivers' strike. As a result, the year-long airport taxi strike ended in failure. By the time the strike began, I had already turned 65, the official retirement age in Canada. After the strike ended, I left the Ottawa taxi industry and fully retired.

Chapter 12   Mother's Love and Family Ties

Around midnight on April 25th, 2000, a sudden and urgent phone call woke me from a deep sleep. I quickly got up and answered the phone, only to find that it was my old brother calling from our hometown in Guizhou, China. He had gone to the Liuzhi Special District Telecommunications Bureau to make an international long-distance call to tell me that our mother was critically ill and might not have much time left. He urged me to return to our hometown as soon as possible to see her one last time, stressing that if I delayed any further, I might not make it in time to say goodbye. After receiving the call from home, I couldn't sleep at all that night. At the time, I was working at JDS Uniphase in Ottawa. The next morning, as long as I arrived JDS Company, I immediately applied for a four-week leave of absence from the HR department, explaining that I needed to return to China for a family emergency. I then began calling around to book the earliest available international flight back to China. Back then, flights from Canada to China were not as frequent, with only two or three flights per week. I booked the earliest possible flight and hastily packed my luggage. By April 28th, I was on my way. I flew from Ottawa to Vancouver, then transferred to a flight bound for Beijing, and from there, I took another flight to Guiyang, Guizhou Province. Once I arrived in Guiyang, I took a train to Liuzhi. Despite all my efforts to rush back, by the time I finally arrived in my hometown of Shanmu village, four or five days had already passed. It was already May 2nd, and my mother had not only passed away but, due to the hot climate, had already been buried. Since the moment I received the news that my mother was critically ill, I had been overcome with anxiety and heartache. Being so far away, separated by a vast ocean, I did everything I could to hurry home, but it was still too late. In the end, I couldn't see my mother one last time. This became the greatest regret of my life and, I believe, the greatest regret for my mother as well. To this day, whenever I think back on it, the pain feels as sharp as ever. Therefore, I dedicate this chapter to my beloved mother in remembrance of her.

(I)

My mom's name was Fengying Tan (谭凤英). She was born on April 14, 1911, and passed away on April 27, 2000, living to the age of 90 according to the lunar calendar. She was born in

The author with his mother and daughter in Guiyang, Guizhou, China in November 1985.

Naqi Village, Dianzi Township, in Liuzhi Special District, Guizhou Province. The Tan family in Naqi was also part of the Hakka people (i.e., Han people), who migrated to Guizhou during the Ming or Qing dynasties as part of the campaign to resettle the southern regions. My maternal grandfather, Zhongyun Tan, came from a long line of farmers. He and my grandmother had six children---two boys and four girls. My mother was the second among the four daughters. When I was young, my mother often told me stories about her childhood. My grandfather and eldest uncle passed away early, leaving my grandmother, who was a bound-footed woman, unable to do heavy farm work. My eldest aunt also had bound feet and was raising two small children, so she, too, was unable to help much. With eight or nine people in the household, the family's meagre farmland could barely provide enough food. It was up to my mother and her three sisters, along with their youngest brother, to shoulder the heavy burden of farming and managing the household. As the saying goes: "the children of the poor learn early to take on responsibilities." My mother and her siblings were no exception. During the busy planting season each spring, when it was time to transplant rice seedlings, my uncle was too small to handle the plow, so my mother and her sisters would carry the heavy plow and set it up in the paddy field for him. Once the plow and ox were in place, only then could my uncle stand on the plow and begin tilling the field. After my uncle finished levelling the fields, my mother and her sisters would then transplant the seedlings. Farming in Guizhou was always challenging and backbreaking. For example, after planting corn in February or March, the fields needed to be weeded and hoed two or three times during the midsummer. Similarly, after rice seedlings were transplanted, the fields had to be weeded and fertilized once or twice during the summer. All of this work was done by my mother and her sisters, along with their little brother. During the harvest season in autumn, the siblings toiled day and night, only finishing the fall harvest and winter planting by late October or early November. Even during the slack season in the dead of winter, my mother and her sisters never took a break. They would spin thread, sew soles, cut fabric, and make shoes and clothes for the whole family. In short, they never had a single day of leisure throughout the entire year. Because of the physically demanding work they endured from a young age, my mother became skilled in farming and was just as capable of doing heavy labor---such as cutting firewood, carrying loads, or hauling---typically done by men. When it came to household chores like tailoring, cooking, or making tea, she was equally proficient and quick. Perhaps due to this lifelong hard work, she developed a strong constitution. Among her sisters, she was the healthiest. Even in her old age, my mother remained remarkably robust. As far as I can remember, despite decades of working in the fields, she never suffered from common ailments like arthritis, which many rural women often had. Throughout my childhood and until she passed away, she never had any major health issues, except for one time in her seventies when I took her to the hospital in Guiyang to treat her cataracts. Other than that, she never needed to go to the hospital.

My mother was a hardworking, kind, self-sacrificing, and compassionate woman. She and her sisters went through so much together, and their bond remained strong throughout their lives. Whether it was in childhood, adulthood, or old age, they always supported each other. When my mother's sisters faced difficulties, they would all rally to help. After the four sisters grew up and got married, my eldest aunt settled in Ganhe Village, my third aunt married into the Zhangjiaping Village, and my youngest aunt married into Tuji Village. My mother originally married into the Chen family in Naqi Village. After her first husband passed away, she remarried into my father's family in Shanmu Village at around the age of 26 or 27, bringing along her two-year-old daughter (my half-sister, Lianxiu Chen). Despite the fact that our family lived relatively far away in a remote area with dangerous mountain roads, this did not deter my mother from maintaining close ties with her siblings. Whenever there was a town market day or if something happened at my grandmother's or one of her sisters' homes, my mother would go to visit, offering help with farm work or household chores.

Back then, rural areas in Guizhou severely lacked medical care, and hygiene conditions were very poor. Many people suffered from a common eye disease called "Luoyuzi," which is actually a form of pterygium caused by chronic inflammation or exposure to intense sunlight and overuse of the eyes. If untreated, the condition would worsen and severely impair vision. My mother had learned a remedy for this condition from my grandmother, and when she remarried into Shanmu Village, she would often prepare the treatment for neighbors or villagers who came to ask for help. If the patient's condition was severe, she would even apply the treatment herself. Because of my mother's generosity, those who came for treatment would sometimes bring a bowl of rice as a token of gratitude. Even though it was a modest offering, my mother would often politely decline.

My mother's industrious, simple, and charitable nature not only left a positive impression on neighbours and relatives but also deeply influenced me from an early age through her actions and example, imprinting these virtues on my young mind (I still vividly remember how she would carry me on her back while preparing and applying medicine for sick villagers). When I was a schoolteacher in the countryside, I noticed that many of my elementary school students had very long hair and lacked both the money and time to visit barbershops. So, I bought a set of hair-cutting tools at my own expense and began offering free haircuts to the students. Later, when I went to university, I took the set of tools with me and continued to give free haircuts to my classmates in my spare time. After graduating and joining the research institute, I became part of our research lab's volunteer

The author with his mother and wife in Guiyang, Guizhou, China in November 1986.

haircutting team, offering free haircuts to my colleagues on weekends. When I went abroad in the mid-1990s, the set of hair-cutting tools traveled across the ocean with me to Canada. There, I continued to give free haircuts to my roommates and friends for many years. Now that my friends are financially secure and living comfortably, no one comes to me for free haircuts anymore. However, this set of tools and my skills haven't gone idle. Occasionally, besides cutting hair for my children and grandchildren when they visit from Toronto, I also give myself a trim every month or two, using a mirror to guide me. After twenty minutes or so of careful cutting and grooming, I'm able to achieve a hairstyle that would have cost about twenty Canadian dollars at a barbershop. Why not save time and money while keeping control of my appearance all on my own?

(Ⅱ)

As I was the only surviving son out of the four or five children my parents had together, and as my father had me in his later years, I was as precious as a gem in my parents' eyes. It wouldn't be an exaggeration to say that they treated me like a treasure, afraid to hold me in their hands for fear of smothering me, and afraid to keep me in their mouths for fear I'd be melt. When it came to food, they always did their best to meet my needs, offering me the very best they had at home. For example, whenever my mom cooked chicken soup, the liver and drumsticks were always set aside for me. When our family made meat dishes, my parents would trim off the fatty parts and give me only the lean meat. During the Lunar New Year or other holidays, our family would make a variety of traditional sticky rice cakes, with glutinous rice cakes being the most delicious but limited in quantity. During these times, my parents would reserve the sticky rice cakes for me, while they ate the coarser and less tasty mixed-grain cakes themselves. Regarding clothing, when I was four or five years old, my mother sewed me a long robe and shirt, making me look like a little gentleman. Whenever my parents went to the market or visited relatives, they would always return with candy or fruit in their pockets just for me. In their hearts and minds, they thought about their child at every moment, without a thought for themselves.

Although my parents took meticulous care of me in my daily life, they did not spoil or overly indulge me. Instead, they consciously guided and nurtured my interest in reading, ambition, and love for labor from an early age. When I was only two or three years old, my father would sit me on his lap and teach me to recite the "**Three Character Classic** (《三字经》)" or the "**Hundred Family Surnames** (《百家姓》)". Although I did not understand the meaning of what I was reading at the time, this undoubtedly sparked my interest in learning and reading from a young age.

When I grew a little older, my mother began teaching me to dress myself, button my shirts, and tie my shoelaces. When she taught me to wash my face, she would say: "Washing your face means washing your ears as well; sweeping the floor means sweeping the corners too." In other words, washing your face thoroughly requires attention to every part, not just the obvious areas. By the time I was five or six, my parents would send me out to the hills with other children to herd cattle, cut grass, or collect firewood, fostering a love for labor early on. I gladly joined in, as working alongside my playmates was both productive and fun.

In the rural areas of the past, there was no electricity and no machines for processing rice or flour. The rice and flour we ate were ground using stone mills and pounders, usually during the evenings or whenever there was free time. Whenever my parents were pounding rice or turning the millstone, they would call me to lend a hand. During the busy harvest seasons, when the adults couldn't manage all the work alone, we children would also help gather the crops. In short, as children from farming families, under the influence and guidance of our parents, we were never spoiled. From a young age, we naturally took the initiative to participate in any farm work we were capable of doing. In short, as children in a farming household, we were never pampered. Thanks to my parents' guidance and influence, we naturally took the initiative to help out with the farm work whenever we could.

When I was eight or nine years old, in the second or third grade of elementary school, our rural village had already transitioned to the advanced stage of agricultural cooperatives. My mother and older siblings were extremely busy with farm work. During winter and summer vacations, not only did I have to help my siblings take care of their two young children (the oldest nephew was five years younger than me), but I also had to learn to cook meals and prepare pig feed. In our area, the main crops were rice, which made up about 60-70%, and corn, which accounted for about 30-40%. As a result, when cooking, we often mixed corn grits or cornmeal with rice to make what we called "corn rice" (actually a blend of two types of grains). Cooking corn grits with rice was relatively simple: you just needed to boil the grits until they were half-cooked, then add the rice and continue cooking until both were about 80% done. After that, the mixture was drained and steamed in a bamboo steamer

The author (right) and his wife in the Huaxi Park, Guiyang, Guizhou, China in July, 1994.

for about 25 minutes. However, cooking rice with cornmeal was more complicated, as it required pre-treating the cornmeal by moistening and steaming it. If the amount of water wasn't just right, the rice could turn out either undercooked or too soft, making it unpleasant to eat. To help me master the technique, my mother taught me step by step. She demonstrated each process while allowing me to practice. First, you take an appropriate amount of cornmeal and place it in a bamboo basket, sprinkle it with cold water, and mix it with chopsticks until it's evenly moistened but not clumpy. Then, pour the moistened cornmeal into the steamer and steam it on high heat for about ten minutes until it's halfcooked. Afterward, you transfer the steamed cornmeal back into the bamboo basket, break it apart with chopsticks, and sprinkle it again with water to mix evenly. Finally, combine the partially cooked rice and the twice-moistened cornmeal, mixing them thoroughly before steaming them together for another 25 minutes. The result was a fragrant, goldencoloured corn and rice blend that not only tasted great but was also nutritious and filling---a favourite among the rural people. If fresh rice and fresh corn were used, it tasted even much better. But in the beginning, my attempts to cook this meal weren't very successful. Sometimes I added too much water to the cornmeal, and other times not enough, resulting in the meal that was either too soft or too hard. But my mother and siblings never blamed me. Instead, they praised and encouraged me to keep trying. Through repeated practice, I gradually became better at it, and the meals improved with each attempt. After that, during every winter or summer vacation, while my mother and siblings were out working in the production team, I stayed home to cook and take care of my nephews and nieces. By the time they returned from work, the meal was ready, and all that was left was to stir-fry the vegetables.

Looking back now, I realize that the experience of learning to cook under my mother's guidance as a child had a profound impact on my later studies and career. The process of learning to cook and taking care of the children helped me develop patience and attention to detail. For example, preparing the cornmeal and rice required several precise steps, each one crucial for success. Later, in university, when I studied analytical chemistry, and in my career working in research and conducting experiments, the procedures were even more intricate, requiring precision at every stage. My ability to handle complex and delicate tasks in the lab can be traced back to the careful training and guidance my mother gave me during those early years.

(Ⅲ)

According to traditional rural customs, when boys and girls reached the age of 14 or 15, parents would start seeking marriage prospects for their children through matchmakers who are generally relatives and friends. After finding a suitable match, they would typically marry around the ages of 17 or 18 and start a family. Such arrangements were mostly the result of parental matchmaking, leaving little room for romantic freedom. Even though it was the "new society" by then, this custom was still prevalent in rural Guizhou during the 1950s and 60s. As I was the only son in the family and my father had passed away early, my mother was especially concerned about my marriage prospects. I remember that when I was only eight or nine year's old and attending elementary school, I vaguely heard my mother talking about finding a match for me. Perhaps I was too young at the time, so the idea was eventually abandoned. When I was 14 or 15 years old, in the third year of junior high, my mother asked relatives to find a match for me with a girl from Yeyatang Village in Dianzi Township, Liuzhi District, who was two or three years younger than me and had the surname Guo. I was young and naïve then, thinking it was just a joke. During the Lunar New Year, I occasionally accompanied my mother to visit the girl's family once or twice, but I didn't take it seriously at all. To my surprise, about a year or two later, during the first semester of my second year in high school, my family, without my knowledge, arranged people to send betrothal gifts to the girl's family and to formally establish the engagement. Only then did I realize the situation had become serious. In the rural tradition, according to the elders' customs, before a couple got engaged, a fortune-teller would be consulted to match their birth dates and other astrological signs. If the signs were compatible, an auspicious day would be chosen for the matchmaker and several people from the young man's family to deliver betrothal gifts to the young girl's family, a process called "sending the eight characters" (known as "Na Ba Zi" in our local dialect). If the girl's family accepted, the engagement would be considered officially established. The young man's family typically sent generous gifts, which included food items (such as fresh pork, ham, chickens, ducks, and sticky rice cakes), clothings (including several outfits, fabrics, or even silk for the young girl), and other necessities (such as a sum of cash money). When the matchmaker and the man's family arrived with the gifts, they would set off firecrackers at the entrance of the village and in front of the girl's home, making it a grand occasion. After the "eight characters" were delivered, the couple would usually marry within a year or two on an auspicious date. I suspected that my family's plan was to wait until I graduated from high school at 18 or 19 and then proceed with the marriage. At this time, I was in my second year of high school, fully focused on my studies and aiming for higher education. I had no interest in getting married early in the countryside, starting a family, or having children. When I heard that my family had already sent the betrothal gifts, I knew that if I didn't put a stop to it right away, I would be pressured to marry after high school graduation. What would I do then?

Getting married in the countryside would certainly derail my future plans. So, I decided that I must end this engagement. When I returned home for winter vacation after the first semester of my second year, I resolutely told my mother, brother, and sister: "I don't agree with this engagement! You arranged everything without asking me. You must go and cancel it!" My mother and sister said: "But we've already sent the gifts, which cost us seventy to eighty yuan in total. How can we cancel it now?" I responded: "That's not my concern! You should have asked me before making the decision. Whoever arranged it must go and undo it!" Seeing my firm stance, my mother and sister realized that I would never agree to this marriage, so they had no choice but to ask the matchmaker to withdraw the engagement. But none of the betrothal gifts were returned. To put things in perspective, seventy or eighty yuan was no small amount for a rural family in Guizhou in the mid-1960s. I knew that canceling this engagement meant wasting several years of hard-earned savings from my mother and siblings. But this was a matter of my future, something I couldn't take lightly. I felt deeply guilty for a long time. From that point on, my mother and sister never dared to arrange a match for me without my consent.

In June 1966, I graduated from high school and was preparing for the university entrance exams when the Cultural Revolution broke out, shattering my university dreams. After drifting aimlessly in school for more than two years, the government launched the "Up to the Mountains and Down to the Countryside" campaign in late 1968, and in January 1969, I had no choice but to return to my rural hometown's production team. By then, I was a young man in my early twenties. When I returned home, my mother and siblings were overjoyed, thinking I would probably stay in the countryside for the rest of my life. They thought I was at the right age for marriage, so they began actively seeking a girl for me, asking friends and relatives to introduce potential matches. However, after returning to my rural hometown, I felt utterly disheartened. After studying for more than ten years and almost making it to university, the Cultural Revolution shattered my dream. Now, I was back to square one in the countryside, facing a bleak and uncertain future. I was so dejected that I had no interest in finding a partner. Yet, feeling pressured by local customs, I reluctantly went on a few blind dates, hoping I might come across a girl I liked. Unfortunately, things didn't turn out as I had hoped. The rural folks were practical and valued whether the girl was hardworking and virtuous. They didn't care much about her education or appearance. After meeting two or three girls, I turned them all down. Either they hadn't been to school, or they weren't very attractive---qualities that differed significantly from what I had imagined. After that, I stopped going on any more arranged dates, much to the displeasure of my relatives. They felt unappreciated, thinking, "We're doing this out of goodwill, and yet you're not grateful." This also led some villagers to misunderstand me, speculating, "Why doesn't a young man in his twenties want to find a wife? Is there something wrong with him?" My mother was deeply worried but didn't dare ask me directly. I wasn't one to share my feelings easily, and I became even more withdrawn at home, appearing melancholic and taciturn.

Seeing this situation, my mother asked my cousin Mingliang Wu, with whom I was very close, to talk to me and find out what I really thought. One evening, Mingliang came over to chat. As someone who was well-read and knowledgeable, we had a lot in common, and I confided in him completely. I told him: "First, although I'm back in the countryside now, I haven't decided to stay here for whole life, so I don't want to get married yet. Second, when choosing a partner, I believe in finding someone who is compatible--someone who shares common values and interests. Right now, I can't find that in the countryside. Third, I'm only 21 or 22 and would like to wait a few more years to see if any opportunities arise. I don't want to consider marriage until I'm at least 25." After hearing my thoughts, Mingliang was thrilled. He happily said: "Youngest brother, you are absolutely right! Marriage is a lifelong decision and shouldn't be rushed. I'll explain this to your mother and family, so they'll stop pressuring you. We all want you to have a bright future and to be a role model for our younger generation." From that day on, my mother and siblings stopped mentioning marriage. As it turned out, my judgment was correct. Just a year and a half after returning to the countryside, I was selected to work at the local commune office. In July 1972, I was recommended to study at Guizhou University, fulfilling my long-cherished dream and bringing about a complete turnaround in my life. Had I given up on my dreams and settled for a life in the countryside, my path would have been entirely different.

(IV)

In mid-July of 1972, six years after graduating from high school and having given up all hope of attending college, I miraculously found myself stepping into the university campus I had dreamed of for so long. The joy and excitement I felt at that time were indescribable. So, once I started university, I made up my mind to study hard and try to make up for the six lost years. Although my three years of university life passed quickly, I did not disappoint my mother and siblings back home. I consistently ranked at the top of my class, and I also secured a desirable job assignment upon graduation.

During my time at university, although I was busy with both my studies and various social responsibilities, I did occasionally think about finding a girlfriend in my class so that I could get married and settle down after graduation. Our class had about 40 students, nearly half of whom were female. I did have my eyes on one or two girls, but perhaps it just wasn't meant to be. By the time we graduated and were assigned jobs, I still hadn't managed to start a romantic relationship, which left me with a slight sense of regret. After graduation, I was assigned to a research institute, and in no time, I found myself at the age of 27 or 28. The promise I had made to my mother back then --- "I'll start looking for a partner after turning 25" --- was something she never forgot, but I had yet to show any signs of progress. Every time I returned home during the Lunar New Year or on occasional visits, my mother would ask me anxiously: "My youngest son, have you found girlfriend yet? When are you getting married?" I would always reply: "Soon, soon!" Initially, my mother would cheer up and say: "Then bring her back home next time so we can meet her. If she's a good match, you should settle down sooner rather than later!" But finding a life partner wasn't as simple as shopping. Perhaps because I was approaching 30, I didn't want to settle for just anyone. I had my heart set on finding someone who truly matched my ideals. But love, as the saying goes, cannot be forced, and the more anxious you are, the less likely it is to happen. Despite having worked for two or three years since graduation, I still hadn't found the right person. Eventually, my mother stopped believing my "soon" promises and, with deep concern, would earnestly sayto me: "My youngest son, what kind of girl are you looking for? Are you waiting for a fairy or what? You're already 28 or 29. From my perspective, it's enough if you find a girl who is educated, diligent, and can manage the household well. You're not getting any younger; it's time to settle down! While my health is still good, if you get married and have children soon, I can help you take care of them." After some serious consideration, I realized my mother was right. Marriage and family life are indeed made up of the mundane realities of life, and having a hardworking and virtuous wife is what matters most. Then, in the spring of 1978, through an introduction, I met a young lady named Xiao Teng from Sichuan Province. My first impression of her was quite positive. She was not only gentle and wellmannered but also hardworking and down-to-earth. I brought her home to meet my mother and siblings, and they all took a liking to her. After further interactions and getting to know each other better, we both felt satisfied, and our relationship was officially confirmed.

In July 1978, I was accepted into the graduate program at the University of the Chinese Academy of Sciences. In September of the same year, I went to the China University of Science and Technology in Hefei, Anhui Province, to attend the foundational courses for graduate students. After completing a year of study, I returned to Guiyang in July 1979. Finally, the matter of marriage was put on the agenda. On September 30th of that year, Xiao Teng and I officially registered our marriage at the civil affairs office of Nanming District, Guiyang City. Housing at the institute was extremely scarce at the time. Despite being legally married and even considered a "late marriage" by official standards, we were not allocated a separate residence. Instead, we lived in a shared one-bedroom unit with another couple from my workplace. They occupied the inner room, and we lived in the outer area. We used several large plastic sheets and a wardrobe to partition off a small corridor for them to pass through. When we got married, my brother and sister back in our hometown did everything they could to support us. They hired a local carpenter to make us a bed, a wardrobe, a small square dining table, and four stools using lumber from home. These pieces of furniture were transported to Guiyang for us. Due to our limited resources, we couldn't afford a lavish wedding celebration. Instead, we spent a modest amount of about ¥100 yuan on some basic household necessities, bought a few pounds of candy, and distributed them to our colleagues at work. That was how we formally announced our marriage. To make up for the modest wedding and to show my appreciation for my new wife, in mid-January 1980, I seized the opportunity of a business trip to the Institute of Oceanology at the Chinese Academy of Sciences in Qingdao to collect geological samples for my graduate thesis. On my way back, I stopped in Shanghai and sent a telegram to my wife in Guiyang, inviting her to join me in Shanghai. This trip to Shanghai served as a belated honeymoon. After our marriage, my mother was undoubtedly the happiest. During that year's Spring Festival, when I brought my new wife home, my mother and siblings organized several banquets in our hometown, inviting all the relatives and friends they could. We joyfully celebrated the Lunar New Year together as a family.

In early January 1981, my wife was about to give birth, yet we were still living in that cramped shared apartment with no heating system. When our baby was born, we would need a stove for heating and cooking. However, given the limited space, this seemed impossible. Out of desperation, I sought help from my old classmate, Daonai Wang, and borrowed the kitchen  in his back building for my wife to use during her confinement. This arrangement provided us with some muchneeded relief. On January 14th, in the early hours of the morning, our daughter was born in the hospital. During the first few days of my wife's confinement, our newborn daughter would cry incessantly from around 10 p.m. until 1 or 2 a.m. every night, but she would sleep soundly during the day. We were first-time parents and had no idea how to handle her constant night crying. Fortunately, our colleague Zhengzhen Wang, who had extensive experience in childcare, noticed our struggle and came over to help. She stayed with us for several nights, bathing and feeding the baby. After a few days, our daughter stopped crying at night and began to settle into a regular sleep routine.

After our daughter was born, our whole family was overjoyed. Although my mother was already in her seventies at the time, she was eager to come to Guiyang to help us take care of the baby. Soon after, we were allocated a small onebedroom unit of about 18 square meters at my workplace. Though the space was limited, it was well-equipped, so we brought my mother to Guiyang to live with us. While we were at work, she would look after the baby and cook for us. As people often say: "An elderly person at home is like a treasure," which certainly proved true. Ever since we had the baby, having my mother around to help made things so much easier for us. No matter when we came home from work, the house was always warm and cozy, the baby was well-fed, and dinner was ready, waiting for us to just stir-fry the dishes. I never had to worry about washing the baby's diapers or clothes---my mother took care of everything.

After all, my mother not only raised four or five children herself, including me, but she also helped raise six or seven grandchildren for my brother and sister. She was highly experienced in childcare, and under her meticulous care, our daughter grew up strong and healthy. By the time our daughter was eight or nine months old, she was already beginning to babble her first words. By the age of two or three years old, when she met our neighbors, she could correctly guess their titles based on their appearance ---calling women "Grandma," "Auntie," or "Sister," and men "Grandpa," "Uncle," or "Brother." Our neighbours were all very fond of her. When our daughter was 11 months old, my wife got pregnant again. However, China had already implemented the one-child policy, and according to the policy, we as state employees were not allowed to have a

second child. As a result, my wife had to go to the hospital for an abortion. My mother simply could not understand this. She would say: "If you're already pregnant, why not just have the baby?" But how could we not want another child? It was just that the national policy didn't allow it. What could we do as government employees? My mother was deeply troubled by this and held onto the regret for a very long time.

After our daughter was born, my mother came to Guiyang to help us care for her. I thought that since my mother had worked so hard all her life in the countryside, she should be able to enjoy a peaceful and comfortable life now. Moreover, I believed that showing filial piety should not be delayed. So, around 1985, after our living conditions had further improved, we transferred her household registration from the countryside to Guiyang. Living with us, she would stay in Guiyang for a year or so, and when she started missing the cats, dogs, and grandchildren back in the village, we would send her back to her hometown to alleviate her homesickness. After spending two or three months in her hometown, she would start missing us and her granddaughter, so my brother or sister would send her back to Guiyang. In our small home in Guiyang, in addition to cooking and caring for our daughter, she also made a few friends in the research institute's compound who were in similar situations---elderly ladies who had come from the countryside to help look after their grandchildren. In her spare time, she would go for walks with Granny Zeng, Granny He, and Granny Xiao, sometimes strolling around the city and even visiting the temple on Dongshan Mountain for incense and sightseeing. Whenever they went out together and one of them bought some candies or snacks, they would offer them around, happily sharing just like innocent children. In this way, coming and going, my mother lived with us in Guiyang for more than a decade. These ten-plus years were probably the happiest and most fulfilling years of her life. Although she was never idle for a single day---either caring for her granddaughter or washing and cooking---she felt content. For her, having something to do at home made her feel useful, and being idle would have been unbearable. It was clear that these years living with us, enjoying the company of her children and grandchildren, were the most joyful and blessed times of her life.

Time flew by, and by around 1993, my mother was more than her eighties. She probably felt that she was growing old and frail, and she didn't want to burden us if she fell ill. Meanwhile, our daughter was growing up and no longer needed as much care. So, she proactively suggested that she wanted to return to our hometown to spend her later years, and that she no longer wished to stay with us in Guiyang. Originally, we had hoped to keep her in Guiyang for the rest of her life, but having lived and worked in the countryside her entire life, she has been firmly determined to return to our hometown for retirement. It seems she wishes to "fall leaves return to their roots," seeking comfort in spending her final years in her liveplace. Respecting her wishes, in late 1993, we sent her back to our village.

After my mother returned to the village, it took us some time to get used to the change. Firstly, it felt as if the house had become much quieter without her presence. Secondly, in the past, when we came home from work, the stove would always be warm and the rice ready; we only needed to stir-fry some vegetables. Now, after returning from work, we had to start cooking from scratch and sometimes even light the stove. Thirdly, since my father had passed away when I was young, my mother and I had relied on each other, and our bond was especially deep. Having my mother by my side made me feel like I truly had a home, filling my heart with warmth and a sense of happiness. After she returned to the countryside, my sister told me that she too had a hard time adjusting at first. She would often talk about the family in Guiyang and her little granddaughter. Because of this, I made a point to visit her several times each year during those first few years. Each time I went back, I would buy some of the snacks she had liked in Guiyang---bananas, candies, tangerines, or biscuits---just like she had done for me when I was a child. This back-and-forth continued until May 1995, when I left for Canada for the first time as a visiting scholar.

Each time I visited, I saw that although her health was gradually declining, she remained generally well, and my brother and sister took very good care of her. This gave me peace of mind when I left for Canada, as I had no worries about her well-being in her later years.

(V)

In mid-June 1996, after completing my one-year term as a visiting scholar in Canada and returning to Guiyang, I immediately went back to my hometown to visit my mother. As soon as we met, she said to me: "My youngest, you're back from abroad! How far is that place? Why did you stay away for such a long time?" I replied: "The country I went to is called Canada. It's about 20,000 to 30,000 li(1 km = 2 lis) away from here! It

takes over 20 hours to fly there, and I worked there for a year."
She then asked: "Why go so far to work? Isn't working here in
Guiyang good enough?" I responded: "My workplace is still in
Guiyang; going to Canada was just temporary." My mother
sighed and said: "Guiyang is much better, it's very closer. If
anything happens, you can be home in half a day." It was clear
that she didn't fully understand or agree with my decision to
travel so far abroad. She worried that if we were separated by
such a great distance, it would be difficult for us to see each other,
even if just once in a while.

By February 1997, I decided to go abroad again. Before
leaving, I went back to my hometown to bid farewell to my
mother and family. I told her I was going to Canada again for
work and that I would be back in about six months. My mother
replied: "But you just came back a few months ago! Why are
you going so far away again? There's work here in Guiyang,
why not just work here? I'm getting old now, and my health isn't
good. If I get sick, I might not be able to see you!" I comforted
her by saying: "Mom, don't worry! Transportation is very
convenient now. If anything happens at home, my brother can
come to Guiyang and find Xia Wu and her mom. If you fall ill,
just have my brother call me, and I can be back in two or three
days." I knew, of course, that I was only saying this to reassure
her. When the time came and if my mother did fall ill, I hadn't
really thought about whether I'd be able to make it back in time.
I was hopeful because, although she was already 86 or 87 years
old, her health seemed relatively stable, and I figured she could
live to over 90 without any major issues. After comforting her, I
reluctantly parted from her and my siblings and left for Canada
again in mid-February 1997.

This time, shortly after arriving back in Canada, an
unexpected event completely disrupted my original plans. One
or two days after I returned to Ottawa, I found out that Professor
Geldsetzer the head of the international collaboration project,
had passed away from liver cancer in early January 1997. This
sudden news shocked me. With his passing, I lost the project's
sponsorship and support. I was faced with a dilemma: should I
stay or return to China? I thought to myself, I came all the way
to Canada out of necessity; it would be difficult to explain my
return to the institute so soon. If I wanted to stay, I needed to
resolve my immigration status quickly. Fortunately, I managed

to do so successfully, and the next issue was finding a job. However, while handling my family's immigration paperwork, there were several setbacks related to the health check process, which delayed the matter. Since I had already established myself in Canada, I was confident that the family immigration issue would eventually be resolved. As expected, by May 1999, my wife and daughter finally received their immigration visas, and in late July of that year, our family was joyfully reunited in Ottawa. Before my wife and daughter left for Canada, they visited my mother back home and informed my siblings that they were leaving China to join me. Based on my wife's feedback and the photos taken with my mother, it seemed that her health was not as good as it had been. Even so, I still believed that nothing serious would happen within the next two to three years. My plan was to go back and visit her in 2001.

By mid-April 2000, Easter was approaching. One morning over the weekend, I went to the Food Basic Supermarket and saw that the lilieflowers for sale were blooming beautifully, so I bought a pot and brought it home to place in our living room. However, this pot of originally vibrant lilies withered and died within less than a week, even though we hadn't neglected it in any way. My wife and I found this very strange since we often bought flowers before, and this had never happened. Just a few days after the flowers died, something else strange happened. On the night of April 22nd or 23rd, a small animal (which seemed like a chipmunk) suddenly appeared in the gap of our kitchen ceiling, frantically scratching as if trying to squeeze out. Since the gap was too narrow for its head to get through, so we could only see its paws clawing around. It made a racket all night, preventing us from sleeping. The little creature kept this up for two consecutive nights before disappearing. At the time, we were living on the first floor of a three-story house, with the kitchen located in the middle. In front of the kitchen were our daughter's room and the living room, and behind the kitchen was our bedroom. Above us were two more floors. It was almost impossible for a chipmunk to enter the ceiling of our first-floor kitchen from the roof or sides, but it happened. Just two days after the chipmunk disappeared, on the night of April 25th, we received an urgent international call from my brother in China, telling me that our mother was critically ill and that I needed to come home immediately. Then another inexplicable incident happened soon after receiving the call. One or two days later, since I worked the mid-shift started at 3:00 p.m., I was washing dishes at home after lunch. I was holding a blue-and-white porcelain bowl under the kitchen faucet, gently rinsing it, when suddenly, the bowl split cleanly in two in my hands as if it had been deliberately broken. The fracture looks very fresh and smooth. I was suddenly stunned and thought: "Could it be that something has happened to my mother?" Panic welled up inside me. Looking back at these strange occurrences, I realized that the withering lilies, the frantic chipmunk, and the broken bowl might have been signals related to my mother's critical condition. My mother passed away on April 27th, the very day I broke the bowl. These bizarre events would seem unbelievable to most, but they happened one after another during my mother's final days. It seemed that, in moments of life and death, deeply connected family members could communicate through some magnetic field or unknown energy, something akin to what people call "telepathy."

Since receiving my brother's phone call, I had been extremely anxious, but at that time, there weren't daily flights from Canada to China (only two or three flights per week), and Ottawa was a smaller city without direct flights to China, often requiring transfers through Vancouver or Toronto. By the time I finally boarded a flight to China on April 28th, after multiple layovers and delays, I didn't reach my hometown until May 2nd. By then, my mother had not only passed away, but she had already been buried for several days. I never got to see her one last time. My sister later told me that our mother had fallen ill in mid-April and had been constantly asking for me. Initially, no one took it seriously, thinking it was like before, where she would recover after a week or two. But after April 20th, her condition worsened, and she probably realized she didn't have much time left. She insisted that my family notify me and have me come home to see her. In her final days, she repeatedly asked my sister: "Did you notify my youngest? Why hasn't he come back yet? Please get him back quickly. If he's late, I'm afraid I won't get to see him!" She passed away, still anxiously waiting for me. This truly shows that, no matter how far the son travels, a mother's heart is always with him. Reflecting on it now, not being able to see my mother one last time is both her lifelong regret and mine as her son.

Looking back on my life, the person I am most grateful to and indebted to is my dear mother. Not only did she give me life, but she also nurtured me and guided me to grow up healthy and strong. In my childhood, she taught me the skills of labor and the principles of being a good person, lessons that have inspired and shaped my entire life. During those difficult years when everyone struggled to get enough to eat, it was my mother and my elder sister who endured the scorching heat and bitter cold year-round, tirelessly gathering wild vegetables to sell during weekends and spare moments, enduring hardships to support my education and ensure that I completed my secondary schooling. After I got married and had a child, it was my mother, despite her advanced age and frail health, who willingly took on the responsibility of caring for our child, cooking, and washing for us, quietly dedicating herself to our small family. Therefore, it is no exaggeration to say that throughout her life, my mother's every thought and concern were always for her children, and never for herself. Without my mother, I wouldn't have the life I have today, nor would I have achieved even the smallest of successes. Every bit of progress or accomplishment I've made is thanks to my mother's dedication and sacrifice.

The poem says: "Who can say that the heart of grass can ever repay the warmth of spring?" A mother's love knows no bounds, and her kindness is difficult to repay. Yet, even though it is impossible to fully return a mother's selfless love, the bond of family endures forever! Mother, your boundless love and kindness to your son can never be forgotten in this lifetime. I will forever cherish and be grateful to you, my dearest mother!

Chapter 13   Enjoying a Peaceful Old Age

(I)

In recent years, some friends who know about my work experience in China often ask me: "Mr. Wu, do you think you gained or lost by immigrating to Canada?" I reply: "Well, it depends. Different people will have different answers depending on their perspectives. It's not something that can be explained in just a few words." If viewed from the perspective of status and professional achievements, then perhaps I did lose. Had I not left, I would likely have retired with the rank of a senior researcher or professor. But after coming to Canada, due to the passing of my collaborating professor, my research work was interrupted, and I switched to a general job, making me an ordinary citizen here. If judged from this angle, then I did lose. However, living as an ordinary citizen in Canada, I feel extremely relaxed and content. Here, as an ordinary person, nobody looks down on you. People here lack that restlessness for status and comparison that is common back in China. In Canada, whether you are a government official or an ordinary citizen, no one has any special privileges. When you go to a government office or elsewhere for services, everything gets handled promptly. Sometimes a phone call or a simple click on a website solves the issue. No one gives you a hard time, and there's absolutely no need to entertain, send gifts, or rely on personal connections. In other words, even if you are just an ordinary citizen here, you live with dignity. Moreover, Canada has a universal healthcare system. Every citizen or permanent resident (those with a green card) holds a health card issued by the province, allowing them to see a doctor, undergo treatments or surgeries in the hospital without paying a single penny. Even meals during hospitalization are provided for free, and there's no need for family members to accompany the patient for care. For elderly citizens aged 65 and above, most prescription medications are also covered by the government. Canadians or permanent residents aged 65 and above who have lived in Canada for more than 10 years are eligible for a government pension. The amount depends on the length of time lived in Canada, but for elderly couples without any other income, each person can receive about

$1,500 CAD per month, amounting to a combined monthly pension of about $3,000 CAD. While this pension isn't substantial, it is more than sufficient for basic living expenses. Here, the cost of living is generally affordable and prices are relatively stable, so there's no sense of financial pressure. Since coming to Canada, perhaps because of the peace of mind or the excellent natural environment, I've been in good health for the past almost thirty years. If I had stayed in China, I would have likely been subjected to the high-stress work environment and the frequent social gatherings with colleagues and friends due to the local food and drinking culture. By the time I retired, my health would have been seriously affected. I would never have the good health I enjoy today. So, from the perspective of personal physical and mental well-being, the answer to whether coming to Canada was a loss or a gain should be as clear as a bright spot on a bald head---self-evident!

Additionally, let's take a look at Canada's national conditions to further understand the benefits of immigrating to Canada. Canada is located in the northern part of North America, bordered by the Atlantic Ocean to the east, the Pacific Ocean to the west, the United States to the south, and the Arctic Ocean to the north. Its land area is nearly 10 million square kilometers, making it the second-largest country in the world. Apart from the Rocky Mountains in the west, most of central and eastern Canada consists of low plateaus and plains, with flat terrain and numerous lakes, and is extremely rich in natural resources. Canada has a highly developed agricultural and livestock industry, making it one of the world's leading wheat exporters and the largest exporter of seafood products. Its mineral resources are equally abundant, with oil reserves ranking third in the world, only behind Venezuela and Saudi Arabia. With a population of about 38 million, Canada has only about onefortieth the population of China, making it a country with vast land and sparse population. Its per capita resources--such as mineral reserves, forest area, arable land, and freshwater resources--- are among the highest in the world. In contrast, although China is also a vast and resource-rich country, its large population base results in a much lower per capita share of resources. Living in a country that is both resource-rich and sparsely populated, it's much easier for people to live in harmony with one another and with nature. It is precisely due to these exceptional natural conditions that Canada has rightfully become one of the most soughtafter destinations for international immigrants.

The author by the shores of Dow's Lake, Ottawa, Ontario, Canada in November, 2001.

Secondly, Canada is a highly developed capitalist country with a well-established manufacturing, high-tech, and service industry. Its resource industry, manufacturing, and agriculture are major pillars of the national economy, supporting a high standard of living for its people. With a comprehensive social welfare system, Canadians have no worries regarding pensions, healthcare, or children's education. Furthermore, Canada is an immigrant country that practices multiculturalism, allowing minority groups the right to use their own languages and maintain their cultural customs. Canadians are warm and friendly, and the society is stable and safe with a very low crime rate. Out of nearly 200 countries in the world, Canada consistently ranks among the best in terms of quality of life. The United Nations Development Programme's Human Development Reports have named Canada the most suitable place for human habitation for many consecutive years. For these reasons, Canada remains one of the most desirable destinations for international immigrants.

In summary, the main reason I chose to settle in Canada during the peak of my career in my late forties was largely due to the prolonged unfair treatment and unreasonable suppression I experienced at my previous workplace in China, which led to major setbacks in my professional path. On the other hand, Canada's beautiful natural environment, friendly citizens, and peaceful social atmosphere deeply attracted me. Between these two factors, the primary reason for my decision was undoubtedly the first one. I thought, since the powers-that-be at my original workplace were persistently making things difficult, then, "If this place doesn't want me, there must be another that does," so why not just leave and put an end to my troubles and unhappiness? Additionally, before my first trip abroad in 1995, I had a life-threatening incident while undergoing gallbladder

surgery due to gallstones. I nearly didn't make it off the operating table and was saved only through intensive emergency care. This neardeath experience undoubtedly had an undeniable impact on the choices I made in the latter half of my life. After recovering from surgery, I reflected deeply on my life and repeatedly asked myself: What is the purpose of living? What is truly the most valuable thing in life? Is it wealth, fame, or status? If one's health and life are gone, then what meaning do wealth, fame, and status hold? After much contemplation and self-reflection, I finally understood that the most precious things in life are health and life itself, everything else, whether it's wealth, fame, or status, is just external and fleeting. After surviving that surgery, I became grateful simply to be alive and healthy. I have since faced any hardship with serenity and an attitude of gratitude for the blessings I have received. Even though I faced significant challenges on my life path, I knew that I could not let obstacles hold me back. I had to keep moving forward to the best of my ability and be ready to embrace new challenges. Therefore, when I decided to settle in Canada, I was fully aware that I might lose my professional career and need to start anew, which is no small feat for a man nearing fifty. But for someone who has faced death and hardship from an early age, what is this in comparison? At worst, I would simply reboot my life. Who knows, taking this new path might even lead to new and exciting opportunities, and along the way, I might get to enjoy new and unexpected experiences. So, I decided to let go of the pursuit of wealth, fame, and status. A healthy body and a relaxed, happy life became my ultimate goals. Canada, with its ideal living conditions, became the place where I could pursue this vision of a healthy and peaceful life. This is the true reason why I chose to leave during the peak of my career and settle in Canada.

Some friends have often asked me: "Since you were treated unfairly in China for such a long time, do you still hold any fondness for the country?" I tell them: "You're mistaken! The people who made things difficult for me were just a few petty individuals at my workplace. They do not represent the whole institution, let alone China as a whole. On the contrary, I still have a deep sense of affection and appreciation for my former workplace. As for China, it is my ancestral homeland, the place where I was born, raised, and educated, it's the root of my identity. I will always cherish and love her. Canada is now my country. From the moment I set foot on this land, I developed a deep affection and respect for it. In other words, I love both my homeland, China, and my new home, Canada, equally. I will never do anything to harm either of these two countries."

(Ⅱ)

After nearly 30 years of work in China, and another 20 years of work in Canada, I officially retired in 2015. Time flies like an arrow, and before I knew it, I was in my seventies, entering the twilight of my life. A few years ago, friends started asking me how I planned to spend my retirement. I told them that I didn't have any detailed plans; my general principle was to do what I enjoy and live a happy and contented life. The things I enjoy are simple: reading, traveling, fishing, and exercising---hobbies I had to put aside in my younger years due to work and family responsibilities. Now that I am retired, I have plenty of time and still maintain good health and energy. Thus, reading, traveling, fishing, exercising, and occasionally writing have become the main themes of my life. It's been five or six years since I retired. During this time, I've read a lot of books, traveled domestically and internationally several times, caught many fish, and kept up with regular exercise. If it hadn't been for the COVID-19 pandemic, I would still be making annual trips back to China and abroad. Even though I'm in my seventies now, I can still eat and sleep well, and I'm free from major health issues. I feel physically and mentally great, my memory and writing skills have improved, and I always find time flying by so quickly each day that sometimes I even feel like there isn't enough of it. Perhaps influenced by my father from an early age, I've always had a strong passion for learning and reading. During my youth, apart from the formal education I received in primary and secondary schools, I read many literary works in my spare time, including the four great classical Chinese novel: *Romance of the Three Kingdoms* (《三国演义》),*Journey to the West* (《西游记》,*Water Margin* (《水浒传》) and *Dream of the Red Chamber* (《红楼梦》), as well as other classic historical novels like *The Sui-Tang Romance* (《隋唐演义》), *The Yang Family Generals* (《杨家将》) and *The Complete Biography of Yue Fei* (《说岳全传》). I also read numerous modern literary works such as *Tracks in the Snowy Forest* (《林海雪原》), *The Guerrillas behind Enemy Lines* (《敌后武工队》), *The Song of Youth* (《青春之歌》), and other novels I could find at the time. During the Cultural Revolution, the school library was almost entirely open, and any interested student could find books to read. I read many so-called "forbidden books" of the time, such as *The Dream of Nanjing* (《金陵春梦》), *The Biography of Khrushchev* (《赫鲁晓夫传》**), The Plum in the Golden Vase** (《金瓶梅》), and many others. I also read some world classics, such as *The author with his mother and wife in November 1986. War and Peace (*《战争与和平》),

The Red and the Black (《红与黑》) and ***The Count of Monte Cristo*** (《基督山伯爵》). This extensive extracurricular reading not only enriched my literary knowledge but also indirectly improved my Chinese language skills and writing proficiency. After graduating from university, and especially after completing my postgraduate studies and starting work, I found myself occupied with administrative and professional responsibilities, leaving little time for reading. I missed out on

The author participated in the celebration of Canada Day in Ottawa, Ontario, Canada in July 1st, 1997.

many popular TV series and movies of that time. After moving abroad, I initially struggled to adapt and build a new life, so I didn't have much time to read either. However, starting from 2016, before and after retirement, I made use of trips back to China to buy a large collection of Chinese books, which I either shipped back to Canada or brought back in my luggage. Thanks to this effort, my home library has grown to over a hundred books. These include Chinese classics like ***Records of the Grand Historian*** (《史记》) and ***Zizhi Tongjian*** (《资治通鉴》), world classics such as ***War and Peace*** (《战争与和平》)

and *The Hunchback of Notre-Dame* (《巴黎圣母院》),
scientific works like *A Brief History of Time* (《时间简史》)
and *Sapiens: A Brief History of Humankind* (《人类简史》),
as well as books on world natural geography, health, and
wellness. I now have a well-rounded collection that allows me
to read whatever I want at any time, fully satisfying my
intellectual needs and enriching my spiritual life.

Traveling has always been one of my dreams and passions
since childhood. After starting
my career, due to work demands,
I traveled extensively across
China for business trips. Over
those twenty-some years, my
footprints almost covered the
entire country. During these
business trips, I took the
opportunity to visit many famous
mountains, rivers, and historical
sites. However, due to the busy
nature of work, my main purpose
was not leisure travel but rather
to unwind briefly from the hectic
schedule. Moreover, the tourism
infrastructure at that time was
relatively basic, so these trips
were mostly like quick glances

rather than in-depth experiences. Thus, after retiring, I aspired to
embark on more extensive journeys, both within China and
abroad, to make up for the many regrets I had when I was
younger.

My first international trip took place in mid-December 2016
when I went on a luxurious Caribbean cruise with my daughter,
son-in-law, and their family, which was sponsored and
organized by my son-in-law's company. Our group of nine
people (my daughter's family of five, my son-in-law's parents,
and my wife and I) joined over twenty others from my
daughter's company, setting off from Miami on December 10,
2016, aboard the luxurious Norwegian Getaway cruise ship to
explore the Eastern Caribbean. This cruise ship, built by
Norwegian Cruise Line in 2014, is a massive luxury vessel

weighing approximately 150,000 tons, with a crew of around 1,700 and a passenger capacity of 4,000. The ship has a total of 19 decks, with five decks below the main deck and 15 decks above. At the top, there are large swimming pools, surfing facilities, a basketball court, minigolf, climbing walls, and various fitness and entertainment amenities, ensuring that people of all ages can find activities they enjoy. The ship also features multiple restaurants, including large buffet-style eateries and à la carte dining options, all operating 24 hours a day. Passengers can eat whatever they want, whenever they want, in any quantity, all entirely free of charge. The cruise typically sails overnight and docks during the day, allowing passengers to disembark and explore the islands. Over the six-day journey, we visited the British Virgin Islands and the U. S. Virgin Islands, enjoying the stunning natural scenery of the Eastern Caribbean islands and experiencing the local culture. It was a uniquely unforgettable trip, one I had never experienced before and one that left a lasting impression. Large luxury cruises like this one are particularly suitable for families with elderly members and young children because cruising requires minimal physical exertion (in fact, one can get by without much walking), while still allowing passengers to take in the beautiful scenery and enjoy six-star service on board---a comfortable and effortless

2017.9.摄于英国爱丁堡

new way to travel.

My second international trip took place from mid-September to early October 2017, a European adventure. Europe is not only the birthplace of modern civilization but also home to the ancient Greek and Roman civilizations, boasting countless well-preserved historical sites and cultural relics. It is one of the most sought-after destinations for international travellers. This trip was organized by a Chinese tour company based in France, and all the travellers were of Chinese descent, coming from various parts of the world. Our tour group had about 40 people, traveling in a luxury coach bus for ten days. The first three days were spent in the United Kingdom, and the remaining seven days were dedicated to touring France, Switzerland, Italy, and Monaco.

The trip began in London, England, and ended in Paris, France. I flew from Ottawa to London on the evening of September 19, and on the 20th, I joined the other tour members in London. During our three days in England, we visited iconic British cities and towns, including London, Cambridge, York Minster, Edinburgh, Rochester, Windermere, and Manchester.

The author visited Shakespeare's former residence in England, UK, in Oct. 2017.

We concluded our time in England with a visit to Stratford-upon-Avon in Warwickshire, the birthplace and former residence of the great playwright William Shakespeare. England, the birthplace of the Industrial Revolution, truly lives up to its reputation with its rich history, advanced industrial and agricultural sectors, and highly developed technology industry. The standard of living in England is notably higher than that of continental Europe, and the UK's decision to leave the European

Union evidently has its reasons. Along the highways, vast farmlands stretch out on either side, and the hills are dotted with lush green pastures. The residential buildings in towns and cities may not be very tall, but they are exquisitely designed and harmoniously arranged.

2017.9.意大利比萨斜塔

The author visited the Leaning Tower of Pisa in Italy in September, 2017.

After finishing our tour of the UK, our coach crossed the Channel Tunnel to Paris, France. Over the next few days, we traveled from Paris to various destinations, visiting the beautiful city of Lucerne in Switzerland, and iconic Italian cities such as Milan, Venice, Rome, Vatican City, Florence, and Pisa. We then followed the Mediterranean coast back into France, visiting Monaco, Nice, and the charming town country, its natural of Cannes. The entire European journey left deep impressions. Although Switzerland is a small mountainous landscapes are like a paradise. Entering Switzerland feels like stepping into a fairytale world, with snow-capped mountains, forests, meadows, and lakes everywhere. The mountain peaks are blanketed in white snow, the mid- slopes are covered with forests, and the lower slopes are lush pastures, making the whole country resemble a giant park. It is no wonder Switzerland is known as

Europe's backyard garden. Italy, on the other hand, truly deserves its title as the cradle of European culture. It nurtured the brilliant ancient Roman civilization and the Etruscan culture and later gave birth to the Renaissance in the Middle Ages. Italy is home to numerous historical and cultural sites that have been remarkably well-preserved, making it the country with the most UNESCO World Heritage Sites in the world. These sites form an inexhaustible treasure trove of tourism resources, offering visitors an unparalleled opportunity to immerse themselves in the rich cultural heritage of the region.

My most recent international trip was to Japan in early October 2019, just before the outbreak of the COVID-19 pandemic. This was actually my second visit to Japan. Back in October 1985, I accompanied my supervisor, Academician Chengji Guo, on a month-long visit to Japan. At that time, we visited Tokyo, Kyoto, Nara, and Osaka. The contrast between China and Japan was stark back then: Japan was a highly developed capitalist society, with skyscrapers everywhere, a wealth of material goods, and clean streets filled with well-dressed pedestrians. In contrast, China had just begun its reform and opening-up phase, with rundown urban buildings, scarce supplies, and streets bustling with bicycles as the primary means of transportation. People's clothing in China was plain and monotonous. That visit to Japan left a deep impression on me. Now, more than thirty years later, China has undergone a dramatic transformation, so I had long wanted to revisit Japan again to see how it has changed after all these decades. Finally, in early October 2019, I joined a tour group, fulfilling my wish to return to Japan.

On October 4, 2019, I flew from Toronto, Canada, to Tokyo, Japan, with a short layover at Calgary Airport, arriving at Narita Airport around 3 p.m. on October 5. That evening, I stayed at the Radisson Hotel in Chiba, which is just a step away from Tokyo. The next day, we toured Tokyo, visiting Asakusa Temple, the park in front of the Imperial Palace, and the Ginza district. In the following days, we continued to visit the famous sights in cities such as Mount Fuji and the renowned Oshino Hakkai village at its foot, Gamagori City, Nagoya, Kyoto, Nara, and Osaka. Overall, my impression from this revisit to Japan, three decades later, was that the municipal construction and cityscape of Japan's major cities had not undergone any noticeable changes. If we were to compare purely based on urban appearance and the grandeur of municipal infrastructure, Chinese cities might have surpassed their Japanese counterparts, especially in the area of airport and train station construction, which have become a dazzling showcase of modern China. However, it cannot be denied that most of Japan's major cities were severely damaged during World War II, and since the economic boom of the 1960s and 1970s, their municipal and infrastructural development has essentially been complete. Despite the passage of several decades, these structures are still fully functional today, although they do appear somewhat outdated.

(Ⅲ)

Yunnan Province, which borders my home province of Guizhou, boasts a wealth of tourist resources and is one of China's major travel destinations. My university classmate and good friend, Mr. Yuchun Xu, worked at the Yunnan Provincial Public Security Bureau after graduation and retired in 2010. Since then, he has extended numerous invitations for me to visit him in Kunming and to tour various parts of Yunnan together. I finally accepted his gracious invitation and visited Yunnan twice, first in April 2018 and again in April 2019. During these visits, we toured the western regions of Yunnan, including Baoshan, Mangshi, Ruili, Dali, and Lijiang, allowing me to experience firsthand the unique customs and cultures of ethnic minorities in the southwestern border regions and to appreciate the stunning scenery of Yunnan Province.

During our trip to Ruili in April 2018, we were joined by another classmate from the Chemistry Department at Guizhou University, Mr. Tianlu Xiao. After meeting in Kunming,

Yuchun specially arranged for a driver to take the three of us on a westward journey. Our first stop was Baoshan, a border town approximately 500 kilometers from Kunming. Baoshan is a strategic frontier town in southwest China and has been a site of military importance since ancient times. Baoshan also boasts a long history and a rich cultural heritage, serving as a key stop along the Southern Silk Road, known as the Ancient Bonan Road. Historically, Baoshan was known as Yongchang Commandery and later Yongchang Prefecture. One of the town's most renowned products is the "Yongchang Go," also known as the "Yongzi," which is a high-quality type of Go stone that has been produced for over five hundred years. The Yongzi stones are considered the finest Go stones, celebrated since the Ming and Qing dynasties. The city has built the Yongzi Chess Institute, a grand six-story pagoda-style structure that is majestic and exudes the opulence of a royal garden.

Our second stop was Mangshi, the capital of Dehong Dai and Jingpo Autonomous Prefecture in Yunnan Province. Mangshi, formerly known as Luxi, was renamed in July 2010 with approval from the State Council. Luxi was the first choice for our

old classmate Yuchun during the Cultural Revolution for the "Down to the Countryside" movement. Decades have passed, but Yuchun still holds a special and indescribable affection for this place. On the evening we arrived in Mangshi, we stayed at the Mangshi Hotel, a landmark building in the city. The Mangshi Hotel was built in 1956 and has a history of over 60 years. It has hosted many national leaders, including Premier Zhou Enlai and Myanmar's Prime Minister U Nu. In the botanical garden in front of the hotel, there are two Michelia champaca trees planted by Premier Zhou and Prime Minister U Nu, symbolizing the friendship between China and Myanmar. In addition to visiting the historic sites of Mangshi, we also sampled the local Jingpo cuisine, which included fried bamboo worms and other insect dishes---a unique and special culinary experience.

Our final stop on this trip was the border town of Ruili, located just across the river from Myanmar. Situated at the southwestern tip of Yunnan Province, Ruili is bordered on three sides by Myanmar and is a border city full of exotic charm. There is a Dai village here that is divided by the national border, with the Chinese side called Yinjin and the Myanmar side called Mangxiu---this is the famous "**One Village, Two Countries** (一寨两国)." Other well known tourist attractions in Ruili include the Jiegao Border Gate, the Wanding Bridge, and the "**One Tree Forest** (独树成林)." The Wanding Bridge is a memorial bridge commemorating the victory of the War of Resistance against Japan. During World War II, when the Japanese army blocked all of China's access to the sea, the Burma Road became the only route for strategic supplies from the international anti-fascist alliance to reach China. As a crucial point on the Burma Road, the Wanding Bridge played a vital role in China's victory in the war.

On our way back to Kunming from Ruili, we made a stop in Dali. Located on the Erhai Plain in western Yunnan, Dali is flanked by the Cangshan Mountains to the west and Erhai Lake to the east. Once the capital of the ancient Nanzhao Kingdom and later the Dali Kingdom, Dali served as the political, economic, and cultural center of the region for over 500 years, boasting a rich cultural heritage. It is also one of China's first Top Ten Charming Cities. Dali is home to numerous historical sites and tourist attractions, among which the most famous include the ancient capital ruins of the Nanzhao Kingdom, Dali Old Town, the Three Pagodas of Dali, and Butterfly Spring. However, taking the cable car up Cangshan Mountain was a unique and exhilarating experience. We began our journey from the foot of Cangshan at the "Tianlong Babu" film set, ascended past the Seven Dragon Maiden Pool, and arrived at the Wash Horse Flat on the summit of Yujufeng Peak, a total vertical ascent of nearly 2,000 meters. The cable car route is equipped with boardwalks, pavilions, and medical aid stations along the way. From the cable car, visitors can enjoy a panoramic view of the snow-capped peaks at the top of Cangshan and the ancient city of Dali at its base, showcasing the grandeur of the mountain and the unique landscape of dwarf rhododendron forests and fir trees at the summit. One particularly noteworthy aspect of this trip was the dramatic change in temperature. Standing at the foot of Cangshan, at an elevation of about 2,200 meters, the temperature was a sweltering 25 to 26 degrees Celsius, making

it feel like a hot summer day. However, after a short 20-minute ride to the summit, over 4,000 meters above sea level, the temperature suddenly dropped to below -10 degrees Celsius, making visitors feel as if they had plunged into an ice cellar. Within just twenty minutes, we experienced a drastic "fire and ice" transformation, a rare phenomenon that left a lasting impression on everyone.

In April 2019, I, along with Yuchun and his old friend Lao Zhang, set out for Lijiang by train. We departed from Kunming at around 8:30 a.m. and arrived in Lijiang at around 1:30 p.m. in the afternoon. We were warmly welcomed at Lijiang Railway Station by Yunlong He, a Naxi friend of Yuchun. Yunlong He, a typical Naxi man in his forties, has a medium build, a bronze complexion, and an unassuming and modest demeanor. Mr. He is also warm-hearted and friendly. As our host and guide for the Lijiang trip, He accompanied and took care of us throughout our stay in Lijiang. That evening, Yunlong He hosted us at a local restaurant and arranged our accommodation at Shuhe Ancient Town, adjacent to Lijiang Old City. In the Naxi language, Shuhe is known as "Shaowu," which means "village under the high mountains." It is one of the earliest settlements of the Naxi people in Lijiang and a well-preserved trading post along the

Ancient Tea Horse Road. Shuhe's architectural layout is best represented by the typical Naxi residential structure of "three rooms and a shining wall," which symbolizes a distinct and characteristic design of Naxi homes. Lijiang Old City, also known as Dayan Old Town, is a renowned historic and cultural city in China, combining natural heritage, cultural heritage, and intangible memory. It is a rare example of a well-preserved multi-ethnic residential city in China, filled with vibrant local customs and unique recreational activities, such as Naxi Ancient Music, Dongba rituals, divination culture, and the Naxi Torch Festival. Lijiang Old City, with its Naxi-style architecture, reflects the distinct characteristics of the Naxi people while integrating the essence of various ethnic groups in its overall city planning and architectural style. The town's buildings are primarily made of wood, and its streets are paved with flagstones and stone slabs, giving the entire city a quaint and elegant charm. The clear and pristine water that flows through the town originates from the melting snow of Yulong Snow Mountain, creating a network of canals throughout Lijiang, forming a unique spatial layout of water systems that permeate every street and alley. Walking through the ancient town, one can see blooming flowers and hear the gentle flow of water under small bridges, making it a perfect picture of tranquil beauty. On a weekly basis or during traditional festivals, the town releases water to flush the streets, keeping them spotless and free of dust. Fifteen kilometers north of Lijiang Old City is Yushuizhai Village, known as the "Sacred Place of Dongba Culture" and the "Cradle of Dongba Culture." Yushuizhai Village is home to a clear, emerald spring that flows down the mountain, forming the "Three Stacked Waterfalls of the Sacred Dragon"---the "Emerging Dragon Waterfall," "Dancing Dragon Waterfall," and "Sending Dragon Waterfall"---creating a breathtaking and spectacular scene.

During our four-day stay in Lijiang, we explored Shuhe Ancient Town, Lijiang Old Town, the Mu Residence, and Yushuizhai Village. We also sampled various Naxi delicacies, such as Lijiang Baba, Naxi-style barbecue, and rice sausage. Lijiang truly lives up to its reputation as a serene, elegant, and unique border town, where tranquility blends with vibrancy and antiquity intertwines with modern prosperity. It is a place that leaves you longing to visit again.

Another noteworthy domestic trip took place in mid-October 2018, when I attended the 40th anniversary celebration of the University Of Chinese Academy of Sciences (UCAS) in Beijing, along with a reunion of the 1978 graduate class and a post-celebration tour to Hami, Xinjiang, and Zhangye, Gansu Province.

A group photo of the class of 1978 alumni celebrating the 40th anniversary of the University of Chinese Academy of Sciences in Beijing in October 2018 (The 4th in the front row is the author).

The University of Chinese Academy of Sciences, formerly known as the Beijing Graduate School of the University of Science and Technology of China, was established in October 1978, making our class the first cohort of graduate students. For this reason, UCAS specially invited our 1978 graduate cohort to attend the 40th-anniversary celebration in Beijing. In 1978, around 1,000 graduate students were recruited from various research institutes under the Chinese Academy of Sciences, and almost all of us were gathered at the Beijing Graduate School to study the foundational courses. After 40 years, many classmates have passed away, some have lost touch, and others were unable to attend due to health reasons, so only a few hundred of us were able to make it. We arrived at the UCAS campus in Huairou, Beijing, on October 12 to register, and the celebration events took place on October 13 and 14. The event was held with great pomp, with leaders from the National Science and Technology Commission and the Chinese Academy of Sciences attending to extend their congratulations. This deeply moved and inspired us,

A group photo (local part same above pgoto) of the class of 1978 alumni celebrating the 40th anniversary of UCAS in Beijing, China in October 2018 (The 3rd person from the left in the front is the author).

the old alumni of the institution. The celebrations concluded on October 15, and I initially planned to leave early that morning to catch the direct train from downtown Beijing to Urumqi in Xinjiang to visit my wife's third aunt family in Hami, and to tour the area. However, due to heavy traffic during Beijing's morning rush hour, I arrived at Beijing West Railway Station 20 minutes late and missed the train. As a result, I had to take the next available direct train the following morning (October 16). The train arrived safely and on time at Hami Railway Station on the afternoon of October 17, where my wife's third uncle and his son-in-law warmly welcomed me at the station.

Hami, Xinjiang, is a familiar place for me because, back in July and August of 1987, while working on the National 305 Project and conducting field geological surveys in the northern Xinjiang region, I made a brief stop in Hami with my wife and daughter to visit my wife's third uncle and aunt. Located in eastern Xinjiang, Hami is a major gateway to Xinjiang and is known as the "Eastern Gate of Xinjiang." Historically, it has been a crucial choke point on the Silk Road and is often referred to as the "Throat of the Western Regions" and the "Gateway to Xinjiang." My wife's third uncle came to Hami in the late 1950s as part of the initiative to develop the Northwest. At that time, he worked at the Hami Steel Plant, dedicating his efforts to the development of China's northwest. Now, he is a silver-haired elderly man in his twilight years, spending his days peacefully at home enjoying the company of his grandchildren. During my visit in 1987, most of Hami consisted of low, flat houses, and rammed earth dwellings could be seen everywhere. Now, more than 30 years later, Hami has undergone a transformation just like cities across the country. The streets are wide and straight, tall buildings are everywhere, and people now live in high-rise apartments, with many residents even owning standalone or semi-detached villas. In 1987, when our family visited Hami, my wife's third uncle and his family lived in a small courtyard house with earthen walls. At that time, his four children were still in school---the oldest was in high school, and the youngest in elementary school. This time, however, all four of his children

The author (right) and his 4th uncle visited Zhangye Danxia National Geopark in Zhangye, Gansu, China in October 2018.

have established their own careers, and some of his eldest grandchildren have even graduated from university and are working. His eldest daughter now lives in a standalone villa, embodying the saying "a happy family with many descendants living in prosperity." I stayed in Hami for three days and was warmly hosted by the entire family. On October 20th, I took a train from Hami to Zhangye, Gansu Province, to visit my wife's fourth uncle and aunt, and to explore this historic cultural city and the Danxia Landform National Geopark. The train arrived safely in Zhangye in the afternoon, where I was greeted by my wife's fourth uncle and his son-in-law, Xiao Chen.

Zhangye is located in the middle of the Hexi Corridor in Gansu Province. To the south, it is bordered by the Qilian Mountains, and to the north, it is flanked by the Heli and Longshou Mountains, with the Zhangye Plain lying in between, offering magnificent natural scenery. Historically known as Ganzhou, Zhangye has long been a strategic frontier stronghold safeguarding the Central Plains, and it has served as a key hub on the Silk Road, connecting China to Central Asia. In 121 B.C., **Emperor Wu** (汉武帝) of the Han Dynasty dispatched **General Huo Qubing** (霍去病) to launch a westward campaign. Following his victorious conquest, Zhangye Commandery was established, named after the phrase "Cut off the arms of the Xiongnu and expand the arms of China." **The *Book of Han*** (《汉书》) records: "***Extend the arms of the nation to reach the Western Regions, block the Xiongnu and Southern Qiang, and cut off the Xiongnu's right arm***." This description highlights the critical geographic importance of Zhangye. Today, Zhangye is recognized as a national historic and cultural city. It has been traversed by historical figures such as **Zhang Qian** (张骞), **Ban Chao** (班超), **Faxian** (法显), and **Xuanzang** (玄奘), all of whom traveled   through Zhang-ye on their way to the Western Regions. In A.D. 609, **Emperor Yang** (隋炀帝) of the Sui Dynasty convened a gathering of rulers or envoys from 27 Western Regions states in Zhangye, holding an event akin to a "World Expo." Furthermore, ***Marco Polo*** (马可波罗) stayed here for an entire year. Zhangye boasts rich tourism resources, including the Giant Buddha Temple, Wooden Pagoda Temple, and Zhenyuan Tower. About 40 kilometers from the city lies the

Zhangye Danxia Landform National Geopark (张掖丹霞地貌国家地质公园), renowned as one of the world's most extraordinary Danxia landscapes.

The author visited Zhangye Danxia National Geopark in Zhangye, Gansu, China in Oct. 2018.

During my stay in Zhangye, I was warmly hosted by my wife's fourth uncle and his entire family. Despite his advanced age and frail health, my wife's fourth uncle personally accompanied me throughout my visit to the Zhangye Danxia Landform National Geopark and various scenic spots and historical sites, including the Wetland Park. Although Zhangye is located deep in the hinterland of the northwestern desert, it was already late autumn, bordering on early winter by mid-to-late October. Yet, the climate in Zhangye remained as warm and welcoming as my wife's fourth uncle's family. The midday sun still felt as warm as spring.

My wife's fourth uncle, named Chengda Zhang, hails from Hebei Province. His father, Renzhi Zhang, joined the Chinese Communist Party in 1925 and was sent by the Party to Moscow Sun Yat-sen University in 1926. Upon his return to China in 1928, Zhang Renzhi lost contact with the Party due to unforeseen circumstances and later drifted to the Northwest, where he made a living as a teacher in Zhangye. During the Anti-Japanese War, Renzhi Zhang actively supported the war efforts in Zhangye, contributing significantly to the nation. Had he not lost contact with the Party, he would likely have become one of the country's leaders after the founding of the People's Republic of China. In the early 1960s, my wife's fourth uncle graduated from junior high school in Zhangye. Responding to the national call for the "Development and Construction of the Great Northwest," he left his hometown as a young man and went alone to Korla, Xinjiang, where he joined a military reclamation farm under the Xinjiang Production and Construction Corps. There, he worked diligently for over 20 to 30 years, dedicating his youth to the construction of Xinjiang. In the early 1980s, moved by a longing for his hometown, he and his family eventually relocated back to Zhangye. Now retired, he and his wife are enjoying their twilight years in Zhangye.

The author (left) visited Huangshan Mount with old friends Bing Rao (middle) and Yuansheng Li (right) in Oct 2019.

My most recent domestic trip was to Huangshan in midOctober 2019. After concluding my trip to Japan on October 9, I flew from Osaka, Japan, to Shanghai at noon on October 10 to join a three-day tour to Huangshan organized by my former colleagues and old friends, including Mr. Yuansheng Li from my previous institute. My flight landed at Shanghai Pudong Airport around 2 p.m., and it took over an hour to clear customs and immigration. Around 4 p.m., I met Mr. Li and his wife at the

airport exit, and then Mr. Li drove us directly to Huangshan. The distance from Shanghai to Huangshan is about 400 kilometers, and after nearly five hours of driving, we finally arrived at the pre-booked hotel at the foot of Huangshan around 9p.m. By that time, the rest of the group had already started dinner. At the dinner table, I met my old friend, Professor Rao Bing from the Geology Department of Nanjing University. That night, I spent a delightful evening in the company of long-time friends like Bing Rao and Yuansheng Li, along with some new acquaintances, exchanging toasts and rekindling old memories.

The next morning, after breakfast, our group of 14 took a cable car up to tour Huangshan. Huangshan, historically known as Yishan, is located in southern Anhui Province. It is renowned for its "Five Wonders"---peculiar pines, oddly shaped rocks, seas of clouds, hot springs, and winter snow--and is known as "the most wonderful mountain under heaven." It is also one of China's top ten famous mountains. Since ancient times, poets and scholars have been drawn to Huangshan to admire the sea of clouds, leaving behind a wealth of poetic inscriptions and couplets that have been passed down through the ages. Therefore, in addition to its unparalleled natural landscapes, Huangshan also boasts a rich cultural heritage, including ancient stone paths, bridges, pavilions, temples, towers, couplets, and numerous cliff inscriptions. It is known for the saying: "After seeing the Five Sacred Mountains, no need to see other mountains; after seeing Huangshan, no need to see the Five Sacred Mountains."In 1982, Huangshan Scenic Area was designated as one of the first national scenic spots by the State Council. In December 1990 and February 2004, it was listed as a UNESCO World Cultural and Natural Heritage site and a UNESCO Global Geopark, respectively. Visiting Huangshan has long been a dream of mine, and thanks to the meticulous planning of my old colleague and friend, Mr. Yuansheng Li, my wish finally came true.

After taking the cable car up to Huangshan, we visited several famous peaks and scenic spots, including Tiandu Peak, Lotus Peak, Shixin Peak, and the Xihai Grand Canyon. Huangshan's scenery is truly extraordinary. The mountain peaks rise sharply and stretch endlessly, blending the grandeur of Mount Tai, the steepness of Mount Hua, the waterfalls of Mount Lu, and the clouds of Mount Heng. After touring Huangshan, one can truly appreciate the saying: "After seeing Huangshan, there is no need to see other mountains." That night, our group stayed at the Bright Summit Hotel, hoping to catch the sunrise atop Huangshan the next morning. However, nature did not cooperate. When we woke up, it was drizzling, and our plan to watch the sunrise on Huangshan was unfortunately ruined. Although we missed the sunrise, the rain stopped quickly, allowing us to continue our tour of famous spots such as the Greeting Pine, the Farewell Pine, and the HundredStep Cloud Ladder. After descending the mountain around noon, I accepted an invitation from my old friend Professor Bing Rao to take a train together to Nanjing. The following day in Nanjing, Professor Rao warmly accompanied me on a tour of Wangjiang Tower and the ancient city walls. We then visited Ms. Zhengzhen Wang, a former colleague from our rare earth research team at the Institute of Geochemistry, who had since transferred to Nanjing University.

On the morning of October 15, I took a high-speed train from Nanjing to Shanghai and met my old classmate Yuchun Xu, who had flown in from Kunming, at Shanghai Hongqiao Airport at noon. On the morning of the 16th, Yuchun Xu and I met our classmate Weiming Chen, who currently works in Shanghai, at the Kempinski Hotel in Pudong, where we were staying. In the afternoon, the three of us toured the Yuyuan Garden and the Lujiazui area in Pudong. On the morning of October 17, I bid farewell to Yuchun Xu and boarded an international flight back to Canada, safely returning home. This trip, lasting just over two weeks, allowed me to visit cities such as Tokyo, Nagoya, Kyoto, Nara, and Osaka in Japan, as well as Huangshan, Nanjing, and

Shanghai in China. It was one of the most efficient and comprehensive trips I have taken in recent years.

(IV)

In the past few years since retirement, apart from reading and traveling, my daily activities mainly include walking, exercising, and fishing. When I was younger, I hardly had time for exercise due to my busy work schedule. Moreover, I had good physical fitness back then and rarely fell ill, so I did not place much importance on physical exercise. However, as I grew older, I started to feel uncomfortable if I didn't engage in some form of physical activity each day. Therefore, since retirement, I've

2020.8.小银湖 (收获一条12磅重的pike)

The author caught a 12-pound pike in Ontario, Canada in August, 2020.

developed the habit of going out for a daily walk, covering 8,000 to 9,000 steps (about an hour), and have managed to keep up with this routine consistently throughout the four seasons. After sticking to this routine for a few years, the benefits have become evident: I now feel even healthier than I did before I retired. I remember when I was in my early 60s, I gradually developed a few minor health issues, such as an enlarged prostate that often got inflamed. During winter, I also felt cold in my feet, and my left hand occasionally experienced numbness. I went to see a Doctor and underwent a series of check-ups. Although nothing serious was found, the doctor prescribed some medication. Later, I thought it would be better to proactively strengthen my body through exercise rather than relying on medications. After a few years of exercise, my prostate condition improved, and the discomfort and inconvenience caused by the illness disappeared. Exercise not only cured some of my health issues but also improved my cardiovascular health, boosted blood circulation, and increased my resistance to cold and illness. My feet are no longer cold, my fingers are no longer numb, and even when I go for a walk in temperatures as low as -20 to -30 degrees Celsius in the winter, I don't feel very cold. Since 2014, it has been seven or eight years without a single cold. All my physiological indicators are normal, and I can eat well, sleep soundly, and feel mentally refreshed every day.

In addition to walking and exercising, my favourite activity is fishing. During the spring, summer, and fall, I often go fishing in the wild with my old friend, Lao Yang. Typically, we go fishing almost every week, making it one of my main hobbies. In fact, I knew nothing about fishing and had no interest in it before. But after coming to Canada, where the vast land, sparse population, and numerous rivers and lakes provide excellent fishing conditions, my outlook changed. My old friend Lao Yang (actually, He is Xiao Yang, as he's more than ten years

The author caught two large pike in Ontario, Canada in August, 2020.

younger than me, but we old friends often address each other with "Lao Zhang(i.e., Old Zhang)" or "Lao Li(i.e., Old Li)") is named Zhengping Yang. He is from Changde, Hunan Province, and was a graduate student at the Shanxi Institute of Coal Chemistry of the Chinese Academy of Sciences. In the mid-1980s, he transferred to the Chinese Academy of Sciences in Beijing and served as the secretary to Vice President Honglie Sun. In 1990, he went to Australia to study, and after earning his PhD degree in 1996, he immigrated to Canada. After more than 20 years of hard work in Ottawa, he has become a well-established Chinese entrepreneur in the city and is a close friend of mine. Because he grew up in a region known for its abundance of fish and rice, he was accustomed to catching fish and shrimp since childhood and is quite skilled at fishing. Since we met in 2001, we have become good friends due to our shared backgrounds and common topics of interest. Sometimes I would follow him to the river to learn fishing techniques. Over time, after two or three years of practice, I gradually mastered fishing and started to enjoy the sport. Before retirement, both of us were busy with our respective jobs and rarely had time to fish together. But after my retirement, Lao Yang also stepped back from his work responsibilities, and we have since often gone fishing together.

In the spring, we usually fish by the river for a type of fish called "sucker," which is similar to the Chinese grass carp. The name "sucker" comes from its long, slightly curved mouth that resembles a suction cup. This fish is delicate and tasty, but due to the numerous small bones, it is not very popular. In the summer, we row out to the lake to fish for bass or pike (also known as the northern pike in North America). Compared to bass and pike, sucker fish are relatively easy to catch. The first reason is that rivers are narrower than lakes, and sucker fish have a high reproductive rate, making them more abundant in the rivers. Secondly, because their mouths are long and soft, once they bite, they are less likely to slip off the hook. Fishing in the lakes, on the other hand, is much more challenging. The lakes are vast, and the fish are constantly moving, making it difficult to predict their location. Therefore, lake fishing often requires not only skill and experience but also a bit of luck.

In Canada, fishing must strictly adhere to each province's fishing regulations; otherwise, one could face penalties for breaking the law. First, people aged 18 to 65 must purchase a fishing license. Those caught fishing without a license can face hefty fines. Secondly, each angler is only allowed to hold one fishing rod at a time. Violators will be fined based on the number of rods in use. Thirdly, different fish species have varying closed

Author (2nd one from left at the front row) and some good friends in Markham, Ontario, Canada in July 1st, 2017.

seasons based on their reproductive rates each year (the fishing regulations specify the start and end dates for when a certain fish species can be fished). There are also rules on how many fish one can take home each time (exceeding the quota results in fines). For example, because bass have relatively low reproductive rates, they are protected from December 15th to mid-June the following year. Even after the season opens in late June, one can only take up to six fish home per trip. Thus, before fishing, one must fully understand the relevant fishing laws and strictly abide by them. The sucker fish's habits are similar to those of carp or grass carp, and worms are their preferred bait, which can be bought at gas stations---about 18 worms per box for $6 to $7 CAD. However, we often catch our own worms at night on rainy days. As for bass and pike, they are predatory fish that mainly feed on small fish and shrimp in the lakes and rivers. The ideal bait for such fish is a type of small fish called "minnow," which is usually sold in tackle shops. It used to cost $10 CAD per dozen (12 fish), but in recent years, the price has risen to $20-25 CAD per dozen. Considering the high cost of buying minnows, in recent years, we have taken to catching our

Author (the 6th one from the left) and some good friends in Ottawa, Ontario, Canada in September, 2019.

own minnow bait in nearby ponds during the evenings. Minnows are relatively easy to catch in May and June, but by July and August, they become scarce, sometimes taking an hour to catch just a few. To ensure we have enough minnows (typically 30-40) for a day of bass fishing in the lake, we often spend our evenings at local ponds catching bait. Therefore, aside from walking and exercising, fishing has become one of my main daily activities during the summer. Some people may probably ask: What's so good about fishing? Why are so many people fond of it? In fact, fishing is a unique form of exercise and a highly enjoyable "soft sport" that greatly benefits one's physical and mental health. First, fishing typically takes place in remote riversides or lakeshores, where the air is fresh and the sunlight is abundant. Fishing in such an environment is naturally very beneficial for one's physical and mental well-being. Secondly, when fishing, it often requires a long wait before a fish bites the bait. If an angler lacks patience and keeps moving the fishing rod, it's likely that no fish will be caught. Therefore, patience is essential for fishing enthusiasts. Some beginners might initially lack patience, but after some time, their patience increases, their fishing skills improve, and they become more attentive in other areas as well. In other words, fishing is highly effective for cultivating patience. Thirdly, the greatest pleasure in fishing is the sensation and joy of reeling in a fish when it bites. It brings an indescribable sense of accomplishment, putting the brain into a state of extreme excitement. During this time, the central nervous system releases a large amount of dopamine and other excitatory substances, which is highly beneficial for both mental and physical health. Finally, fishing also offers the opportunity to enjoy fresh and delicious fish. Over the past years, I have not only caught but also savoured a good amount of wild bass during the summer and fall seasons. In summary, fishing is an activity that greatly benefits both physical and mental health. It helps relieve stress, cultivates patience and character, enhances life's pleasures, and improves physiological functions, promoting overall well-being. It's an activity that has countless benefits without a single harm and is suitable for people of all ages.

In recent years, whether familiar or not, anyone who has interacted with me often asks the same question: "Lao Wu, you're in your seventies, yet your hair hasn't turned white, you have no wrinkles at the corners of your eyes, and your energy level seems like that of a person in their fifties or sixties. You look much younger than your actual age. What's your secret to staying so youthful? Can you share it with us so that we can learn from you?" Every time this happens, I find it hard to give a satisfying answer. I usually respond: "What secret could I possibly have? I'm just like everyone else, eating the same grains and staples every day, never having undergone any special treatments, and I don't even know much about health preservation." But anyway, since people often ask me this question, and when I worked at JDS in the past, I had indeed incountered some misunderstandings and unnecessary troubles because my appearance did not seem to match my actual age. Therefore, I have sometimes seriously thought about why people often say I look younger. However, I haven't really figured it out. My understanding is that whether a person looks young should be closely related to their mindset. Simply put, a person's mentality is directly linked to their health and outward appearance. If a person is constantly worried, their mental burden must be heavy, and when the mind is burdened, it naturally shows on the face, making them look unhappy. If a person is unhappy, they are bound to have a gloomy face, and if this goes on for a long time, they will inevitably look older. Conversely, if a person is cheerful every day, and even if they have troubles in life, they can pick up and put down things easily without holding onto worries, their mood will naturally be light and joyful. When a person is happy, their face will naturally be adorned with smiles. Over time, such a person will undoubtedly appear youthful and energetic, which is the meaning behind the saying "appearance comes from the heart." As for myself, I am an ordinary person, just like everyone else. I eat the same daily grains and experience the same worries as others. If there is any difference, it might be that I have survived a life-anddeath ordeal. Due to a surgical error during my gallbladder operation, I had a close brush with death---a deeply unforgettable experience that profoundly altered my outlook on life and values, whether consciously or unconsciously. Once a person has experienced life and death, they develop a serene and peaceful attitude and a sense of fearlessness. This state of mind allows one to let go of burdens, to live without the usual anxieties, and to face life with a relaxed and carefree disposition. It is precisely this mindset that makes me carry a sense of gratitude every day, living in selfcontentment and joy. When interacting with others at work or in daily life, I am always happy and open-hearted, with a smiling face. For over twenty years, whenever people who know me or have met me greet me, they often say: "Look at Mr. Wu! Whenever he meets someone, he's always smiling! I wonder what makes him so happy all the time." And at moments like this, I would burst out laughing and say: "If I see you and don't smile, should I cry? What sense does that make?" Therefore, after settling in Canada, perhaps because I have completely distanced myself from the kind of backstabbing work environment where people shake hands in front but kick each other behind the scenes, I have fewer worries in daily life. Coupled with the positive mindset from surviving a near-death experience due to the gallbladder surgery mishap, I have felt mentally refreshed and motivated in whatever environment or work I engage in. With such a mentality and living environment, I believe that for anyone, it would be hard not to look young over time. This might be what people refer to as my secret to staying healthy!

2020.2.春节全家福

A full Family portrait was taken during the 2020 Chinese New Year in Toronto, Ontario, Canada.

Now, as this autobiographical summary of my life comes to an end, it can be considered a concluding chapter. I am already 74 years old. In 74 years, there have been more than 26,000 days---neither too long nor too short. The ancient saying goes: "Reaching seventy is rare." But in today's era of highly advanced medical care and technology, living to 80, 90, or even a hundred years old is not uncommon. Although no one can predict whether tomorrow or accidents come first, judging by my current physical condition, if no unexpected event occurs, living another 20 years should not be a problem. Since my retirement, reading, traveling, fishing, and exercising have become the main themes of my life. Although I have read quite a few books and traveled to many countries over the years, there are still many worthwhile books left to read and plenty of countries and regions I still want to visit. Thus, in my future retirement life, I will continue reading the books I love and traveling to the places I want to go, as long as my health allows. I will still take my daily walks and exercise, and I will continue to fish. In short, I will, as always, live each day happily and enjoy my retirement life to the fullest.

Completed in August 2022
Finalized in December 2022

Ottawa, Canada

Afterword

After a year and half of arduous effort in recollecting and writing, this autobiographical memoir, spanning 250,000 to 300,000 words, has finally been completed, and my once tightly strung nerves have completely relaxed. Actually, I feel a bit tired. Indeed, spending more than a year to finish a memoir covering over 70 years is not an easy task. Having a myriad of fragmented memories in one's mind is one thing, but weaving these fragments together into coherent text that accurately conveys them is quite another. Thus, to write this memoir, I began drafting right after the Chinese New Year in 2021. I went through three versions: the first draft was mainly focused on structuring and selecting content to build the framework of the memoir. The second draft was based on the first, supplementing and refining the material and language. The third draft, built on the second, polished and systematized the manuscript, making the narrative more fluid and engaging. After that, I repeatedly reviewed and revised the entire manuscript more than ten times to ensure that not a single typo or incorrect word remained. However, selfproofreading is not an easy task; despite multiple reviews, minor errors may still have escaped notice. Therefore, although this book is only around 250,000 to 300,000 words long, after writing three drafts, the total text amounted to as much as over 700,000 words---making it quite a significant undertaking.

After completing the third draft in August 2021, the next issue was how to input all this text into a computer. Since I hadn't been very proficient with computers throughout my working life and had never composed any articles on one, and as a Southerner, my Mandarin pronunciation is often imprecise, I found typing characters into a computer using pinyin challenging, making it hard to locate the right characters. Even inputting a short essay of several hundred characters was time-consuming and labor-intensive. Additionally, I had an old computer, over a decade old, but it had long since stopped functioning due to disuse. I initially considered asking someone else to help input the text. However, for a manuscript of closed to 300,000 characters, typing it into the computer would be a significant workload. Not only would it require payment, but the quality of the text might not meet my standards. Thus, I thought, why not do it myself? After all, the one thing I have in abundance now is time. If I don't know how to type, I can learn gradually-- practice makes perfect. With enough repetition, I should be able to handle the task competently. So, after my daughter bought me a laptop, I began practicing typing. After three to four months of diligent effort, I managed to input the entire manuscript. Later, I also learned how to format and insert pictures on the computer. By August 2022, a complete memoir, rich in both text and images, was finally finished. When I saw the manuscript I had painstakingly written, with each word and picture carefully selected and inserted, I felt as proud and joyous as if looking at my own child.

Because I was born and raised in a relatively unique family environment---not only losing my father in childhood but also having a half-sister and an adopted elder brother--my personal experiences are more complex and winding compared to those of my peers. Therefore, when writing a memoir, the first consideration was how to segment the timeline and events, i.e., how to design the chapters. Initially, I planned to write six or seven chapters, or seven or eight chapters, totalling around 100,000 characters enough. One chapter for childhood, one for adolescence, and one for youth (the period of the Cultural Revolution and the "Down to the Countryside" movement), followed by three or four chapters on adulthood. However, once I began writing, life events flashed before my eyes like scenes from a movie. Some events even had their exact dates clearly imprinted in my mind, and once I started writing, I could not stop. I especially felt that my experiences after graduating from graduate school and entering the workforce contained too much that was worth recording. Thus, on top of the initial seven or eight chapters, I added three or four more, ultimately ending up with eleven or twelve chapters. After finishing the entire text, I felt the earlier chapters recalling my mother seemed rather thin, and the depiction of my small family life and my wife and children was also insufficient. Therefore, I specifically added a chapter dedicated to the memory of my mother and included details of my family life. The final chapter describes my post-retirement life, focusing on the theme of "enjoyment," including reading, writing, international travel, visiting relatives in China, fishing, and fitness.

Another significant issue was how to title this memoir. When I began writing, I did not have a definitive title in mind. The current title 《Unforgettable Years》, was only settled upon after multiple changes. Before moving abroad in 1997, I had worked at the Institute of Geochemistry of the Chinese Academy of Sciences for more than 20 years, making some achievements in my research. However, at this peak of my career, I chose to move abroad. Many of my old colleagues and friends, familiar with my journey, felt that settling abroad seemed a loss, and some even thought I might have regretted it. But after careful consideration and weighing the pros and cons, I felt that the choice I made back then was clearly wise and correct. Frankly speaking, if I had stayed in China, I might have had greater advancements in scientific research and personal career development. Yet, life is unpredictable, and any choices made at crucial moments can never be perfect---gains always come with losses. Choosing to live abroad is no exception, with both pros and cons, benefits and drawbacks. Simply put, no choice allows you to have the best of both worlds. For me personally, having gone through a life-and-death ordeal due to a gallbladder surgery mishap, I have long since viewed fame and fortune with indifference. Therefore, no matter what choice I made, I've always felt at peace. Whether I am in one place or another, "Where the heart finds peace is my homeland," so there's never been a question of regret. Thus, my initial working title was "No Regrets in This Life", meaning that looking back on my life, I have no regrets about the choices I've made or my current circumstances (although there may be some disappointments). I am quite content. But after finishing the entire manuscript and reflecting on it, I felt that this title did not fully harmonize with the content. So I changed it to "No Wasted Years", implying that although I haven't achieved any monumental successes, I have always strived and never wasted my time. Yet, after making the change, I still felt that the title didn't perfectly align with the content too. I kept ruminating on the overall essence of the memoir, pondering what title could accurately summarize and reflect the text. Then it suddenly occurred to me to use "Unforgettable Years", which might better capture the essence of the entire work. After all, in my decades-long life journey, there indeed have been many hard years that I will never forget. When I proposed this title to my good friend Kaiyuan Li for feedback, he said: "The title 'Unforgettable Years' is great! It carried a subtle meaning and closely matched the content of your book." Thus, the title *"Unforgettable Years"* was finally settled upon.

After completing the manuscript, I shared it with some friends for feedback and received many valuable suggestions for revisions. A few friends specifically asked about the later lives of certain key figures mentioned repeatedly in my memoir, who were closely tied to my upbringing and fate, such as my cousin Mingliang Wu, the former director of our commune Revolutionary Committee, Delong Ma, as well as my brother and sister. They hoped I could provide a brief account of their later fates at the end of the memoir. Thus, I want to briefly introduce the subsequent circumstances of these individuals here to address my friends' concerns.

Objectively speaking, my cousin, Brother Mingliang Wu, had a significant impact on my education and growth during my childhood and teenage years. If it hadn't been for his guidance and inspiration, my path might have been very different. Therefore, Mingliang Wu could be considered the first "benefactor" in my life. Because of his landlord family background, he was unjustly persecuted during the Cultural Revolution and lived in exile under an assumed identity for nearly ten years. Given his education equivalent to a middleschool level, along with his eloquence and talent, Mingliang should have been a prominent intellectual in the rural areas of underdeveloped Guizhou. Unfortunately, due to his family background, his talent was suppressed or persecuted, and he couldn't make use of his abilities. After the downfall of the Gang of Four and the end of the Cultural Revolution, he dared to reveal his true identity once the nation restored order. In the early 1980s, his youngest son, Yun Wu, was admitted to Guiyang Institute of Traditional Chinese Medicine, which brought him immense pride and joy. Sadly, he passed away unexpectedly in 1985 at the age of 58, before he could enjoy many peaceful years---an unfortunate and regrettable end.

The second "benefactor" in my life was Mr. Delong Ma, the former director of our commune Revolutionary Committee. Anyone who experienced the "Down to the Countryside" movement during the Cultural Revolution knows that the fate of educated youths lay entirely in the hands of others. At that time, whether one could secure a job, join the army, or go to university required the recommendation of the production brigade and the commune, which in reality meant having the right connections. Without such connections, even a small brigade party secretary could trap you in the countryside for a life. In my case, as I mentioned in the memoir, if I hadn't worked at the commune office and developed ties with the commune leaders such as director Delong Ma, I would never have had the opportunity to go to university, and my life path would have been entirely different. Therefore, Director Ma was the second benefactor in my life and one of the most crucial influences on my personal development. Mr. Ma was from Dayong Township in Liuzhi District (formerly part of Puding County before Liuzhi District was established), around 50 years old at the time, a capable and upright man who valued talent and placed the right people in the right positions. He was highly regarded by the people of our entire commune. After the Cultural Revolution ended, he retired from his position as director and secretary of the commune in the mid-1990s.

Of course, throughout my 70-plus years of life, I have encountered many benefactors beyond Mingliang Wu and Director Ma. Many others, such as my first-year junior high school homeroom teacher Xianzhong Huang, my cousin Zhongmei Yu, and Zhongxue Guo who helped me transfer schools in my second year of junior high, Professor Ming Li, head of the Central Analytical Laboratory at the Institute of Geochemistry, Director Ziyuan Ouyang, and my graduate advisor, Academician Chengji Guo, all had a profound influence on my growth. However, due to space constraints, I will not elaborate on each one here.

Lastly, I would like to speak about my brother and sister. Without a doubt, my brother and sister were crucial to my development. Without their support, I wouldn't have reached where I am today. Although my brother was adopted and my sister and I are half-siblings, they treated me as if we were born of the same parents. When I first started junior high, I was only 12 or 13, and had to walk more than 30 kilometers to the county seat. Carrying luggage, or even walking the distance empty-handed, was a daunting challenge for a child of that age. Every time school started or ended, it was my brother who carried my luggage, taking me to school or picking me up. In addition, in the 1960s, even though prices were relatively low, the ¥3-5 yuan monthly board and a little pocket money was a significant burden for a family without any steady income. Every weekend, my sister would accompany our mother, toiling hard, collecting and selling wild vegetables at the town market to accumulate ¥2-3 yuans at a time, which were then used to cover my school expenses. If not for their help and support, it would have been nearly impossible for my mother alone to fund my education. Therefore, besides being grateful to my mother, I am also deeply grateful to my brother and sister. They were both benefactors in my life. Since getting married in the early 1950s, my brother and sister have supported and cared for each other through thick and thin for seventy years. They had nine children in total. Unfortunately, one of the children died shortly after birth, but the remaining eight (two boys and six girls) were raised to adulthood. They were a truly happy and blessed large family. However, in her later years, my sister suffered from retinal detachment due to years of hard work, which left her blind. In addition, her legs became crippled by worsening arthritis, making her completely dependent on my brother's care. On May 23, 2022, drained by a lifetime of toil, my sister suddenly passed away peacefully in her sleep at the age of 86. After my sister's death, my brother, though surrounded by children and grandchildren, felt spiritually desolate and restless. His appetite dwindled, and his mental state declined. On the night of August 13, 2022, while turning in his sleep, he accidentally fell off the bed, fracturing his right hip. When my nephew took him to the hospital the next day, the doctor deemed him too old and frail for surgery and recommended bed rest and recuperation at home. Thereafter, my brother remained bedridden, and his condition continued to deteriorate. In early September, he developed urinary retention due to prostate enlargement and had to be readmitted to the hospital for catheterization. After lying in bed for over a month, suffering immense physical and emotional pain from the hip fracture and prostate condition, he finally refused to eat. About a week later, he peacefully passed away, following my sister just four months after her death, on September 20, 2022, at the age of 91.

People often say: "What you think about during the day, you dream about at night." Since retiring, I have been contemplating whether and how to write this autobiography, and thus memories of my past often resurfaced in my mind. In the years before I began writing this book, I would sometimes dream of climbing various mountains while sleeping. The narrow paths up the mountains were always winding, and when I was almost at the summit, the last few steps would often be on unstable stones or frail branches that seemed ready to break. Only after struggling with all my might would I finally reach the top. Each time I awoke from these dreams, I would often find myself gasping for breath and drenched in sweat. However, after completing this book, I have not had any similar dreams of climbing or danger in the past couple of years. I believe that by finally writing this memoir with my own hands, the challenging and tortuous memories of my life have found their ideal resting place, bringing a sense of closure that allows me to sleep more peacefully from now on.

During the writing process, I received encouragement and support from many old classmates and friends. Special thanks go to my dear friends Kaiyuan Li and Xiang Wang, who provided numerous valuable suggestions and advice during the drafting process. At the same time, I would like to extend my special thanks to Ms. Dudu for taking the time out of her busy schedule to write a very touching preface for this book.

Mingqing Wu
Ottawa
April 30, 2023

Appendix (1) The List of Publications

[1]   Qizhong Wen, Jinshou Yan, Guiyi Diao, Suhua Yu, Mingqing Wu: Changes in trace elements during the transformation of loess. Geochimica, 1979, 2: 145-155.

[2]   Mingqing Wu, Jianquan Lei: Continuous determination of trace scandium and rare earth elements in marine sediments. Proceedings of the Symposium on Marine and Limnological Chemistry, Xiamen, 1981, 79-86.

[3]   Wan Xianjue, Yuwei Chen, Mingqing Wu: Study on the chemical composition of ferromanganese nodules. Proceedings of the Symposium on Chemical Analysis of Minerals and Rocks, Geological Publishing House, Beijing, 1982, 487-492.

[4]   Mingqing Wu, Jianquan Lei: Continuous determination of trace scandium and rare earth elements in marine shell fossils. Geology and Geochemistry, 1982, 11: 53-56.

[5]   Yuwei Chen, Xianjue Wang, Mingqing Wu: Geochemistry and material sources of sediments in the East China Sea. Proceedings of the International Symposium on Sedimentology of the East China Sea Continental Shelf, Volume 2, Hangzhou, Ocean Press, 1983, 846-855.

[6]   Mingqing Wu: Geochemical study of rare earth elements in seabed sediments of the Taiwan Shoal. Geochimica, 1983, 3: 303-313.

[7]   Xianjue Wang, Yuwei Chen, Mingqing Wu: Geochemistry of rare earth trace elements in ferromanganese nodules and their genesis. Oceanologia et Limnologia Sinica, 1984, 15(6): 501-514.

[8]   Xianjue Wang, Mingqing Wu, Dehua Liang: Some geochemical characteristics of basalts in the South China Sea. Geochimica, 1984, 4: 332-340.

[9]   Mingqing Wu, Xianjue Wang: Rare earth elements in the biosphere. Geology and Geochemistry (Supplement), 1984, 51-54.

[10]   Mingqing Wu: Overview of rare earth elment geochemistry research in Japan. Bulletin of Mineralogy, Petrology and Geochemistry, 1986, 1: 25-27.

[11]   WuMingqing, Jianquan Lei: Research on methods for continuous determination of trace scandium and rare earth elements in marine sediments and shell fossils. Journal of Guizhou University, 1987, 4(3): 135-143.

[12]   Mingqing Wu: A new radiometric dating method — La-Ba chronometry. Geology and Geochemistry, 1987, 3: 70-72.

[13]   Mingqing Wu, Xiaofeng Xiao: Ion exchange separation and determination of trace uranium, thorium, and rare earth elements in marine sediments. Marine Sciences, 1988, 34-39.

[14]   Mingqing Wu, Xianjue Wang: Chemical composition characteristics of sediments in the Okinawa Trough and their geological significance. Oceanologia et Limnologia Sinica, 1988, 19(3): 34-45.

[15]   Xianjue Wang, Mingqing Wu: Rare earth elements in the hydrosphere. Geochemistry of Rare Earth Elements, Science Press, Beijing, 1989, 284-304.

[16]   Mingqing Wu, Xianjue Wang: Biogeochemistry of rare earth elements. Geochemistry of Rare Earth Elements, Science Press, Beijing, 1989, 305-320.

[17]   Mingqing Wu, Xianjue Wang: Chemical composition characteristics of sediments in the Okinawa Trough. Proceedings of the Third ChinaSoviet Symposium on Geology, Geophysics, Geochemistry, and Mineral Resources of Pacific Marginal Seas, September 1989, Vladivostok, USSR, 136-144.

[18]   Mingqing Wu: Some geochemical characteristics of trace elements in Okinawa Trough sediments. Acta Oceanologica Sinica, 1991, 13(1): 71-81.

[19]   Mingqing Wu, Ziyuan Ouyang, Yunhua Song: Thermodynamic analysis of the mineral assemblage in shell fossils. Acta Sedimentologica Sinica, 1991, 9(1): 129-135.

[20]   Mingqing Wu, Xianjue Wang: Rare earth and trace elements in East China Sea sediments. Geochimica, 1991, 1: 40-46.

[21]   Mingqing Wu, Qizhong Wen, Jinyu Pan, Guiyi Diao: Rare earth elements in the Malan Loess of the middle reaches of the Yellow River. Chinese Science Bulletin, 1991, 5: 366-369.

[22]   Mingqing Wu, Qizhong Wen, Jinyu Pan, Guiyi Diao: Rare earth elements in the Malan Loess from the middle reaches of the Huanghe River. Chinese Science Bulletin, 1991, (4): 405-410.

[23]   Mingqing Wu, Ziyuan Ouyang, Yunhua Song: Changes in paleo-ocean redox conditions at the western margin of the Tarim Basin — Evidence from Ce anomalies in shell fossils. Science in China (Series B), 1992, 2: 206-215.

[24]   Mingqing Wu, Ziyuan Ouyang, Yunhua Song, et al.: Redox variations of the ancient ocean at the western margin of the Tarim Basin — Evidence from Ce anomalies in shell fossils. Science in China, 1992, 35(9): 1110-1120.

[25]   Mingqing Wu, Ziyuan Ouyang: Ce anomaly — A chemical tracer for paleo-ocean redox variations. Chinese Science Bulletin, 1992, 3: 242-244.

[26]   Mingqing Wu and Ziyuan Ouyang: Ce anomaly — A chemical tracer for paleo-ocean redox variations. Chinese Science Bulletin, 1992, 37(15): 1293-1296.

[27]   Mingqing Wu, Chuzhen Chen, Yaoqi Zhou, et al.: Distribution characteristics of trace elements in the P/T boundary section at SelongXishan, Tibet. Advances in Mineralogy, Petrology, and Geochemistry, Lanzhou University Press, 1994, 125-134.

[28]   Mingqing Wu, Qizhong Wen, Jinyu Pan, and Guiyi Diao: The average chemical composition of Loess in North China and its comparison with elemental abundance in the upper continental crust. Chinese Journal of Geochemistry, 1995, 3: 35-44.

[29]   Mingqing Wu: Geochemistry of rare earth elements, in Rare Earth and Their Applications (ed. Yu Zhongsheng), 1996, Beijing, Metallurgical Industry Publishing House, pp. 356-386.

[30]   Mingqing Wu, Qizhong Wen, Jinyu Pan, et al.: Reinvestigation of the major chemical composition of Malan Loess in the middle reaches of the Yellow River. Progress in Nature Science, 1996, 6(1): 80-85.

[31]   Mingqing Wu, Qizhong Wen, Jinyu Pan, et al.: Mass-weighted average of major chemical compositions of the Malan Loess in North China. Progress in Nature Science, 1996, 6(5): 602-610.

[32]   Mingqing Wu, Chuzhen Chen, Zhou Yaoqi, Zhifang Chai: Geochemistry of REE and trace elements in the P/T boundary section at Selong-Xishan, South Tibet. Progress in Nature Science, 1996, 6(2): 213-221.

[33]   Mingqing Wu, Chuzhen Chen, Yaoqi Zhou, et al.: REE and trace element geochemistry of the P/T boundary section at Selong-Xishan, South Tibet, China. Chinese Journal of Geochemistry, 1995, 4: 135-142.

[34]   Mingqing Wu, Kun Wang, Wayne Goodfellow, et al.: Negative organic carbon isotope anomalies at the Permian-Triassic boundary section in Lekang, Guizhou, and their geological significance. Acta Mineralogica Sinica, 1997, 1: 35-43.

[35]   Mingqing Wu, Kun Wang, Wayne Goodfellow, et al.: Organic carbon isotope records of the Permian-Triassic boundary mass extinction event in Southern China. 1997 (Unpublished).

[36]   Mingqing Wu, Kun Wang, Wayne Goodfellow, et al.: Organic carbon isotope record of Permian-Triassic boundary mass extinction events in Southern China. 1997 (English).

[37]   Mingqing Wu, Kun Wang, Wayne Goodfellow, et al.: Anomaly of PGEs across the Devonian-Carboniferous boundary at the Dapoushang section, Muhua, Guizhou, South China, and its geological significance. 1997 (English).

(Email of the author: qingming.wu11@gmail.com)

Appendix (2) The Reference Letters

I✦I Energy, Mines and   Énergie, Mines et
Resources Canada   Ressources Canada
Geological Survey   Secteur de la Commission
of Canada Sector   géologique du Canada

May 22nd, 1996

To whom it may concern:

Dr. Mingqing Wu is currently completing a one-year stay as a Visiting Scientist at the Geological Survey of Canada and the University of Ottawa, Ottawa, Canada. His principal objective during his stay in Canada was to better understand the cause and consequences of Phanerozoic biological mass extinction events. To this end, Dr. Wu has analyzed more than one hundred and sixty rock samples that were carefully collected from Permian-Triassic (P-T) and Devonian-Carboniferous (D-C) boundary sections in China. During the past twelve months, Dr. Wu has carried out highly specialized analyses of platinoid element abundances by Inductive Coupled Plasma - Mass Spectrometry and of carbon and oxygen isotopes by conventional mass spectrometry at the University of Ottawa. The results for the D-C boundary are world-class and have been described in a manuscript prepared by Dr. Wu. Carbon isotopes in organic matter and carbonate show conclusively that this boundary coincides with a major faunal turnover and associated biomass reduction. Platinoid element anomalies at the D-C boundaries demonstrate a causal link between mass extinction and the impact of a large meteorite with the earth's surface 345 million years ago. Results for the P-T boundary likewise show that this extinction event was sudden and of high magnitude. Although the cause of this extinction is still debated, cosmic micro spheres from the boundary interval indicate an extraterrestrial process.

Dr. Wu has proved to be a capable, dedicated and highly cooperative fellow research scientist during his stay at the Geological Survey of Canada. He has mastered several specialized analytical techniques and contributed significantly to joint research on the cause and consequences of mass biological extinctions.

Sincerely,

Dr. Wayne D. Goodfellow
Senior Research Scientist
Geological Survey of Canada
601 Booth Street
Ottawa, Ontario K1A 0E8
Tel: 613-~~666-8185~~
and
Adjunct Professor
Department of Geology
University of Ottawa

Canada

Natural Resources
Canada

Ressources naturelles
Canada

Geological Survey
of Canada

Commission géologique
du Canada

May 31, 1996

To whom it may concern,

Dr. Mingqing Wu has been a visiting scientist working in my laboratory for the past year. He has been working with me in the capacity of analytical chemist carrying out determinations for the platinum group elements in geological samples.

During the course of his collaboration, Dr. Wu learned and successfully applied a technique for the determination of the PGEs which involved chemical purifications, sample dissolutions, separations, and analysis by Inductively Coupled Plasma Mass Spectrometry. The procedure, developed at the Geological Survey of Canada, is demanding from the point of view of contamination control and attention paid to detail. Detection limits for the method used are limited by contamination levels and not by instrument sensitivity and thus a high standard of laboratory practice is essential. Detection limits for the PGEs were in the 50 ppt concentration range. Dr. Wu was able to master the technique and successfully complete the analysis of scores of samples.

Dr. Wu impressed me with his ability to quickly learn a difficult procedure related to a field outside his own area of training. He was an extremely hard and diligent worker who didn't get discouraged, even when there were challenges to overcome. Dr. Wu is an affable person, capable of getting along will with others and is a team player. It has been a pleasure to have worked with him during his stay in Canada.

Sincerely,

D. Conrad Grégoire
Head,
Analytical Chemistry Laboratories
Geological Survey of Canada

tel: 613-995-4213
fax: 613-943-1286
e-mail: gregoire@emr.ca

Adjunct Professor
Department of Chemistry
Carleton University

Canada

地调所化学分
析室室主任的
推荐信

Appendix (3) International Project Mandate

RESPONSE OF THE OCEAN/ATMOSPHERE SYSTEM TO PAST GLOBAL CHANGES
IGCP PROJECT 386

Helmut H.J. Geldsetzer
Geological Survey of Canada
3303-33rd St. NW
Calgary, Alberta T2L 2A7
Canada
EMAIL: hgeldsetzer@gsc.emr.ca
FAX: (403) 292-5377
TEL: (403) 292-7155

Dhiraj M. Banerjee
Department of Geology
University of Delhi
Delhi 110007
India
EMAIL: cscc@.isc.ernet.in
FAX: 91-11-725541
TEL: 91-11-7257073

Louis A. Derry
Department of Geological Sciences
Cornell University
2122 Snell Hall
Ithaca, NY 14853-1504
U.S.A.
EMAIL: derry@geology.cornell.edu
FAX: (607) 254-4780
TEL: (607) 233-9355

Zbigniew Sawlowicz
Institute of Geological Sciences
Jagiellonian University
ul. Oleandry 2a
30-060 Krakow
Poland
EMAIL: ZBYSZEK@ing.uj.edu.pl
FAX: 48-12-332270
TEL: 48-12-336465

Harald Strauss
Institute of Geology
Ruhr-University, Bochum
Universitätsstr. 150
D-44801 Bochum
Germany
EMAIL: HARALD.STRAUSS@ruhr-uni-bochum.de
FAX: 49-234-7094571
TEL: 49-234-7023227

September 17, 1996

Secretary Office
China National Committee
International Geological Correlation Program
Ministry of Geology and Mineral Resources of China
64 Funeidajie Street, Xisi 100812
Beijing, China

RE: IGCP Project 386

Dear Sir:

As the coordinator and secretary of the new IGCP Project 386 "Response of the ocean/atmosphere system to past global changes" I would like to inform you that the Institute of Geochemistry, Chinese Academy of Sciences, Guiyang has been proposed as the official representative of the new IGCP Project 386. The Institute of Geochemistry is represented by Drs. Ming-Qing Wu, Jun-Ya Nan and Wei-Dong Yang. The three scientists are experienced researchers; Dr. Ming-Qing Wu recently completed a successful stay as a visiting scientist in Canada where he conducted complex geochemical analyses on very sophisticated instruments such as an Inductive Coupled Plasma Mass Spectometre. The same standard of equipment is available at the Institute of Geochemistry in Guiyang and I am certain that Drs. Ming-Qing Wu, Jun-Ya Nan and Wei-Dong Yang will make significant contributions to the objectives of IGCP Project 386.

I look forward to the formal approval of the Institute of Geochemistry, Chinese Academy of Sciences, Guiyang as the formal representative of IGCP Project 386. I also hope that one of the formal annual meetings of IGCP Project 386 can be held in China.

A copy of the approved proposal of IGCP Project 386 and a brief summary of the project (Episodes, volume 18/4, December 1995) are enclosed.

Sincerely,

H.H.J. Geldsetzer, Coordinator and Secretary of IGCP Project 386
c.c.   Drs. Ming-Qing Wu, Jun-Ya Nan, Wei-Dong Yang

国际合作项目委托书

Appendix (4) The Certificate of Special Allowance

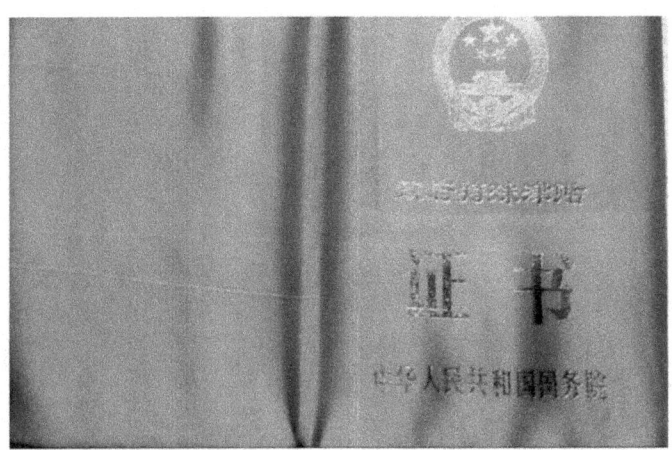

CERTIFICATE
(Translation)

Comrade Mingqing Wu:

In recognition of your outstanding contributions to the development of China's scientific and technological undertakings, it has been decided to grant you a special government allowance starting from October 1993, along with this certificate.

The State Council of
The People's Republic of China

October 1, 1993

Special Government Allowance No. 491932723

www.ingramcontent.com/pod-product-compliance
Lightning Source LLC
Chambersburg PA
CBHW071700120626
46550CB00001B/56